The Junior Classics

A · LIBRARY · FOR
BOYS · AND · GIRLS

P. F. Collier · & · Son
New · York

"EVERYTHING'S GOT A MORAL, IF ONLY YOU CAN
FIND IT"   —page 479
From the painting by Beatrice Stevens

THE
JUNIOR CLASSICS

SELECTED AND ARRANGED BY
WILLIAM PATTEN
MANAGING EDITOR OF THE HARVARD CLASSICS

INTRODUCTION BY
CHARLES W. ELIOT, LL.D.
PRESIDENT EMERITUS OF HARVARD UNIVERSITY

WITH A READING GUIDE BY
WILLIAM ALLAN NEILSON, Ph.D.
PROFESSOR OF ENGLISH, HARVARD UNIVERSITY
PRESIDENT SMITH COLLEGE, NORTHAMPTON, MASS.,
SINCE 1917

VOLUME SIX

Old-Fashioned Tales

P. F. COLLIER & SON
NEW YORK

"A Fox and a Raven," Rebecca Harding Davis;
Copyright, 1875, by Scribner & Co. "A Case of Coinci-
dence," Rose Terry Cooke; Copyright, 1882, by D.
Lothrop & Co. "Deacon Thomas Wales' Will," Mary
E. Wilkins; Copyright, 1885, by D. Lothrop & Co.
"Dill," Mary E. Wilkins; Copyright, 1888, by D. Lothrop
& Co.

Acknowledgments of permissions given by authors and
publishers for the use of copyright material
appear in Volume 10

The Collier Press, New York
Electrotyped, Printed, and Bound by
P. F. COLLIER & SON

CONTENTS

1-Jun. Cl-6

CONTENTS

ILLUSTRATIONS

THE RACE FOR THE SILVER SKATES

By Mary Mapes Dodge

THE 20th of December came at last, bringing with it the perfection of winter weather. All over the level landscape lay the warm sunlight. It tried its power on lake, canal, and river; but the ice flashed defiance, and showed no sign of melting. The very weather-cocks stood still to enjoy the sight. This gave the windmills a holiday. Nearly all the past week they had been whirling briskly: now, being rather out of breath, they rocked lazily in the clear, still air. Catch a windmill working when the weather-cocks have nothing to do!

There was an end to grinding, crushing, and sawing for that day. It was a good thing for the millers near Broek. Long before noon, they concluded to take in their sails, and go to the race. Everybody would be there. Already the north side of the frozen Y was bordered with eager spectators: the news of the great skating-match had travelled far and wide. Men, women, and children, in holiday attire, were flocking toward the spot. Some wore furs, and wintry cloaks or shawls; but many, consulting their feelings rather than the almanac, were dressed as for an October day.

The site selected for the race was a faultless plain of ice near Amsterdam, on that great *arm* of the

Zuyder-Zee, which Dutchmen, of course, must call the Eye. The townspeople turned out in large numbers. Strangers in the city deemed it a fine chance to see what was to be seen. Many a peasant from the northward had wisely chosen the 20th as the day for the next city-trading. It seemed that everybody, young and old, who had wheels, skates, or feet at command, had hastened to the scene.

There were the gentry in their coaches, dressed like Parisians fresh from the Boulevards; Amsterdam children in charity uniforms; girls from the Roman-Catholic Orphan-House, in sable gowns and white headbands; boys from the Burgher Asylum, with their black tights and short-skirted, harlequin coats.[1] There were old-fashioned gentlemen in cocked hats and velvet knee-breeches; old-fashioned ladies, too, in stiff, quilted skirts, and bodices of dazzling brocade. These were accompanied by servants bearing foot-stoves and cloaks. There were the peasant-folk arrayed in every possible Dutch costume—shy young rustics in brazen buckles; simple village-maidens concealing their flaxen hair under fillets of gold; women whose long, narrow aprons were stiff with embroidery; women with short corkscrew curls hanging over their foreheads; women with shaved heads and close-fitting caps; and women in striped skirts and windmill bonnets; men in leather, in homespun, in velvet and broad-

[1] This is not said in derision. Both the boys and girls of this institution wear garments quartered in red and black alternately. By making the dress thus conspicuous, the children are, in a measure, deterred from wrong-doing while going about the city. The Burgher Orphan-Asylum affords a comfortable home to several hundred boys and girls. Holland is famous for its charitable institutions.

8

cloth; burghers in model European attire, and burghers in short jackets, wide trousers, and steeple-crowned hats.

There were beautiful Friesland girls in wooden shoes and coarse petticoats, with solid gold crescents encircling their heads, finished at each temple with a golden rosette, and hung with lace a century old. Some wore necklaces, pendants, and ear-rings of the purest gold. Many were content with gilt, or even with brass; but it is not an uncommon thing for a Friesland woman to have all the family treasure in her head-gear. More than one rustic lass displayed the value of two thousand guilders upon her head that day.

Scattered throughout the crowd were peasants from the Island of Marken, with sabots, black stockings, and the widest of breeches; also women from Marken, with short blue petticoats, and black jackets gayly figured in front. They wore red sleeves, white aprons, and a cap like a bishop's mitre over their golden hair.

The children, often, were as quaint and odd-looking as their elders. In short, one-third of the crowd seemed to have stepped bodily from a collection of Dutch paintings.

Everywhere could be seen tall women, and stumpy men, lively-faced girls, and youths whose expression never changed from sunrise to sunset.

There seemed to be at least one specimen from every known town in Holland. There were Utrecht water-bearers, Gouda cheese-makers, Delft pottery-men, Schiedam distillers, Amsterdam diamond-cutters, Rotterdam merchants, dried-up herring-packers, and two sleepy-eyed shepherds from Texel. Every man of them had his pipe and tobacco-pouch. Some carried what might be called the smoker's complete outfit,—a pipe, tobacco, a pricker with which to clean the tube, a silver net for protecting the bowl, and a box of the strongest of brimstone-matches.

A true Dutchman, you must remember, is rarely without his pipe on any possible occasion. He may, for a moment, neglect to breathe; but, when the pipe is forgotten, he must be dying, indeed. There were no such sad cases here. Wreaths of smoke were rising from every possible quarter. The more fantastic the smoke-wreath, the more placid and solemn the smoker.

Look at those boys and girls on stilts! That is a good idea. They can see over the heads of the tallest. It is strange to see those little bodies high in the air, carried about on mysterious legs. They have such a resolute look on their round faces, what wonder that nervous old gentlemen, with tender feet, wince and tremble while the long-legged little monsters stride past them!

You will read, in certain books, that the Dutch are a quiet people: so they are generally. But listen! did ever you hear such a din? All made up of human voices—no, the horses are helping somewhat, and the fiddles are squeaking pitifully (how it must pain fiddles to be tuned!); but the mass of the sound comes from the great *vox humana* that belongs to a crowd.

That queer little dwarf, going about with a heavy basket, winding in and out among the people, helps not a little. You can hear his shrill cry above all the other sounds, "Pypen en tabac! Pypen en tabac!"

Another, his big brother, though evidently some years younger, is selling doughnuts and bon-bons. He is calling on all pretty children, far and near, to come quickly, or the cakes will be gone.

You know quite a number among the spectators. High up in yonder pavilion, erected upon the border of the ice, are some persons whom you have seen very lately. In the centre is Madame van Gleck. It is her birthday, you remember: she has the post of honor. There is Mynheer van Gleck, whose meerschaum has not really grown fast to his lips: it only appears so. There are grandfather and grandmother, whom you met at the St. Nicholas *fête*. All the children are with them. It is so mild, they have brought even the baby. The poor little creature is swaddled very much after the manner of an Egyptian mummy; but it can crow with delight, and, when the band is playing, open and shut its animated mittens in perfect time to the music.

Grandfather, with his pipe and spectacles and fur cap, makes quite a picture as he holds baby upon his knee. Perched high upon their canopied platforms, the party can see all that is going on. No wonder the ladies look complacently at the glassy ice: with a stove for a footstool, one might sit cosily beside the North Pole.

There is a gentleman with them who somewhat resembles St. Nicholas as he appeared to the young Van Glecks, on the fifth of December. But the saint had a flowing white beard; and this face is as smooth as a pippin. His saintship was larger around the body, too, and (between ourselves) he had a pair of thimbles in his mouth, which this gentleman certainly has not. It cannot be St. Nicholas, after all.

Near by, in the next pavilion, sit the Van Holps, with their son and daughter (the Van Gends) from The Hague. Peter's sister is not one to forget her promises.

She has brought bouquets of exquisite hot-house flowers for the winners.

These pavilions, and there are others beside, have all been erected since daylight. That semi-circular one, containing Mynheer Korbes's family, is very pretty, and proves that the Hollanders are quite skilled at tent-making; but I like the Van Gleck's best,—the centre one,—striped red and white, and hung with evergreens.

The one with the blue flags contains the musicians. Those pagoda-like affairs, decked with sea-shells, and streamers of every possible hue, are the judges' stands; and those columns and flag-staffs upon the ice mark the limit of the race-course. The two white columns, twined with green, connected at the top by that long, floating strip of drapery, form the starting-point. Those flagstaffs, half a mile off, stand at each end of the boundary line, cut sufficiently deep to be distinct to the skaters, though not enough so to trip them when they turn to come back to the starting-point.

The air is so clear, it seems scarcely possible that the columns and flagstaffs are so far apart. Of course, the judges' stands are but little nearer together.

Half a mile on the ice, when the atmosphere is like this, is but a short distance, after all, especially when fenced with a living chain of spectators.

The music has commenced. How melody seems to enjoy itself in the open air! The fiddles have forgotten their agony; and every thing is harmonious. Until you look at the blue tent, it seems that the music springs from the sunshine, it is so boundless, so joyous. Only when you see the staid-faced musicians, you realize the truth.

Where are the racers? All assembled together near the white columns. It is a beautiful sight,— forty boys and girls in picturesque attire, darting with electric swiftness in and out among each other, or sailing in pairs and triplets, beckoning, chatting, whispering, in the fulness of youthful glee.

A few careful ones are soberly tightening their straps: others, halting on one leg, with flushed, eager faces, suddenly cross the suspected skate over their knee, give it an examining shake, and dart off again. One and all are possessed with the spirit of motion. They cannot stand still. Their skates are a part of them; and every runner seems bewitched.

Holland is the place for skaters, after all. Where else can nearly every boy and girl perform feats on the ice that would attract a crowd if seen on Central Park? Look at Ben! I did not see him before. He is really astonishing the natives; no easy thing to do in the Netherlands. Save your strength, Ben, you will need it soon. Now other boys are trying! Ben is surpassed already. Such jumping, such poising, such spinning, such india-rubber exploits generally! That boy with a red cap is the lion now: his back is a watch-spring, his body is cork—no, it is iron, or it would snap at that. He is a bird, a top, a rabbit, a corkscrew, a sprite, a flesh-ball, all in an instant. When you think he's erect, he is down; and, when you think he is down, he is up. He drops his glove on the ice, and turns a somerset as he picks it up. Without stopping, he snatches the cap from Jacob Poot's astonished head, and claps it back again "hindside before." Lookers-on hurrah and laugh. Foolish boy! It is arctic weather under your feet, but more than temperate overhead. Big drops already are rolling down your forehead. Superb skater, as you are, you may lose the race.

A French traveller, standing with a note-book in his hand, sees our English friend, Ben, buy a doughnut of the dwarf's brother, and eat it. There-upon he writes in his note-book, that the Dutch take enormous mouthfuls, and universally are fond of potatoes boiled in molasses.

There are some familiar faces near the white columns. Lambert, Ludwig, Peter, and Carl are all there, cool, and in good skating-order. Hans is not far off. Evidently he is going to join in the race, for his skates are on,—the very pair that he sold for seven guilders. He had soon suspected that his fairy godmother was the mysterious "friend" who had bought them. This settled, he had boldly charged her with the deed; and she, knowing well that all her little savings had been spent in the pur-

chase, had not had the face to deny it. Through
the fairy godmother, too, he had been rendered
amply able to buy them back again. Therefore
Hans is to be in the race. Carl is more indignant
than ever about it; but, as three other peasant-boys
have entered, Hans is not alone.

Twenty boys and twenty girls. The latter, by
this time, are standing in front, braced for the
start; for they are to have the first "run." Hilda,
Rychie, and Katrinka are among them. Two or
three bend hastily to give a last pull at their skate-
straps. It is pretty to see them stamp to be sure
that all is firm. Hilda is speaking pleasantly to a
graceful little creature in a red jacket and a new
brown petticoat. Why, it is Gretel! What a difference those pretty shoes make, and the skirt, and
the new cap! Annie Bouman is there, too. Even
Janzoon Kolp's sister has been admitted; but Janzoon himself has been voted out by the directors,
because he killed the stork, and only last summer,
was caught in the act of robbing a bird's nest,—a
legal offence in Holland.

This Janzoon Kolp, you see, was— There, I cannot tell the story just now. The race is about to
commence.

Twenty girls are formed in a line. The music
has ceased.

A man, whom we shall call the crier, stands between the columns and the first judges' stand. He
reads the rules in a loud voice:—

"THE GIRLS AND BOYS ARE TO RACE IN TURN,
UNTIL ONE GIRL AND ONE BOY HAS BEATEN TWICE.
THEY ARE TO START IN A LINE FROM THE UNITED

COLUMNS, SKATE TO THE FLAGSTAFF LINE, TURN, AND THEN COME BACK TO THE STARTING-POINT; THUS MAKING A MILE AT EACH RUN."

A flag is waved from the judges' stand. Madame van Gleck rises in her pavilion. She leans forward with a white handkerchief in her hand. When she drops it, a bugler is to give the signal for them to start.

The handkerchief is fluttering to the ground. Hark!

They are off!

No. Back again. Their line was not true in passing the judges' stand.

The signal is repeated.

Off again. No mistake this time. Whew! how fast they go!

The multitude is quiet for an instant, absorbed in eager, breathless watching.

Cheers spring up along the line of spectators. Huzza! five girls are ahead. Who comes flying back from the boundary-mark? We cannot tell. Something red, that is all. There is a blue spot flitting near it, and a dash of yellow nearer still. Spectators at this end of the line strain their eyes, and wish they had taken their post nearer the flag-staff.

The wave of cheers is coming back again. Now we can see. Katrinka is ahead!

She passes the Van Holp pavilion. The next is Madame van Gleck's. That leaning figure gazing from it is a magnet. Hilda shoots past Katrinka, waving her hand to her mother as she passes. Two others are close now, whizzing on like arrows.

16

What is that flash of red and gray? Hurrah, it is Gretel! She, too, waves her hand, but toward no gay pavilion. The crowd is cheering; but she hears only her father's voice,—"Well done, little Gretel!" Soon Katrinka, with a quick, merry laugh, shoots past Hilda. The girl in yellow is gaining now. She passes them all,—all except Gretel. The judges lean forward without seeming to lift their eyes from their watches. Cheer after cheer fills the air: the very columns seem rocking. Gretel has passed them. She has won.

"GRETEL BRINKER, ONE MILE!" shouts the crier.

The judges nod. They write something upon a tablet which each holds in his hand.

While the girls are resting,—some crowding eagerly around our frightened little Gretel, some standing aside in high disdain,—the boys form in line.

Mynheer van Gleck drops the handkerchief, this time. The buglers give a vigorous blast.

The boys have started.

Halfway already. Did ever you see the like!

Three hundred legs flashing by in an instant. But there are only twenty boys. No matter: there were hundreds of legs, I am sure. Where are they now? There is such a noise, one gets bewildered. What are the people laughing at? Oh! at that fat boy in the rear. See him go! See him! He'll be down in an instant: no, he won't. I wonder if he knows he is all alone: the other boys are nearly at the boundary-line. Yes, he knows it. He stops. He wipes his hot face. He takes off his cap, and looks about him. Better to give up with a good grace. He has made a hundred friends by that hearty, astonished laugh. Good Jacob Poot!

The fine fellow is already among the spectators, gazing as eagerly as the rest.

A cloud of feathery ice flies from the heels of the skaters as they "bring to," and turn at the flag-staffs.

Something black is coming now, one of the boys: it is all we know. He has touched the *vox humana* stop of the crowd: it fairly roars. Now they come nearer: we can see the red cap. There's Ben, there's Peter, there's Hans!

Hans is ahead. Young Madame van Gend almost crushes the flowers in her hand: she had been quite sure that Peter would be first. Carl Schummel is next, then Ben, and the youth with the red cap. The others are pressing close. A tall figure darts from among them. He passes the red cap, he passes Ben, then Carl. Now it is an even race between him and Hans. Madame van Gend catches her breath.

It is Peter! He is ahead! Hans shoots past him. Hilda's eyes fill with tears: Peter *must* beat. Annie's eyes flash proudly. Gretel gazes with clasped hands: four strokes more will take her brother to the columns.

He is there! Yes; but so was young Schummel just a second before. At the last instant, Carl, gathering his powers, had whizzed between them, and passed the goal.

"Carl Schummel, one mile!" shouts the crier.

Soon Madame van Gleck rises again. The falling handkerchief starts the bugle; and the bugle, using its voice as a bow-string, shoots off twenty girls like so many arrows.

It is a beautiful sight; but one has not long to look: before we can fairly distinguish them, they are far in the distance. This time they are close upon one another. It is hard to say, as they come speeding back from the flagstaff, which will reach the columns first. There are new faces among the foremost,—eager, glowing faces, unnoticed before. Katrinka is there, and Hilda; but Gretel and Rychie are in the rear. Gretel is wavering, but, when Rychie passes her, she starts forward afresh. Now they are nearly beside Katrinka. Hilda is still in advance: she is almost "home." She has not faltered since that bugle-note sent her flying: like an arrow, still she is speeding toward the goal. Cheer after cheer rises in the air. Peter is silent; but his eyes shine like stars. "Huzza! Huzza!"

The crier's voice is heard again.

"HILDA VAN GLECK, ONE MILE!"

A loud murmur of approval runs through the crowd, catching the music in its course, till all seems one sound, with a glad rhythmic throbbing in its depths. When the flag waves, all is still.

Once more the bugle blows a terrific blast. It sends off the boys like chaff before the wind,—dark chaff, I admit, and in big pieces.

It is whisked around at the flagstaff, driven faster yet by the cheers and shouts along the line. We begin to see what is coming. There are three boys in advance, this time, and all abreast,—Hans, Peter, and Lambert. Carl soon breaks the ranks.

19

rushing through with a whiff. Fly, Hans; fly, Peter: don't let Carl beat again!—Carl the bitter, Carl the insolent. Van Mounen is flagging; but you are as strong as ever. Hans and Peter, Peter and Hans: which is foremost? We love them both. We scarcely care which is the fleeter.

Hilda, Annie, and Gretel, seated upon the long crimson bench, can remain quiet no longer. They spring to their feet, so different! and yet one in eagerness. Hilda instantly reseats herself: none shall know how interested she is; none shall know how anxious, how filled with one hope. Shut your eyes, then, Hilda, hide your face rippling with joy. Peter has beaten.

"PETER VAN HOLP, ONE MILE!" calls the crier.

The same buzz of excitement as before, while the judges take notes, the same throbbing of music through the din; but something is different. A little crowd presses close about some object near the column. Carl has fallen. He is not hurt, though somewhat stunned. If he were less sullen, he would find more sympathy in these warm young hearts. As it is, they forget him as soon as he is fairly on his feet again.

The girls are to skate their third mile.

How resolute the little maidens look as they stand in a line! Some are solemn with a sense of responsibility; some wear a smile half-bashful, half-provoked: but one air of determination pervades them all.

This third mile may decide the race. Still, if neither Gretel nor Hilda win, there is yet a chance among the rest for the silver skates.

Each girl feels sure, that, this time, she will accomplish the distance in one-half the time. How they stamp to try their runners! How nervously they examine each strap! How erect they stand at last, every eye upon Madame van Gleck!

The bugle thrills through them again. With quivering eagerness they spring forward, bending, but in perfect balance. Each flashing stroke seems longer than the last.

Now they are skimming off in the distance.

Again the eager straining of eyes; again the shouts and cheering; again the thrill of excitement, as, after a few moments, four or five, in advance of the rest, come speeding back, nearer, nearer, to the white columns.

Who is first? Not Rychie, Katrinka, Annie, nor Hilda, nor the girl in yellow, but Gretel,—Gretel, the fleetest sprite of a girl that ever skated. She was but playing in the earlier race: *now* she is in earnest, or, rather, something within her has determined to win. That lithe little form makes no effort; but it cannot stop,—not until the goal is passed!

In vain the crier lifts his voice: he cannot be heard. He has no news to tell: it is already ringing through the crowd,—*Gretel has won the silver skates!*

Like a bird, she has flown over the ice; like a bird, she looks about her in a timid, startled way. She longs to dart to the sheltered nook where her father and mother stand. But Hans is beside her: the girls are crowding round. Hilda's kind, joyous voice breathes in her ear. From that hour, none will despise her. Goose-girl, or not, Gretel stands acknowledged Queen of the Skaters.

With natural pride, Hans turns to see if Peter van Holp is witnessing his sister's triumph. Peter is not looking toward them at all. He is kneeling, bending his troubled face low, and working hastily at his skate-strap. Hans is beside him at once.

"Are you in trouble, mynheer?"

"Ah, Hans! that you? Yes, my fun is over. I tried to tighten my strap, to make a new hole; and this botheration of a knife has cut it nearly in two."

"Mynheer," said Hans, at the same time pulling off a skate, "you must use my strap!"

"Not I, indeed, Hans Brinker!" cried Peter, looking up, "though I thank you warmly. Go to your post, my friend: the bugle will sound in a minute."

"Mynheer!" pleaded Hans in a husky voice. "You have called me your friend. Take this strap —quick! There is not an instant to lose. I shall not skate this time: indeed, I am out of practice. Mynheer, you *must* take it;" and Hans, blind and deaf to any remonstrance, slipped his strap into Peter's skate, and implored him to put it on.

"Come, Peter!" cried Lambert from the line: "we are waiting for you."

"For madame's sake," pleaded Hans, "be quick! She is motioning to you to join the racers. There, the skate is almost on: quick, mynheer, fasten it. I could not possibly win. The race lies between Master Schummel and yourself."

"You are a noble fellow, Hans!" cried Peter, yielding at last. He sprang to his post just as the white handkerchief fell to the ground. The bugle sends forth its blast, loud, clear, and ringing.

Off go the boys.

"Mein Gott!" cries a tough old fellow from Delft. "They beat every thing,—these Amsterdam youngsters. See them!"

See them, indeed! They are winged Mercuries, every one of them. What mad errand are they on?

Ah, I know: they are hunting Peter van Holp. He is some fleet-footed runaway from Olympus. Mercury and his troop of winged cousins are in full chase. They will catch him! Now Carl is the runaway. The pursuit grows furious. Ben is foremost.

The chase turns in a cloud of mist. It is coming this way. Who is hunted now? Mercury himself. It is Peter, Peter van Holp! Fly, Peter! Hans is watching you. He is sending all his fleetness, all his strength, into your feet. Your mother and sister are pale with eagerness. Hilda is trembling, and dare not look up. Fly, Peter! The crowd has not gone deranged: it is only cheering. The pursuers are close upon you. Touch the white column! It beckons; it is reeling before you—it—

"Huzza! Huzza! Peter has won the silver skates!"

"PETER VAN HOLP!" shouted the crier. But who heard him? "Peter van Holp!" shouted a hundred voices; for he was the favorite boy of the place. "Huzza! Huzza!"

Now the music was resolved to be heard. It struck up a lively air, then a tremendous march.

23

The spectators, thinking something new was about to happen, deigned to listen and to look.

The racers formed in single file. Peter, being tallest, stood first. Gretel, the smallest of all, took her place at the end. Hans, who had borrowed a strap from the cake-boy, was near the head.

Three gayly-twined arches were placed at intervals upon the river, facing the Van Gleck pavilion.

Skating slowly, and in perfect time to the music, the boys and girls moved forward, led on by Peter. It was beautiful to see the bright procession glide along like a living creature. It curved and doubled, and drew its graceful length in and out among the arches: whichever way Peter, the head, went, the body was sure to follow. Sometimes it steered direct for the centre arch; then, as if seized with a new impulse, turned away and curled itself about the first one; then unwound slowly, and bending low, with quick, snake-like curvings, crossed the river, passing at length through the farthest arch.

When the music was slow, the procession seemed to crawl like a thing afraid: it grew livelier, and the creature darted forward with a spring, gliding rapidly among the arches, in and out, curling, twisting, turning, never losing form, until at the shrill call of the bugle rising above the music, it suddenly resolved itself into boys and girls standing in double semicircle before Madame van Gleck's pavilion.

Peter and Gretel stand in the centre, in advance of the others. Madame van Gleck rises majestically. Gretel trembles, but feels that she must look at the beautiful lady. She cannot hear what is said, there is such a buzzing all around her. She is thinking that she ought to try and make a courtesy, such as her mother makes to the *meester*, when suddenly something so dazzling is placed in her hand that she gives a cry of joy.

Then she ventures to look about her. Peter, too, has something in his hands. "Oh, Oh! how splendid!" she cries; and "Oh! how splendid!" is echoed as far as people can see.

Meantime the silver skates flash in the sunshine, throwing dashes of light upon those two happy faces.

Mevrouw van Gend sends a little messenger with her bouquets,—one for Hilda, one for Carl, and others for Peter and Gretel.

At sight of the flowers, the Queen of the Skaters becomes uncontrollable. With a bright stare of gratitude, she gathers skates and bouquet in her apron, hugs them to her bosom, and darts off to search for her father and mother in the scattering crowd.

NELLY'S HOSPITAL

By Louisa M. Alcott

NELLY sat beside her mother picking lint; but while her fingers flew, her eyes often looked wistfully out into the meadow, golden with buttercups, and bright with sunshine. Presently she said, rather bashfully, but very earnestly, "Mamma, I want to tell you a little plan I've made, if you'll please not laugh."

"I think I can safely promise that, my dear," said her mother, putting down her work that she might listen quite respectfully.

Nelly looked pleased, and went on confidingly.

"Since brother Will came home with his lame foot, and I've helped you tend him, I've heard a great deal about hospitals, and liked it very much. To-day I said I wanted to go and be a nurse, like Aunt Mercy; but Will laughed, and told me I'd better begin by nursing sick birds and butterflies and pussies before I tried to take care of men. I did not like to be made fun of, but I've been thinking that it would be very pleasant to have a little hospital all my own, and be a nurse in it, because, if I took pains, so many pretty creatures might be made well, perhaps. Could I, mamma?"

Her mother wanted to smile at the idea, but did not, for Nelly looked up with her heart and eyes so full of tender compassion, both for the unknown men for whom her little hands had done their best, and for the smaller sufferers nearer home, that she stroked the shining head, and answered readily:

"Yes, Nelly, it will be a proper charity for such a young Samaritan, and you may learn much if you are in earnest. You must study how to feed and nurse your little patients, else your pity will do no good, and your hospital become a prison. I will help you, and Tony shall be your surgeon."

"O mamma, how good you always are to me! Indeed, I am in truly earnest; I will learn, I will be kind, and may I go now and begin?"

"You may, but tell me first where will you have your hospital?"

"In my room, mamma; it is so snug and sunny, and I never should forget it there," said Nelly.

"You must not forget it anywhere. I think that plan will not do. How would you like to find caterpillars walking in your bed, to hear sick pussies mewing in the night, to have beetles clinging to your clothes, or see mice, bugs, and birds tumbling downstairs whenever the door was open?" said her mother.

Nelly laughed at that thought a minute, then clapped her hands, and cried: "Let us have the old summer-house! My doves only use the upper part, and it would be so like Frank in the story-book. Please say yes again, mamma."

Her mother did say yes, and, snatching up her hat, Nelly ran to find Tony, the gardener's son, a pleasant lad of twelve, who was Nelly's favorite playmate. Tony pronounced the plan a "jolly" one, and, leaving his work, followed his young mistress to the summer-house, for she could not wait one minute.

"What must we do first?" she asked, as they stood looking in at the dim, dusty room, full of garden tools, bags of seeds, old flower-pots, and watering-cans.

"Clear out the rubbish, miss," answered Tony.

"Here it goes, then," and Nelly began bundling everything out in such haste that she broke two flower-pots, scattered all the squash-seeds, and brought a pile of rakes and hoes clattering down about her ears.

"Just wait a bit, and let me take the lead, miss. You hand me things, I'll pile 'em in the barrow and wheel 'em off to the barn; then it will save time, and be finished up tidy."

Nelly did as he advised, and very soon nothing but dust remained.

"What next?" she asked, not knowing in the least.

"I'll sweep up while you see if Polly can come and scrub the room out. It ought to be done before you stay here, let alone the patients."

"So it had," said Nelly, looking very wise all of a sudden. "Will says the wards—that means the rooms, Tony—are scrubbed every day or two, and kept very clean, and well venti—something—I can't say it; but it means having a plenty of air come in. I can clean windows while Polly mops, and then we shall soon be done."

Away she ran, feeling very busy and important. Polly came, and very soon the room looked like another place. The four latticed windows were set wide open, so the sunshine came dancing through the vines that grew outside, and curious roses peeped in to see what frolic was afoot. The walls shone white again, for not a spider dared to stay; the wide seat which encircled the room was dustless now,—the floor as nice as willing hands could make it; and the south wind blew away all musty odors with its fragrant breath.

"How fine it looks!" cried Nelly, dancing on the doorstep, lest a foot-print should mar the still damp floor.

"I'd almost like to fall sick for the sake of staying here," said Tony, admiringly. "Now, what sort of beds are you going to have, miss?"

"I suppose it won't do to put butterflies and toads and worms into beds like the real soldiers where Will was?" answered Nelly, looking anxious.

Tony could hardly help shouting at the idea; but, rather than trouble his little mistress, he said very soberly: "I'm afraid they wouldn't lay easy, not being used to it. Tucking up a butterfly would about kill him; the worms would be apt to get lost among the bed-clothes; and the toads would tumble out the first thing."

"I shall have to ask mamma about it. What will you do while I'm gone?" said Nelly, unwilling that a moment should be lost.

"I'll make frames for nettings to the windows, else the doves will come in and eat up the sick people."

"I think they will know that it is a hospital, and be too kind to hurt or frighten their neighbors," began Nelly; but as she spoke, a plump white dove walked in, looked about with its red-winged eyes, and quietly pecked up a tiny bug that had just ventured out from the crack where it had taken refuge when the deluge came.

"Yes, we must have the nettings. I'll ask mamma for some lace," said Nelly, when she saw that; and, taking her pet dove on her shoulder, told it about her hospital as she went toward the house; for, loving all little creatures as she did, it grieved her to have any harm befall even the least or plainest of them. She had a sweet child-fancy that her playmates understood her language as she did theirs, and that birds, flowers, animals, and insects felt for her the same affection which she felt for them. Love always makes friends, and nothing seemed to fear the gentle child; but welcomed her like a little sun who shone alike on all, and never suffered an eclipse.

She was gone some time, and when she came back her mind was full of new plans, one hand full of rushes, the other of books, while over her head floated the lace, and a bright green ribbon hung across her arm.

"Mamma says that the best beds will be little baskets, boxes, cages, and any sort of thing that suits the patients; for each will need different care and food and medicine. I have not baskets enough, so, as I cannot have pretty white beds, I am going to braid pretty green nests for my patients, and, while I do it, mamma thought you'd read to me the pages she has marked, so that we may begin right."

"Yes, miss; I like that. But what is the ribbon for?" asked Tony.

"O, that's for you. Will says that, if you are to be an army surgeon, you must have a green band on your arm; so I got this to tie on when we play hospital."

Tony let her decorate the sleeve of his gray jacket, and when the nettings were done, the welcome books were opened and enjoyed. It was a happy time, sitting in the sunshine, with leaves pleasantly astir all about them, doves cooing overhead, and flowers sweetly gossiping together through the

about. Does this look like an amb'lance, Will?"

"Not a bit, but it shall, if you and mamma like to help me. I want four long bits of cane, a square of white cloth, some pieces of thin wood, and the gum-pot," said Will, sitting up to examine the little cart, feeling like a boy again as he took out his knife and began to whittle.

Upstairs and downstairs ran Nelly till all necessary materials were collected, and almost breathlessly she watched her brother arch the canes over the cart, cover them with the cloth, and fit an upper shelf of small compartments, each lined with cotton-wool to serve as beds for wounded insects, lest they should hurt one another or jostle out. The lower part was left free for any larger creatures which Nelly might find. Among her toys she had a tiny cask which only needed a peg to be water-tight; this was filled and fitted in before, because, as the small sufferers needed no seats, there was no place for it behind, and, as Nelly was both horse and driver, it was more convenient in front.

On each side of it stood a box of stores. In one were minute rollers, as bandages are called, a few bottles not yet filled, and a wee doll's jar of cold-cream, because Nelly could not feel that her outfit was complete without a medicine-chest. The other box was full of crumbs, bits of sugar, bird-seed, and grains of wheat and corn, lest any famished stranger should die for want of food before she got it home. Then mamma painted "U. S. San. Com." in bright letters on the cover, and Nelly received her charitable plaything with a long sigh of satisfaction.

"Nine o'clock already. Bless me, what a short evening this has been," exclaimed Will, as Nelly came to give him her good-night kiss.

"And such a happy one," she answered. "Thank you very, very much, dear Will. I only wish my little amb'lance was big enough for you to go in,—I'd so like to give you the first ride."

"Nothing I should like better, if it were possible, though I've a prejudice against ambulances in general. But as I cannot ride, I'll try and hop out to your hospital to-morrow, and see how you get on,"—which was a great deal for Captain Will to say, because he had been too listless to leave his sofa for several days.

That promise sent Nelly happily away to bed, only stopping to pop her head out of the window to see if it was likely to be a fair day to-morrow, and to tell Tony about the new plan as he passed below.

"Where shall you go to look for your first load of sick folks, miss?" he asked.

"All round the garden first, then through the grove, and home across the brook. Do you think I can find any patients so?" said Nelly.

"I know you will. Good night, miss," and Tony walked away with a merry look on his face, that Nelly would not have understood if she had seen it.

Up rose the sun bright and early, and up rose Nurse Nelly almost as early and as bright. Breakfast was taken in a great hurry, and before the dew was off the grass this branch of the S. C. was all astir. Papa, mamma, big brother and baby sister, men and maids, all looked out to see the funny little ambulance depart, and nowhere in all the summer fields was there a happier child than Nelly, as she went smiling down the garden path, where tall flowers kissed her as she passed and every blithe bird seemed singing a "Good speed!"

"How I wonder what I shall find first," she thought, looking sharply on all sides as she went. Crickets chirped, grasshoppers leaped, ants worked busily at their subterranean houses, spiders spun shining webs from twig to twig, bees were coming for their bags of gold, and butterflies had just begun their holiday. A large white one alighted on the top of the ambulance, walked over the inscription as if spelling it letter by letter, then floated away from flower to flower, like one carrying the good news far and wide.

"Now every one will know about the hospital and be glad to see me coming," thought Nelly. And indeed it seemed so, for just then a blackbird, sitting on the garden wall, burst out with a song full of musical joy, Nelly's kitten came running after to stare at the wagon and rub her soft side against it, a bright-eyed toad looked out from his cool bower among the lily-leaves, and at that minute Nelly found her first patient. In one of the dewy cobwebs hanging from a shrub near by sat a fat black and yellow spider, watching a fly whose delicate wings were just caught in the net. The poor fly buzzed pitifully, and struggled so hard that the whole web shook; but the more he struggled, the more he entangled himself, and the fierce spider was preparing to descend that it might weave a shroud about its prey, when a little finger broke the threads and lifted the fly safely into the palm of a hand, where he lay faintly humming his thanks.

Nelly had heard much about contrabands, knew who they were, and was very much interested in them; so, when she freed the poor black fly, she played he was her contraband, and felt glad that her first patient was one that needed help so much. Carefully brushing away as much of the web as she could, she left small Pompey, as she named him, to free his own legs, lest her clumsy fingers should hurt him; then she laid him in one of the soft beds with a grain or two of sugar if he needed refreshment, and bade him rest and recover from his fright, remembering that he was at liberty to fly away whenever he liked, because she had no wish to make a slave of him.

Feeling very happy over this new friend, Nelly went on singing softly as she walked, and presently she found a pretty caterpillar dressed in brown fur, although the day was warm. He lay so still she thought him dead, till he rolled himself into a ball as she touched him.

"I think you are either faint from the heat of this thick coat of yours, or that you are going to make a cocoon of yourself, Mr. Fuzz," said Nelly. "Now I want to see you turn into a butterfly, so I shall take you, and if you get lively again I will let you go. I shall play that you have given out on a march, as the soldiers sometimes do, and been left behind for the Sanitary people to see to."

In went sulky Mr. Fuzz, and on trundled the ambulance till a golden green rose-beetle was discovered, lying on his back kicking as if in a fit.

"Dear me, what shall I do for him?" thought Nelly. "He acts as baby did when she was so ill, and mamma put her in a warm bath. I haven't got my little tub here, or any hot water, and I'm afraid the beetle would not like it if I had. Perhaps he has pain in his stomach; I'll turn him over, and pat his back, as nurse does baby's when she cries for pain like that."

She set the beetle on his legs, and did her best to comfort him; but he was evidently in great distress, for he could not walk, and instead of lifting his emerald overcoat, and spreading the wings that lay underneath, he turned over again, and kicked more violently than before. Not knowing what to do, Nelly put him into one of her soft nests for Tony to cure if possible. She found no more patients in the garden except a dead bee, which she wrapped in a leaf, and took home to bury. When she came to the grove, it was so green and cool she longed to sit and listen to the whisper of the pines, and watch the larch-tassels wave in the wind. But, recollecting her charitable errand, she went rustling along the pleasant path till she came to another patient, over which she stood considering several minutes before she could decide whether it was best to take it to her hospital, because it was a little gray snake, with a bruised tail. She knew it would not hurt her, yet she was afraid of it; she thought it pretty, yet could not like it; she pitied its pain, yet shrunk from helping it, for it had a fiery eye, and a keen quivering tongue, that looked as if longing to bite.

"He is a rebel, I wonder if I ought to be good to him," thought Nelly, watching the reptile writhe with pain. "Will said there were sick rebels in his hospital, and one was very kind to him. It says, too, in my little book, 'Love your enemies.' I think snakes are mine, but I guess I'll try and love him because God made him. Some boy will kill him if I leave him here, and then perhaps his mother will be very sad about it. Come, poor worm, I wish to help you, so be patient, and don't frighten me."

Then Nelly laid her little handkerchief on the ground, and with a stick gently lifted the wounded snake upon it, and, folding it together, laid it in the ambulance. She was thoughtful after that, and so busy puzzling her young head about the duty of loving those who hate us, and being kind to those who are disagreeable or unkind, that she went through the rest of the wood quite forgetful of her work. A soft "Queek, queek!" made her look up and listen. The sound came from the long meadow-grass, and, bending it carefully back, she found a half-fledged bird, with one wing trailing on the ground, and its eyes dim with pain or hunger.

"You darling thing, did you fall out of your nest and hurt your wing?" cried Nelly, looking up into the single tree that stood near by. No nest was to be seen, no parent birds hovered overhead, and little Robin could only tell its troubles in that mournful "Queek, queek, queek!"

38

Nelly ran to get both her chests, and, sitting down beside the bird, tried to feed it. To her great joy it ate crumb after crumb, as if it were half starved, and soon fluttered nearer with a confiding fearlessness that made her very proud. Soon baby Robin seemed quite comfortable, his eye brightened, he "queeked" no more, and but for the drooping wing would have been himself again. With one of her bandages Nelly bound both wings closely to his sides for fear he should hurt himself by trying to fly; and though he seemed amazed at her proceedings, he behaved very well, only staring at her, and ruffling up his few feathers in a funny way that made her laugh. Then she had to discover some way of accommodating her two larger patients so that neither should hurt nor alarm the other. A bright thought came to her after much pondering. Carefully lifting the handkerchief, she pinned the two ends to the roof of the cart, and there swung little Forked-tongue, while Rob lay easily below.

By this time Nelly began to wonder how it happened that she found so many more injured things than ever before. But it never entered her innocent head that Tony had searched the wood and meadow before she was up, and laid most of these creatures ready to her hands, that she might not be disappointed. She had not yet lost her faith in fairies, so she fancied they too belonged to her small sisterhood, and presently it did really seem impossible to doubt that the good folk had been at work.

Coming to the bridge that crossed the brook,

she stopped a moment to watch the water ripple over the bright pebbles, the ferns bend down to drink, and the funny tadpoles frolic in quieter nooks, where the sun shone, and the dragon-flies swung among the rushes. When Nelly turned to go on, her blue eyes opened wide, and the handle of the ambulance dropped with a noise that caused a stout frog to skip into the water heels over head.

Directly in the middle of the bridge was a pretty green tent, made of two tall burdock leaves. The stems were stuck into cracks between the boards, the tips were pinned together with a thorn, and one great buttercup nodded in the doorway like a sleepy sentinel. Nelly stared and smiled, listened, and looked about on every side. Nothing was seen but the quiet meadow and the shady grove, nothing was heard but the babble of the brook and the cheery music of the bobolinks.

"Yes," said Nelly softly to herself, "that is a fairy tent, and in it I may find a baby elf sick with whooping-cough or scarlet-fever. How splendid it would be! only I could never nurse such a dainty thing."

Stooping eagerly, she peeped over the buttercup's drowsy head, and saw what seemed a tiny cock of hay. She had no time to feel disappointed, for the haycock began to stir, and, looking nearer, she beheld two silvery gray mites, who wagged wee tails, and stretched themselves as if they had just waked up. Nelly knew that they were young field-mice, and rejoiced over them, feeling rather relieved that no fairy had appeared, though she still believed them to have had a hand in the matter.

"I shall call the mice my Babes in the Wood, because they are lost and covered up with leaves," said Nelly, as she laid them in her snuggest bed, where they nestled close together, and fell fast asleep again.

Being very anxious to get home, that she might tell her adventures, and show how great was the need of a sanitary commission in that region, Nelly marched proudly up the avenue, and, having displayed her load, hurried to the hospital, where another applicant was waiting for her. On the step of the door lay a large turtle, with one claw gone, and on his back was pasted a bit of paper, with his name,—"Commodore Waddle, U. S. N." Nelly knew this was a joke of Will's, but welcomed the ancient mariner, and called Tony to help her get him in.

All that morning they were very busy settling the new-comer, for both people and books had to be consulted before they could decide what diet and treatment was best for each. The winged contraband had taken Nelly at her word, and flown away on the journey home. Little Rob was put in a large cage, where he could use his legs, yet not injure his lame wing. Forked-tongue lay under a wire cover, on sprigs of fennel, for the gardener said that snakes were fond of it. The Babes in the Wood were put to bed in one of the rush baskets, under a cotton-wool coverlet. Greenback, the beetle, found ease for his unknown aches in the warm heart of a rose, where he sunned himself all

41

day. The Commodore was made happy in a tub of water, grass, and stones, and Mr. Fuzz was put in a well-ventilated glass box to decide whether he would be a cocoon or not.

Tony had not been idle while his mistress was away, and he showed her the hospital garden he had made close by, in which were cabbage, nettle, and mignonette plants for the butterflies, flowering herbs for the bees, chick-weed and hemp for the birds, catnip for the pussies, and plenty of room left for whatever other patients might need. In the afternoon, while Nelly did her task at lint-picking, talking busily to Will as she worked, and interesting him in her affairs, Tony cleared a pretty spot in the grove for the burying-ground, and made ready some small bits of slate on which to write the names of those who died. He did not have it ready an hour too soon, for at sunset two little graves were needed, and Nurse Nelly shed tender tears for her first losses as she laid the motherless mice in one smooth hollow, and the gray-coated rebel in the other. She had learned to care for him already, and when she found him dead, was very glad she had been kind to him, hoping that he knew it, and died happier in her hospital than all alone in the shadowy wood.

The rest of Nelly's patients prospered, and of the many added afterward few died, because of Tony's skilful treatment and her own faithful care. Every morning when the day proved fair the little ambulance went out upon its charitable errand; every afternoon Nelly worked for the human sufferers whom she loved; and every evening brother

Will read aloud to her from useful books, showed
her wonders with his microscope, or prescribed
remedies for the patients, whom he soon knew by
name and took much interest in. It was Nelly's
holiday; but, though she studied no lessons, she
learned much, and unconsciously made her pretty
play both an example and a rebuke for others.

At first it seemed a childish pastime, and people laughed. But there was something in the familiar words "sanitary," "hospital," and "ambulance" that made them pleasant sounds to many
ears. As reports of Nelly's work went through the
neighborhood, other children came to see and copy
her design. Rough lads looked ashamed when in
her wards they found harmless creatures hurt by
them, and going out they said among themselves,
"We won't stone birds, chase butterflies, and
drown the girls' little cats any more, though we
won't tell them so." And most of the lads kept
their word so well that people said there never had
been so many birds before as all that summer
haunted wood and field. Tender-hearted playmates brought their pets to be cured; even busy
farmers had a friendly word for the small charity,
which reminded them so sweetly of the great one
which should never be forgotten; lonely mothers
sometimes looked out with wet eyes as the little ambulance went by, recalling thoughts of absent sons
who might be journeying painfully to some far-off
hospital, where brave women waited to tend them
with hands as willing, hearts as tender, as those the
gentle child gave to her self-appointed task.

At home the charm worked also. No more idle

days for Nelly, or fretful ones for Will, because
the little sister would not neglect the helpless creatures so dependent upon her, and the big brother
was ashamed to complain after watching the patience of these lesser sufferers, and merrily said he
would try to bear his own wound as quietly and
bravely as the "Commodore" bore his. Nelly
never knew how much good she had done Captain
Will till he went away again in the early autumn.
Then he thanked her for it, and though she cried
for joy and sorrow she never forgot it, because he
left something behind him which always pleasantly
reminded her of the double success her little hospital had won.

When Will was gone and she had prayed softly
in her heart that God would keep him safe and
bring him home again, she dried her tears and went
away to find comfort in the place where he had
spent so many happy hours with her. She had not
been there before that day, and when she reached
the door she stood quite still and wanted very much
to cry again, for something beautiful had happened. She had often asked Will for a motto for
her hospital, and he had promised to find her one.
She thought he had forgotten it; but even in the
hurry of that busy day he had found time to do
more than keep his word, while Nelly sat indoors,
lovingly brightening the tarnished buttons on the
blue coat that had seen so many battles.

Above the roof, where the doves cooed in the
sun, now rustled a white flag with the golden "S.
C." shining on it as the wind tossed it to and fro.
Below, on the smooth panel of the door, a skilful

pencil had drawn two arching ferns, in whose soft shadow, poised upon a mushroom, stood a little figure of Nurse Nelly, and underneath it another of Dr. Tony bottling medicine, with spectacles upon his nose. Both hands of the miniature Nelly were outstretched, as if beckoning to a train of insects, birds and beasts, which was so long that it not only circled round the lower rim of this fine sketch, but dwindled in the distance to mere dots and lines. Such merry conceits as one found there! A mouse bringing the tail it had lost in some cruel trap, a dor-bug with a shade over its eyes, an invalid butterfly carried in a tiny litter by long-legged spiders, a fat frog with gouty feet hopping upon crutches, Jenny Wren sobbing in a nice handkerchief, as she brought dear dead Cock Robin to be restored to life. Rabbits, lambs, cats, calves, and turtles, all came trooping up to be healed by the benevolent little maid who welcomed them so heartily.

Nelly laughed at these comical mites till the tears ran down her cheeks, and thought she never could be tired of looking at them. But presently she saw four lines clearly printed underneath her picture, and her childish face grew sweetly serious as she read the words of a great poet, which Will had made both compliment and motto:—

> "He prayeth best who loveth best
>   All things, both great and small;
> For the dear God who loveth us,
>   He made and loveth all."

A FOX AND A RAVEN

By Rebecca Harding Davis

[A raven, sitting high up on a limb, had a fine piece of cheese. He was just going to enjoy it, when along came Mr. Fox. Now the fox wanted the cheese, and he knew he could not catch the raven. So he began to flatter the raven's croaking voice, and to beg the raven for one of his "sweet songs." At last the poor raven, silly with flattery, opened his mouth to sing—when lo! the cheese dropped to the ground, and off ran the wily fox with the stolen treasure in his mouth. The raven flew away, and never was heard of again.]

DONEE was a king's daughter. She had heard her father talk of the battles into which he had led his mighty warriors, and of how all the world that she knew had once been his, from the hills behind which the sun rose to the broad rushing river where it set. Now all of this account was strictly true.

But the king, as he talked, wore no clothes but a muddy pair of cotton trousers, and sat on a log in the sun, a pig rooting about his bare feet. Black Joe, going by, called him a lazy old red-skin; and that was true, too. But these differing accounts naturally confused Donee's mind. When the old chief was dead, however, there was an end of all talk of his warriors or battles. A large part of the land was left, though; a long stretch of river bottom and forests, with but very little swamp. Donee's brother, Oostogah, when he was in a good humor, planted and hoed a field of corn (as he had no wife to do it for him), and with a little fish and game,

46

they managed to find enough to eat. Oostogah and
the little girl lived in a hut built of logs and mud,
and, as the floor of it never had been scrubbed, the
grass actually began to grow out of the dirt in the
corners. There was a log smouldering on the
hearth, where Donee baked cakes of pounded corn
and beans in the ashes, and on the other side of the
dark room was the heap of straw where she slept.
Besides this, there were two hacked stumps of
trees which served for chairs, and an iron pot out
of which they ate; and there you have the royal
plenishing of *that* palace.

All the other Indians had long ago gone West.
Donee had nothing and nobody to play with. She
was as easily scared as a rabbit; yet sometimes,
when Oostogah was gone for days together, she
was so lonely that she would venture down through
the swamp to peep out at the water-mill and the two
or three houses which the white people had built.
The miller, of all the white people, was the one
that she liked best to watch, he was so big and
round, and jolly; and one day, when he had met her
in the path, he did not call her "Injun," or "red
nigger," as the others did, but had said: "Where's
your brother, my dear?" just as if she were white.
She saw, sometimes, his two little girls and boy
playing about the mill-door, and they were round
and fat, and jolly, just like their father.

At last, one day Oostogah went down to the mill,
and Donee plucked up her courage and followed
him. When she was there hiding close behind the
trough in which the horses were watered, so that
nobody could see her, she heard the miller say to

her brother: "You ought to go to work to clear
your land, my lad. In two years there will be
hundreds of people moving in here, and you own
the best part of the valley."

Oostogah nodded. "The whole country once belonged to my people."

"That's neither here nor there," said the miller.
"Dead chickens don't count for hatching. You go
to work now and clear your land, and you can sell
it for enough to give you and this little girl behind
the trough an education. Enough to give you both
a chance equal to any white children."

Oostogah nodded again, but said nothing. He
was shrewd enough, and could work, too, when he
was in the humor. "Come, Donee," he said.

But the miller's little Thad. and Jenny had
found Donee behind the trough, and the three were
making a nettle basket together, and were very
well acquainted already.

"Let the child stay till you come back from fish-
ing, Oostogah," said the miller.

So Donee staid all the afternoon. Jenny and
Betty rolled and shouted, and could not talk fast
enough with delight because they had this new little
girl to play with, and Thad. climbed all the trees,
as Jenny said, to "show off," and Betty tumbled
into the trough head over heels and was taken out
dripping.

Donee was very quiet, but it was to her as if the
end of the world had come, all this was so happy
and wonderful. She never had had anybody to
play with before.

Then, when Betty was carried in to be dried and

dressed, there was, too, the bright, cheerful room, with a lovely blue carpet on the floor, and a white spread on the bed with fringe, and red dahlias that shone in the sun, putting their heads in at the window. Betty's mother did not scold when she took her wet clothes off, but said some funny things which made them laugh. She looked at Donee now and then, standing with her little hands clasped behind her back.

"Does your mother *never* wash or dress you, Donee?" said Betty.

"She is dead," said Donee.

Betty's mother did not say any more funny things after that. When she had finished dressing Betty, to the tying of her shoes, she called the little Indian girl up to her.

"What can you do?" she said. "Sew? Make moccasins?"

She had the pleasantest voice. Donee was not at all afraid. "I can sew. I can make baskets," she said. "I am going to make a basket for every one of you."

"Very well. You can have a tea-party, Jenny, out of doors." Then she opened a cupboard. "Here are the dishes," taking out a little box. "And bread, jam, milk, sugar, and candy."

"Candy!" cried Betty, rushing out to tell Thad.

"Candy? Hooray!" shouted Thad.

For there are no shops out in that wild country where a boy can run for a stick of lemon or gumdrops every time he gets a penny. It was very seldom that Thad. or Betty could have a taste of those red and white "bull's eyes" which their mother now took out of the jar in the locked cupboard. They knew she brought it out to please the little Indian girl, whose own mother was dead.

Jenny set the table for the tea-party under a big oak. There was a flat place on one of the round roots that rose out of the moss, which was the very thing for a table. So there she spread the little white and gold plates and cups and saucers, with the meat dish (every bit as large as your hand), in the middle, full of candy. The milk, of course, was put in the pot for coffee, and set on three dead leaves to boil; and Jenny allowed Donee to fill the jam dishes herself, with her own hands. Donee could hardly get her breath as she did it.

When they were all ready they sat down. The sun shone, and the wind was blowing, and the water of the mill-race flashed and gurgled as it went by, and a song-sparrow perched himself on the fence close to them and sang, and sang, just as if he knew what was going on.

"He wants to come to the party!" said Betty, and then they all laughed. Donee laughed too.

The shining plates just fitted into the moss, and there was a little pitcher, the round-bellied part of which was covered with sand, while the handle and top were, Jenny said, of solid gold; that was put in the middle of all.

Donee did not think it was like fairy-land or heaven, because she had never in her life heard of fairy-land or heaven. She had never seen anything but her own filthy hut, with its iron pot and wooden spoons.

When it was all over, the children's mother

(Donee felt as if she was her mother too) called her in, and took out of that same cupboard a roll of the loveliest red calico.

"Now, Donee," she said, "if you can make yourself a dress of this I will give you this box," and she opened a box, just like Jenny's. Inside, packed in thin slips of paper, was a set of dishes; pure white, with the tiniest rose-bud in the middle of each; cups, saucers, meat-dish, coffee-pot, and all; and, below all, a pitcher, with sand on the brown bottom, but the top and handle of solid gold!

Donee went back to the hut, trotting along beside Oostogah, her roll of calico under her arm. The next day she cut it out into a slip and began to sew.

Oostogah was at work all day cutting down dead trees. When he came in at night, Donee said: "If you sold the land for much money, could we have a home like the miller's?"

Oostogah was as much astonished as if a chicken had asked him a question, but he said, "Yes."

"Would I be like Jenny and Betty?"

"You're a chief's daughter," grunted Oostogah.

One day in the next week she went down to the river far in the woods, and took a bath, combing her long straight black hair down her shoulders. Then she put on her new dress, and went down to the miller's house. It was all very quiet, for the children were not there, but their mother came to the door. She laughed out loud with pleasure when she saw Donee. The red dress was just the right color for her to wear with her dark skin and black hair. Her eyes were soft and shy, and her bare feet and arms (like most Indian women's) pretty enough to be copied in marble.

"You are a good child—you're a very good child! Here are the dishes. I wish the children were at home. Sit right down on the step now and eat a piece of pie."

But Donee could not eat the pie, her heart was so full.

"Hillo!" called the miller, when he saw her. "Why, what a nice girl you are to-day, Dony! Your brother's hard at work, eh? It will all come right, then."

Donee stood around for a long time, afraid to say what she wanted.

"What is it?" asked the miller's wife.

Donee managed to whisper, if she were to have a party the next day, could the children come to it? and their mother said: "Certainly, in the evening."

When the little girl ran down the hill, the miller said: "Seems as if't would be easy to make Christians out of them two."

"I'm going to do what I can for Donee," said the miller's wife.

It was not so easy for the little red-skinned girl to have a party, for she had neither jam nor bread, nor butter, not to mention candy. But she was up very early the next morning, and made tiny little cakes of corn, no bigger than your thumbnail, and she went to a hollow tree she knew of and got a cupful of honey, and brought some red haws, and heaps of nuts, hickory and chestnuts. When Oostogah had gone, she set out her little dishes under a big oak, and dressed herself in her lovely frock, though she knew the party could not begin for hours and hours. The brown cakes and honey, and scarlet haws, were in the white dishes, and the gold pitcher, with a big purple flower, was in the middle. Donee sat down and looked at it all. In a year or two Oostogah would build a house like the miller's, and she should have a blue carpet on the floor, and a white bed, and wear red frocks every day, like Betty.

Just then she heard voices talking. Oostogah had come back; he sat upon a log; and the trader, who came around once a year, stood beside him, a pack open at his feet. It was this peddler, Hawk, who was talking.

"I tell you, Oostogy, the miller's a fool. There's no new settlers coming here, and nobody wants your land. There's hundreds and thousands of acres beyond better than this. You'd better take my offer. Look at that suit!"

He held up short trousers of blue cloth worked with colored porcupine quills, and a scarlet mantle glittering with beads and gold fringe.

"I don't want it," grunted Oostogah. "Sell my land for big pile money."

"Oh, very well. I don't want to buy your land. There's thousands of acres to be had for the asking, but there's not such a dress as that in the United States. I had that dress made on purpose for you, Oostogy. I said: 'Make me a dress for the son of a great chief. The handsomest man'" (eying the lad from head to foot) "'that lives this side of the great water.'"

Oostogah grunted, but his eyes began to sparkle.

"Here now, Oostogy, just try it on to please me. I'd like to see you dressed like a chief for once."

Oostogah, nothing loth, dropped his dirty blanket, and was soon rigged in the glittering finery, while Hawk nodded in rapt admiration.

"There's not a man in the country, red-skin or pale-face, but would know you for the son of the great Denomah. Go look down in the creek, Oostogy."

Oostogah went, and came back, walking more slowly. He began to take off his mantle.

"There's a deputation from these Northern tribes going this winter to see the Great Father at Washington. If Oostogy had a proper dress he could go. But shall the son of Denomah come before the Great Father in a torn horse-blanket?"

"Your words are too many," said Oostogah. "I have made up my mind. I will sell you the land for the clothes."

Donee came up then, and stood directly before him, looking up at him. But she said nothing. It is not the habit of Indian women and children to speak concerning matters of importance.

Oostogah pushed her out of the way, and, with the trader, went into the hut to finish their bargain.

In an hour or two her brother came to Donee. He had his new clothes in a pack on his back. "Come," he said, pointing beyond the great river to the dark woods.

"We will come back here again, Oostogah?"

"No; we will never come back."

Donee went to the tree and looked down at the party she had made; at the little dishes with the

A FOX AND A RAVEN

rose on each. But she did not lift one of them up. She took off her pretty dress and laid it beside them, and, going to the hut, put on her old rags again. Then she came out and followed her brother, whose face was turned toward the great dark woods in the west.

When the miller's children came to the party that afternoon, a pig was lying on Donee's red dress, and the dishes were scattered and broken. But the hut was empty.

*   *   *   *   *   *   *   *

A year afterward, the miller came back from a long journey. After he had kissed and hugged his wife and little ones, he said: "You remember, wife, how Hawk cheated that poor Indian lad out of his land?"

"Yes; I always said it was the old story of the fox and the foolish raven over again."

"It was the old story of the white and the red man over again. But out in an Indian village I found Donee sick and starving."

The miller's wife jumped to her feet. The tears rushed to her eyes. "What did you do? What did you do?"

"Well, there wasn't but one thing to do, and I did that." He went out to the wagon and carried in the little Indian girl, and laid her on the bed.

"Poor child! Poor child! Where is Oostogah?"

The miller shook his head. "Don't ask any questions about him. The raven flew away to the woods, and was never heard of again. Better if that were the end of Oostogah."

Donee, opening her tired eyes, saw the blue

carpet and the white bed where she lay, and the red dahlias shining in the sun and looking in at the window, and beside her were the children, and the children's mother smiling down on her with tears in her eyes.

THE PRIVATE THEATRICALS

By Mrs. A. D. T. Whitney

SATURDAY was a day of hammering, basting, draping, dressing, rehearsing, running from room to room. Upstairs, in Mrs. Green's garret, Leslie Goldthwaite and Dakie Thayne, with a third party never before introduced upon the stage, had a private practising; and at tea-time, when the great hall was cleared, they got up there with Sin Saxon and Frank Scherman, locked the doors, and in costume, with regular accompaniment of bell and curtain, the performance was repeated.

Dakie Thayne was stage-manager and curtain-puller; Sin Saxon and Frank Scherman represented audience, with clapping and stamping, and laughter that suspended both,—making as nearly the noise of two hundred as two could,—this being an essential part of the rehearsal in respect to the untried nerves of the *debutant,* which might easily be a little uncertain.

"He stands fire like a Yankee veteran."

"It's inimitable," said Sin Saxon, wiping the moist merriment from her eyes. "And your cap, Leslie! And that bonnet! And this unutterable old oddity of a gown! Who did contrive it all?

and where did they come from? You'll carry off the glory of the evening. It ought to be the last."

"No, indeed," said Leslie. "Barbara Frietchie must be last, of course. But I'm so glad you think it will do. I hope they'll be amused."

"Amused! If you could only see your own face!"

"I see Sir Charles's, and that makes mine."

The new performer, you perceive, was an actor with a title.

That night's coach, driving up while the dress-rehearsal of the other tableaux was going on at the hall, brought Cousin Delight to the Green Cottage, and Leslie met her at the door.

Sunday morning was a pause and rest and hush of beauty and joy. They sat—Delight and Leslie —by their open window, where the smell of the lately harvested hay came over from the wide, sun-shiny entrance of the great barn, and away beyond stretched the pine woods, and the hills swelled near in dusky evergreen, and indigo shadows, and less-ened far down toward Winnipiseogee, to where, faint and tender and blue, the outline of little Os-sipee peeped in between great shoulders so mod-estly,—seen only through the clearest air on days like this. Leslie's little table, with fresh white cover, held a vase of ferns and white convolvulus and beside this Cousin Delight's two books that came out always from the top of her trunk,—her Bible and her little "Daily Food." To-day the verses from Old and New Testaments were these: —"The steps of a good man are ordered by the Lord, and he delighteth in his way." "Walk circumspectly, not as fools, but as wise, redeeming the time."

They had a talk about the first,—"The steps,"—the little details,—not merely the general trend and final issue; if, indeed, these could be directed without the other.

"You always make me see things, Cousin Delight," Leslie said.

"It is very plain," Delight answered; "if people only would read the Bible as they read even a careless letter from a friend, counting each word of value, and searching for more meaning and fresh inference to draw out the most. One word often answers great doubts and askings that have troubled the world."

Afterward, they walked round by a still wood-path under the Ledge to the North Village, where there was a service. It was a plain little church, with unpainted pews; but the windows looked forth upon a green mountain-side, and whispers of oaks and pines and river-music crept in, and the breath of sweet water-lilies, heaped in a great bowl upon the communion-table of common stained cherry-wood, floated up and filled the place. The minister, a quiet, gray-haired man, stayed his foot an instant at that simple altar, before he went up the few steps to the desk. He had a sermon in his pocket from the text, "The hairs of your heads are all numbered." He changed it at the moment in his mind, and, when presently he rose to preach, gave forth, in a tone touched, through the fresh presence of that reminding beauty, with the very spontaneousness of the Master's own saying,—"Consider the lilies." And then he told them of God's momently thought and care.

There were scattered strangers, from various houses, among the simple rural congregation. Walking home through the pines again, Delight and Leslie and Dakie Thayne found themselves preceded and followed along the narrow way. Sin Saxon and Frank Scherman came up and joined them when the wider openings permitted.

Two persons just in front were commenting upon the sermon.

"Very fair for a country parson," said a tall, elegant-looking man, whose broad, intellectual brow was touched by dark hair slightly frosted, and whose lip had the curve that betokens self-reliance and strong decision,—"very fair. All the better for not flying too high. Narrow, of course. He seems to think the Almighty has nothing grander to do than to finger every little cog of the tremendous machinery of the universe,—that he measures out the ocean of his purposes as we drop a liquid from a phial. To me it seems belittling the Infinite."

"I don't know whether it is littleness or greatness, Robert, that must escape minutiæ," said his companion, apparently his wife. "If we could reach to the particles, perhaps we might move the mountains."

"We never agree upon this, Margie. We won't begin again. To my mind, the grand plan of things was settled ages ago,—the impulses generated that must needs work on. Foreknowledge and intention, doubtless: in that sense the hairs *were* numbered. But that there is a special direction and interference to-day for you and me—well, we won't argue, as I said; but I never can conceive it so; and I think a wider look at the world brings a question to all such primitive faith."

The speakers turned down a side-way with this, leaving the ledge path and their subject to our friends. Only to their thoughts at first; but presently Cousin Delight said, in a quiet tone, to Leslie, "That doesn't account for the steps, does it?"

"I am glad it *can't,*" said Leslie.

Dakie Thayne turned a look toward Leslie, as if he would gladly know of what she spoke,—a look in which a kind of gentle reverence was strangely mingled with the open friendliness. I cannot easily indicate to you the sort of feeling with which the boy had come to regard this young girl, just above him in years and thought and in the attitude which true womanhood, young or old, takes toward man. He had no sisters; he had been intimately associated with no girl-companions; he had lived with his brother and an uncle and a young aunt, Rose. Leslie Goldthwaite's kindness had drawn him into the sphere of a new and powerful influence,—something different in thought and purpose from the apparent unthought about her; and this lifted her up in his regard and enshrined her with a sort of pure sanctity. He was sometimes really timid before her, in the midst of his frank chivalry.

"I wish you'd tell me," he said suddenly, falling back with her as the path narrowed again. "What are the 'steps?'"

"It was a verse we found this morning,—Cousin Delight and I," Leslie answered; and as she spoke the color came up full in her cheeks, and her voice was a little shy and tremulous. " 'The steps of a good man are ordered by the Lord.' That one word seemed to make one certain. 'Steps,'—not path, nor the end of it; but all the way." Somehow she was quite out of breath as she finished.

Meantime Sin Saxon and Frank had got with Miss Goldthwaite, and were talking too.

"Set spinning," they heard Sin Saxon say, "and then let go. That was his idea. Well! Only it seems to me there's been especial pains taken to show us it can't be done. Or else, why don't they find out perpetual motion? Everything stops after a while, unless—I can't talk theologically, but I mean all right—you hit it again."

"You've a way of your own of putting things, Asenath," said Frank Scherman—with a glance that beamed kindly and admiringly upon her and "her way,"—"but you've put that clear to me as nobody else ever did. A proof set in the very laws themselves,—momentum that must lessen and lose itself with the square of the distance. The machinery cavil won't do."

"Wheels; but a living spirit within the wheels," said Cousin Delight.

"Every instant a fresh impulse; to think of it so makes it real, Miss Goldthwaite,—and grand and awful." The young man spoke with a strength in the clear voice that could be so light and gay.

"And tender, too. 'Thou layest Thine hand upon me,' " said Delight Goldthwaite.

Sin Saxon was quiet; her own thought coming back upon her with a reflective force, and a thrill

61

at her heart at Frank Scherman's words. Had these two only planned tableaux and danced Germans together before?

Dakie Thayne walked on by Leslie Goldthwaite's side, in his happy content touched with something higher and brighter through that instant's approach and confidence. If I were to write down his thought as he walked, it would be with phrase and distinction peculiar to himself and to the boy-mind, —"It's the real thing with her; it don't make a fellow squirm like a pin put out at a caterpillar. She's *good;* but she isn't *pious!*"

This was the Sunday that lay between the busy Saturday and Monday. "It is always so wherever Cousin Delight is," Leslie Goldthwaite said to herself, comparing it with other Sundays that had gone. Yet she too, for weeks before, by the truth that had come into her own life and gone out from it, had been helping to make these moments possible. She had been shone upon, and had put forth; henceforth she should scarcely know when the fruit was ripening or sowing itself anew, or the good and gladness of it were at human lips.

She was in Mrs. Linceford's room on Monday morning, putting high velvet-covered corks to the heels of her slippers, when Sin Saxon came over hurriedly, and tapped at the door.

"*Could* you be *two* old women?" she asked, the instant Leslie opened. "Ginevra Thoresby has given out. She says it's her cold,—that she doesn't feel equal to it; but the amount of it is, she got her chill with the Shannons going away so suddenly, and the Amy Robsart and Queen Elizabeth picture

62

being dropped. There was nothing else to put her in, and so she won't be Barbara."

"Won't be Barbara Frietchie!" cried Leslie, with an astonishment as if it had been angelhood refused.

"No. Barbara Frietchie is only an old woman in a cap and kerchief, and she just puts her head out of a window: the *flag* is the whole of it, Ginevra Thoresby says."

"*May* I do it? Do you think I can be different enough in the two? Will there be time?" Leslie questioned eagerly.

"We'll change the programme, and put 'Taking the Oath' between. The caps can be different, and you can powder your hair for one, and—*would* it do to ask Miss Craydocke for a front for the other?" Sin Saxon had grown delicate in her feeling for the dear old friend whose hair had once been golden.

"I'll tell her about it, and ask her to help me contrive. She'll be sure to think of anything that can be thought of."

"Only there's the dance afterward, and you had so much more costume for the other," Sin Saxon said, demurringly.

"Never mind. I shall *be* Barbara; and Barbara wouldn't dance, I suppose."

"Mother Hubbard would, marvellously."

"Never mind," Leslie answered again, laying down the little slipper, finished.

"She don't care *what* she is, so that she helps along," Sin Saxon said of her, rejoining the others in the hall. "I'm ashamed of myself and all the rest of you, beside her. Now make yourselves as fine as you please."

We must pass over the hours as only stories and dreams do, and put ourselves, at ten of the clock that night, behind the green curtain and the footlights, in the blaze of the three rows of bright lamps, that, one above another, poured their illumination from the left upon the stage, behind the wide picture-frame.

Susan Josselyn and Frank Scherman were just "posed" for "Consolation." They had given Susan this part, after all, because they wanted Martha for "Taking the Oath," afterward. Leslie Goldthwaite was giving a hasty touch to the tent drapery and the gray blanket; Leonard Brookhouse and Dakie Thayne manned the halyards for raising the curtain; there was the usual scuttling about the stage for hasty clearance; and Sin Saxon's hand was on the bell, when Grahame Lowe sprang hastily in through the dressing-room upon the scene.

"Hold on a minute," he said to Brookhouse. "Miss Saxon, General Ingleside and party are over at Green's,—been there since nine o'clock. Oughtn't we to send compliments or something, before we finish up?"

Then there was a pressing forward and an excitement. The wounded soldier sprang from his couch; the nun came nearer, with a quick light in her eye; Leslie Goldthwaite, in her mob cap, quilted petticoat, big-flowered calico train, and high-heeled shoes; two or three supernumeraries, in Rebel gray, with bayonets, coming on in "Barbara Frietchie"; and Sir Charles, bouncing out from somewhere behind, to the great hazard of the frame of lights,—huddled together upon the stage and consulted. Dakie Thayne had dropped his cord and almost made a rush off at the first announcement; but he stood now, with a repressed eagerness that trembled through every fibre, and waited.

"Would he come?" "Isn't it too late?" "Would it be any compliment?" "Won't it be rude not to?" "All the patriotic pieces are just coming!" "Will the audience like to wait?" "Make a speech and tell 'em. You, Brookhouse." "O, he *must* come! Barbara Frietchie and the flag! Just think!" "Isn't it grand?" "O, I'm so frightened!" These were the hurried sentences that made the buzz behind the scenes; while in front "all the world wondered." Meanwhile, lamps trembled, the curtain vibrated, the very framework swayed.

"What is it? Fire?" queried a nervous voice from near the footlights.

"This won't do," said Frank Scherman. "Speak to them, Brookhouse. Dakie Thayne, run over to Green's, and say,—The ladies' compliments to General Ingleside and friends, and beg the honor of their presence at the concluding tableaux."

Dakie was off with a glowing face, something like an odd, knowing smile twinkling out from the glow also, as he looked up at Scherman and took his orders. All this while he had said nothing.

Leonard Brookhouse made his little speech, received with applause and a cheer. Then they quieted down behind the scenes, and a rustle and buzz began in front,—kept up for five minutes or so, in gentle fashion, till two gentlemen, in plain clothes, walked quietly in at the open door; at sight of whom, with instinctive certainty, the whole assembly rose. Leslie Goldthwaite, peeping through the folds of the curtain, saw a tall, grand-looking man, in what may be called the youth of middle age, every inch a soldier, bowing as he was ushered forward to a seat vacated for him, and followed by one younger, who modestly ignored the notice intended for his chief. Dakie Thayne was making his way, with eyes alight and excited, down a side passage to his post.

Then the two actors hurried once more into position; the stage was cleared by a whispered peremptory order; the bell rung once, the tent trembling with some one whisking further out of sight behind it,—twice, and the curtain rose upon "Consolation."

Lovely as the picture is, it was lovelier in the living tableau. There was something deep and intense in the pale calm of Susan Josselyn's face, which they had not counted on even when they discovered that hers was the very face for the "Sister." Something made you thrill at the thought of what those eyes would show, if the downcast, quiet lids were raised. The earnest gaze of the dying soldier met more, perhaps, in its uplifting; for Frank Scherman had a look, in this instant of enacting, that he had never got before in all his practisings. The picture was too real for applause,—almost, it suddenly seemed, for representation.

"Don't I know that face, Noll?" General Ingleside asked, in a low tone, of his companion.

Instead of answering at once, the younger man

bent further forward toward the stage, and his own very plain, broad, honest face, full over against the downcast one of the Sister of Mercy, took upon itself that force of magnetic expression which makes a look felt even across a crowd of other glances, as if there were but one straight line of vision, and that between such two. The curtain was going slowly down; the veiling lids trembled, and the paleness replaced itself with a slow-mounting flush of color over the features, still held motionless. They let the cords run more quickly then. She was getting tired, they said; the curtain had been up too long. Be that as it might, nothing could persuade Susan Josselyn to sit again, and "Consolation" could not be repeated.

So then came "Mother Hubbard and her dog," —the slow old lady and the knowing beast that was always getting one step ahead of her. The possibility had occurred to Leslie Goldthwaite as she and Dakie Thayne amused themselves one day with Captain Green's sagacious Sir Charles Grandison, a handsome black spaniel, whose trained accomplishment was to hold himself patiently in any posture in which he might be placed, until the word of release was given. You might stand him on his hind legs, with paws folded on his breast; you might extend him on his back, with helpless legs in air; you might put him in any attitude possible to be maintained, and maintain it he would, faithfully, until the signal was made. From this prompting came the Illustration of Mother Hubbard. Also, Leslie Goldthwaite had seized the hidden suggestion of application, and hinted it in

certain touches of costume and order of performance. Nobody would think, perhaps, at first, that
the striped scarlet and white petticoat under the
tucked-up train, or the common print apron of
dark blue, figured with innumerable little white
stars, meant anything beyond the ordinary adjuncts
of a traditional old woman's dress; but when, in the
second scene, the bonnet went on,—an ancient
marvel of exasperated front and crown, pitched
over the forehead like an enormous helmet, and
decorated, upon the side next the audience, with
black and white eagle plumes springing straight
up from the fastening of an American shield,—
above all, when the dog himself appeared, "dressed
in his clothes" (a cane, an all-round white collar
and a natty little tie, a pair of three-dollar tasselled
kid-gloves dangling from his left paw, and a small
monitor hat with a big spread-eagle stuck above
the brim,—the remaining details of costume being
of no consequence),—when he stood "reading the
news" from a huge bulletin,—"LATEST BY CABLE
FROM EUROPE,"—nobody could mistake the personi-
fication of Old and Young America.

It had cost much pains and many dainty morsels,
to drill Sir Charles, with all the aid of his excellent
fundamental education; and the great fear had been
that he might fail them at the last. But the scenes
were rapid, in consideration of canine infirmity.
If the cupboard was empty, Mother Hubbard's
basket behind was not; he got his morsels duly; and
the audience was "requested to refrain from applause until the end." Refrain from laughter they
could not, as the idea dawned upon them and

developed; but Sir Charles was used to that in the execution of his ordinary tricks; he could hardly have done without it better than any other old actor. A dog knows when he is having his day, to say nothing of doing his duty; and these things are as sustaining to him as to anybody. This state of his mind, manifest in his air, helped also to complete the Young America expression. Mother Hubbard's mingled consternation and pride at each successive achievement of her astonishing puppy were inimitable. Each separate illustration made its point. Patriotism, especially, came in when the undertaker, bearing the pall with red-lettered border,—Rebellion,—finds the dog, with upturned, knowing eye, and parted jaws, suggestive as much of a good grip as of laughter, half risen upon fore-paws, as far from "dead" as ever, mounting guard over the old bone "Constitution."

The curtain fell at last, amid peals of applause and calls for the actors.

Dakie Thayne had accompanied with the reading of the ballad, slightly transposed and adapted. As Leslie led Sir Charles before the curtain, in response to the continued demand, he added the concluding stanza,—

> "The dame made a courtesy,
>   The dog made a bow;
> The dame said, 'Your servant,'
>   The dog said, 'Bow-wow.'"

Which, with a suppressed "Speak, sir!" from Frank Scherman, was brought properly to pass. Done with cleverness and quickness from beginning to end, and taking the audience utterly by surprise, Leslie's little combination of wit and sagacity had been throughout a signal success. The actors crowded round her. "We'd no idea of it!" "Capital!" "A great hit!" they exclaimed. "Mother Hubbard is the star of the evening," said Leonard Brookhouse. "No, indeed," returned Leslie, patting Sir Charles's head,—"this is the dog-star." "Rather a Sirius reflection upon the rest of us," rejoined Brookhouse, shrugging his shoulders, as he walked off to take his place in the "Oath," and Leslie disappeared to make ready for "Barbara Frietchie."

Several persons, before and behind the curtain, were making up their minds, just now, to a fresh opinion. There was nothing so very slow or tame, after all, about Leslie Goldthwaite. Several others had known that long ago.

"Taking the Oath" was piquant and spirited. The touch of restive scorn that could come out on Martha Josselyn's face just suited her part; and Leonard Brookhouse was very cool and courteous, and handsome and gentlemanly-triumphant as the Union officer.

"Barbara Frietchie" was grand. Grahame Lowe played Stonewall Jackson. They had improvised a pretty bit of scenery at the back, with a few sticks, some paint, brown carpet-paper, and a couple of mosquito-bars;—a Dutch gable with a lattice window, vines trained up over it, and bushes below. It was a moving tableau, enacted to the reading of Whittier's glorious ballad. "Only an old woman in a cap and kerchief, putting her head out at a garret window,"—that was all; but the fire was in the young eyes under the painted wrinkles and the snowy hair; the arm stretched itself out quick and bravely at the very instant of the pistol-shot that startled timid ears; one skilful movement detached and seized the staff in its apparent fall, and the liberty-colors flashed full in Rebel faces, as the broken lower fragment went clattering to the stage. All depended on the one instant action and expression. These were perfect. The very spirit of Barbara stirred her representative. The curtain began to descend slowly, and the applause broke forth before the reading ended. But a hand, held up, hushed it till the concluding lines were given in thrilling tones, as the tableau was covered from sight.

"Barbara Frietchie's work is o'er,
And the Rebel rides on his raids no more.

"Honor to her! and let a tear
Fall, for her sake, on Stonewall's bier.

"Over Barbara Frietchie's grave,
Flag of Freedom and Union, wave!

"Peace and order and beauty draw
Round thy symbol of light and law;

"And ever the stars above look down
On thy stars below in Frederick town!"

Then one great cheer broke forth, and was prolonged to three.

"Not be Barbara Frietchie!" Leslie would not have missed that thrill for the finest beauty-part of all. For the applause—that was for the flag, of course, as Ginevra Thoresby said.

The benches were slid out at a window upon a lower roof, the curtain was looped up, and the footlights carried away; the "music" came up, and took possession of the stage; and the audience hall resolved itself into a ballroom. Under the chandelier, in the middle, a tableau not set forth in the programme was rehearsed and added a few minutes after.

Mrs. Thoresby, of course, had been introduced to the general; Mrs. Thoresby, with her bright, full, gray curls and her handsome figure, stood holding him in conversation between introductions, graciously waiving her privilege as new-comers claimed their modest word. Mrs. Thoresby took possession; had praised the tableaux, as "quite creditable, really, considering the resources we had," and was following a slight lead into a long talk, of information and advice on her part, about Dixville Notch. The general thought he should go there, after a day or two at Outledge.

Just here came up Dakie Thayne. The actors, in costume, were gradually mingling among the audience, and Barbara Frietchie, in white hair, from which there was not time to remove the powder, plain cap and kerchief, and brown woolen gown, with her silken flag yet in her hand, came with him. This boy, who "was always everywhere," made no hesitation, but walked straight up to the central group, taking Leslie by the hand. Close to the general, he waited courteously for a long sentence of Mrs. Thoresby's to be ended, and then said, simply,—"Uncle James, this is my friend, Miss Leslie Goldthwaite. My brother, Dr. Ingleside—why, where is Noll?"

Dr. Oliver Ingleside had stepped out of the circle in the last half of the long sentence. The Sister of Mercy—no longer in costume, however—had come down the little flight of steps that led from the stage to the floor. At their foot the young army surgeon was shaking hands with Susan Josselyn. These two had had the chess-practice together—and other practice—down there among the Southern hospitals.

Mrs. Thoresby's face was very like some fabric subjected to chemical experiment, from which one color and aspect has been suddenly and utterly discharged to make room for something different and new. Between the first and last there waits a blank. With this blank full upon her, she stood there for one brief, unprecedented instant in her life, a figure without presence or effect. I have seen a daguerreotype in which were cap, hair, and collar, quite correct,—what should have been a face rubbed out. Mrs. Thoresby rubbed herself out, and so performed her involuntary tableau.

"Of course I might have guessed. I wonder it never occurred to me," Mrs. Linceford was replying, presently, to her vacuous inquiry. "The name seemed familiar, too; only he called himself 'Dakie.' I remember perfectly now. Old Jacob Thayne, the Chicago millionaire. He married pretty little Mrs. Ingleside, the Illinois Representative's widow, that first winter I was in Washington. Why, Dakie must be a dollar prince!"

He was just Dakie Thayne, though, for all that. He and Leslie and Cousin Delight,—the Josselyns and the Inglesides,—dear Miss Craydocke, hurrying up to congratulate,—Marmaduke Wharne looking on without a shade of cynicism in the gladness of his face, and Sin Saxon and Frank Scherman flitting up in the pauses of dance and promenade,—well, after all, these were the central group that night. The pivot of the little solar system was changed; but the chief planets made but slight account of that; they just felt that it had grown very warm and bright.

"O Chicken Little!" Mrs. Linceford cried to Leslie Goldthwaite, giving her a small shake with her good-night kiss at her door. "How did you know the way was going to fall? And how have you led us all this chase to cheat Fox Lox at last?"

But that wasn't the way Chicken Little looked at it. She didn't care much for the bit of dramatic *dénouement* that had come about by accident,— like a story, Elinor said,—or the touch of poetic justice that tickled Mrs. Linceford's world-instructed sense of fun. Dakie Thayne wasn't a sum that needed proving. It was very nice that this famous general should be his uncle,—but not at all strange: they were just the sort of people he *must* belong to. And it was nicest of all that Dr. Ingleside and Susan Josselyn should have known each other,—"in the glory of their lives," she phrased it to herself, with a little flash of girl-enthusiasm and a vague suggestion of romance.

"Why didn't you tell us?" Mrs. Linceford said to Dakie Thayne next morning. "Everybody would have—" She stopped. She could not tell this boy to his frank face that everybody would have thought more and made more of him because his uncle had got brave stars on his shoulders, and his father had died leaving two millions or so of dollars.

"I know they would have," said Dakie Thayne. "That was just it. What is the use of telling things? I'll wait till I've done something that tells itself."

There was a pretty general break-up at Outledge during the week following. The tableaux were the *finale* of the season's gayety,—of this particular little episode, at least, which grew out of the association together of these personages of our story. There might come a later set, and later doings; but this last week of August sent the mere summer-birds fluttering. Madam Routh must be back in New York, to prepare for the reopening of her school; Mrs. Linceford had letters from her husband, proposing to meet her by the first, in N——, and so the Haddens would be off; the Thoresbys had stayed as long as they cared to in any one place where there seemed no special inducement; General Ingleside was going through the mountains to Dixville Notch. Rose Ingleside,—bright and charming as her name,—just a fit flower to put beside our Ladies' Delight,—finding out, at once, as all girls and women did, her sweetness, and leaning more and more to the rare and delicate sphere of her quiet attraction,—Oliver and Dakie Thayne,— these were his family party; but there came to be question about Leslie and Delight. Would not they make six? And since Mrs. Linceford and her sisters must go, it seemed so exactly the thing for them to fall into; otherwise Miss Goldthwaite's journey hither would hardly seem to have been worth while. Early September was so lovely among the hills; opportunities for a party to Dixville Notch would not come every day; in short, Dakie had set his heart upon it, Rose begged, the general was as pressing as true politeness would allow, and it was settled.

"Only," Sin Saxon said, suddenly, on being told, "I should like if you would tell me, General Ingleside, the precise military expression synonymous with 'taking the wind out of one's sails.' Because that's just what you've done for me."

"My dear Miss Saxon! In what way?"

"Invited my party,—some of them,—and taken my road. That's all. I spoke first, though I didn't speak out loud. See here!" And she produced a letter from her mother, received that morning. "Observe the date, if you please,—August 24. 'Your letter reached me yesterday.' And it had travelled round, as usual, two days in papa's pocket, beside. I always allow for that. 'I quite approve your plan; provided, as you say, the party be properly matronized. I'—h'm ——That refers to little explanations of my own. Well, all is, I was going to do this very thing,—with enlargements. And now Miss Craydocke and I may collapse."

"Why? when with you and your enlargements we might make the most admirable combination? At least, the Dixville road is open to all."

"Very kind of you to say so,—the first part, I mean,—if you could possibly have helped it. But there are insurmountable obstacles on that Dixville road—to us. There's a lion in the way. Don't you see we should be like the little ragged boys running after the soldier-company? We couldn't think of putting ourselves in that 'bony light,' especially before the eyes of Mrs.—Grundy." This last, as Mrs. Thoresby swept impressively along the piazza in full dinner costume.

"Unless you go first, and we run after you," suggested the general.

"All the same. You talked Dixville to her the very first evening, you know. No, nobody can have an original Dixville idea any more. And I've been asking them,—the Josselyns, and Mr. Wharne and all, and was just coming to the Goldthwaites; and now I've got them on my hands, and I don't know where in the world to take them. That comes of keeping an inspiration to ripen. Well, it's a lesson of wisdom! Only, as Effie says about her housekeeping, the two dearest things in living are butter and experience!"

Amidst laughter and banter and repartee, they came to it, of course; the most delightful combination and joint arrangement. Two wagons, the general's and Dr. Ingleside's two saddle-horses, Frank Scherman's little mountain mare, that climbed like a cat, and was sure-footed as a chamois, —these with a side-saddle for the use of a lady sometimes upon the last, make up the general equipment of the expedition.

All Mrs. Grundy knew was that they were won-

derfully merry and excited together, until this plan
came out as the upshot.

The Josselyns had not quite consented at once,
though their faces were bright with a most thankful appreciation of the kindness that offered them
such a pleasure; nay, that entreated their compan-
ionship as a thing so genuinely coveted to make
its own pleasure complete. Somehow, when the
whole plan developed, there was a little sudden
shrinking on Sue's part, perhaps on similar grounds
to Sin Saxon's perception of insurmountable
obstacles; but she was shyer than Sin of putting
forth her objections, and the general zeal and delight, and Martha's longing look, unconscious of
cause why not, carried the day.

There had never been a blither setting off from
the Giant's Cairn. All the remaining guests were
gathered to see them go. There was not a mote
in the blue air between Outledge and the crest of
Washington. All the subtile strength of the hills
—ores and sweet waters and resinous perfumes and
breath of healing leaf and root distilled to absolute
purity in the clear ether that only sweeps from such
bare, thunder-scoured summits—made up the ex-
hilarant draught in which they drank the mountain-
joy and received afar off its baptism of delight.

It was beautiful to see the Josselyns so girlish
and gay; it was lovely to look at old Miss Craydocke, with her little tremors of pleasure, and the
sudden glistenings in her eyes; Sin Saxon's pretty
face was clear and noble, with its pure impulse of
kindliness, and her fun was like a sparkle upon
deep waters. Dakie Thayne rushed about in a sort

of general satisfaction which would not let him be quiet anywhere. Outsiders looked with a kind of new, half-jealous respect on these privileged few who had so suddenly become the "General's party." Sin Saxon whispered to Leslie Goldthwaite,— "It's neither his nor mine, honeysuckle; it's yours, —Henny-penny and all the rest of it, as Mrs. Linceford said." Leslie was glad with the crowning gladness of her bright summer.

"That girl has played her cards well," Mrs. Thoresby said of her, a little below her voice, as she saw the general himself making her especially comfortable with Cousin Delight in a back seat.

"Particularly, my dear madam," said Marmaduke Wharne, coming close and speaking with clear emphasis, "as she could not possibly have known that she had a trump in her hand!"

To tell of all that week's journeying, and of Dixville Notch,—the adventure, the brightness, the beauty, and the glory,—the sympathy of abounding enjoyment, the waking of new life that it was to some of them,—the interchange of thought, the cementing of friendships,—would be to begin another story, possibly a yet longer one. Leslie's summer, according to the calendar, is already ended. Much in this world must pause unfinished, or come to abrupt conclusion. People "die suddenly at last," after the most tedious illnesses. "Married and lived happy ever after," is the inclusive summary that winds up many an old tale whose time of action only runs through hours. If in this summer-time with Leslie Goldthwaite your thoughts have broadened somewhat with hers, some questions for you have been partly answered; if it has appeared to you how a life enriches itself by drawing toward and going forth into the life of others through seeing how this began with her, it is no unfinished tale that I leave with you.

A little picture I will give you farther on, a hint of something farther yet, and say good by.

Some of them came back to Outledge, and stayed far into the still rich September. Delight and Leslie sat before the Green Cottage one morning, in the heart of a golden haze and a gorgeous bloom. All around the feet of the great hills lay the garlands of early-ripened autumn. You see nothing like it in the lowlands;—nothing like the fire of the maples, the carbuncle-splendor of the oaks, the flash of scarlet sumachs and creepers, the illumination of every kind of little leaf, in its own way, upon which the frost-touch comes down from those tremendous heights that stand rimy in each morning's sun, trying on white caps that by and by they shall pull down heavily over their brows, till they cloak all their shoulders also in the like sculptured folds, to stand and wait, blind, awful chrysalides, through the long winter of their death and silence.

Delight and Leslie had got letters from the Josselyns and Dakie Thayne. There was news in them such as thrills always the half-comprehending sympathies of girlhood. Leslie's vague suggestion of romance had become fulfilment. Dakie Thayne was wild with rejoicing that dear old Noll was to marry Sue. "She had always made him think of

Noll, and his ways and likings, ever since that day of the game of chess that by his means came to grief. It was awful slang, but he could not help it: it was just the very jolliest go!"

Susan Josselyn's quiet letter said,—"That kindness which kept us on and made it beautiful for us, strangers, at Outledge, has brought to me, by God's providence, this great happiness of my life."

After a long pause of trying to take it in, Leslie looked up. "What a summer this has been! So full,—so much has happened! I feel as if I had been living such a great deal!"

"You have been living in others' lives. You have had a great deal to do with what has happened."

"O Cousin Delight! I have only been *among* it! I could not *do*—except such a very little."

"There is a working from us beyond our own. But if our working runs with that—? You have done more than you will ever know, little one." Delight Goldthwaite spoke very tenderly. Her own life, somehow, had been closely touched, through that which had grown and gathered about Leslie. "It depends on that abiding. 'In me, and I in you; so shall ye bear much fruit.'"

She stopped. She would not say more. Leslie thought her talking rather wide of the first suggestion; but this child would never know, as Delight had said, what a centre, in her simple, loving way, she had been for the working of a purpose beyond her thought.

Sin Saxon came across the lawn, crowned with gold and scarlet, trailing creepers twined about her shoulders, and flames of beauty in her full hands.

course, and Dakie
rom a great school
ping for West Point
, who is Dakie's in-
er, our Pansie, our
f innumerable sweet

all, says the brave
eman, is that which
for life,—Delight

CIDENCE

ooke

was Grandmother
like other grand-
nd rosy as a winter
-white hair set up in
nd eyes as black as
up with smiles or

." she said: and
as determined her
'look half-way de-
ttle mob caps, soft
satin bow, one lav-
o show where the
them on right; the
l, or the cap itself
lled them off and

stuck them on a china jar in the parlor, or a tin canister on the kitchen shelf, and left them there till flies and dust ruined them.

"Amelia's as obstinate as a pig!" said the old lady: "she would have me wear 'em, and I wouldn't!"

That was all, but it was enough; not a grand-child ever made her another cap. Moreover Grand-mother Grant always dressed in one fashion; she had a calico dress for morning and a black silk for the afternoon, made with an old-fashioned surplice waist, with a thick plaited ruff about her throat; she sometimes tied a large white apron on, but only when she went into the kitchen; and she wore a pocket as big as three of yours, Matilda, tied on underneath and reached through a slit in her gown. Therein she kept her keys, her smelling-bottle, her pocket-book, her handkerchief and her spectacles, a bit of flagroot and some liquorice stick. I mean when I say this, that all these things belonged in her pocket, and she meant to keep them there; but it was one peculiarity of the dear old lady, that she always lost her necessary conveniences, and lost them every day.

"Maria!" she would call out to her daughter in the next room, "have you seen my spectacles?"

"No, mother; when did you have them?"

"Five minutes ago, darning Harry's stockings; but never mind, there's another pair in the basket."

In half an hour when Gerty came into her room for something she needed, Grandmother would say:

"Gerty, do look on the floor and see if my specs lie anywhere around."

A CASE OF COINCIDENCE

Gerty couldn't find them, and then Grandma would say:

"Probably they dropped out on the grass under the window, you can see when you go down; but give me my gold pair out of my upper drawer."

And when Mrs. Maria went to call her mother down to dinner she would find her hunting all about the room, turning her cushions over, peering into the wood-basket, shaking out the silk quilt, and say "What is it you want, mother?"

"My specs, dear. I can't find one pair."

"But there are three on your head now!" and Grandma would sit down and laugh till she shook all over, as if it were the best joke in the world to push your spectacles up over the short white curls on your forehead, one pair after another, and forget all about them.

She mislaid her handkerchief still oftener. Gerty would sometimes pick up six of these useful articles in one day where the old lady dropped them as she went about the house; but the most troublesome of all her habits was a way she had of putting her pocket-book in some queer place every night, or if ever she left home in the day-time, and then utterly forgetting where she had secreted it from the burglars or thieves she had all her life expected.

The house she lived in was her own, but Doctor White who had married her daughter Maria, rented it of her, and the rent paid her board; she had a thousand dollars a year beside, half of which she reserved for her dress and her charities, keeping the other half for her Christmas gifts to her children and grandchildren. There were ten of these

85

last, and the ten always needed something. Gerty White, the doctor's daughter, was twelve years old; she had three brothers: Tom, John, and Harry, all older than she was. Mrs. Rutledge, who had been Annie Grant, was a widow with three daughters—Sylvia, Amelia, and Anne, these latter two now out in society and always glad of new dresses, gloves, bonnets, ribbons, lace, and the thousand small fineries girls never have to their full satisfaction. There were Thomas Grant's two girls of thirteen and fifteen, Rosamond and Kate, and his little boy Hal, crippled in his babyhood so that he must always go on crutches, but as bright and happy as Grandma herself, and her prime favorite.

Now it was Grandma's way to draw her money out of the bank two weeks before Christmas, and go into Boston with Mrs. White to buy all the things she had previously thought over for these ten and their parents; and one winter she had made herself all ready to take the ten-o'clock train, and had just taken her pocket-book out of the drawer when she was called down-stairs to see a poor woman who had come begging for some clothes for her husband.

"Come right upstairs, Mrs. Slack," said Grandma. "I don't have many applications for men's things, so I guess there's a coat of Mr. Grant's put away in the camphor chest, and maybe a vest or so; you sit right down by my fire whilst I go up to the garret and look."

It took Grandma some time to find the clothes under all the shawls and blankets in the chest, and when she had given them to Mrs. Slack she had to hurry to the station with her daughter, and the cars being on the track they did not stop to get tickets, but were barely in time to find seats when the train rolled off. The conductor came round in a few minutes and Grandma put her hand in her pocket, suddenly turned pale, opened her big satchel and turned out all its contents, stood up and shook her dress, looked on the floor, and when Mrs. White said in amazement, "What *is* the matter, mother?" she answered curtly, "I've lost my pocket-book."

"Was it in your pocket?" asked Maria.

"Yes; at least I s'pose so: I certainly took it out of my drawer, for I noticed how heavy 'twas; that new cashier gave me gold for most of it, you see."

"You'd have known then if you dropped it on the way, mother."

"I should think so: any way, I can't go to Boston without it! We may as well stop at the next station and go back."

So back they went; asked at the ticket office if any such thing had been picked up on the platform, and leaving a description of it, went rather forlornly back to the house. Here a terrible upturning of everything took place; drawers were emptied, cupboards ransacked, trunks explored, even the camphor chest examined to its depths, and everything in it shaken out.

"You don't suspect Mrs. Slack?" inquired Maria.

"Sally Slack! no, indeed. I've known her thirty year, Maria; she's honest as the daylight."

Still Maria thought it best to send for Mrs. Slack and inquire if she had seen it when she was at the house.

A CASE OF COINCIDENCE

"Certain, certain!" answered the good woman. "I see Mis' Grant hev it into her hand when she went up charmber; I hedn't took no notice of it before, but she spoke up an' says, says she, 'I'll go right up now, Mis' Slack, for I'm in some of a hurry, bein' that I'm a goin' in the cars to Bosstown for to buy our folkses' Christmas things;' so then I took notice 't she hed a pocket-book into her hand."

This was valuable testimony, and Mrs. Slack's face of honest concern and sympathy showed her innocence in the matter. Next day there was an advertisement put in the paper, for the family concluded Grandma must have dropped her money in the street going to the station, but the advertisement proved as fruitless as the search, and for once in her life the dear old lady was downcast enough.

"The first time I never gave 'em a thing on Christmas! I do feel real downhearted about it, Maria. There's Annie's three girls lotted so on their gloves an' nicknacks for parties this winter, for I was goin' to give them gold pieces so's they could get what they wanted sort of fresh when they *did* want it; and poor Gerty's new cloak!"

"Oh, never mind that, mother. I can sponge and turn and fix over the old one; a plush collar and cuffs will make it all right."

"But there's the boys. Tom did want that set of tools and a bench for 'em; and I reckoned on seeing Harry's eyes shine over a real Newfoundland dog. That makes me think; won't you write to that man in New York? I've changed my mind about the dog. And Jack can't go to Thomas's now for vacation; oh dear!"

"*Don't* worry, mother," said Maria; but Grandma went on:

"Kate and Rosy too, they won't get their seal muffs and caps, and dear little Hal! how he will long for the books I promised him. It's real trying, Maria!" and Grandma wiped a tear from her eyes, a most unusual symptom.

But it was her way to make the best of things, and she sat down at once to tell Thomas of her loss, and then put it out of her mind as well as she might.

It spoke well for all those ten grandchildren that they each felt far more sorry for Grandmother Grant's disappointment than their own, and all resolved to give her a present much nicer and more expensive than ever before, pinching a little on their other gifts to the end; and because they had to spare from their own presents for this laudable purpose, it was natural enough that not one should tell another what they meant to send her, lest it should seem too extravagant in proportion to what the rest of the family received. Christmas morning the arrival began. The stocking of Grandpa's which Gerty had insisted on hanging to the knob of Grandma's door was full, and when she came down to breakfast she brought it with her still unsearched, that the family might enjoy her surprise.

At the top a square parcel tied with blue ribbon was marked "from Gerty," and proved to be a little velvet porte-monnaie.

"Dear child! how thoughtful!" said Grandma,

giving her a kiss, and not observing that the doctor looked funnily at Mrs. White across the table.

The next package bore John's name and disclosed a pocket-book of Russia leather.

"So useful!" said Grandma, with a twinkle of gratitude in her kind old eyes.

Harry emitted a long low whistle, and his eyes shone as the next paper parcel with his name on it showed an honest black leather pocket-book with a steel clasp.

Grandma had to laugh. Doctor White roared, and Tom looked a little rueful as his bundle produced another wallet as like to Harry's as two peas in a pod:

"Dear boys!" said Grandma, shaking like a liberal bowl of jelly with the laughter she tried to suppress in vain; but it was the boys' turn to shout as further explorations into the foot of the old blue stocking brought up a lovely seal-skin wallet from their mother, and a voluminous yellow leather one from the doctor.

> "Six souls with but a single thought;
> Six hearts that beat as one;"

misquoted Mrs. Maria, and a chorus of laughter that almost rattled the windows followed her. They were still holding their sides and bursting out afresh every other minute, when little Sylvia Rutledge sailed into the dining-room with a delicate basket in her hand.

"Merry Christmas!" said she, "but you seem to have it already."

The boys all rushed at once to explain.

"Wait a minute," said she, "till I have given Grandma her gifts," and she produced successively from her basket four parcels.

Sylvia's held another velvet. porte-monnaie; Annie's contained a second of hand-painted kid, daisies on a black ground; and Amelia's was a third pocket-book of gray canvas with Russia leather corners and straps; while Mrs. Rutledge's tiny packet produced an old-fashioned short purse, with steel fringe and clasp, which she had knit herself for her mother.

How can words tell the laughter which hailed this repetition?

The boys rolled off their chairs and roared till their very sides ached; tears streamed down Mrs. White's fair face; Grace gazed at the presents with a look half rueful and half funny, while the doctor's vigorous "haw! haw! haw!" could have been heard half a mile had it not been happily the season of shut doors and windows, while Sylvia herself perceiving the six pocket-books which had preceded her basketful, appreciated the situation and laughed all the harder because she was not tired with a previous fit of mirth, and Grandma sat shaking and chuckling in her chair, out of breath to be sure, but her face rosy and her eyes shining more than ever.

Suddenly a loud knock at the front door interrupted their laughter. Tom ran to admit the intruder; it was the expressman with a box from New York directed in uncle Tom's hand to Mrs. J. G. Grant.

"Something better than pocket-books this time,

mother!" said the doctor, as Tom ran for the screw-driver; but alas! the very first bundle that rolled out and fell heavily to the floor, proved when picked up to be indeed another pocket-book, cornered and clasped with silver, and Grandma's initials on the clasp; beautiful as the gift was it was thrust aside with a certain impatience, for the next package, labelled "from Rosamond," but opened only to display the very counterpart of Amelia's gift; and a paper box with Kate's script outside held the recurrent pocket-book again in black velvet and gilt corners, while a little carved white-wood box, the work of Hal's patient fingers, showed within its lid a purse of silvered links which had cost all his year's savings.

This was the last touch. Hitherto their curiosity as one thing was displayed after another had kept them in a sort of bubbling quiet, but this final development was too much; they laughed so loud and so long that old Hannah, hurrying from the kitchen and opening the door to see what was the matter, looked thunderstruck as she beheld the whole family shaking, choking, rolling about or holding on to each other in roars of side-splitting laughter, while fourteen purses and pocket-books made the breakfast table look like a fancy fair.

"I thought I heard a crackling of thorns, as scripter says," she growled. "Be you a-going to set up a fancy store, Mis' White?"

"Bring in breakfast, Hannah," said the doctor, recovering himself. "It's a melancholy truth that we can't eat pocket-books!"

For the satisfaction of the curious I must explain that the next May, when a certain old clock on the landing of the garret stairs was taken down to be put in order and made into a household god after the modern rage for such things, right under it lay Grandma's pocket-book intact.

"Well, now I remember!" said the astonished old lady, who never did remember where she had hidden anything till somebody else found it.

"I was goin' up to the chest to get out those things of husband's for Sally Slack, and I thought I wouldn't leave my pocket-book in my room, 'twould be putting temptation in her way, which isn't really right if a person is ever so honest; we're all frail as you may say when our time comes, and I didn't have my cloak on to put it in the pocket, and my under pocket was full, so I just slipped it under the clock case as I went up, feeling certain sure I should remember it because I never put it there before."

But the family voted that no harm had been done after all, for next Christmas the Rutledge girls each had a lovely silk party dress from the double fund; Gracie's cloak was mated by the prettiest hat and muff; Tom had his wild desire for a bicycle fulfilled; Harry owned a real gold watch which was far better than a dog; and Jack's ten gold eagles took him in the spring to Niagara and down the St. Lawrence, a journey never to be forgotten. Kate and Rosamond had their sealskin caps with muffs, gloves and velvet skirts to correspond with and supplement their last year's jackets; and Hal not only had his precious books, but a bookcase for them, and the pocket-books were redistributed among their givers; so that in the end good and not evil came of Grandma's losing her Christmas pocket-book!

THE FLIGHT OF THE DOLLS

By Lucretia P. Hale

HOW could the heart of doll wish for anything more in such a baby-house! It was fitted up in the most complete style; there were coal-hods for all the grates, and gas-fixtures in the drawing-rooms, and a register (which would not *rege.,* however!), carpets on all the floors, books on the centre-table; everything to make a sensible doll comfortable. But they were not happy, these dolls, seven of them, not counting the paper dolls. They were very discontented. They had always been happy till the Spanish Doll had come among them, dressed in a gypsy dress, yellow and black lace. But she had talked to them so much about the world that all were anxious to go abroad and see it, all,—from the large one that could open and shut her eyes, to the littlest China that could not sit down.

So they set out, one clear night. The Spanish Doll had put a chip in the play-room window that made it easier to open; and the Large Doll had slept outside the baby-house, so she opened the doors and let out the others. All stepped safely upon the piazza. Where should they go first?

The first plan was for the lamb-pen, and they made for it directly. The Spanish Doll walked through its slats; the Large Doll pushed in the little ones, but when she came to go in herself, horrible to say—she *stuck!* The Spanish Doll pulled, and the little dolls ran out and pushed. No use!

If Angelica Maria could have seen her Large Doll now! But no, Angelica Maria's head was asleep on its pillow; she little knew of the escape of her dolls!

At last said the Large Doll, "Wake up the Lamb and tell him!" Which they did, and he came and butted, till he butted the Large Doll out. "It is no use," said the Large Doll, "we must try something else," and the rest all came out of the pen. They went to the dovecote. The Spanish Doll quickly climbed the ladder; so could the Large Doll. But when she turned to help the little ones, her head was too heavy, and she was not stiff enough to stoop. "We must try something else," said she, and the Spanish Doll had to come down, scolding Spanish all the way. Then they walked down the garden walk, all in a procession, the Large Doll leading the way; they reached the arbor at the foot of the garden. "Let us all sit in a row here," said the Large Doll. So they got upon the seat, facing the door, running up a board that was laid against the seat. Here they sat till the morning began to dawn. Angelica Maria could have seen them now, but she was still fast asleep on her pillow.

"This will never do," exclaimed the Large Doll, as soon as light came, "for they can see us from the play room, our eyes all in a row." They must hide during the day time, and start on their journey

when night should come again. But where should
they go? They walked up and down the green
alleys. The scarlet poppies nodded to them sleep-
ily, and the roses put out a thorn or two, to get
them to stop. The little China would have been
very tired, but a broad-backed Toad kindly offered
to carry her. If Angelica Maria could have seen
them now!

"Let us speak to some of the animals," said the
Large Doll, "and ask where we shall hide."

"Not the Cat," said a middle-sized Doll, "for
she makes up faces."

"Suppose we ask the birds," said the Large Doll,
for they were just waking up. The Spanish Doll
soon made acquaintance with an Oriole, who agreed
to take her up to his nest for the day. It was just
fitted up, and Mrs. had not moved in. Fortunately
the Spanish Doll was quite slender, so the Oriole
could lift her, and her dress matched his feathers.
The squirrels kindly took some of the others into
their nests under the beech-tree, and the Large
Doll tucked the littlest China into a fox-glove.
"Where shall I go myself?" thought she. "There
is one comfort; if I want to go to sleep, I can shut
my eyes, which none of the rest can do wherever
they are." So she walked round till she came to a
water-melon, with a three-cornered piece cut out.
She climbed up on a Rabbit's back, and looked in.
A cat had eaten out the inside. "This will do very
well for me," said she, "and I feel like having a
nap by this time, if only somebody would pull my
wire!" The Rabbit knew of a dragon-fly who was
strong in his feelers; but the Large Doll had an

objection to dragon-flies, so she flung herself in with a jounce, and that closed her eyes. The Rabbit tucked in her skirts, and there she was.

Could Angelica Maria have seen them now! Some hidden among the low branches of the spruces, where the robins had invited them; some still chatting in the bushes, with the jays; the Spanish Doll swinging in the Oriole's nest, way up in the elm. That was life!

But Angelica Maria was calmly eating her breakfast. A friend had invited her to a picnic for the day, so, instead of thinking of her dolls she was planning what she should carry.

One thought she did give to her Large Doll. She wished to take her to the picnic. But, of course, she could not be found! If the Large Doll had only known, how she would have regretted that she had run away! For she was fond of picnics, and now she was sleeping in this damp melon!

But she knew nothing of it till the Spanish Doll came to wake her, and tell her that all the family had gone away for the day. Far up in the Oriole's nest in the elm tree, the Spanish Doll had seen them go. Now, if ever, was the time for fun. So the Large Doll came out of her melon, jumped open her eyes, assembled the rest, and asked what they should do. A large Dor-bug who was going that way, advised them to try the strawberry bed. "Oh, yes," all exclaimed, "the strawberry bed!"

The procession was formed but two were missing! In passing the fox-gloves, where the little China had been hidden, many had shut up never to open again, and she could not be found. A

middling-sized Doll, with boots, was missing also!
In vain they called; there was no answer.

The Spanish Doll ran up a nasturtium vine, to
see that all was safe. She sat on a scarlet nasturtium at the very top of the post, and declared "all
was quiet in the strawberry bed," and came down.

What a jolly time they had among the strawberries! The Large Doll sat under a vine, and the
strawberries dropped into her mouth, and the
stiffer dolls stood up and helped themselves. Such
fun as they had! They got strawberries all over
their faces, and their hands, and their light dresses!
This they liked so much, for they usually had to be
careful. How they chatted, and one told how the
squirrels lived, and another about the robins. And
the Spanish Doll told how delightful it was up in
the Oriole's nest. She had half a mind to hire it
for the summer. All this was much more charming than their dull baby-house; though the Large
Doll declared she had been used all her life to better society than she had yet found in the melon.

But all this festivity was put an end to by a
sudden shower. The Spanish Doll, afraid for her
black lace, made for a hen-coop, where she had a
battle with a Poland. The rest ran into the summer-house.

As soon as the rain ceased, however, all came
out from their hiding-places. There was a beautiful rainbow in the sky, and as the dolls walked
down the alley, they suddenly saw that the garden
gate was open. They ran eagerly toward it, and
soon were out in the Wide World! They crossed
the broad road, into the fields, into the meadows.

They stumbled through a potato-patch, and ran in
and out of cornstalks. In their hurry they had to
stop to breathe now and then, all but one Doll
whose mouth was always open. They reached a
little stream and ran along its border, and never
stopped till they came to a shady place among some
trees, by mossy rocks. Here they might be safe,
and here they stopped to think.

Hunger was their first sensation. One of the
dolls drew from her pocket a pewter gridiron, which
she had snatched from the kitchen fire when they
fled, the night before. There were three fish on
it, one red, one yellow, one blue. These they shared,
and were satisfied for a little while. How lovely
was the spot, they began to say. How charming
it would be to set up housekeeping among the
rushes. It was even suggested that, from time to
time, one of them might return to the deserted
baby-house, and bring from it comfortable furniture—a dish here, a flat-iron there. But in the
midst of their cheerful talk, a terrible accident!

The Spanish Doll was thirsty, and leaning over
the edge of the brook, she lost her balance, and fell
into the water! The exhausted dolls all rushed to
the rescue. All their efforts were vain; but a large
Bull-frog kindly came to help, and lifted the Spanish Doll's head from the stream, and propped it
up against the reeds. But what a state she was
in! The bright color washed from her cheeks, her
raven hair all dimmed, the lustre of her eyes all
gone. A fashionable Doll in vain attempted consolation, suggesting the greater charms of light
hair and rats; in vain did the Large Doll speak of

the romance of the adventure, and call the Bull-frog their Don Quixote; a heavy gloom hung over all. It was the Spanish Doll that had led them on, that had kept up their spirits; now hers had failed, and with her feet still in the water, she leaned her head wearily against the reeds.

Suddenly voices were heard! Steps approached! Each doll rushed to a hiding place. It was the voice of Angelica Maria herself! Some of the picnic party had decided to walk down the stream, on their way home, and Angelica Maria was among them.

The Spanish Doll had drawn a reed across her face, to hide it, but the Large Doll had not been able to fly quickly enough, and was left in full view, leaning against a mullein. A blush suffused her cheek. What was Angelica Maria's surprise!

"Who can have brought my Large Doll here?" she exclaimed. "It must have been the boys,"—meaning her brothers; "how wicked of them to leave her out in that shower. And here are the twins, Euphrosyne and Calliope, all hidden among the bushes, and dear little Eunice! They look as if they had been in the wars! How could Tom have known we were coming this way? How naughty of him!"

"Perhaps he meant a little surprise," suggested her uncle. But Angelica Maria picked up her dolls and fondled them, and were not they glad of the rest, after that weary march?

All but the Spanish Doll! Why had she not spoken? And would Angelica Maria have known her Spanish Doll if she had? When the trees were left all silent again, and the voices had died away, perhaps the Spanish Doll was sorry she had hidden her face,—that she had not lifted up her arms. But she was very proud. How could she have borne to be recognized? For she felt that one of her feet was washed off by the flowing stream, and her gay yellow and black dress soiled and torn.

The Bull-frog at last succeeded in lifting her to the shore. A kindly Musk-rat begged her to be his housekeeper; limping, she went into his soft-lined house, and was grateful even for this humble abode. Often she thought of the past, and cheered the simple fireside with tales of adventure, with the grandeur of Life in a Baby-house, and how she might have been the bride of an Oriole. But was she not missed in the baby-house? Angelica Maria wept her loss, but her uncle consoled her by telling her the Spanish Doll must have retired to one of her castles in Spain. This cheered Angelica Maria, and she busied herself in fitting new dresses for the poor travel-stained dolls she had left.

So this was the end of the Flight of the Dolls. You can imagine whether they ever tried it again, or rested satisfied with their comfortable home. A few days after, Angelica Maria saw a little head peeping out of a withered fox-glove. It was that of the littlest China. She was much emaciated, having had nothing to eat but a few drops of honey brought her by a benevolent Bee. Even these had cloyed.

Years after, when the spout of the wood-house was cleared out, the boots of a middling-sized Doll were seen. They belonged to the middling-sized

Doll with boots, who had clambered up to the dove-cote, and had lost her balance in the gutter. She had passed a miserable existence, summer and winter, bewailing her fate, and looking at her boots.

SOLOMON JOHN GOES FOR APPLES

By Lucretia P. Hale

SOLOMON JOHN agreed to ride to Farmer Jones's for a basket of apples, and he decided to go on horseback. The horse was brought round to the door. Now he had not ridden for a great while; and, though the little boys were there to help him, he had great trouble in getting on the horse.

He tried a great many times, but always found himself facing the wrong way, looking at the horse's tail. They turned the horse's head, first up the street, then down the street; it made no difference; he always made some mistake, and found himself sitting the wrong way.

"Well," said he, at last, "I don't know as I care. If the horse has his head in the right direction, that is the main thing. Sometimes I ride this way in the cars, because I like it better. I can turn my head easily enough, to see where we are going." So off he went, and the little boys said he looked like a circus-rider, and they were much pleased.

He rode along out of the village, under the elms, very quietly. Pretty soon he came to a bridge, where the road went across a little stream. There was a road at the side, leading down to the stream, because sometimes waggoners watered their horses there. Solomon John's horse turned off, too, to drink of the water.

"Very well," said Solomon John, "I don't blame him for wanting to wet his feet, and to take a drink, this hot day."

When they reached the middle of the stream, the horse bent over his head.

"How far his neck comes into his back!" exclaimed Solomon John; and at that very moment he found he had slid down over the horse's head, and was sitting on a stone, looking into the horse's face. There were two frogs, one on each side of him, sitting just as he was, which pleased Solomon John, so he began to laugh instead of to cry.

But the two frogs jumped into the water.

"It is time for me to go on," said Solomon John. So he gave a jump, as he had seen the frogs do; and this time he came all right on the horse's back, facing the way he was going.

"It is a little pleasanter," said he.

The horse wanted to nibble a little of the grass by the side of the way; but Solomon John remembered what a long neck he had, and would not let him stop.

At last he reached Farmer Jones, who gave him his basket of apples.

Next he was to go on to a cider-mill, up a little lane by Farmer Jones's house, to get a jug of cider. But as soon as the horse was turned into the lane, he began to walk very slowly,—so slowly that Solomon John thought he would not get there before

103

night. He whistled, and shouted, and thrust his knees into the horse, but still he would not go.

"Perhaps the apples are too heavy for him," said he. So he began by throwing one of the apples out of the basket. It hit the fence by the side of the road, and that started up the horse, and he went on merrily.

"That was the trouble," said Solomon John; "that apple was too heavy for him."

But very soon the horse began to go slower and slower.

So Solomon John thought he would try another apple. This hit a large rock, and bounded back under the horse's feet, and sent him off at a great pace. But very soon he fell again into a slow walk.

Solomon John had to try another apple. This time it fell into a pool of water, and made a great splash, and set the horse out again for a little while; he soon returned to a slow walk,—so slow that Solomon John thought it would be to-morrow morning before he got to the cider-mill.

"It is rather a waste of apples," thought he; "but I can pick them up as I come back, because the horse will be going home at a quick pace."

So he flung out another apple; that fell among a party of ducks, and they began to make such a quacking and a waddling, that it frightened the horse into a quick trot.

So the only way Solomon John could make his horse go was by flinging his apples, now on one side, now on the other. One time he frightened a cow, that ran along by the side of the road, while the horse raced with her. Another time he started up a brood of turkeys, that gobbled and strutted enough to startle twenty horses. In another place he came near hitting a boy, who gave such a scream that it sent the horse off at a furious rate.

And Solomon John got quite excited himself, and he did not stop till he had thrown away all his apples, and had reached the corner of the cider-mill.

"Very well," said he, "if the horse is so lazy, he won't mind my stopping to pick up the apples on the way home. And I am not sure but I shall prefer walking a little to riding the beast."

The man came out to meet him from the cider-mill, and reached him the jug. He was just going to take it, when he turned his horse's head round, and, delighted at the idea of going home, the horse set off at a full run without waiting for the jug. Solomon John clung to the reins, and his knees held fast to the horse. He called out "Whoa! whoa!" but the horse would not stop.

He went galloping on past the boy, who stopped, and flung an apple at him; past the turkeys, that came and gobbled at him; by the cow, that turned and ran back in a race with them until her breath gave out; by the ducks, that came and quacked at him; by an old donkey, that brayed over the wall at him; by some hens, that ran into the road under the horse's feet, and clucked at him; by a great rooster, that stood up on a fence, and crowed at him; by Farmer Jones, who looked out to see what had become of him; down the village street, and he never stopped till he had reached the door of the house.

Out came Mr. and Mrs. Peterkin, Agamemnon, Elizabeth Eliza, and the little boys.

Solomon John got off his horse all out of breath. "Where is the jug of cider?" asked Mrs. Peterkin.

"It is at the cider-mill," said Solomon John.

"At the mill!" exclaimed Mrs. Peterkin.

"Yes," said Solomon John; "the little boys had better walk out for it; they will enjoy it; and they had better take a basket; for on the way they will find plenty of apples, scattered all along on either side of the lane, and hens, and ducks, and turkeys, and a donkey."

The little boys looked at each other, and went; but they stopped first, and put on their india-rubber boots.

WILD ROBIN

By Sophie May

IN the green valley of the Yarrow, near the castle-keep of Norham, dwelt an honest sonsy little family, whose only grief was an unhappy son, named Robin.

Janet, with jimp form, bonnie eyes, and cherry cheeks, was the best of daughters: the boys, Sandie and Davie, were swift-footed, brave, kind, and obedient; but Robin, the youngest, had a stormy temper, and, when his will was crossed, he became as reckless as a reeling hurricane. Once, in a passion, he drove two of his father's "kye," or cattle, down a steep hill to their death. He seemed not to care for home or kindred, and often pierced the tender heart of his mother with sharp words. When she came at night, and "happed" the bed-clothes carefully about his form, and then stooped to kiss his nut-brown cheeks, he turned away with a frown, muttering, "Mither, let me be."

It was a sad case with Wild Robin, who seemed to have neither love nor conscience.

"My heart is sair," sighed his mother, "wi' greeting over sich a son."

"He hates our auld cottage and our muckle wark," said the poor father. "Ah, weel! I could a'maist wish the fairies had him for a season, to teach him better manners."

This the gudeman said heedlessly, little knowing there was any danger of Robin's being carried away to Elfland. Whether the fairies were at that instant listening under the eaves, will never be known; but it chanced, one day, that Wild Robin was sent across the moors to fetch the kye.

"I'll rin away," thought the boy: " 'tis hard indeed if ilka day a great lad like me must mind the kye. I'll gae aff; and they'll think me dead."

So he gaed, and he gaed, over round swelling hills, over old battle-fields, past the roofless ruins of houses whose walls were crowned with tall climbing grasses, till he came to a crystal sheet of water, called St. Mary's Loch. Here he paused to take breath. The sky was dull and lowering; but at his feet were yellow flowers, which shone, on that gray day, like freaks of sunshine.

He threw himself wearily upon the grass, not heeding that he had chosen his couch within a little

mossy circle known as a "fairy's ring." Wild
Robin knew that the country people would say
the fays had pressed that green circle with their
light feet. He had heard all the Scottish lore of
brownies, elves, will-o'-the-wisps, and the strange
water-kelpies, who shriek with eldritch laughter.
He had been told that the queen of the fairies had
coveted him from his birth, and would have stolen
him away, only that, just as she was about to seize
him from the cradle, he had *sneezed;* and from
that instant the fairy-spell was over, and she had
no more control of him.

Yet, in spite of all these stories, the boy was not
afraid; and if he had been informed that any of
the uncanny people were, even now, haunting his
footsteps, he would not have believed it.

"I see," said Wild Robin, "the sun is drawing his
night-cap over his eyes, and dropping asleep. I
believe I'll e'en take a nap mysel', and see what
comes o' it."

In two minutes he had forgotten St. Mary's
Loch, the hills, the moors, the yellow flowers. He
heard, or fancied he heard, his sister Janet calling
him home.

"And what have ye for supper?" he muttered
between his teeth.

"Parritch and milk," answered the lassie gently.

"Parritch and milk! Whist! say nae mair!
Lang, lang! may ye wait for Wild Robin: he'll not
gae back for oatmeal parritch!"

Next a sad voice fell on his ear.

"Mither's; and she mourns me dead!" thought
he; but it was only the far-off village-bell, which

sounded like the echo of music he had heard lang syne, but might never hear again.

"D'ye think I'm not alive?" tolled the bell. "I sit all day in my little wooden temple, brooding over the sins of the parish."

"A brazen lie!" cried Robin.

"Nay, the truth, as I'm a living soul! Wae worth ye, Robin Telfer: ye think yersel' hardly used. Say, have your brithers softer beds than yours? Is your ain father served with larger potatoes or creamier buttermilk? Whose mither sae kind as yours, ungrateful chiel? Gae to Elfland, Wild Robin; and dool and wae follow ye! dool and wae follow ye!"

The round yellow sun had dropped behind the hills; the evening breezes began to blow; and now could be heard the faint trampling of small hoofs, and the tinkling of tiny bridle-bells: the fairies were trooping over the ground. First of all rode the queen.

> "Her skirt was of the grass-green silk,
> Her mantle of the velvet fine;
> At ilka tress of her horse's mane
> Hung fifty silver bells and nine."

But Wild Robin's closed eyes saw nothing; his sleep-sealed ears heard nothing. The queen of the fairies dismounted, stole up to him, and laid her soft fingers on his cheeks.

"Here is a little man after my ain heart," said she: "I like his knitted brow, and the downward curve of his lips. Knights, lift him gently, set him on a red-roan steed, and waft him away to Fairyland."

Wild Robin was lifted as gently as a brown leaf borne by the wind; he rode as softly as if the red-roan steed had been saddled with satin, and shod with velvet. It even may be that the faint tinkling of the bridle-bells lulled him into a deeper slumber; for when he awoke it was morning in Fairy-land.

Robin sprang from his mossy couch, and stared about him. Where was he? He rubbed his eyes, and looked again. Dreaming, no doubt; but what meant all these nimble little beings bustling hither and thither in hot haste? What meant these pearl-bedecked caves, scarcely larger than swallows' nests? these green canopies, overgrown with moss? He pinched himself, and gazed again. Countless flowers nodded to him, and seemed, like himself, on tiptoe with curiosity, he thought. He beckoned one of the busy, dwarfish little brownies toward him.

"I ken I'm talking in my sleep," said the lad; "but can ye tell me what dell is this, and how I chanced to be in it?"

The brownie might or might not have heard; but, at any rate, he deigned no reply, and went on with his task, which was pounding seeds in a stone mortar.

"Am I Robin Telfer, of the Valley of Yarrow, and yet canna shake aff my silly dreams?"

"Weel, my lad," quoth the queen of the fairies, giving him a smart tap with her wand, "stir yersel', and be at work; for naebody idles in Elf-land."

Bewildered Robin ventured a look at the little queen. By daylight she seemed somewhat sleepy and tired; and was withal so tiny, that he might almost have taken her between his thumb and finger, and twirled her above his head; yet she poised herself before him on a mullein-stalk and looked every inch a queen.

Robin found her gaze oppressive; for her eyes were hard and cold and gray, as if they had been little orbs of granite.

"Get ye to work, Wild Robin!"

"What to do?" meekly asked the boy, hungrily glancing at a few kernels of rye which had rolled out of one of the brownie's mortars.

"Are ye hungry, my laddie? Touch a grain of rye if ye dare! Shell these dry beans; and if so be ye're starving, eat as many as ye can boil in an acorn-cup."

With these words she gave the boy a withered bean-pod, and, summoning a meek little brownie, bade him see that the lad did not over-fill the acorn-cup, and that he did not so much as peck at a grain of rye.

Then glancing sternly at her prisoner, she withdrew, sweeping after her the long train of her green robe.

The dull days crept by, and still there seemed no hope that Wild Robin would ever escape from his beautiful but detested prison. He had no wings, poor laddie; and he could neither become invisible nor draw himself through a keyhole bodily.

It is true, he had mortal companions: many chubby babies; many bright-eyed boys and girls, whose distracted parents were still seeking them, far and wide, upon the earth. It would almost seem that the wonders of Fairy-land might make the little prisoners happy. There were countless treasures to be had for the taking, and the very dust in the little streets was precious with specks of gold: but the poor children shivered for the want of a mother's love; they all pined for the dear home-people.

If a certain task seemed to them particularly irksome, the heartless queen was sure to find it out, and oblige them to perform it, day after day. If they disliked any article of food, that, and no other, were they forced to eat, or starve.

Wild Robin, loathing his withered beans and unsalted broths, longed intensely for one little breath of fragrant steam from the toothsome parritch on his father's table, one glance at a roasted potato. He was homesick for the gentle sister he had neglected, the rough brothers whose cheeks he had pelted black and blue; and yearned for the very chinks in the walls, the very thatch on the home-roof.

Gladly would he have given every fairy-flower, at the root of which clung a lump of gold ore, if he might have had his own coverlet "happed" about him once more by the gentle hands he had despised.

"Mither," he whispered in his dreams, "my shoon are worn, and my feet bleed; but I'll soon creep hame, if I can. Keep the parritch warm for me."

Robin was as strong as a mountain-goat; and his strength was put to the task of threshing rye, grinding oats and corn, or drawing water from a brook.

Every night, troops of gay fairies and plodding brownies stole off on a visit to the upper world, leaving Robin and his companions in ever-deeper despair. Poor Robin! he was fain to sing,—

"Oh that my father had ne'er on me smiled!
Oh that my mother had ne'er to me sung!
Oh that my cradle had never been rocked,
But that I had died when I was young!"

Now, there was one good-natured brownie who pitied Robin. When he took a journey to earth with his fellow-brownies, he often threshed rye for the laddie's father, or churned butter in his good mother's dairy, unseen and unsuspected. If the little creature had been watched, and paid for these good offices, he would have left the farmhouse forever in sore displeasure.

To homesick Robin he brought news of the family who mourned him as dead. He stole a silky tress of Janet's fair hair, and wondered to see the boy weep over it; for brotherly affection is a sentiment which never yet penetrated the heart of a brownie. The dull little sprite would gladly have helped the poor lad to his freedom, but told him that only on one night of the year was there the least hope, and that was on Hallow-e'en, when the whole nation of fairies ride in procession through the streets of earth.

So Robin was instructed to spin a dream, which the kind brownie would hum in Janet's ear while she slept. By this means the lassie would not only learn that her brother was in the power of the elves, but would also learn how to release him.

Accordingly, the night before Hallow-e'en, the bonnie Janet dreamed that the long-lost Robin

was living in Elf-land, and that he was to pass
through the streets with a cavalcade of fairies. But,
alas! how should even a sister know him in the dim
starlight, and among the passing troops of elfish
and mortal riders? The dream assured her that
she might let the first company go by, and the second; but Robin would be one of the third:—

"First let pass the black, Janet,
    And syne let pass the brown;
But grip ye to the milk-white steed,
    And pull the rider down.

For *I* ride on the milk-white steed,
    And aye nearest the town:
Because I was a christened lad
    They gave me that renown.

My right hand will be gloved, Janet;
    My left hand will be bare;
And these the tokens I give thee,
    No doubt I will be there.

They'll shape me in your arms, Janet,
    A toad, snake, and an eel;
But hold me fast, nor let me gang,
    As you do love me weel.

They'll shape me in your arms, Janet,
    A dove, bat, and a swan:
Cast your green mantle over me,
    I'll be myself again."

The good sister Janet, far from remembering
any of the old sins of her brother, wept for joy to
know that he was yet among the living. She told
no one of her strange dream; but hastened secretly

to the Miles Cross, saw the strange cavalcade pricking through the greenwood, and pulled down the rider on the milk-white steed, holding him fast through all his changing shapes. But when she had thrown her green mantle over him, and clasped him in her arms as her own brother Robin, the angry voice of the fairy queen was heard:—

"Up then spake the queen of fairies,
    Out of a bush of rye,
'You've taken away the bonniest lad
    In all my companie.

'Had I but had the wit, yestreen,
    That I have learned to-day,
I'd pinned the sister to her bed
    Ere he'd been won away!' "

However, it was too late now. Wild Robin was safe, and the elves had lost their power over him forever. His forgiving parents and his leal-hearted brothers welcomed him home with more than the old love.

So grateful and happy was the poor laddie, that he nevermore grumbled at his oatmeal parritch, or minded his kye with a scowling brow.

But to the end of his days, when he heard mention of fairies and brownies, his mind wandered off in a mizmaze. He died in peace, and was buried on the banks of the Yarrow.

DEACON THOMAS WALES' WILL

By Mary E. Wilkins Freeman

IN the Name of God Amen! the Thirteenth Day
of September One Thousand Seven Hundred
Fifty & eight, I, Thomas Wales of Braintree, in
the County of Suffolk & Province of the Massachu-
setts Bay in New England, Gent—being in good
health of Body and of Sound Disposing mind and
Memory, Thanks be given to God—Calling to
mind my mortality, Do therefore in my health
make and ordain this my Last Will and Testament.
And First I Recommend my Soul into the hand of
God who gave it—Hoping through grace to obtain
Salvation thro' the merits and Mediation of Jesus
Christ my only Lord and Dear Redeemer, and my
body to be Decently inter^d, at the Discretion of my
Executer, believing at the General Resurection to
receive the Same again by the mighty Power of
God—And such worldly estate as God in his good-
ness hath graciously given me after Debts, funeral
Expenses &c, are Paid I give & Dispose of the
Same as Followeth—

Imprimis—I Give to my beloved Wife Sarah a
good Sute of mourning apparrel Such as she may
Choose—also if she acquit my estate of Dower and
third-therin (as we have agreed) Then that my Executer return all of Household movables she bought
at our marriage & since that are remaining, also to
Pay to her or Her Heirs That Note of Forty
Pound I gave to her, when she acquited my estate
and I hers. Before Division to be made as herein

116

exprest, also the Southwest fire-Room in my House, a right in my Cellar, Halfe the Garden, also the Privilege of water at the well & yard room and to bake in the oven what she hath need of to improve her Life-time by her.

After this, followed a division of his property amongst his children, five sons, and two daughters. The "Homeplace" was given to his sons Ephraim and Atherton. Ephraim had a good house of his own, so he took his share of the property in land, and Atherton went to live in the old homestead. His quarters had been poor enough; he had not been so successful as his brothers, and had been unable to live as well. It had been a great cross to his wife, Dorcas, who was very high spirited. She had compared, bitterly, the poverty of her household arrangements with the abundant comfort of her sisters-in-law.

Now, she seized eagerly at the opportunity of improving her style of living. The old Wales house was quite a pretentious edifice for those times. All the drawback to her delight was, that Grandma should have the southwest fire-room. She wanted to set up her high-posted bedstead with its enormous feather-bed in that, and have it for her fore-room. Properly, it was the fore-room, being right across the entry from the family sitting room. There was a tall chest of drawers that would fit in so nicely between the windows, too. Take it altogether, she was chagrined at having to give up the southwest room; but there was no help for it—there it was in Deacon Wales' will.

Mrs. Dorcas was the youngest of all the sons' wives, as her husband was the latest born. She was quite a girl to some of them. Grandma had never more than half approved of her. Dorcas was high-strung and flighty, she said. She had her doubts about living happily with her. But Atherton was anxious for this division of the property, and he was her youngest darling, so she gave in. She felt lonely, and out of her element, when everything was arranged, she established in the southwest fire-room, and Atherton's family keeping house in the others, though things started pleasantly and peaceably enough.

It occurred to her that her son Samuel might have her own "help," a stout woman, who had worked in her kitchen for many years, and she take in exchange his little bound girl, Ann Ginnins. She had always taken a great fancy to the child. There was a large closet out of the southwest room, where she could sleep, and she could be made very useful, taking steps, and running "arrants" for her.

Mr. Samuel and his wife hesitated a little, when this plan was proposed. In spite of the trouble she gave them, they were attached to Ann, and did not like to part with her, and Mrs. Polly was just getting her "larnt" her own ways, as she put it. Privately, she feared Grandma would undo all the good she had done, in teaching Ann to be smart and capable. Finally they gave in, with the understanding that it was not to be considered necessarily a permanent arrangement, and Ann went to live with the old lady.

Mrs. Dorcas did not relish this any more than

she did the appropriation of the southwest fire-room. She had never liked Ann very well. Besides she had two little girls of her own, and she fancied Ann rivaled them in Grandma's affection. So, soon after the girl was established in the house, she began to *show out* in various little ways.

Thirsey, her youngest child, was a mere baby, a round fat dumpling of a thing. She was sweet, and good-natured, and the pet of the whole family. Ann was very fond of playing with her, and tending her, and Mrs. Dorcas began to take advantage of it. The minute Ann was at liberty she was called upon to take care of Thirsey. The constant carrying about such a heavy child soon began to make her shoulders stoop and ache. Then Grandma took up the cudgels. She was smart and high-spirited, but she was a very peaceable old lady on her own account, and fully resolved "to put up with every thing from Dorcas, rather than have strife in the family." She was not going to see this helpless little girl imposed on, however. "The little gal ain't goin' to get bent all over, tendin' that heavy baby, Dorcas," she proclaimed. "You can jist make up your mind to it. She didn't come here to do sech work."

Dorcas had to make up her mind to it, but it rankled.

Ann's principal duties were scouring "the brasses" in Grandma's room, taking steps for her, and spinning her stint every day. Grandma set smaller stints than Mrs. Polly. As time went on, she helped about the cooking. She and Grandma cooked their own victuals, and ate from a little separate table in the common kitchen. It was a very large room, and might have accommodated several families, if they could have agreed. There was a big oven, and a roomy fire-place. Good Deacon Wales had probably seen no reason at all why his "beloved wife" should not have her right therein with the greatest peace and concord.

But it soon came to pass that Mrs. Dorcas' pots and kettles were all prepared to hang on the trammels when Grandma's were, and an army of cakes and pies marshalled to go in the oven when Grandma had proposed to do some baking. Grandma bore it patiently for a long time; but Ann was with difficulty restrained from freeing her small mind, and her black eyes snapped more dangerously at every new offence.

One morning, Grandma had two loaves of "riz bread," and some election cakes, rising, and was intending to bake them in about an hour, when they should be sufficiently light. What should Mrs. Dorcas do, but mix up sour milk bread and some pies with the greatest speed, and fill up the oven, before Grandma's cookery was ready!

Grandma sent Ann out into the kitchen to put the loaves in the oven and lo and behold! the oven was full. Ann stood staring for a minute, with a loaf of election cake in her hands; that and the bread would be ruined if they were not baked immediately, as they were raised enough. Mrs. Dorcas had taken Thirsey and stepped out somewhere, and there was no one in the kitchen. Ann set the election cake back on the table. Then, with the aid of the tongs, she reached into the brick oven

and took out every one of Mrs. Dorcas' pies and
loaves. Then she arranged them deliberately in
a pitiful semicircle on the hearth, and put Grandma's cookery in the oven.

She went back to the southwest room then, and
sat quietly down to her spinning. Grandma asked
if she had put the things in, and she said "Yes,
ma'am," meekly. There was a bright red spot on
each of her dark cheeks.

When Mrs. Dorcas entered the kitchen, carrying
Thirsey wrapped up in an old homespun blanket,
she nearly dropped as her gaze fell on the fire-
place and the hearth. There sat her bread and
pies, in the most lamentable half-baked, sticky,
doughy condition imaginable. She opened the
oven, and peered in. There were Grandma's
loaves, all a lovely brown. Out they came, with a
twitch. Luckily, they were done. Her own went
in, but they were irretrievable failures.

Of course, quite a commotion came from this.
Dorcas raised her shrill voice pretty high, and
Grandma, though she had been innocent of the
whole transaction, was so blamed that she gave
Dorcas a piece of her mind at last. Ann surveyed
the nice brown loaves, and listened to the talk in
secret satisfaction; but she had to suffer for it afterward. Grandma punished her for the first time,
and she discovered that that kind old hand was
pretty firm and strong. "No matter what you
think, or whether you air in the rights on't, or not,
a little gal mustn't ever sass her elders," said
Grandma.

But if Ann's interference was blamable, it was

productive of one good result—the matter came to Mr. Atherton's ears, and he had a stern sense of justice when roused, and a great veneration for his mother. His father's will should be carried out to the letter, he declared; and it was. Grandma baked and boiled in peace, outwardly, at least, after that.

Ann was a great comfort to her; she was outgrowing her wild, mischievous ways, and she was so bright and quick. She promised to be pretty, too. Grandma compared her favorably with her own grandchildren, especially Mrs. Dorcas' eldest daughter Martha, who was nearly Ann's age. "Marthy's a pretty little gal enough," she used to say, "but she ain't got the *snap* to her that Ann has, though I wouldn't tell Atherton's wife so, for the world."

She promised Ann her gold beads, when she should be done with them, under strict injunctions not to say anything about it till the time came; for the others might feel hard as she wasn't her own flesh and blood. The gold beads were Ann's ideals of beauty, and richness, though she did not like to hear Grandma talk about being "done with them." Grandma always wore them around her fair, plump old neck; she had never seen her without her string of beads.

As before said, Ann was now very seldom mischievous enough to make herself serious trouble; but, once in a while, her natural propensities would crop out. When they did, Mrs. Dorcas was exceedingly bitter. Indeed, her dislike of Ann was, at all times, smouldering, and needed only a slight fanning to break out.

One stormy winter day, Mrs. Dorcas had been working till dark, making candle-wicks. When she came to get tea, she tied the white fleecy rolls together, a great bundle of them, and hung them up in the cellar-way, over the stairs, to be out of the way. They were extra fine wicks, being made of flax for the company candles. "I've got a good job done," said Mrs. Dorcas, surveying them complacently. Her husband had gone to Boston, and was not coming home till the next day, so she had had a nice chance to work at them, without as much interruption as usual.

Ann, going down the cellar-stairs, with a lighted candle, after some butter for tea, spied the beautiful rolls swinging overhead. What possessed her to, she could not herself have told—she certainly had no wish to injure Mrs. Dorcas' wicks—but she pinched up a little end of the fluffy flax and touched her candle to it. She thought she would see how that little bit would burn off. She soon found out. The flame caught, and ran like lightning through the whole bundle. There was a great puff of fire and smoke, and poor Mrs. Dorcas' fine candle-wicks were gone. Ann screamed, and sprang down stairs. She barely escaped the whole blaze coming in her face.

"What's that!" shrieked Mrs. Dorcas, rushing to the cellar-door. Words can not describe her feeling when she saw that her nice candle-wicks, the fruit of her day's toil, were burnt up.

If ever there was a wretched culprit that night, Ann was. She had not meant to do wrong, but that, maybe, made it worse for her in one way. She had not even gratified malice to sustain her. Grandma blamed her, almost as severely as Mrs. Dorcas. She said she didn't know what would "become of a little gal, that was so keerless," and decreed that she must stay at home from school and work on candle-wicks till Mrs. Dorcas' loss was made good to her. Ann listened ruefully. She was scared and sorry, but that did not seem to help matters any. She did not want any supper, and she went to bed early and cried herself to sleep.

Somewhere about midnight, a strange sound woke her up. She called out to Grandma in alarm. The same sound had awakened her. "Get up, an' light a candle, child," said she; "I'm afeard the baby's sick."

Ann scarcely had the candle lighted, before the door opened, and Mrs. Dorcas appeared in her nightdress—she was very pale, and trembling all over. "Oh!" she gasped, "it's the baby. Thirsey's got the croup, an' Atherton's away, and there ain't anybody to go for the doctor. O what shall I do, what shall I do!" She fairly wrung her hands.

"*Hev* you tried the skunk's oil?" asked Grandma eagerly, preparing to get up.

"Yes, I have, I have! It's a good hour since she woke up, an' I've tried everything. It hasn't done any good. I thought I wouldn't call you, if I could help it, but she's worse—only hear her! An' Atherton's away! Oh! what shall I do, what shall I do?"

"Don't take on so, Dorcas," said Grandma, tremulously, but cheeringly. "I'll come right along, an'—why, child, what air you goin' to do?"

Ann had finished dressing herself, and now she was pinning a heavy homespun blanket over her head, as if she were preparing to go out doors.

"I'm going after the doctor for Thirsey," said Ann, her black eyes flashing with determination.

"O will you, will you!" cried Mrs. Dorcas, catching at this new help.

"Hush, Dorcas," said Grandma, sternly. "It's an awful storm out—jist hear the wind blow! It ain't fit fur her to go. Her life's jist as precious as Thirsey's."

Ann said nothing more, but she went into her own little room with the same determined look in her eyes. There was a door leading from this room into the kitchen. Ann slipped through it hastily, lit a lantern which was hanging beside the kitchen chimney, and was out doors in a minute.

The storm was one of sharp, driving sleet, which struck her face like so many needles. The first blast, as she stepped outside the door, seemed to almost force her back, but her heart did not fail her. The snow was not so very deep, but it was hard walking. There was no pretense of a path. The doctor lived half a mile away, and there was not a house in the whole distance, save the Meeting House and schoolhouse. It was very dark. Lucky it was that she had taken the lantern; she could not have found her way without it.

On kept the little slender, erect figure, with the fierce determination in its heart, through the snow and sleet, holding the blanket close over its head, and swinging the feeble lantern bravely.

When she reached the doctor's house, he was

gone. He had started for the North Precinct early in the evening, his good wife said; he was called down to Captain Isaac Lovejoy's, the house next to the North Precinct Meeting House. She'd been sitting up waiting for him, it was such an awful storm, and such a lonely road. She was worried, but she didn't think he'd start for home that night; she guessed he'd stay at Captain Lovejoy's till morning.

The doctor's wife, holding her door open, as best she could, in the violent wind, had hardly given this information to the little snow-bedraggled object standing out there in the inky darkness, through which the lantern made a faint circle of light, before she had disappeared.

"She went like a speerit," said the good woman, staring out into the blackness in amazement. She never dreamed of such a thing as Ann's going to the North Precinct after the doctor, but that was what the daring girl had determined to do. She had listened to the doctor's wife in dismay, but with never one doubt as to her own course of proceeding.

Straight along the road to the North Precinct she kept. It would have been an awful journey that night for a strong man. It seemed incredible that a little girl could have the strength or courage to accomplish it. There were four miles to traverse in a black, howling storm, over a pathless road, through forests, with hardly a house by the way.

When she reached Captain Isaac Lovejoy's house, next to the Meeting House in the North Precinct of Braintree, stumbling blindly into the warm, lighted kitchen, the captain and the doctor could hardly believe their senses. She told the doctor about Thirsey; then she almost fainted from cold and exhaustion.

Good wife Lovejoy laid her on the settee, and brewed her some hot herb tea. She almost forgot her own sick little girl, for a few minutes, in trying to restore this brave child who had come from the South Precinct in this dreadful storm to save little Thirsey Wales' life.

When Ann came to herself a little, her first question was, if the doctor were ready to go.

"He's gone," said Mrs. Lovejoy, cheeringly.

Ann felt disappointed. She had thought she was going back with him. But that would have been impossible. She could not have stood the journey for the second time that night, even on horseback behind the doctor, as she had planned.

She drank a second bowlful of herb tea, and went to bed with a hot stone at her feet, and a great many blankets and coverlids over her.

The next morning, Captain Lovejoy carried her home. He had a rough wood sled, and she rode on that, on an old quilt; it was easier than horseback, and she was pretty lame and tired.

Mrs. Dorcas saw her coming and opened the door. When Ann came up on the stoop, she just threw her arms around her and kissed her.

"You needn't make the candle-wicks," said she. "It's no matter about them at all. Thirsey's better this morning, an' I guess you saved her life."

Grandma was fairly bursting with pride and delight in her little gal's brave feat, now that she saw her safe. She untied the gold beads on her neck, and fastened them around Ann's. "There," said she, "you may wear them to school to-day, if you'll be keerful."

That day, with the gold beads by way of celebration, began a new era in Ann's life. There was no more secret animosity between her and Mrs. Dorcas. The doctor had come that night in the very nick of time. Thirsey was almost dying. Her mother was fully convinced that Ann had saved her life, and she never forgot it. She was a woman of strong feelings, who never did things by halves, and she not only treated Ann with kindness, but she seemed to smother her grudge against Grandma for robbing her of the southwest fire-room.

DILL

By Mary E. Wilkins Freeman

DAME CLEMENTINA was in her dairy, churning, and her little daughter Nan was out in the flower-garden. The flower-garden was a little plot back of the cottage, full of all the sweet, old-fashioned herbs. There were sweet marjoram, sage, summersavory, lavender, and ever so many others. Up in one corner, there was a little green bed of dill.

Nan was a dainty, slim little maiden, with yellow, flossy hair in short curls all over her head. Her eyes were very sweet and round and blue, and she wore a quaint little snuff-colored gown. It had a very short full waist, with low neck and puffed sleeves, and the skirt was straight and narrow and down to her little heels.

She danced around the garden, picking a flower here and there. She was making a nosegay for her mother. She picked lavender and sweet-william and pinks, and bunched them up together.

Finally she pulled a little sprig of dill and ran, with that and the nosegay, to her mother in the dairy.

"Mother dear," said she, "here is a little nosegay for you; and what was it I overheard you telling Dame Elizabeth about dill last night?"

Dame Clementina stopped churning and took the nosegay. "Thank you, Sweetheart, it is lovely," said she, "and, as for the dill—it is a charmed plant, you know, like four-leaved clover."

"Do you put it over the door?" asked Nan.

"Yes. Nobody who is envious or ill-disposed, can enter into the house if there is a sprig of dill over the door. Then I know another charm which makes it stronger. If one just writes this verse:

> 'Alva, aden, winira mir,
>   Villawissen lingen;
> Sanchta, wanchta, attazir,
>   Hor de mussen wingen'

under the sprig of dill, every one envious, or evil-disposed, who attempts to enter the house, will have to stop short, just where they are, and stand there; they cannot move."

"What does the verse mean?" asked Nan, with great eyes.

"That, I do not know. It is written in a foreign language. But it is a powerful charm."

"O mother, will you write it off for me, if I will bring you a bit of paper and a pen?"

"Certainly," replied her mother, and wrote it off when Nan brought pen and paper.

"Now," said she, "you must run off and play again, and not hinder me any longer, or I shall not get my butter made to-day."

So Nan danced away with the verse, and the sprig of dill, and her mother went on churning.

She had a beautiful tall stone churn, with the sides all carved with figures in relief. There were milkmaids and cows as natural as life all around the churn. The dairy was charming too. The shelves were carved stone; and the floor had a little silvery rill running right through the middle of it, with green ferns at the sides. All along the stone shelves were set pans full of yellow cream, and the pans were all of solid silver, with a chasing of buttercups and daisies around the brims.

It was not a common dairy, and Dame Clementina was not a common dairy-woman. She was very tall and stately, and wore her silver-white hair braided around her head like a crown, with a high silver comb at the top. She walked like a queen; indeed she was a noble count's daughter. In her early youth, she had married a pretty young dairyman, against her father's wishes; so she had been disinherited. The dairyman had been so very poor and low down in the world, that the count felt it his duty to cast off his daughter, lest she should do discredit to his noble line. There was a much pleasanter, easier way out of the difficulty, which the count did not see. Indeed, it was a peculiarity of all his family that they never could see a way out of a difficulty, high and noble as they were. The count only needed to have given the poor young dairyman a few acres of his own land, and a few bags of his own gold, and begged the king, with whom he had great influence, to knight him, and all the obstacles would have been removed; the dairyman would have been quite rich and noble enough for his son-in-law. But he never thought of that, and his daughter was disinherited. However, he made all the amends to her that he could, and fitted her out royally for her humble station in life. He caused this beautiful dairy to be built for her, and gave her the silver milk-pans, and the carved stone churn.

"My daughter shall not churn in a common wooden churn, or skim the cream from wooden pans," he had said.

The dairyman had been dead a good many years now, and Dame Clementina managed the dairy alone. She never saw anything of her father, though he lived in his castle not far off on a neighboring height. When the sky was clear, she could see its stone towers against it. She had four beautiful white cows, and Nan drove them to pasture; they were very gentle.

When Dame Clementina had finished churning, she went into the cottage. As she stepped through the little door with clumps of sweet peas on each side, she looked up. There was the sprig of dill, and the magic verse she had written under it.

DILL

Nan was sitting at the window inside, knitting her stent on a blue stocking. "Ah, Sweetheart," said her mother, laughing, "you have little cause to pin the dill and the verse over our door. None is likely to envy us, or to be ill disposed toward us."

"O mother," said Nan, "I know it, but I thought it would be so nice to feel sure. O there is Dame Golding coming after some milk. *Do* you suppose she will have to stop?"

"What nonsense!" said her mother. They both of them watched Dame Golding coming. All of a sudden, she stopped short, just outside. She could go no further. She tried to lift her feet, but could not.

"O mother!" cried Nan, "she has stopped!"

The poor woman began to scream. She was frightened almost to death. Nan and her mother were not much less frightened, but they did not know what to do. They ran out, and tried to comfort her, and gave her some cream to drink; but it did not amount to much. Dame Golding had secretly envied Dame Clementina for her silver milk-pans. Nan and her mother knew why their visitor was so suddenly rooted to the spot, of course, but she did not. She thought her feet were paralyzed, and she kept begging them to send for her husband.

"Perhaps he can pull her away," said Nan, crying. How she wished she had never pinned the dill and the verse over the door! So she set off for Dame Golding's husband. He came running in a great hurry; but when he had nearly reached his wife, and had his arms reached out to grasp her, he, too, stopped short. He had envied Dame Clementina for her beautiful white cows, and there he was fast, also.

He began to groan and scream too. Nan and her mother ran into the house and shut the door. They could not bear it. "What shall we do, if any one else comes?" sobbed Nan. "O mother, there is Dame Dorothy coming! And—yes— O she has stopped too!" Poor Dame Dorothy had envied Dame Clementina a little for her flower-garden, which was finer than hers, as she had to join Dame Golding and her husband.

Pretty soon, another woman came, who had looked with envious eyes at Dame Clementina, because she was a count's daughter; and another, who had grudged her a fine damask petticoat which she had had before she was disinherited, and still wore on holidays; and they both had to stop.

Then came three rough-looking men in velvet jackets and slouched hats, who brought up short at the gate with a great jerk that nearly took their breath away. They were robbers who were prowling about with a view to stealing Dame Clementina's silver milk-pans some dark night.

All through the day the people kept coming and stopping. It was wonderful how many things poor Dame Clementina had to be envied by men and women, and even children. They envied Nan for her yellow curls or her blue eyes, or her pretty snuff-colored gown. When the sun set, the yard in front of Dame Clementina's cottage was full of people. Lastly, just before dark, the count himself came ambling up on a coal-black horse. The count was a majestic old man dressed in velvet, with stars on his breast. His white hair fell in long curls on his shoulders, and he had a pointed beard. As he came to the gate, he caught a glimpse of Nan in the door.

"How I wish that little maiden was my child," said he.

And, straightway, he stopped. His horse pawed and trembled when he lashed him with a jewelled whip to make him go on; but he could not stir forward one step. Neither could the count dismount from his saddle; he sat there fuming with rage.

Meanwhile, poor Dame Clementina and little Nan were overcome with distress. The sight of their yard full of all these weeping people was dreadful. Neither of them had any idea how to do away with the trouble, because of their family inability to see their way out of a difficulty.

When supper time came, Nan went for the cows, and her mother milked them into her silver milk pails, and strained off the milk into her silver pans. Then they kindled up a fire and cooked some beautiful milk porridge for the poor people in the yard, and then carried them each a bowlful.

It was a beautiful warm moonlight night, and all the winds were sweet with roses and pinks; so the people could not suffer out of doors; but the next morning it rained.

"O mother," said Nan, "it is raining, and what will the poor people do?"

Dame Clementina would never have seen her way out of this difficulty, had not Dame Golding cried out that her bonnet was getting wet, and she wanted an umbrella.

"Why you must go around to their houses of course, and get their umbrellas for them," said Dame Clementina, "but first, give ours to that old man on horseback." She did not know her father, so many years had passed since she had seen him, and he had altered so.

So Nan carried out their great yellow umbrella to the count, and went around to the others' houses for their own umbrellas. It was pitiful enough to see them standing all alone behind the doors. She could not find three extra ones for the three robbers, and she felt badly about that.

Somebody suggested, however, that milk pans turned over their heads would keep the rain off their slouched hats, at least; so she got a silver milk-pan for an umbrella for each. They made such frantic efforts to get away then, that they looked like jumping-jacks; but it was of no use.

Poor Dame Clementina and Nan after they had given more milk porridge to the people, and done all they could for their comfort, stood staring disconsolately out of the window at them under their dripping umbrellas. The yard was fairly green and black and blue and yellow with umbrellas. They wept at the sight, but they could not think of any way out of the difficulty. The people themselves might have suggested one, had they known the real cause; but they did not dare to tell them how they were responsible for all the trouble; they seemed so angry.

About noon Nan spied their most particular

friend, Dame Elizabeth, coming. She lived a little way out of the village. Nan saw her approaching the gate through the rain and mist, with her great blue umbrella, and her long blue double cape and her poke bonnet; and she cried out in the greatest dismay: "O mother, mother, there is our dear Dame Elizabeth coming; she will have to stop too!"

Then they watched her with beating hearts. Dame Elizabeth stared with astonishment at the people, and stopped to ask them questions. But she passed quite through their midst, and entered the cottage under the sprig of dill, and the verse. She did not envy Dame Clementina or Nan, anything.

"Tell me what this means," said she. "Why are all these people standing in your yard in the rain with umbrellas?"

Then Dame Clementina and Nan told her. "And O what shall we do?" said they. "Will these people have to stand in our yard forever?"

Dame Elizabeth stared at them. The way out of the difficulty was so plain to her, that she could not credit its not being plain to them.

"Why," said she, "don't you *take down the sprig of dill and the verse?*"

"Why, sure enough!" said they in amazement. "Why didn't we think of that before?"

So Dame Clementina ran out quickly, and pulled down the sprig of dill and the verse.

Then the way the people hurried out of the yard! They fairly danced and flourished their heels, old folks and all. They were so delighted to be able to move, and they wanted to be sure they could move. The robbers tried to get away unseen with their silver milk-pans, but some of the people stopped them, and set the pans safely inside the dairy. All the people, except the count, were so eager to get away, that they did not stop to inquire into the cause of the trouble then.

Afterward, when they did, they were too much ashamed to say anything about it.

It was a good lesson to them; they were not quite so envious after that. Always, on entering any cottage, they would glance at the door, to see if, perchance, there might be a sprig of dill over it. And, if there was not, they were reminded to put away any envious feeling they might have toward the inmates out of their hearts.

As for the count, he had not been so much alarmed as the others, since he had been to the wars and was braver. Moreover, he felt that his dignity as a noble had been insulted. So he dismounted and fastened his horse to the gate, and strode up to the door with his sword clanking and the plumes on his hat nodding.

"What," he begun; then he stopped short. He had recognized his daughter in Dame Clementina. She recognized him at the same moment. "O my dear daughter!" said he. "O my dear father!" said she.

"And this is my little grandchild?" said the count; and he took Nan upon his knee, and covered her with caresses.

Then the story of the dill and the verse was told. "Yes," said the count, "I truly was envious of you, Clementina, when I saw Nan."

After a little, he looked at his daughter sorrowfully. "I should dearly love to take you up to the castle with me, Clementina," said he, "and let you live there always, and make you and the little child my heirs. But how can I? You are disinherited, you know?"

"I don't see any way," assented Dame Clementina, sadly.

Dame Elizabeth was still there, and she spoke up to the count with a curtesy. "Noble sir," said she, "why don't you make another will?"

"Why, sure enough," cried the count with great delight, "why don't I? I'll have my lawyer up to the castle to-morrow."

He did immediately alter his will, and his daughter was no longer disinherited. She and Nan went to live at the castle, and were very rich and happy. Nan learned to play on the harp, and wore snuff-colored satin gowns. She was called Lady Nan, and she lived a long time, and everybody loved her. But never, so long as she lived, did she pin the sprig of dill and the verse over the door again. She kept them at the very bottom of a little satinwood box—the faded sprig of dill wrapped round with the bit of paper on which was written the charm-verse:

"Alva, aden, winira mir,
  Villawissen lingen;
Sanchta, wanchta, attazir,
  Hor de mussen wingen."

BROWNIE AND THE COOK

By Mrs. Dinah Mulock Craik

THERE was once a little Brownie, who lived —where do you think he lived?—in a coal cellar.

Now a coal cellar may seem a most curious place to choose to live in; but then a Brownie is a curious creature—a fairy and yet not one of that sort of fairies who fly about on gossamer wings, and dance in the moonlight, and so on. He never dances; and as to wings, what use would they be to him in a coal cellar? He is a sober, stay-at-home, household elf—nothing much to look at, even if you did see him, which you are not likely to do—only a little old man, about a foot high, all dressed in brown, with a brown face and hands, and a brown peaked cap, just the color of a brown mouse. And, like a mouse, he hides in corners—especially kitchen corners, and only comes out after dark when nobody is about, and so sometimes people call him Mr. Nobody.

I said you were not likely to see him. I never did, certainly, and never knew anybody that did; but still, if you were to go into Devonshire, you would hear many funny stories about Brownies in general, and so I may as well tell you the adventures of this particular Brownie, who belonged to a family there; which family he had followed from house to house most faithfully, for years and years.

A good many people had heard him—or supposed they had—when there were extraordinary noises about the house; noises which must have come from a mouse or a rat—or a Brownie. But nobody had ever seen him except the children,—the three little boys and three little girls,—who declared he often came to play with them when they were alone, and was the nicest companion in the world, though he was such an old man—hundreds of years old! He was full of fun and mischief, and up to all sorts of tricks, but he never did anybody any harm unless they deserved it.

Brownie was supposed to live under one particular coal, in the darkest corner of the cellar, which was never allowed to be disturbed. Why he had chosen it nobody knew, and how he lived there nobody knew either, nor what he lived upon. Except that, ever since the family could remember, there had always been a bowl of milk put behind the coal-cellar door for the Brownie's supper. Perhaps he drank it—perhaps he didn't: anyhow the bowl was always found empty next morning. The old Cook, who had lived all her life in the family, had never once forgotten to give Brownie his supper; but at last she died, and a young Cook came in her stead, who was very apt to forget everything. She was also both careless and lazy, and disliked taking the trouble to put a bowl of milk in the same place every night for Mr. Nobody. "She didn't believe in Brownies," she said; "she had never seen one, and seeing's believing." So she laughed at the other servants, who looked very grave, and put the bowl of milk in its place as often as they could, without saying much about it.

But once, when Brownie woke up, at his usual hour for rising—ten o'clock at night, and looked round in search of his supper—which was, in fact, his breakfast—he found nothing there. At first he could not imagine such neglect, and went smelling and smelling about for his bowl of milk—it was not always placed in the same corner now—but in vain.

"This will never do," said he; and being extremely hungry, began running about the coal cellar to see what he could find. His eyes were as useful in the dark as in the light—like a pussy-cat's; but there was nothing to be seen—not even a potato paring, or a dry crust, or a well-gnawed bone, such as Tiny, the terrier, sometimes brought into the coal cellar and left on the floor—nothing, in short, but heaps of coals and coal-dust; and even a Brownie cannot eat that, you know.

"Can't stand this; quite impossible!" said the Brownie, tightening his belt to make his poor little inside feel less empty. He had been asleep so long—about a week I believe, as was his habit when there was nothing to do—that he seemed ready to eat his own head, or his boots, or anything. "What's to be done? Since nobody brings my supper, I must go and fetch it."

He spoke quickly, for he always thought quickly, and made up his mind in a minute. To be sure, it was a very little mind, like his little body; but he did the best he could with it, and was not a bad sort of old fellow, after all. In the house he had never done any harm, and often some good, for he frightened away all the rats, mice, and black beetles. Not the crickets—he liked them, as the old Cook had done: she said they were such cheerful creatures, and always brought luck to the house. But the young Cook could not bear them, and used to pour boiling water down their holes, and set basins of beer for them with little wooden bridges up to the rim, that they might walk up, tumble in, and be drowned.

So there was not even a cricket singing in the silent house when Brownie put his head out of his coal-cellar door, which, to his surprise, he found open. Old Cook used to lock it every night, but the young Cook had left that key, and the kitchen and pantry keys, too, all dangling in the lock, so that any thief might have got in, and wandered all over the house without being found out.

"Hurrah, here's luck!" cried Brownie, tossing his cap up in the air, and bounding right through the scullery into the kitchen. It was quite empty, but there was a good fire burning itself out—just for its own amusement, and the remains of a capital supper spread on the table—enough for half a dozen people being left still.

Would you like to know what there was? Devonshire cream, of course; and part of a large dish of junket, which is something like curds and whey. Lots of bread and butter and cheese, and half an apple pudding. Also a great jug of cider and another of milk, and several half-full glasses, and no end of dirty plates, knives, and forks. All were scattered about the table in the most untidy fashion, just as the servants had risen from their supper, without thinking to put anything away.

Brownie screwed up his little old face and turned up his button of a nose, and gave a long whistle. You might not believe it, seeing he lived in a coal cellar; but really he liked tidiness, and always played his pranks upon disorderly or slovenly folk.

"Whew!" said he; "here's a chance. What a supper I'll get now!"

And he jumped on to a chair and thence to the table, but so quietly that the large black cat with four white paws, called Muff, because she was so fat and soft and her fur so long, who sat dozing in front of the fire, just opened one eye and went to sleep again. She had tried to get her nose into the milk jug, but it was too small; and the junket dish was too deep for her to reach, except with one paw. She didn't care much for bread and cheese and apple pudding, and was very well fed besides; so, after just wandering round the table she had jumped down from it again, and settled herself to sleep on the hearth.

But Brownie had no notion of going to sleep. He wanted his supper, and oh! what a supper he did eat! first one thing and then another, and then trying everything all over again. And oh! what a lot he drank!—first milk and then cider, and then mixed the two together in a way that would have disagreed with anybody except a Brownie. As it was, he was obliged to slacken his belt several times, and at last took it off altogether. But he must have had a most extraordinary capacity for eating and drinking—since, after he had nearly cleared the table, he was just as lively as ever, and began jumping about on the table as if he had had no supper at all.

Now his jumping was a little awkward, for there happened to be a clean white tablecloth: as this was only Monday, it had had no time to get dirty—untidy as the Cook was. And you know Brownie lived in a coal cellar, and his feet were black with running about in coal dust. So, wherever he trod, he left the impression behind, until, at last, the whole tablecloth was covered with black marks.

Not that he minded this: in fact, he took great pains to make the cloth as dirty as possible; and then laughing loudly, "Ho, ho, ho!" leaped on to the hearth, and began teasing the cat; squeaking like a mouse, or chirping like a cricket, or buzzing like a fly; and altogether disturbing poor Pussy's mind so much that she went and hid herself in the farthest corner and left him the hearth all to himself, where he lay at ease till daybreak.

Then, hearing a slight noise overhead, which might be the servants getting up, he jumped on to the table again—gobbled up the few remaining crumbs for his breakfast, and scampered off to his coal cellar; where he hid himself under his big coal, and fell asleep for the day.

Well, the Cook came downstairs rather earlier than usual, for she remembered she had to clear off the remains of supper; but lo and behold, there was nothing left to clear! Every bit of food was eaten up—the cheese looked as if a dozen mice had been nibbling at it, and nibbled it down to the very rind; the milk and cider were all drunk—and mice don't care for milk and cider, you know. As for the apple pudding, it had vanished altogether; and the dish was licked as clean as if Boxer, the yard dog, had been at it in his hungriest mood.

"And my white tablecloth—oh, my clean white tablecloth! What can have been done to it?" cried she in amazement. For it was all over little black footmarks, just the size of a baby's foot—only babies don't wear shoes with nails in them, and don't run about and climb on kitchen tables after all the family have gone to bed.

Cook was a little frightened; but her fright changed to anger when she saw the large black cat stretched comfortably on the hearth. Poor Muff had crept there for a little snooze after Brownie went away.

"You nasty cat! I see it all now; it's you that have eaten up all the supper; it's you that have been on my clean tablecloth with your dirty paws."

They were white paws, and as clean as possible; but Cook never thought of that, any more than she did of the fact that cats don't usually drink cider or eat apple pudding.

"I'll teach you to come stealing food in this way; take that—and that—and that!"

Cook got hold of a broom and beat poor Pussy till the creature ran mewing away. She couldn't speak, you know—unfortunate cat! and tell people that it was Brownie who had done it all.

Next night Cook thought she would make all safe and sure; so, instead of letting the cat sleep by the fire, she shut her up in the chilly coal cellar, locked the door, put the key in her pocket, and went off to bed—leaving the supper as before.

BROWNIE AND THE COOK

When Brownie woke up and looked out of his hole, there was, as usual, no supper for him, and the cellar was close shut. He peered about, to try and find some cranny under the door to creep out at, but there was none. And he felt so hungry that he could almost have eaten the cat, who kept walking to and fro in a melancholy manner—only she was alive, and he couldn't well eat her alive; besides, he knew she was old, and had an idea she might be too tough; so he merely said politely, "How do you do, Mrs. Pussy?" to which she answered nothing—of course.

Something must be done, and luckily Brownies can do things which nobody else can do. So he thought he would change himself into a mouse, and gnaw a hole through the door. But then he suddenly remembered the cat, who, though he had decided not to eat her, might take this opportunity of eating him. So he thought it advisable to wait till she was fast asleep, which did not happen for a good while.

At length, quite tired with walking about, Pussy turned round on her tail six times, curled down in a corner, and fell fast asleep.

Immediately Brownie changed himself into the smallest mouse possible; and, taking care not to make the least noise, gnawed a hole in the door, and squeezed himself through, immediately turning into his proper shape again, for fear of accidents.

The kitchen fire was at its last glimmer; but it showed a better supper than even last night, for the Cook had had friends with her—a brother and two cousins—and they had been exceedingly merry. The food they had left behind was enough for three Brownies at least, but this one managed to eat it all up. Only once, in trying to cut a great slice of beef, he let the carving-knife and fork fall with such a clatter that Tiny, the terrier, who was tied up at the foot of the stairs, began to bark furiously. However, he brought her her puppy, which had been left in a basket in a corner of the kitchen, and so succeeded in quieting her.

After that he enjoyed himself amazingly, and made more marks than ever on the white table-cloth; for he began jumping about like a pea on a trencher, in order to make his particularly large supper agree with him.

Then, in the absence of the cat, he teased the puppy for an hour or two, till, hearing the clock strike five, he thought it as well to turn into a mouse again, and creep back cautiously into his cellar. He was only just in time, for Muff opened one eye, and was just going to pounce upon him, when he changed himself back into a Brownie. She was so startled that she bounded away, her tail growing into twice its natural size, and her eyes gleaming like round green globes. But Brownie only said, "Ha, ha, ho!" and walked deliberately into his hole.

When Cook came downstairs and saw that the same thing had happened again—that the supper was all eaten, and the tablecloth blacker than ever with the extraordinary footmarks, she was greatly puzzled. Who could have done all this? Not the cat, who came mewing out of the coal cellar the minute she unlocked the door. Possibly a rat—

but then would a rat have come within reach of Tiny?

"It must have been Tiny herself, or her puppy," which just came rolling out of its basket over Cook's feet. "You little wretch! You and your mother are the greatest nuisance imaginable. I'll punish you!"

And, quite forgetting that Tiny had been safely tied up all night, and that her poor little puppy was so fat and helpless it could scarcely stand on its legs, to say nothing of jumping on chairs and tables, she gave them both such a thrashing that they ran howling together out of the kitchen door, where the kind little kitchen maid took them up in her arms.

"You ought to have beaten the Brownie, if you could catch him," said she in a whisper. "He'll do it again and again, you'll see, for he can't bear an untidy kitchen. You'd better do as poor old Cook did, and clear the supper things away, and put the odds and ends safe in the larder; also," she added mysteriously, "if I were you, I'd put a bowl of milk behind the coal-cellar door."

"Nonsense!" answered the young Cook, and flounced away. But afterward she thought better of it, and did as she was advised, grumbling all the time, but doing it.

Next morning the milk was gone! Perhaps Brownie had drunk it up; anyhow nobody could say that he hadn't. As for the supper, Cook having safely laid it on the shelves of the larder, nobody touched it. And the tablecloth, which was wrapped up tidily and put in the dresser drawer, came out as clean as ever, with not a single black footmark upon it. No mischief being done, the cat and the dog both escaped beating, and Brownie played no more tricks with anybody—till the next time.

BROWNIE AND THE CHERRY TREE

By Mrs. Dinah Mulock Craik

THE "next time" was quick in coming, which was not wonderful, considering there was a Brownie in the house. Otherwise the house was like most other houses, and the family like most other families. The children also: they were sometimes good, sometimes naughty, like other children; but, on the whole, they deserved to have the pleasure of a Brownie to play with them, as they declared he did—many and many a time.

A favorite play-place was the orchard, where grew the biggest cherry tree you ever saw. They called it their "castle," because it rose up ten feet from the ground in one thick stem, and then branched out into a circle of boughs, with a flat place in the middle, where two or three children could sit at once. There they often did sit, turn by turn, or one at a time—sometimes with a book, reading; and the biggest boy made a sort of rope ladder by which they could climb up and down—which they did all winter, and enjoyed their "castle" very much.

But one day in spring they found their ladder cut away! The Gardener had done it, saying it injured the tree, which was just coming into blossom. Now this Gardener was a rather gruff man, with a growling voice. He did not mean to be unkind, but he disliked children; he said they bothered him. But when they complained to their mother about the ladder, she agreed with Gardener that the tree must not be injured, as it bore the biggest cherries in all the neighborhood—so big that the old saying of "taking two bites at a cherry" came really true.

"Wait till the cherries are ripe," said she; and so the little people waited, and watched it through its leafing and blossoming—such sheets of blossoms, white as snow!—till the fruit began to show, and grew large and red on every bough.

At last one morning the mother said, "Children, should you like to help gather the cherries to-day?"

"Hurrah!" they cried, "and not a day too soon; for we saw a flock of starlings in the next field—and if we don't clear the tree, they will."

"Very well; clear it, then. Only mind and fill my baskets quite full, for preserving. What is over you may eat, if you like."

"Thank you, thank you!" and the children were eager to be off; but the mother stopped them till she could get the Gardener and his ladder.

"For it is he must climb the tree, not you; and you must do exactly as he tells you; and he will stop with you all the time and see that you don't come to harm."

This was no slight cloud on the children's happiness, and they begged hard to go alone.

"Please, might we? We will be so good!"

THE CHERRY TREE

The mother shook her head. All the goodness in the world would not help them if they tumbled off the tree, or ate themselves sick with cherries. "You would not be safe, and I should be so unhappy!"

To make mother "unhappy" was the worst rebuke possible to these children; so they choked down their disappointment, and followed the Gardener as he walked on ahead, carrying his ladder on his shoulder. He looked very cross, and as if he did not like the children's company at all.

They were pretty good, on the whole, though they chattered a good deal; but Gardener said not a word to them all the way to the orchard. When they reached it, he just told them to "keep out of his way and not worrit him," which they politely promised, saying among themselves that they should not enjoy their cherry-gathering at all. But children who make the best of things, and try to be as good as they can, sometimes have fun unawares.

When the Gardener was steadying his ladder against the trunk of the cherry tree, there was suddenly heard the barking of a dog, and a very fierce dog, too. First it seemed close beside them, then in the flower garden, then in the fowl yard.

Gardener dropped the ladder out of his hands. "It's that Boxer! He has got loose again! He will be running after my chickens, and dragging his broken chain all over my borders. And he is so fierce, and so delighted to get free. He'll bite anybody who ties him up, except me."

"Hadn't you better go and see after him?"

THE CHERRY TREE

Gardener thought it was the eldest boy who spoke, and turned around angrily; but the little fellow had never opened his lips.

Here there was heard a still louder bark, and from a quite different part of the garden.

"There he is—I'm sure of it! jumping over my bedding-out plants, and breaking my cucumber frames. Abominable beast!—just let me catch him!"

Off Gardener darted in a violent passion, throwing the ladder down upon the grass, and forgetting all about the cherries and the children.

The instant he was gone, a shrill laugh, loud and merry, was heard close by, and a little brown old man's face peeped from behind the cherry tree.

"How d'ye do?—Boxer was me. Didn't I bark well? Now I'm come to play with you."

The children clapped their hands; for they knew that they were going to have some fun if Brownie was there—he was the best little playfellow in the world. And then they had him all to themselves. Nobody ever saw him except the children.

"Come on!" cried he, in his shrill voice, half like an old man's, half like a baby's. "Who'll begin to gather the cherries?"

They all looked blank; for the tree was so high to where the branches sprung, and besides, their mother had said that they were not to climb. And the ladder lay flat upon the grass—far too heavy for little hands to move.

"What! you big boys don't expect a poor little fellow like me to lift the ladder all by myself? Try! I'll help you."

THE CHERRY TREE

Whether he helped or not, no sooner had they taken hold of the ladder than it rose up, almost of its own accord, and fixed itself quite safely against the tree.

"But we must not climb—mother told us not," said the boys ruefully. "Mother said we were to stand at the bottom and pick up the cherries."

"Very well. Obey your mother. I'll just run up the tree myself."

Before the words were out of his mouth Brownie had darted up the ladder like a monkey, and disappeared among the fruit-laden branches.

The children looked dismayed for a minute, till they saw a merry brown face peeping out from the green leaves at the very top of the tree.

"Biggest fruit always grows highest," cried the Brownie. "Stand in a row, all you children. Little boys, hold out your caps: little girls, make a bag of your pinafores. Open your mouths and shut your eyes, and see what the queen will send you."

They laughed and did as they were told; whereupon they were drowned in a shower of cherries— cherries falling like hailstones, hitting them on their heads, their cheeks, their noses—filling their caps and pinafores and then rolling and tumbling on to the grass, till it was strewn thick as leaves in autumn with the rosy fruit.

What a glorious scramble they had—these three little boys and three little girls! How they laughed and jumped and knocked heads together in picking up the cherries, yet never quarreled—for there were such heaps, it would have been ridiculous to squabble over them; and besides, whenever they began to quarrel, Brownie always ran away. Now he was the merriest of the lot; ran up and down the tree like a cat, helped to pick up the cherries, and was first-rate at filling the large market basket.

"We were to eat as many as we liked, only we must first fill the basket," conscientiously said the eldest girl; upon which they all set to at once, and filled it to the brim.

"Now we'll have a dinner-party," cried the Brownie; and squatted down like a Turk, crossing his queer little legs, and sticking his elbows upon his knees, in a way that nobody but a Brownie could manage. "Sit in a ring! sit in a ring! and we'll see who can eat the fastest."

The children obeyed. How many cherries they devoured, and how fast they did it, passes my capacity of telling. I only hope they were not ill next day, and that all the cherry-stones they swallowed by mistake did not disagree with them. But perhaps nothing does disagree with one when one dines with a Brownie. They ate so much, laughing in equal proportion, that they had quite forgotten the Gardener—when, all of a sudden, they heard him clicking angrily the orchard gate, and talking to himself as he walked through.

"That nasty dog! It wasn't Boxer, after all. A nice joke! to find him quietly asleep in his kennel after having hunted him, as I thought, from one end of the garden to the other! Now for the cherries and the children—bless us! where are the children? And the cherries? Why, the tree is as bare as a blackthorn in February! The starlings have been at it, after all. Oh, dear! oh, dear!"

THE CHERRY TREE

"Oh, dear! oh, dear!" echoed a voice from behind the tree, followed by shouts of mocking laughter. Not from the children—they sat as demure as possible, all in a ring, with their hands before them, and in the center the huge basket of cherries, piled as full as it could possibly hold. But the Brownie had disappeared.

"You naughty brats, I'll have you punished!" cried the Gardener, furious at the laughter, for he never laughed himself. But as there was nothing wrong, the cherries being gathered—a very large crop—and the ladder found safe in its place—it was difficult to say what had been the harm done and who had done it.

So he went growling back to the house, carrying the cherries to the mistress, who coaxed him into good temper again, as she sometimes did; bidding also the children to behave well to him, since he was an old man, and not really bad—only cross. As for the little folks, she had not the slightest intention of punishing them; and, as for the Brownie, it was impossible to catch him. So nobody was punished at all.

THE OUPHE[1] OF THE WOOD

By Jean Ingelow

"AN Ouphe!" perhaps you exclaim, "and pray what might that be?"

An Ouphe, fair questioner,—though you may never have heard of him,—was a creature well known (by hearsay, at least) to your great-great-grandmother. It was currently reported that every forest had one within its precincts, who ruled over the woodmen, and exacted tribute from them in the shape of little blocks of wood ready hewn for the fire of his underground palace,—such blocks as are bought at shops in these degenerate days, and called "kindling."

It was said that he had a silver axe, with which he marked those trees that he did not object to have cut down; moreover, he was supposed to possess great riches, and to appear but seldom above ground, and when he did to look like an old man in all respects but one, which was that he always carried some green ash-keys about with him which he could not conceal, and by which he might be known.

Do I hear you say that you don't believe he ever existed?

It matters not at all to my story whether you do or not. He certainly does not exist now. The Commissioners of Woods and Forests have much to answer for, if it was they who put an end to his reign; but I do not think they did; it is

[1] *Ouphe,* pronounced "oof," is an old-fashioned word for goblin or elf.

more likely that the spelling-book used in woodland districts disagreed with his constitution.

After this short preface please to listen while I tell you that once in a little black-timbered cottage, at the skirts of a wood, a young woman sat before the fire rocking her baby, and, as she did so, building a castle in the air: "What a good thing it would be," she thought to herself, "if we were rich!"

It had been a bright day, but the evening was chilly; and, as she watched the glowing logs that were blazing on her hearth, she wished that all the lighted part of them would turn to gold.

She was very much in the habit—this little wife —of building castles in the air, particularly when she had nothing else to do, or her husband was late in coming home to his supper. Just as she was thinking how late he was there was a tap at the door, and an old man walked in, who said:

"Mistress, will you give a poor man a warm at your fire?"

"And welcome," said the young woman, setting him a chair.

So he sat down as close to the fire as he could, and spread out his hands to the flames.

He had a little knapsack on his back, and the young woman did not doubt that he was an old soldier.

"Maybe you are used to the hot countries," she said.

"All countries are much the same to me," replied the stranger. "I see nothing to find fault with in this one. You have fine hawthorn-trees hereabouts; just now they are as white as snow; and then you have a noble wood behind you."

"Ah, you may well say that," said the young woman. "It is a noble wood to us; it gets us bread. My husband works in it."

"And a fine sheet of water there is in it," continued the old man. "As I sat by it to-day it was pretty to see those cranes, with red legs, stepping from leaf to leaf of the water-lilies so lightly."

As he spoke he looked rather wistfully at a little saucepan which stood upon the hearth.

"Why, I shouldn't wonder if you were hungry," said the young woman, laying her baby in the cradle, and spreading a cloth on the round table. "My husband will be home soon, and if you like to stay and sup with him and me, you will be kindly welcome."

The old man's eyes sparkled when she said this, and he looked so very old and seemed so weak that she pitied him. He turned a little aside from the fire, and watched her while she set a brown loaf on the table, and fried a few slices of bacon; but all was ready, and the kettle had been boiling some time before there were any signs of the husband's return.

"I never knew Will to be so late before," said the stranger. "Perhaps he is carrying his logs to the saw-pits."

"Will!" exclaimed the wife. "What, you know my husband, then? I thought you were a stranger in these parts."

"Oh, I have been past this place several times," said the old man, looking rather confused; "and so, of course, I have heard of your husband. Nobody's stroke in the wood is so regular and strong as his."

"And I can tell you he is the handiest man at home," began his wife.

"Ah, ah," said the old man, smiling at her eagerness; "and here he comes, if I am not mistaken."

At that moment the woodman entered.

"Will," said his wife, as she took his bill-book from him, and hung up his hat, "here's an old soldier come to sup with us, my dear." And as she spoke, she gave her husband a gentle push toward the old man, and made a sign that he should speak to him.

"Kindly welcome, master," said the woodman. "Wife, I'm hungry; let's to supper."

The wife turned some potatoes out of the little saucepan, set a jug of beer on the table, and they all began to sup. The best of everything was offered by the wife to the stranger. The husband, after looking earnestly at him for a few minutes, kept silence.

"And where might you be going to lodge tonight, good man, if I'm not too bold?" asked she.

The old man heaved a deep sigh, and said he supposed he must lie out in the forest.

"Well, that would be a great pity," remarked his kind hostess. "No wonder your bones ache if you have no better shelter." As she said this, she looked appealingly at her husband.

"My wife, I'm thinking, would like to offer you a bed," said the woodman; "at least, if you don't mind sleeping in this clean kitchen, I think that we could toss you up something of that sort that you need not disdain."

"Disdain, indeed!" said the wife. "Why, Will, when there's not a tighter cottage than ours in all the wood, and with a curtain, as we have, and a brick floor, and everything so good about us——"

The husband laughed; the old man looked on with a twinkle in his eye.

"I'm sure I shall be humbly grateful," said he.

Accordingly, when supper was over, they made him up a bed on the floor, and spread clean sheets upon it of the young wife's own spinning, and heaped several fresh logs on the fire. Then they wished the stranger good night, and crept up the ladder to their own snug little chamber.

"Disdain, indeed!" laughed the wife, as soon as they shut the door. "Why, Will, how could you say it? I should like to see him disdain me and mine. It isn't often, I'll engage to say, that he sleeps in such a well-furnished kitchen."

The husband said nothing, but secretly laughed to himself.

"What are you laughing at, Will?" said his wife, as she put out the candle.

"Why, you soft little thing," answered the woodman, "didn't you see that bunch of green ash-keys in his cap; and don't you know that nobody would dare to wear them but the Ouphe of the Wood? I saw him cutting those very keys for himself as I passed to the sawmill this morning, and I knew him again directly, though he has disguised himself as an old man."

"Bless us!" exclaimed the little wife; "is the

Wood Ouphe in our cottage? How frightened I am! I wish I hadn't put the candle out."

The husband laughed more and more.

"Will," said his wife, in a solemn voice, "I wonder how you dare laugh, and that powerful creature under the very bed where you lie!"

"And she to be so pitiful over him," said the woodman, laughing till the floor shook under him, "and to talk and boast of our house, and insist on helping him to more potatoes, when he has a palace of his own, and heaps of riches! Oh, dear! oh, dear!"

"Don't laugh, Will," said the wife, "and I'll make you the most beautiful firmity[1] you ever tasted to-morrow. Don't let him hear you laughing."

"Why, he comes for no harm," said the woodman. "I've never cut down any trees that he had not marked, and I've always laid his toll of the wood, neatly cut up, beside his foot-path, so I am not afraid. Besides, don't you know that he always pays where he lodges, and very handsomely, too?"

"Pays, does he?" said the wife. "Well, but he is an awful creature to have so near one. I would much rather he had really been an old soldier. I hope he is not looking after my baby; he shall not have him, let him offer ever so much."

The more the wife talked, the more the husband laughed at her fears, till at length he fell asleep, whilst she lay awake, thinking and thinking, till by degrees she forgot her fears, and began to wonder

---

[1]*Firmity:* generally written frumenty; wheat boiled in milk with sugar and fruit.

what they might expect by way of reward. Hours appeared to pass away during these thoughts. At length, to her great surprise, while it was still quite dark, her husband called to her from below:

"Come down, Kitty; only come down to see what the Ouphe has left us."

As quickly as possible Kitty started up and dressed herself, and ran down the ladder, and then she saw her husband kneeling on the floor over the knapsack, which the Ouphe had left behind him. Kitty rushed to the spot, and saw the knapsack bursting open with gold coins, which were rolling out over the brick floor. Here was good fortune! She began to pick them up, and count them into her apron. The more she gathered, the faster they rolled, till she left off counting, out of breath with joy and surprise.

"What shall we do with all this money?" said the delighted woodman.

They consulted for some time. At last they decided to bury it in the garden, all but twenty pieces, which they would spend directly. Accordingly they dug a hole and carefully hid the rest of the money, and then the woodman went to the town, and soon returned laden with the things they had agreed upon as desirable possessions; namely, a leg of mutton, two bottles of wine, a necklace for Kitty, some tea and sugar, a grand velvet waistcoat, a silver watch, a large clock, a red silk cloak, and a hat and feather for the baby, a quilted petticoat, a great many muffins and crumpets, a rattle, and two new pairs of shoes.

How enchanted they both were! Kitty cooked

the nice things, and they dressed themselves in the finery, and sat down to a very good dinner. But, alas! the woodman drank so much of the wine that he soon got quite tipsy, and began to dance and sing. Kitty was very much shocked; but when he proposed to dig up some more of the gold, and go to market for some more wine and some more blue velvet waistcoats, she remonstrated very strongly. Such was the change that had come over this loving couple, that they presently began to quarrel, and from words the woodman soon got to blows, and, after beating his little wife, lay down on the floor and fell fast asleep, while she sat crying in a corner.

The next day they both felt very miserable, and the woodman had such a terrible headache that he could neither eat nor work; but the day after, being pretty well again, he dug up some more gold and went to town, where he bought such quantities of fine clothes and furniture and so many good things to eat, that in the end he was obliged to buy a wagon to bring them home in, and great was the delight of his wife when she saw him coming home on the top of it, driving the four gray horses himself.

They soon began to unpack the goods and lay them out on the grass, for the cottage was far too small to hold them.

"There are some red silk curtains with gold rods," said the woodman.

"And grand indeed they are!" exclaimed his wife, spreading them over the onion bed.

"And here's a great looking-glass," continued the woodman, setting one up against the outside of the cottage, for it would not go in the door.

THE OUPHE

So they went on handing down the things, and it took nearly the whole afternoon to empty the wagon. No wonder, when it contained, among other things, a coral and bells for the baby, and five very large tea-trays adorned with handsome pictures of impossible scenery, two large sofas covered with green damask, three bonnets trimmed with feathers and flowers, two glass tumblers for them to drink out of,—for Kitty had decided that mugs were very vulgar things,—six books bound in handsome red morocco, a mahogany table, a large tin saucepan, a spit and silver waiter, a blue coat with gilt buttons, a yellow waistcoat, some pictures, a dozen bottles of wine, a quarter of lamb, cakes, tarts, pies, ale, porter, gin, silk stockings, blue and red and white shoes, lace, ham, mirrors, three clocks, a four-post bedstead, and a bag of sugar candy.

These articles filled the cottage and garden; the wagon stood outside the paling. Though the little kitchen was very much encumbered with furniture, they contrived to make a fire in it; and, having eaten a sumptuous dinner, they drank each other's health, using the new tumblers to their great satisfaction.

"All these things remind me that we must have another house built," said Kitty.

"You may do just as you please about that, my dear," replied her husband, with a bottle of wine in his hand.

"My dear," said Kitty, "how vulgar you are! Why don't you drink out of one of our new tumblers, like a gentleman?"

The woodman refused, and said it was much more handy to drink it out of the bottle.

"Handy, indeed!" retorted Kitty; "yes, and by that means none will be left for me."

Thereupon another quarrel ensued, and the woodman, being by this time quite tipsy, beat his wife again. The next day they went and got numbers of workmen to build them a new house in their garden. It was quite astonishing even to Kitty, who did not know much about building, to see how quick these workmen were; in one week the house was ready. But in the meantime the woodman, who had very often been tipsy, felt so unwell that he could not look after them; therefore it is not surprising that they stole a great many of his fine things while he lay smoking on the green damask sofa which stood on the carrot bed. Those articles which the workmen did not steal the rain and dust spoilt; but that they thought did not much matter, for still more than half the gold was left; so they soon furnished the new house. And now Kitty had a servant, and used to sit every morning on a couch dressed in silks and jewels till dinner-time, when the most delicious hot beefsteaks and sausage pudding or roast goose were served up, with more sweet pies, fritters, tarts, and cheese-cakes than they could possibly eat. As for the baby, he had three elegant cots, in which he was put to sleep by turns; he was allowed to tear his picture-books as often as he pleased, and to eat so many sugar-plums and macaroons that they often made him quite ill.

The woodman looked very pale and miserable, though he often said what a fine thing it was to be rich. He never thought of going to his work, and used generally to sit in the kitchen till dinner was ready, watching the spit. Kitty wished she could see him looking as well and cheerful as in old days, though she felt naturally proud that her husband should always be dressed like a gentleman, namely, in a blue coat, red waistcoat, and top-boots.

He and Kitty could never agree as to what should be done with the rest of the money; in fact, no one would have known them for the same people; they quarrelled almost every day, and lost nearly all their love for one another. Kitty often cried herself to sleep—a thing she had never done when they were poor; she thought it was very strange that she should be a lady, and yet not be happy. Every morning when the woodman was sober they invented new plans for making themselves happy, yet, strange to say, none of them succeeded, and matters grew worse and worse. At last Kitty thought she should be happy if she had a coach; so she went to the place where the knapsack was buried, and began to dig; but the garden was so trodden down that she could not dig deep enough, and soon got tired of trying. At last she called the servant, and told her the secret as to where the money was, promising her a gold piece if she could dig it up. The servant dug with all her strength, and with a great deal of trouble they got the knapsack up, and Kitty found that not many gold pieces were left.

However, she resolved to have the coach, so she took them and went to the town, where she bought a yellow chariot, with a most beautiful coat of arms upon it, and two cream-colored horses to draw it.

In the meantime the maid ran to the magistrates, and told them she had discovered something very dreadful, which was, that her mistress had nothing to do but dig in the ground and that she could make money come—coined money: "which," said the maid, "is a very terrible thing, and it proves that she must be a witch."

The mayor and aldermen were very much shocked, for witches were commonly believed in in those days; and when they heard that Kitty had dug up money that very morning, and bought a yellow coach with it, they decided that the matter must be investigated.

When Kitty drove up to her own door, she saw the mayor and aldermen standing in the kitchen waiting for her.

She demanded what they wanted, and they said they were come in the king's name to search the house.

Kitty immediately ran up-stairs and took the baby out of his cradle, lest any of them should steal him, which, of course, seemed a very probable thing for them to do. Then she went to look for her husband, who, shocking to relate, was quite tipsy, quarrelling and arguing with the mayor, and she actually saw him box an alderman's ears.

"The thing is proved," said the indignant mayor; "this woman is certainly a witch."

Kitty was very much bewildered at this; but how much more when she saw her husband seize the mayor—yes, the very mayor himself—and shake him so hard that he actually shook his head off, and it rolled under the dresser! "If I had not seen this with my own eyes," said Kitty, "I could not have believed it—even now it does not seem at all real."

All the aldermen wrung their hands.

"Murder! murder!" cried the maid.

"Yes," said the aldermen, "this woman and her husband must immediately be put to death, and the baby must be taken from them and made a slave."

In vain Kitty fell on her knees; the proofs of their guilt were so plain that there was no hope for mercy; and they were just going to be led out to execution when—why, then she opened her eyes, and saw that she was lying in bed in her own little chamber where she had lived and been so happy; her baby beside her in his wicker[1] cradle was crowing and sucking his fingers.

"So, then, I have never been rich, after all," said Kitty; "and it was all only a dream! I thought it was very strange at the time that a man's head should roll off."

And she heaved a deep sigh, and put her hand to her face, which was wet with the tears she had shed when she thought that she and her husband were going to be executed.

"I am very glad, then, my husband is not a drunken man; and he does *not* beat me; but he goes to work every day, and I am as happy as a queen."

Just then she heard her husband's good-tempered voice whistling as he went down the ladder.

[1] *Wicker:* made of willow twigs like a basket.

"Kitty, Kitty," said he, "come, get up, my little woman; it's later than usual, and our good visitor will want his breakfast."

"Oh, Will, Will, do come here," answered the wife; and presently her husband came up again, dressed in his fustian jacket, and looking quite healthy and good-tempered—not at all like the pale man in the blue coat, who sat watching the meat while it roasted.

"Oh, Will, I have had such a frightful dream," said Kitty, and she began to cry; "we are not going to quarrel and hate each other, are we?"

"Why, what a silly little thing thou art to cry about a dream," said the woodman, smiling. "No, we are not going to quarrel as I know of. Come, Kitty, remember the Ouphe."

"Oh, yes, yes, I remember," said Kitty, and she made haste to dress herself and come down.

"Good morning, mistress; how have you slept?" said the Ouphe, in a gentle voice, to her.

"Not so well as I could have wished, sir," said Kitty.

The Ouphe smiled. "*I* slept very well," he said. "The supper was good, and kindly given, without any thought of reward."

"And that is the certain truth," interrupted Kitty: "I never had the least thought what you were till my husband told me."

The woodman had gone out to cut some fresh cresses for his guest's breakfast.

"I am sorry, mistress," said the Ouphe, "that you slept uneasily—my race are said sometimes by their presence to affect the dreams of you mortals.

Where is my knapsack? Shall I leave it behind me in payment of bed and board?"

"Oh, no, no, I pray you don't," said the little wife, blushing and stepping back; "you are kindly welcome to all you have had, I'm sure: don't repay us so, sir."

"What, mistress, and why not?" asked the Ouphe, smiling. "It is as full of gold pieces as it can hold, and I shall never miss them."

"No, I entreat you, do not," said Kitty, "and do not offer it to my husband, for maybe he has not been warned as I have."

Just then the woodman came in.

"I have been thanking your wife for my good entertainment," said the Ouphe, "and if there is anything in reason that I can give either of you—"

"Will, we do very well as we are," said his wife, going up to him and looking anxiously in his face.

"I don't deny," said the woodman, thoughtfully, "that there are one or two things I should like my wife to have, but somehow I've not been able to get them for her yet."

"What are they?" asked the Ouphe.

"One is a spinning-wheel," answered the woodman; "she used to spin a good deal when she was at home with her mother."

"She shall have a spinning-wheel," replied the Ouphe; "and is there nothing else, my good host?"

"Well," said the woodman, frankly, "since you are so obliging, we should like a hive of bees."

"The bees you shall have also; and now, good morning both, and a thousand thanks to you."

So saying, he took his leave, and no pressing could make him stay to breakfast.

"Well," thought Kitty, when she had had a little time for reflection, "a spinning-wheel is just what I wanted; but if people had told me this time yesterday morning that I should be offered a knapsack full of money, and should refuse it, I could not possibly have believed them!"

THE PRINCE'S DREAM

By Jean Ingelow

IF we may credit the fable, there is a tower in the midst of a great Asiatic plain, wherein is confined a prince who was placed there in his earliest infancy, with many slaves and attendants, and all the luxuries that are compatible with imprisonment. Whether he was brought there from some motive of state, whether to conceal him from enemies, or to deprive him of rights, has not transpired; but it is certain that up to the date of this little history he had never set his foot outside the walls of that high tower, and that of the vast world without he knew only the green plains which surrounded it; the flocks and the birds of that region were all his experience of living creatures, and all the men he saw outside were shepherds.

And yet he was not utterly deprived of change, for sometimes one of his attendants would be ordered away, and his place would be supplied by a new one. The prince would never weary of ques-

171

tioning this fresh companion, and of letting him talk of cities, of ships, of forests, of merchandise, of kings; but though in turns they all tried to satisfy his curiosity, they could not succeed in conveying very distinct notions to his mind; partly because there was nothing in the tower to which they could compare the external world, partly because, having chiefly lived lives of seclusion and indolence in Eastern palaces, they knew it only by hearsay themselves.

At length, one day, a venerable man of a noble presence was brought to the tower, with soldiers to guard him and slaves to attend him. The prince was glad of his presence, though at first he seldom opened his lips, and it was manifest that confinement made him miserable. With restless feet he would wander from window to window of the stone tower, and mount from story to story; but mount as high as he would there was still nothing to be seen but the vast, unvarying plain, clothed with scanty grass, and flooded with the glaring sunshine; flocks and herds and shepherds moved across it sometimes, but nothing else, not even a shadow, for there was no cloud in the sky to cast one. The old man, however, always treated the prince with respect, and answered his questions with a great deal of patience, till at length he found a pleasure in satisfying his curiosity, which so much pleased the poor young prisoner, that, as a great condescension, he invited him to come out on the roof of the tower and drink sherbet with him in the cool of the evening, and tell him of the country beyond the desert, and what seas are like, and mountains, and towns.

two houses and I have none; lend me one of thy houses to live in, and I will give thee my gold;' thus again they exchange."

"It is well," said the prince; "but in time of drought, if there is no bread in a city, can they make it of gold?"

"Not so," answered the old man, "but they must send their gold to a city where there is food, and bring that back instead of it."

"But if there was a famine all over the world," asked the prince, "what would they do then?"

"Why, then, and only then," said the old man, "they must starve, and the gold would be nought, for it can only be changed for that which *is;* it cannot make that which *is not.*"

"And where do they get gold?" asked the prince. "Is it the precious fruit of some rare tree, or have they whereby they can draw it down from the sky at sunset?"

"Some of it," said the old man, "they dig out of the ground."

Then he told the prince of ancient rivers running through terrible deserts, whose sands glitter with golden grains and are yellow in the fierce heat of the sun, and of dreary mines where the Indian slaves work in gangs tied together, never seeing the light of day; and lastly (for he was a man of much knowledge, and had travelled far), he told him of the valley of the Sacramento in the New World, and of those mountains where the people of Europe send their criminals, and where now their free men pour forth to gather gold, and dig for it as hard as if for life; sitting up by it at night lest any should take it from them, giving up houses and country, and wife and children, for the sake of a few feet of mud, whence they dig clay that glitters as they wash it; and how they sift it and rock it as patiently as if it were their own children in the cradle, and afterward carry it in their bosoms, and forego on account of it safety and rest.

"But, prince," he went on, seeing that the young man was absorbed in his narrative, "if you would pass your word to me never to betray me, I would procure for you a sight of the external world, and in a trance you should see those places where gold is dug, and traverse those regions forbidden to your mortal footsteps."

Upon this, the prince threw himself at the old man's feet, and promised heartily to observe the secrecy required, and entreated that, for however short a time, he might be suffered to see this wonderful world.

Then, if we may credit the story, the old man drew nearer to the chafing-dish which stood between them, and having fanned the dying embers in it, cast upon them a certain powder and some herbs, from whence as they burnt a peculiar smoke arose. As their vapors spread, he desired the prince to draw near and inhale them, and then (says the fable) assured him that when he should sleep he would find himself, in his dream, at whatever place he might desire, with this strange advantage, that he should see things in their truth and reality as well as in their outward shows.

So the prince, not without some fear, prepared to obey; but first he drank his sherbet, and handed over the golden cup to the old man by way of recompense; then he reclined beside the chafing-dish and inhaled the heavy perfume till he became overpowered with sleep, and sank down upon the carpet in a dream.

The prince knew not where he was, but a green country was floating before him, and he found himself standing in a marshy valley where a few wretched cottages were scattered here and there with no means of communication. There was a river, but it had overflowed its banks and made the central land impassable, the fences had been broken down by it, and the fields of corn laid low; a few wretched peasants were wandering about there; they looked half-clad and half-starved. "A miserable valley, indeed!" exclaimed the prince; but as he said it a man came down from the hills with a great bag of gold in his hand.

"This valley is mine," said he to the people; "I have bought it for gold. Now make banks that the river may not overflow, and I will give you gold; also make fences and plant fields, and cover in the roofs of your houses, and buy yourselves richer clothing." So the people did so, and as the gold got lower in the bag the valley grew fairer and greener, till the prince exclaimed, "O gold, I see your value now! O wonderful, beneficent gold!"

But presently the valley melted away like a mist, and the prince saw an army besieging a city; he heard a general haranguing his soldiers to urge them on, and the soldiers shouting and battering the walls; but shortly, when the city was well-nigh taken, he saw some men secretly giving gold among the soldiers, so much of it that they threw down their arms to pick it up, and said that the walls were so strong that they could not throw them down. "O powerful gold!" thought the prince; "thou art stronger than the city walls!"

After that it seemed to him that he was walking about in a desert country, and in his dream he thought, "Now I know what labor is, for I have seen it, and its benefits; and I know what liberty is, for I have tasted it; I can wander where I will, and no man questions me; but gold is more strange to me than ever, for I have seen it buy both liberty and labor." Shortly after this he saw a great crowd digging upon a barren hill, and when he drew near he understood that he was to see the place whence the gold came.

He came up and stood a long time watching the people as they toiled ready to faint in the sun, so great was the labor of digging up the gold.

He saw some who had much and could not trust any one to help them to carry it, binding it in bundles over their shoulders, and bending and groaning under its weight; he saw others hide it in the ground, and watch the place, clothed in rags, that none might suspect that they were rich; but some, on the contrary, who had dug up an unusual quantity, he saw dancing and singing, and vaunting their success, till robbers waylaid them when they slept, and rifled their bundles and carried their golden sand away.

"All these men are mad," thought the prince, "and this pernicious gold has made them so."

After this, as he wandered here and there, he saw groups of people smelting the gold under the shadow of the trees, and he observed that a dancing, quivering vapor rose up from it which dazzled their eyes, and distorted everything that they looked at; arraying it also in different colors from the true one.

He observed that this vapor from the gold caused all things to rock and reel before the eyes of those who looked through it, and also, by some strange affinity, it drew their hearts toward those who carried much gold on their persons, so that they called them good and beautiful; it also caused them to see darkness and dulness in the faces of those who had carried none. "This," thought the prince, "is very strange;" but not being able to explain it, he went still farther, and there he saw more people. Each of these had adorned himself with a broad golden girdle, and was sitting in the shade, while other men waited on them.

"What ails these people?" he inquired of one who was looking on, for he observed a peculiar air of weariness and dulness in their faces. He was answered that the girdles were very tight and heavy, and being bound over the regions of the heart, were supposed to impede its action, and prevent it from beating high, and also to chill the wearer, as, being of opaque material, the warm sunshine of the earth could not get through to warm them.

"Why, then, do they not break them asunder," exclaimed the prince, "and fling them away?"

"Break them asunder!" cried the man; "why,

what a madman you must be; they are made of the purest gold!"

"Forgive my ignorance," replied the prince; "I am a stranger."

So he walked on, for feelings of delicacy prevented him from gazing any longer at the men with the golden girdles; but as he went he pondered on the misery he had seen, and thought to himself that this golden sand did more mischief than all the poisons of the apothecary; for it dazzled the eyes of some, it strained the hearts of others, it bowed down the heads of many to the earth with its weight; it was a sore labor to gather it, and when it was gathered the robber might carry it away; it would be a good thing, he thought, if there were none of it.

After this he came to a place where were sitting some aged widows and some orphan children of the gold-diggers, who were helpless and destitute; they were weeping and bemoaning themselves, but stopped at the approach of a man whose appearance attracted the prince, for he had a very great bundle of gold on his back, and yet it did not bow him down at all; his apparel was rich, but he had no girdle on, and his face was anything but sad.

"Sir," said the prince to him, "you have a great burden; you are fortunate to be able to stand under it."

"I could not do so," he replied, "only that as I go on I keep lightening it;" and as he passed each of the widows, he threw gold to her, and, stooping down, hid pieces of it in the bosoms of the children.

"You have no girdle," said the prince.

"I once had one," answered the gold-gatherer; "but it was so tight over my breast that my heart grew cold under it, and almost ceased to beat. Having a great quantity of gold on my back, I felt almost at the last gasp; so I threw off my girdle, and being on the bank of a river, which I knew not how to cross, I was about to fling it in, I was so vexed! 'But no,' thought I, 'there are many people waiting here to cross besides myself. I will make my girdle into a bridge, and we will cross over on it.'"

"Turn your girdle into a bridge!" said the prince, doubtfully, for he did not quite understand.

The man explained himself.

"And, then, sir, after that," he continued, "I turned one-half of my burden into bread, and gave it to these poor people. Since then I have not been oppressed by its weight, however heavy it may have been; for few men have a heavier one. In fact, I gather more from day to day."

As the man kept speaking, he scattered his gold right and left with a cheerful countenance, and the prince was about to reply, when suddenly a great trembling under his feet made him fall to the ground. The refining fires of the gold-gatherers sprang up into flames, and then went out; night fell over everything on the earth, and nothing was visible in the sky but the stars of the southern cross.

"It is past midnight," thought the prince, "for the stars of the cross begin to bend."

He raised himself upon his elbow, and tried to pierce the darkness, but could not. At length a slender blue flame darted out, as from ashes in a chafing-dish, and by the light of it he saw the strange pattern of his carpet and the cushions lying about. He did not recognize them at first, but presently he knew that he was lying in his usual place, at the top of his tower.

"Wake up, prince," said the old man.

The prince sat up and sighed, and the old man inquired what he had seen.

"O man of much learning!" answered the prince, "I have seen that this is a wonderful world; I have seen the value of labor, and I know the uses of it; I have tasted the sweetness of liberty, and am grateful, though it was but in a dream; but as for that other word that was so great a mystery to me, I only know this, that it must remain a mystery forever, since I am fain to believe that all men are bent on getting it; though, once gotten, it causeth them endless disquietude, only second to their discomfort that are without it. I am fain to believe that they can procure with it whatever they most desire, and yet that it cankers their hearts and dazzles their eyes; that it is their nature and their duty to gather it; and yet that, when once gathered, the best thing they can do is to scatter it!"

The next morning, when he awoke, the old man was gone. He had taken with him the golden cup. And the sentinel was also gone, none knew whither. Perhaps the old man had turned his golden cup into a golden key.

A LOST WAND

By Jean Ingelow

MORE than a hundred years ago, at the foot of a wild mountain in Norway, stood an old castle, which even at the time I write of was so much out of repair as in some parts to be scarcely habitable.

In a hall of this castle a party of children met once on Twelfth-night to play at Christmas games and dance with little Hulda, the only child of the lord and lady.

The winters in Norway are very cold, and the snow and ice lie for months on the ground; but the night on which these merry children met it froze with more than ordinary severity, and a keen wind shook the trees without, and roared in the wide chimneys like thunder.

Little Hulda's mother, as the evening wore on, kept calling on the servants to heap on fresh logs of wood, and these, when the long flames crept around them, sent up showers of sparks that lit up the brown walls, ornamented with the horns of deer and goats, and made it look as cheerful and gay as the faces of the children. Hulda's grandmother had sent her a great cake, and when the children had played enough at all the games they could think of, the old gray-headed servants brought it in and set it on the table, together with a great many other nice things such as people eat in Norway—pasties made of reindeer meat, and castles of the sweet pastry sparkling with sugar ornaments of ships and flowers and crowns, and cranberry pies, and whipped cream as white as the snow outside; but nothing was admired so much as the great cake, and when the children saw it they set up a shout which woke the two hounds who were sleeping on the hearths, and they began to bark, which roused all the four dogs in the kennels outside who had not been invited to see either the cake or the games, and they barked, too, shaking and shivering with cold, and then a great lump of snow slid down from the roof, and fell with a dull sound like distant thunder on the pavement of the yard.

"Hurrah!" cried the children, "the dogs and the snow are helping us to shout in honor of the cake."

All this time more and more nice things were coming in—fritters, roasted grouse, frosted apples, and buttered crabs. As the old servants came shivering along the passages, they said, "It is a good thing that children are not late with their suppers; if the confects had been kept long in the larder they would have frozen on the dishes."

Nobody wished to wait at all; so, as soon as the supper was ready, they all sat down, more wood was heaped on to the fire, and when the moon shone in at the deep casements, and glittered on the dropping snowflakes outside, it only served to make the children more merry over their supper to think how bright and warm everything was inside.

This cake was a real treasure, such as in the days of the fairies, who still lived in certain parts of Norway, was known to be of the kind they loved. A piece of it was always cut and laid outside in the snow, in case they should wish to taste it.

Hulda's grandmother had also dropped a ring into this cake before it was put into the oven, and it is well known that whoever gets such a ring in his or her slice of cake has only to wish for something directly, and the fairies are bound to give it, *if they possibly can.* There have been cases known when the fairies could not give it, and then, of course, they were not to blame.

On this occasion the children said: "Let us all be ready with our wishes, because sometimes people have been known to lose them from being so long making up their minds when the ring has come to them."

"Yes," cried the eldest boy. "It does not seem fair that only one should wish. I am the eldest. I begin. I shall wish that Twelfth-night would come twice a year."

"They cannot give you that, I am sure," said Friedrich, his brother, who sat by him.

"Then," said the boy, "I wish father may take me with him the next time he goes out bear-shooting."

"I wish for a white kitten with blue eyes," said a little girl whose name was Therese.

"I shall wish to find an amber necklace that does not belong to any one," said another little girl.

"I wish to be a king," said a boy whose name was Karl. "No, I think I shall wish to be the burgomaster, that I may go on board the ships in the harbor, and make their captains show me what is in them. I shall see how the sailors make their sails go up."

"I shall wish to marry Hulda," said another boy; "when I am a man, I mean. And besides that, I

185

wish I may find a black puppy in my room at home, for I love dogs."

"But that is not fair," said the other children. "You must only wish for one thing, as we did."

"But I really wish for both," said the boy.

"If you wish for both perhaps you will get neither," said little Hulda.

"Well, then," answered the boy, "I wish for the puppy."

And so they all went on wishing till at last it came to Hulda's turn.

"What do you wish for, my child?" said her mother.

"Not for anything at all," she answered, shaking her head.

"Oh, but you must wish for something!" cried all the children.

"Yes," said her mother, "and I am now going to cut the cake. See, Hulda, the knife is going into it. Think of something."

"Well, then," answered the little girl, "I cannot think of anything else, so I shall wish that you may all have your wishes."

Upon this the knife went crunching down into the cake, the children gave three cheers, and the white waxen tulip bud at the top came tumbling on the table, and while they were all looking it opened its leaves, and out of the middle of it stepped a beautiful little fairy woman, no taller than your finger.

She had a white robe on, a little crown on her long yellow hair; there were two wings on her shoulders, just like the downy brown wings of a butterfly, and in her hand she had a little sceptre sparkling with precious stones.

"Only one wish," she said, jumping down on to the table, and speaking with the smallest little voice you ever heard. "Your fathers and mothers were always contented if we gave them one wish every year."

As she spoke, Hulda's mother gave a slice of cake to each child, and, when Hulda took hers, out dropped the ring, and fell clattering on her platter.

"Only one wish," repeated the fairy. And the children were all so much astonished (for even in those days fairies were but rarely seen) that none of them spoke a word, not even in a whisper. "Only one wish. Speak, then, little Hulda, for I am one of that race which delights to give pleasure and to do good. Is there really nothing that you wish, for you shall certainly have it if there is?"

"There was nothing, dear fairy, before I saw you," answered the little girl, in a hesitating tone.

"But now there is?" asked the fairy. "Tell it me, then, and you shall have it."

"I wish for that pretty little sceptre of yours," said Hulda, pointing to the fairy's wand.

The moment Hulda said this the fairy shuddered and became pale, her brilliant colors faded, and she looked to the children's eyes like a thin white mist standing still in her place. The sceptre, on the contrary, became brighter than ever, and the precious stones glowed like burning coals.

"Dear child," she sighed, in a faint, mournful voice, "I had better have left you with the gift of your satisfied, contented heart, than thus have

urged you to form a wish to my destruction. Alas!
alas! my power and my happiness fade from me,
and are as if they had never been. My wand must
now go to you, who can make no use of it, and I
must flutter about forlornly and alone in the cold
world, with no more ability to do good, and waste
away my time—a helpless and defenceless thing."

"Oh, no, no!" replied little Hulda. "Do not
speak so mournfully, dear fairy. I did not wish at
first to ask for it. I will not take the wand if it is
of value to you, and I should be grieved to have it
against your will."

"Child," said the fairy, "you do not know our
nature. I have said whatever you wished should
be yours. I cannot alter this decree; it *must* be so.
Take my wand; and I entreat you to guard it carefully, and never to give it away lest it should get
into the hands of my enemy; for if once it should, I
shall become his miserable little slave. Keep my
wand with care; it is of no use to you, but in the
course of years it is possible I may be able to regain
it, and on Midsummer night I shall for a few hours
return to my present shape, and be able for a short
time to talk with you again."

"Dear fairy," said little Hulda, weeping, and
putting out her hand for the wand, which the fairy
held to her, "is there nothing else that I can do
for you?"

"Nothing, nothing," said the fairy, who had now
become so transparent and dim that they could
scarcely see her; only the wings on her shoulders
remained, and their bright colors had changed to a
dusky brown. "I have long contended with my

bitter enemy, the chief of the tribe of the gnomes—
the ill-natured, spiteful gnomes. Their desire is as
much to do harm to mortals as it is mine to do them
good. If now he should find me I shall be at his
mercy. It was decreed long ages ago that I should
one day lose my wand, and it depends in some degree upon you, little Hulda, whether I shall ever
receive it again. Farewell."

And now nothing was visible but the wings: the
fairy had changed into a moth, with large brown
wings freckled with dark eyes, and it stood trembling upon the table, till at length, when the children had watched it some time, it fluttered toward
the window and beat against the panes, as if it
wished to be released, so they opened the casement
and let it out in the wind and cold.

Poor little thing! They were very sorry for it;
but after a while they nearly forgot it, for they
were but children. Little Hulda only remembered
it, and she carefully enclosed the beautiful sceptre
in a small box. But Midsummer day passed by,
and several other Midsummer days, and still Hulda
saw nothing and heard nothing of the fairy. She
then began to fear that she must be dead, and it
was a long time since she had looked at the wand,
when one day in the middle of the Norway summer, as she was playing in one of the deep bay windows of the castle, she saw a pedlar with a pack on
his back coming slowly up the avenue of pine-trees,
and singing a merry song.

"Can I speak to the lady of this castle?" he said
to Hulda, making at the same time a very low bow.

Hulda did not much like him, he had such restless black eyes and such a cunning smile. His face showed that he was a foreigner; it was as brown as a nut. His dress also was very strange; he wore a red turban, and had large earrings in his ears, and silver chains wound round and round his ankles.

Hulda replied that her mother was gone to the fair at Christiania, and would not be back for several days.

"Can I then speak with the lord of the castle?" asked the pedlar.

"My father is gone out to fish in the fiord," replied little Hulda; "he will not return for some time, and the maids and the men are all gone to make hay in the fields; there is no one left at home but me and my old nurse."

The pedlar was very much delighted to hear this. However, he pretended to be disappointed.

"It is very unfortunate," he said, "that your honored parents are not at home, for I have got some things here of such wonderful beauty that nothing could have given them so much pleasure as to have feasted their eyes with the sight of them—rings, bracelets, lockets, pictures—in short, there is nothing beautiful that I have not got in my pack, and if your parents could have seen them they would have given all the money they had in the world rather than not have bought some of them."

"Good pedlar," said little Hulda, "could you not be so very kind as just to let me have a sight of them?"

The pedlar at first pretended to be unwilling, but after he had looked all across the wide heath and seen that there was no one coming, and that the hounds by the doorway were fast asleep in the sun, and the very pigeons on the roof had all got their heads under their wings, he ventured to step across the threshold into the bay window, and begin to open his pack and display all his fine things, taking care to set them out in the sunshine, which made them glitter like glowworms.

Little Hulda had never seen anything half so splendid before. There were little glasses set round with diamonds, and hung with small tinkling bells which made delightful music whenever they were shaken; ropes of pearls which had a more fragrant scent than bean-fields or hyacinths; rings, the precious stones of which changed color as you frowned or smiled upon them; silver boxes that could play tunes; pictures of beautiful ladies and gentlemen, set with emeralds, with devices in coral at the back; little golden snakes, with brilliant eyes that would move about; and so many other rare and splendid jewels that Hulda was quite dazzled, and stood looking at them with blushing cheeks and a beating heart, so much she wished that she might have one of them.

"Well, young lady," said the cunning pedlar, "how do you find these jewels? Did I boast too much of their beauty?"

"Oh, no!" said Hulda, "I did not think there had been anything so beautiful in the world. I did not think even our queen had such fine jewels as these. Thank you, pedlar, for the sight of them."

"Will you buy something, then, of a poor man?" answered the pedlar. "I've travelled a great distance, and not sold anything this many a day."

"I should be very glad to buy," said little Hulda, "but I have scarcely any money; not half the price of one of these jewels, I am sure."

Now there was lying on the table an ancient signet-ring set with a large opal.

"Maybe the young lady would not mind parting with this?" said he, taking it up. "I could give her a new one for it of the latest fashion."

"Oh, no, thank you!" cried Hulda, hastily, "I must not do so. This ring is my mother's, and was left her by my grandmother."

The pedlar looked disappointed. However, he put the ring down, and said, "But if my young lady has no money, perhaps she has some old trinkets or toys that she would not mind parting with—a coral and bells, or a silver mug, or a necklace, or, in short, anything that she keeps put away, and that is of no use to her?"

"No," said the little girl, "I don't think I have got anything of the kind. Oh, yes! to be sure, I have got somewhere up-stairs a little gold wand, which I was told not to give away; but I'm afraid she who gave it me must have been dead a long while, and it is of no use keeping it any longer."

Now this pedlar was the fairy's enemy. He had long suspected that the wand must be concealed somewhere in that region, and near the sea, and he had disguised himself, and gone out wandering among the farmhouses and huts and castles to try if he could hear some tidings of it, and get it if possible into his power. The moment he heard Hulda mention her gold wand, he became excessively anxious to see it. He was a gnome, and when his malicious eyes gleamed with delight they shot out a burning ray, which scorched the hound who was lying asleep close at hand, and he sprang up and barked at him.

"Peace, peace, Rhan!" cried little Hulda; "lie down, you unmannerly hound!" The dog shrank back again growling, and the pedlar said in a careless tone to 'Hulda:

"Well, lady, I have no objection just to look at the little gold wand, and see if it is worth anything."

"But I am not sure that I could part with it," said Hulda.

"Very well," replied the pedlar, "as you please; but I may as well look at it. I should hope these beautiful things need not go begging." As he spoke he began carefully to lock up some of the jewels in their little boxes, as if he meant to go away.

"Oh, don't go," cried Hulda. "I am going upstairs to fetch my wand. I shall not be long; pray wait for me."

Nothing was further from the pedlar's thought than to go away, and while little Hulda was running up to look for the wand he panted so hard for fear that after all he might not be able to get it that he woke the other hound, who came up to him, and smelt his leg.

"What sort of a creature is this?" said the old hound to his companion, speaking, of course, in the dogs' language.

"I'm sure I can't say," answered the other. "I wonder what he is made of,—he smells of mushrooms! quite earthy, I declare! as if he had lived underground all his life."

"Let us stand one on each side of him, and watch that he doesn't steal anything."

So the two dogs stood staring at him; but the pedlar was too cunning for them. He looked out of the window, and said, "I think I see the master coming," upon which they both turned to look across the heath, and the pedlar snatched up the opal ring, and hid it in his vest. When they turned around he was folding up his trinkets again as calmly as possible. "One cannot be too careful to count one's goods," he said, gravely. "Honest people often get cheated in houses like these, and honest as these two dogs look, I know where one of them hid that leg-of-mutton bone that he stole yesterday!" Upon hearing this the dogs sneaked under the table ashamed of themselves. "I would not have it on my conscience that I robbed my master for the best bone in the world," continued the pedlar, and as he said this he took up a little silver horn belonging to the lord of the castle, and, having tapped it with his knuckle to see whether the metal was pure, folded it up in cotton, and put it in his pack with the rest of his curiosities.

Presently Hulda came down with a little box in her hand, out of which she took the fairy's wand.

The pedlar was so transported at the sight of it that he could scarcely conceal his joy; but he knew that unless he could get it by fair means it would be of no use to him.

"How dim it looks!" said little Hulda; "the stones used to be so very bright when first I had it."

A LOST WAND

"Ah! that is a sign that the person who gave it you is dead," said the deceitful pedlar.

"I am sorry to hear she is dead," said Hulda, with a sigh. "Well, then, pedlar, as that is the case, I will part with the wand if you can give me one of your fine bracelets instead of it."

The pedlar's hand trembled with anxiety, as he held it out for the wand, but the moment he had got possession of it all his politeness vanished.

"There," he said, "you have got a very handsome bracelet in your hand. It is worth a great deal more than the wand. You may keep it. I have no time to waste; I must be gone." So saying, he hastily snatched up the rest of his jewels, thrust them into his pack, and slung it over his shoulder, leaving Hulda looking after him with the bracelet in her hand. She saw him walk rapidly along the heath till he came to a gravel-pit, very deep, and with overhanging sides. He swung himself over by the branches of the trees.

"What can he be going to do there?" she said to herself. "But I will run after him, for I don't like this bracelet half so well as some of the others."

So Hulda ran till she came to the edge of the gravel-pit, but was so much surprised that she could not say a word. There were the great footmarks made by the pedlar down the steep sides of the pit; and at the bottom she saw him sitting in the mud, digging a hole with his hands.

"Hi!" he said, putting his head down. "Some of you come up. I've got the wand at last. Come and help me down with my pack."

195

"I'm coming," answered a voice, speaking under the ground; and presently up came a head, all covered with earth, through the hole the pedlar had made. It was shaggy with hair, and had two little bright eyes, like those of a mole. Hulda thought she had never seen such a curious little man. He was dressed in brown clothes, and had a red-peaked cap on his head; and he and the pedlar soon laid the pack at the bottom of the hole, and began to stamp upon it, dancing and singing with great vehemence. As they went on the pack sank lower and lower, till at last, as they still stood upon it, Hulda could see only their heads and shoulders. In a little time longer she could only see the top of the red cap; and then the two little men disappeared altogether, and the ground closed over them, and the white nettles and marsh marigolds waved their heads over the place as if nothing had happened.

Hulda walked away sadly and slowly. She looked at the beautiful bracelet, and wished she had not parted with the wand for it, for she now began to fear that the pedlar had deceived her. Nevertheless, who would not be delighted to have such a fine jewel? It consisted of a gold hoop, set with turquoise, and on the clasp was a beautiful bird, with open wings, all made of gold, and which quivered as Hulda carried it. Hulda looked at its bright eyes—ruby eyes, which sparkled in the sunshine—and at its crest, all powdered with pearls, and she forgot her regret.

"My beautiful bird!" she said, "I will not hide you in a dark box, as the pedlar did. I will wear

you on my wrist, and let you see all my toys, and
you shall be carried every day into the garden, that
the flowers may see how elegant you are. But stop!
I think I see a little dust on your wings. I must
rub it off." So saying, Hulda took up her frock
and began gently rubbing the bird's wings, when,
to her utter astonishment, it opened its pretty beak
and sang:

> "My master, oh, my master,
>   The brown hard-hearted gnome,
> He goes down faster, faster,
>   To his dreary home.
> Little Hulda sold her
>   Golden wand for me,
> Though the fairy told her
>   That must never be—
> Never—she must never
>   Let the treasure go.
> Ah! lost forever,
>   Woe! woe! woe!"

The bird sang in such a sorrowful voice, and fluttered its golden wings so mournfully, that Hulda
wept.

"Alas! alas!" she said, "I have done very wrong.
I have lost the wand forever! Oh, what shall I do,
dear little bird? Do tell me."

But the bird did not sing again, and it was now
time to go to bed. The old nurse came out to fetch
Hulda. She had been looking all over the castle
for her, and been wondering where she could have
hidden herself.

In Norway, at midsummer, the nights are so
short that the sun only dips under the hills time
enough to let one or two stars peep out before he

appears again. The people, therefore, go to bed in the broad sunlight.

"Child," said the old nurse, "look how late you are—it is nearly midnight. Come, it is full time for bed. This is Midsummer day."

"Midsummer day!" repeated Hulda. "Ah, how sorry I am! Then this is a day when I might have seen the fairy. How very, very foolish I have been!"

Hulda laid her beautiful bracelet upon a table in her room, where she could see it, and kissed the little bird before she got into bed. She had been asleep a long time when a little sobbing voice suddenly awoke her, and she sat up to listen. The house was perfectly still; her cat was curled up at the door, fast asleep; her bird's head was under its wing; a long sunbeam was slanting down through an opening in the green window-curtain, and the motes danced merrily in it.

"What could that noise have been?" said little Hulda, lying down again. She had no sooner laid her head on the pillow than she heard it again; and, turning round quickly to look at the bracelet, she saw the little bird fluttering its wings, and close to it, with her hands covering her face, the beautiful, long lost fairy.

"Oh, fairy, fairy! what have I done!" said Hulda. "You will never see your wand again. The gnome has got it, and he has carried it down under the ground, where he will hide it from us forever."

The fairy could not look up, nor answer. She remained weeping, with her hands before her face, till the little golden bird began to chirp.

A LOST WAND

"Sing to us again, I pray you, beautiful bird!" said Hulda; "for you are not friendly to the gnome. I am sure you are sorry for the poor fairy."

"Child," said the fairy, "be cautious what you say—that gnome is my enemy; he disguised himself as a pedlar the better to deceive you, and now he has got my wand he can discover where I am; he will be constantly pursuing me, and I shall have no peace; if once I fall into his hands, I shall be his slave forever. The bird is not his friend, for the race of gnomes have no friends. Speak to it again, and see if it will sing to you, for you are its mistress."

"Sing to me, sweet bird," said Hulda, in a caressing tone, and the little bird quivered its wings and bowed its head several times; then it opened its beak and sang:

> "Where's the ring?
> Oh the ring, my master stole the ring,
>   And he holds it while I sing,
> In the middle of the world.
>   Where's the ring?
> Where the long green Lizard curled
>   All its length, and made a spring
> Fifty leagues along.
>   There he stands,
>   With his brown hands,
> And sings to the Lizard a wonderful song.
>   And he gives the white stone to that Lizard fell,
>   For he fears it—and loves it passing well."

"What!" said Hulda, "did the pedlar steal my mother's ring—that old opal ring which I told him I could not let him have?"

"Child," replied the fairy, "be not sorry for his treachery; this theft I look to for my last hope for recovering the wand."

"How so?" asked Hulda.

"It is a common thing among mortals," replied the fairy, "to say the thing which is not true, and do the thing which is not honest; but among the other races of beings who inhabit this world the penalty of mocking and imitating the vices of you, the superior race, is, that if ever one of us can be convicted of it, that one, be it gnome, sprite, or fairy, is never permitted to appear in the likeness of humanity again, nor to walk about on the face of the land which is your inheritance. Now the gnomes hate one another, and if it should be discovered by the brethren of this my enemy that he stole the opal ring, they will not fail to betray him. There is, therefore, no doubt, little Hulda, that he carries both the ring and the wand about with him wherever he goes, and if in all your walks and during your whole life you should see him again, and go boldly up to him and demand the stolen stone, he will be compelled instantly to burrow his way down again into the earth, and leave behind him all his ill-gotten gains."

"There is, then, still some hope," said Hulda, in a happier voice; "but where, dear fairy, have you hidden yourself so long?"

"I have passed a dreary time," replied the fairy. "I have been compelled to leave Europe and fly across to Africa, for my enemy inhabits that great hollow dome which is the centre of the earth, and he can only come up in Europe; but my poor little brown wings were often so weary in my flight across the sea that I wished, like the birds, I could drop into the waves and die; for what was to me the use of immortality when I could no longer soothe the sorrow of mortals? But I cannot die; and after I had fluttered across into Egypt, where the glaring light of the sun almost blinded me, I was thankful to find a ruined tomb or temple underground, where great marble sarcophagi were ranged around the walls, and where in the dusky light I could rest from my travels, in a place where I only knew the difference between night and day by the redness of the one sunbeam which stole in through a crevice, and the silvery blue of the moonbeam that succeeded it.

"In that temple there was no sound but the rustling of the bat's wings as they flew in before dawn, or sometimes the chirping of a swallow which had lost its way, and was frightened to see all the grim marble faces gazing at it. But the quietness did me good, and I waited, hoping that the young King of Sweden would marry, and that an heir would be born to him (for I am a Swedish fairy), and then I should recover my liberty according to an ancient statute of the fairy realm, and my wand would also come again into my possession; but alas! he is dead, and the reason you see me to-day is, that, like the rest of my race, I am come to strew leaves on his grave and recount his virtues. I must now return, for the birds are stirring; I hear the cows lowing to be milked, and the maids singing as they go out with their pails. Farewell, little Hulda; guard well the bracelet; I must to my ruined temple

again. Happy for me will be the day when you
see my enemy (if that day ever comes); the bird
will warn you of his neighborhood by pecking your
hand.

"One moment stay, dear fairy," said Hulda.
"Where am I most likely to see the gnome?"

"In the south," replied the fairy, "for they love
hot sunshine. I can stay no longer. Farewell."

So saying, the fairy again became a moth and
fluttered to the window. Little Hulda opened it,
the brown moth settled for a moment upon her
lips as if it wished to kiss her, and then it flew out
into the sunshine, away and away.

Little Hulda watched her till her pretty wings
were lost in the blue distance; then she turned and
took her bracelet, and put it on her wrist, where,
from that day forward, she always wore it night
and day.

Hulda now grew tall, and became a fair young
maiden, and she often wished for the day when she
might go down to the south, that she might have a
better chance of seeing the cruel gnome, and as she
sat at work in her room alone she often asked the
bird to sing to her, but he never sang any other
songs than the two she had heard at first.

And now two full years had passed away, and it
was again the height of the Norway summer, but
the fairy had not made her appearance.

As the days began to shorten, Hulda's cheeks
lost their bright color, and her steps their merry
lightness; she became pale and wan. Her parents
were grieved to see her change so fast, but they
hoped, as the weary winter came on, that the cheer-

ful fire and gay company would revive her; but she grew worse and worse, till she could scarcely walk alone through the rooms where she had played so happily, and all the physicians shook their heads and said, "Alas! alas! the lord and lady of the castle may well look sad: nothing can save their fair daughter, and before the spring comes she will sink into an early grave."

The first yellow leaves now began to drop, and showed that winter was near at hand.

"My sweet Hulda," said her mother to her one day, as she was lying upon a couch looking out into the sunshine, "is there anything you can think of that would do you good, or any place we can go to that you think might revive you?"

"I had only one wish," replied Hulda, "but that, dear mother, I cannot have."

"Why not, dear child?" said her father. "Let us hear what your wish was."

"I wished that before I died I might be able to go into the south and see that wicked pedlar, that if possible I might repair the mischief I had done to the fairy by restoring her the wand."

"Does she wish to go into the south?" said the physicians. "Then it will be as well to indulge her, but nothing can save her life; and if she leaves her native country she will return to it no more."

"I am willing to go," said Hulda, "for the fairy's sake."

So they put her on a pillion, and took her slowly on to the south by short distances, as she could bear it. And as she left the old castle, the wind tossed some yellow leaves against her, and then whirled them away across the heath to the forest. Hulda said:

> "Yellow leaves, yellow leaves,
>   Whither away?
>   Through the long wood paths
>   How fast do ye stray!"

The yellow leaves answered:

> "We go to lie down
>   Where the spring snowdrops grow,
>   Their young roots to cherish
>   Through frost and through snow."

Then Hulda said again to the leaves:

> "Yellow leaves, yellow leaves,
>   Faded and few,
>   What will the spring flowers
>   Matter to you?"

And the leaves said:

> "We shall not see them,
>   When gaily they bloom,
>   But sure they will love us
>   For guarding their tomb."

Then Hulda said:

"The yellow leaves are like me: I am going away from my place for the sake of the poor fairy, who now lies hidden in the dark Egyptian ruin; but if I am so happy as to recover her wand by my care, she will come back glad and white, like the snowdrops when winter is over, and she will love my memory when I am laid asleep in my tomb."

So they set out on their journey, and every day went a little distance toward the south, till at last, on Christmas Eve, they came to an ancient city at the foot of a range of mountains.

"What a strange Christmas this is!" said Hulda, when she looked out the next morning. "Let us stay here, mother, for we are far enough to the south. Look how the red berries hang on yonder tree, and these myrtles on the porch are fresh and green, and a few roses bloom still on the sunny side of the window."

It was so fine and warm that the next day they carried Hulda to a green bank where she could sit down.

It was close by some public gardens, and the people were coming and going. She fell into a doze as she sat with her mother watching her, and in her half-dream she heard the voices of the passers-by, and what they said about her, till suddenly a voice which she remembered made her wake with a start, and as she opened her frightened eyes, there, with his pack on his back, and his cunning eyes fixed upon her, stood the pedlar.

"Stop him!" cried Hulda, starting up. "Mother, help me to run after him!"

"After whom, my child?" asked her mother.

"After the pedlar," said Hulda. "He was here but now, but before I had time to speak to him, he stepped behind that thorn-bush and disappeared."

"So that is Hulda," said the pedlar to himself, as he went down the steep path into the middle of the world. "She looks as if a few days more would be all she has to live. I will not come here any more till the spring, and then she will be dead, and I shall have nothing to fear."

But Hulda did not die. See what a good thing it is to be kind. The soft, warm air of the south revived her by degrees—so much, that by the end of the year she could walk in the public garden and delight in the warm sunshine; in another month she could ride with her father to see all the strange old castles in that neighborhood, and by the end of February she was as well as ever she had been in her life; and all this came from her desire to do good to the fairy by going to the south.

"And now," thought the pedlar, "there is no doubt that the daisies are growing on Hulda's grave by this time, so I will go up again to the outside of the world, and sell my wares to the people who resort to those public places."

So one day when in that warm climate the spring flowers were already blooming on the hillsides, up he came close to the ruined walls of a castle, and set his pack down beside him to rest after the fatigues of his journey.

"This is a cool, shady place," he said, looking round, "and these dark yew-trees conceal it very well from the road. I shall come here always in the middle of the day, when the sun is too hot, and count over my gains. How hard my mistress, the Lizard, makes me work! Who would have thought she would have wished to deck her green head with opals down there, where there are only a tribe of brown gnomes to see her? But I have not given her that one out of the ring which I stole, nor three others that I conjured out of the crozier of the priest as I knelt at the altar, and they thought I was rehearsing a prayer to the Virgin."

After resting some time, the pedlar took up his pack and went boldly on to the gardens, never doubting but that Hulda was dead; but it so happened that at that moment Hulda and her mother sat at work in a shady part of the garden under some elder-trees.

"What is the matter, my sweet bird?" said Hulda, for the bird pecked her wrist, and fluttered its wings, and opened its beak as if it were very much frightened.

"Let us go, mother, and look about us," said Hulda.

So they both got up and wandered all over the gardens; but the pedlar, in the meantime, had walked on toward the town, and they saw nothing of him.

"Sing to me, my sweet bird," said Hulda that night as she lay down to sleep. "Tell me *why* you pecked my wrist."

Then the bird sang to her:

"Who came from the ruin, the ivy-clad ruin,
  With old shaking arches, all moss overgrown,
      Where the flitter-bat hideth,
      The limber snake glideth,
  And chill water drips from the slimy green stone?"

"Who did?" asked Hulda. "Not the pedlar, surely? Tell me, my pretty bird." But the bird only chirped a little and fluttered its golden wings, so Hulda ceased to ask it, and presently fell asleep, but the bird woke her by pecking her wrist very early, almost before sunrise, and sang:

> "Who dips a brown hand in the chill shaded water
> The water that drips from a slimy green stone?
> Who flings his red cap
> At the owlets that flap
> Their white wings in his face as he sits there alone?"

Hulda, upon hearing this, arose in great haste and dressed herself; then she went to her father and mother, and entreated that they would come with her to the old ruin. It was now broad day, so they all three set out together. It was a very hot morning, the dust lay thick upon the road, and there was not air enough to stir the thick leaves of the trees which hung overhead.

They had not gone far before they found themselves in a crowd of people, all going toward the castle ruin, for there, they told Hulda, the pedlar, the famous pedlar from the north, who sold such fine wares, was going to perform some feats of jugglery of most surprising cleverness.

"Child," whispered Hulda's mother, "nothing could be more fortunate for us; let us mingle with the crowd and get close to the pedler.

Hulda assented to her mother's wish, but the heat and dust, together with her own intense desire to rescue the lost wand, made her tremble so that she had great difficulty in walking. They went among gypsies, fruit-women, peasant girls, children, travelling musicians, common soldiers, and laborers; the heat increased, and the dust and the noise, and at last Hulda and her parents were borne forward into the old ruin among a rush of people running and huzzaing, and heard the pedlar shout to them:

"Keep back, good people; leave a space before me; leave a large space between me and you."

So they pressed back again, jostling and crowding each other, and left an open space before him from which he looked at them with his cunning black eyes, and with one hand dabbling in the cold water of the spring.

The place was open to the sky, and the broken arches and walls were covered with thick ivy and wall flowers. The pedlar sat on a large gray stone, with his red cap on and his brown fingers adorned with splendid rings, and he spread them out and waved his hands to the people with ostentatious ceremony.

"Now, good people," he said, without rising from his seat, "you are about to see the finest, rarest, and most wonderful exhibition of the conjuring art ever known!"

"Stop!" cried a woman's voice from the crowd, and a young girl rushed wildly forward from the people, who had been trying to hold her back.

"I impeach you before all these witnesses!" she cried, seizing him by the hand. "See justice done, good people. I impeach you, pedlar. Where's the ring—my mother's ring—which you stole on Midsummer's day in the castle?"

"Good people," said the pedlar, pulling his red cap over his face, and speaking in a mild, fawning voice, "I hope you'll protect me. I hope you won't see me insulted."

"My ring, my ring!" cried Hulda; "he wore it on his finger but now!"

"Show your hand like a man!" said the people. "If the lady says falsely, can't you face her and tell her so? Never hold it down so cowardly!"

The pedlar had tucked his feet under him, and when the people cried out to him to let the rings on his hand be seen, he had already burrowed with them up to his knees in the earth.

"Oh, he will go down into the earth!" cried Hulda. "But I will not let go! Pedlar, pedlar, it is useless! If I follow you before the Lizard, your mistress, I will not let go!"

The pedlar turned his terrified, cowardly eyes upon Hulda, and sank lower and lower. The people were too frightened to move.

"Stop, child," cried her mother. "Oh, he will go down and drag thee with him."

But Hulda would not and could not let go. The pedlar had now sunk up to his waist. Her mother wrung her hands, and in an instant the earth closed upon them both, and, after falling in the dark down a steep abyss, they found themselves, not at all the worse, standing in a dimly lighted cave with a large table in it piled with mouldy books. Behind the table was a smooth and perfectly round hole in the wall about the size of a cartwheel.

Hulda looked that way, and saw how intensely dark it was through this hole, and she was wondering where it led to when an enormous green Lizard put its head through into the cave, and gazed at her with its great brown eyes.

"What is thy demand, fine child of the day-light?" said the Lizard.

"Princess," replied Hulda, "I demand that this thy servant should give up to me a ring which he stole in my father's castle when I was a child."

The pedlar no sooner heard Hulda boldly demand her rights than he fell on his knees and began to cry for mercy.

"Mercy rests with this maiden," said the Lizard. At the same time she darted out her tongue, which was several yards in length and like a scarlet thread, and with it stripped the ring from the gnome's finger and gave it to Hulda.

"Speak, maiden, what reparation do you demand of this culprit, and what shall be his punishment?"

"Great princess," replied Hulda, "let him restore to me a golden wand which I sold to him, for it belongs to a fairy whom he has long persecuted."

"Here it is, here it is!" cried the cowardly gnome, putting his hand into his bosom and pulling it out, shaking all the time, and crying out most piteously, "Oh, don't let me be banished from the sunshine!"

"After this double crime no mercy can be shown you," said the Lizard, and she twined her scarlet tongue round him, and drew him through the hole to herself. At the same instant it closed, and a crack came in the roof of the cave, through which the sunshine stole, and as Hulda looked up in flew a brown moth and settled on the magic bracelet. She touched the moth with the wand, and instantly it stood upon her wrist—a beautiful and joyous fairy. She took her wand from Hulda's hand, and stood for a moment looking gratefully in her face without speaking. Then she said to the wand:

"Art thou my own again, and wilt thou serve me?"

"Try me," said the wand.

So she struck the wall with it, and said, "Cleave, wall!" and a hole came in the wall large enough for Hulda to creep through, and she found herself at the foot of a staircase hewn in the rock, and, after walking up it for three hours, she came out in the old ruined castle, and was astonished to see that the sun had set. The moment she appeared her father and mother, who had given her over for lost, clasped her in their arms and wept for joy as they embraced her.

"My child," said her father, "how happy thou lookest, not as if thou hadst been down in the dark earth!"

Hulda kissed her parents and smiled upon them; then she turned to look for the fairy, but she was gone. So they all three walked home in the twilight, and the next day Hulda set out again with her parents to return to the old castle in Norway. As for the fairy, she was happy from that day in the possession of her wand; but the little golden bird folded its wings and never sang any songs again.

SNAP-DRAGONS—A TALE OF CHRISTMAS EVE

By Juliana Horatia Ewing

ONCE upon a time there lived a certain family of the name of Skratdj. (It has a Russian or Polish look, and yet they most certainly lived in England.) They were remarkable for the following peculiarity: They seldom seriously quarrelled, but they never agreed about anything. It is hard to say whether it were more painful for their friends to hear them constantly contradicting each other, or gratifying to discover that it "meant nothing," and was "only their way."

It began with the father and mother. They were a worthy couple, and really attached to each other. They had a habit of contradicting each other's statements, and opposing each other's opinions, which, though mutually understood and allowed for in private, was most trying to the bystanders in public. If one related an anecdote, the other would break in with half a dozen corrections of trivial details of no interest or importance to any one, the speakers included. For instance: Suppose the two dining in a strange house, and Mrs. Skratdj seated by the host, and contributing to the small talk of the dinner-table. Thus:

"Oh, yes. Very changeable weather indeed. It looked quite promising yesterday morning in the town, but it began to rain at noon."

"A quarter-past eleven, my dear," Mr. Skratdj's voice would be heard to say from several chairs down, in the corrective tones of a husband and father; "and really, my dear, so far from being a promising morning, I must say it looked about as threatening as it well could. Your memory is not always accurate in small matters, my love."

But Mrs. Skratdj had not been a wife and a mother for fifteen years, to be snuffed out at one snap of the marital snuffers. As Mr. Skratdj leaned forward in his chair, she leaned forward in hers, and defended herself across the intervening couples.

"Why, my dear Mr. Skratdj, you said yourself the weather had not been so promising for a week."

"What I said, my dear, pardon me, was that the barometer was higher than it had been for a week. But, as you might have observed if these details were in your line, my love, which they are not, the rise was extraordinarily rapid, and there is no surer sign of unsettled weather. But Mrs. Skratdj is apt to forget these unimportant trifles," he added, with a comprehensive smile round the dinner-table; "her thoughts are very properly absorbed by the more important domestic questions of the nursery."

"Now I think that's rather unfair on Mr. Skratdj's part," Mrs. Skratdj would chirp, with a smile quite as affable and as general as her husband's. "I'm sure he's *quite* as forgetful and inaccurate as *I* am. And I don't think *my* memory is at *all* a bad one."

"You forgot the dinner-hour when we were going out to dine last week, nevertheless," said Mr. Skratdj.

"And you couldn't help me when I asked you,"

was the sprightly retort. "And I'm sure it's not like you to forget anything about *dinner,* my dear."

"The letter was addressed to you," said Mr. Skratdj.

"I sent it to you by Jemima," said Mrs. Skratdj.

"I didn't read it," said Mr. Skratdj.

"Well, you burnt it," said Mrs. Skratdj; "and, as I always say, there's nothing more foolish than burning a letter of invitation before the day, for one is certain to forget."

"I've no doubt you always do say it," Mr. Skratdj remarked, with a smile, "but I certainly never remember to have heard the observation from your lips, my love."

"Whose memory's in fault there?" asked Mrs. Skratdj, triumphantly; and as at this point the ladies rose, Mrs. Skratdj had the last word.

Indeed, as may be gathered from this conversation, Mrs. Skratdj was quite able to defend herself. When she was yet a bride, and young and timid, she used to collapse when Mr. Skratdj contradicted her statements, and set her stories straight in public. Then she hardly ever opened her lips without disappearing under the domestic extinguisher. But in the course of fifteen years she had learned that Mr. Skratdj's bark was a great deal worse than his bite. (If, indeed, he had a bite at all.) Thus snubs that made other people's ears tingle, had no effect whatever on the lady to whom they were addressed, for she knew exactly what they were worth, and had by this time become fairly adept at snapping in return. In the days when she succumbed she was occasionally unhappy, but

now she and her husband understood each other,
and, having agreed to differ, they, unfortunately,
agreed also to differ in public.

Indeed, it was the bystanders who had the worst
of it on these occasions. To the worthy couple
themselves the habit had become second nature,
and in no way affected the friendly tenor of their
domestic relations. They would interfere with each
other's conversation, contradicting assertions, and
disputing conclusions for a whole evening; and then,
when all the world and his wife thought that these
ceaseless sparks of bickering must blaze up into a
flaming quarrel as soon as they were alone, they
would bowl amicably home in a cab, criticizing the
friends who were commenting upon them, and as
little agreed about the events of the evening as
about the details of any other events whatever.

Yes; the bystanders certainly had the worst of
it. Those who were near wished themselves anywhere else, especially when appealed to. Those
who were at a distance did not mind so much. A
domestic squabble at a certain distance is interesting, like an engagement viewed from a point
beyond the range of guns. In such a position one
may some day be placed oneself! Moreover, it gives
a touch of excitement to a dull evening to be able
to say *sotto voce* to one's neighbor, "Do listen! The
Skratdjs are at it again!" Their unmarried friends
thought a terrible abyss of tyranny and aggrava-
tion must lie beneath it all, and blessed their stars
that they were still single and able to tell a tale
their own way. The married ones had more idea of
how it really was, and wished in the name of com-

mon sense and good taste that Skratdj and his wife would not make fools of themselves.

So it went on, however; and so, I suppose, it goes on still, for not many bad habits are cured in middle age.

On certain questions of comparative speaking their views were never identical. Such as the temperature being hot or cold, things being light or dark, the apple-tarts being sweet or sour. So one day Mr. Skratdj came into the room, rubbing his hands, and planting himself at the fire with "Bitterly cold it is to-day, to be sure."

"Why, my dear William," said Mrs. Skratdj, "I'm sure you must have got a cold; I feel a fire quite oppressive myself."

"You were wishing you'd a sealskin jacket yesterday, when it wasn't half as cold as it is to-day," said Mr Skratdj.

"My dear William! Why, the children were shivering the whole day, and the wind was in the north."

"Due east, Mrs. Skratdj."

"I know by the smoke," said Mrs. Skratdj, softly, but decidedly.

"I fancy I can tell an east wind when I feel it," said Mr. Skratdj, jocosely, to the company.

"I told Jemima to look at the weathercock," murmured Mrs. Skratdj.

"I don't care a fig for Jemima," said her husband,

On another occasion Mrs. Skratdj and a lady friend were conversing.

* * * "We met him at the Smith's—a gentlemanlike, agreeable man, about forty," said

217

Mrs. Skratdj, in reference to some matter interesting to both ladies.

"Not a day over thirty-five," said Mr. Skratdj, from behind his newspaper.

"Why, my dear William, his hair's gray," said Mrs. Skratdj.

"Plenty of men are gray at thirty," said Mr. Skratdj. "I knew a man who was gray at twenty-five."

"Well, forty or thirty-five, it doesn't much matter," said Mrs. Skratdj, about to resume her narration.

"Five years matters a good deal to most people at thirty-five," said Mr. Skratdj, as he walked towards the door. "They would make a remarkable difference to me, I know;" and with a jocular air Mr. Skratdj departed, and Mrs. Skratdj had the rest of the anecdote her own way.

The Spirit of Contradiction finds a place in most nurseries, though to a very varying degree in different ones. Children snap and snarl by nature, like young puppies; and most of us can remember taking part in some such spirited dialogues as the following:

"I will."	"You daren't."
"You can't."	"I dare."
"You shall."	"I'll tell mamma."
"I won't."	"I don't care if you do."

It is the part of wise parents to repress these squibs and crackers of juvenile contention, and to enforce that slowly learned lesson, that in this world one must often "pass over" and "put up with" things in other people, being oneself by no means perfect. Also that it is a kindness, and almost a duty, to let people think and say and do things in their own way occasionally.

But even if Mr. and Mrs. Skratdj had ever thought of teaching all this to their children, it must be confessed that the lesson would not have come with a good grace from either of them, since they snapped and snarled between themselves as much or more than their children in the nursery.

The two elders were the leaders in the nursery squabbles. Between these, a boy and a girl, a ceaseless war of words was waged from morning to night. And as neither of them lacked ready wit, and both were in constant practice, the art of snapping was cultivated by them to the highest pitch.

It began at breakfast, if not sooner.

"You've taken my chair."

"It's not your chair."

"You know it's the one I like, and it was in my place."

"How do you know it was in your place?"

"Never mind. I do know."

"No, you don't."

"Yes, I do."

"Suppose I say it was in my place."

"You can't, for it wasn't."

"I can, if I like."

"Well, was it?"

"I sha'n't tell you."

"Ah! that shows it wasn't."

"No, it doesn't."

"Yes, it does." Etc., etc., etc.

The direction of their daily walks was a fruitful subject of difference of opinion.

"Let's go on the Common to-day, nurse?"

"Oh, don't let's go there; we're always going on the Common."

"I'm sure we're not. We've not been there for ever so long."

"Oh, what a story! We were there on Wednesday. Let's go down Gipsey Lane. We never go down Gipsey Lane."

"Why, we're always going down Gipsey Lane. And there's nothing to see there."

"I don't care. I won't go on the Common, and I shall go and get papa to say we're to go down Gipsey Lane. I can run faster than you."

"That's very sneaking; but I don't care."

"Papa! papa! Polly's called me a sneak."

"No, I didn't, papa."

"You did."

"No, I didn't. I only said it was sneaking of you to say you'd run faster than me, and get papa to say we were to go down Gipsey Lane."

"Then you did call him sneaking," said Mr. Skratdj. "And you're a very naughty, ill-mannered little girl. You're getting very troublesome, Polly, and I shall have to send you to school, where you'll be kept in order. Go where your brother wishes at once."

For Polly and her brother had reached an age when it was convenient, if possible, to throw the blame of all nursery differences on Polly. In families where domestic discipline is rather fractious than firm, there comes a stage when the girls almost invariably go to the wall, because they will stand snubbing, and the boys will not. Domestic authority, like some other powers, is apt to be magnified on the weaker class.

But Mr. Skratdj would not always listen even to Harry.

"If you don't give it me back directly, I'll tell about your eating the two magnum-bonums in the kitchen garden on Sunday," said Master Harry, on one occasion.

" 'Telltale tit!
　　Your tongue shall be slit,
　　And every dog in the town shall have a little bit,' "

quoted his sister.

"Ah! You've called me a telltale. Now I'll go and tell papa. You got into a fine scrape for calling me names the other day."

"Go, then! I don't care."

"You wouldn't like me to go, I know."

"You daren't. That's what it is."

"I dare."

"Then why don't you?"

"Oh, I am going; but you'll see what will be the end of it."

Polly, however, had her own reasons for remaining stolid, and Harry started. But when he reached the landing he paused. Mr. Skratdj had especially announced that morning that he did not wish to be disturbed, and though he was a favorite, Harry had no desire to invade the dining-room at this crisis. So he returned to the nursery, and said, with a magnanimous air, "I don't want to get you into a scrape, Polly. If you'll beg my pardon I won't go."

"I'm sure I sha'n't," said Polly, who was equally well informed as to the position of affairs at head-quarters. "Go, if you dare."

"I won't if you want me not," said Harry, discreetly waiving the question of apologies.

"But I'd rather you went," said the obdurate Polly. "You're always telling tales. Go and tell now, if you're not afraid."

So Harry went. But at the bottom of the stairs he lingered again, and was meditating how to return with most credit to his dignity, when Polly's face appeared through the banisters, and Polly's sharp tongue goaded him on.

"Ah! I see you. You're stopping. You daren't go."

"I dare," said Harry; and at last he went.

As he turned the handle of the door, Mr. Skratdj turned round.

"Please, papa—" Harry began.

"Get away with you!" cried Mr. Skratdj. "Didn't I tell you I was not to be disturbed this morning? What an extraor—"

But Harry had shut the door, and withdrawn precipitately.

Once outside, he returned to the nursery with dignified steps, and an air of apparent satisfaction, saying:

"You're to give me the bricks, please."

"Who says so?"

"Why, who should say so? Where have I been, pray?"

"I don't know, and I don't care."

"I've been to papa. There!"

"Did he say I was to give up the bricks?"

"I've told you."

"No, you've not."

"I sha'n't tell you any more."

"Then I'll go to papa and ask."

"Go by all means."

"I won't if you'll tell me truly."

"I sha'n't tell you anything. Go and ask, if you dare," said Harry, only too glad to have the tables turned.

Polly's expedition met with the same fate, and she attempted to cover her retreat in a similar manner.

"Ah! you didn't tell."

"I don't believe you asked papa."

"Don't you? Very well!"

"Well, did you?"

"Never mind." Etc., etc., etc.

Meanwhile Mr. Skratdj scolded Mrs. Skratdj for not keeping the children in better order. And Mrs. Skratdj said it was quite impossible to do so when Mr. Skratdj spoilt Harry as he did, and weakened her (Mrs. Skratdj's) authority by constant interference.

Difference of sex gave point to many of these nursery sqabbles, as it so often does to domestic broils.

"Boys never will do what they're asked," Polly would complain.

"Girls ask such unreasonable things," was Harry's retort.

"Not half so unreasonable as the things you ask."

"Ah! that's a different thing! Women have got to do what men tell them, whether it's reasonable or not."

"No, they've not!" said Polly. "At least, that's only husbands and wives."

"All women are inferior animals," said Harry.

"Try ordering mamma to do what you want, and see!" said Polly.

"Men have got to give orders, and women have to obey," said Harry, falling back on the general principle. "And when I get a wife, I'll take care I make her do what I tell her. But you'll have to obey your husband when you get one."

"I won't have a husband, and then I can do as I like."

"Oh, won't you? You'll try to get one, I know. Girls always want to be married."

"I'm sure I don't know why," said Polly; "they must have had enough of men if they have brothers."

And so they went on, *ad infinitum,* with ceaseless arguments that proved nothing and convinced nobody, and a continual stream of contradiction that just fell short of downright quarreling.

Indeed, there was a kind of snapping even less near to a dispute than in the cases just mentioned. The little Skratdjs, like some other children, were under the unfortunate delusion that it sounds clever to hear little boys and girls snap each other up with

"Then you like music?" said the hot-tempered gentleman.

"Yes, I like it very much," said Polly.

"Oh, do you?" Harry broke in. "Then what are you always crying over it for?"

"I'm not always crying over it."

"Yes, you are"

"No, I'm not I only cry sometimes, when I stick fast."

"Your music must be very sticky, for you're always stuck at."

"Hold your tongue!" said the hot-tempered gentleman.

With what he imagined to be a very waggish air, Harry put out his tongue, and held it with his finger and thumb. It was unfortunate that he had not time to draw it in again before the hot-tempered gentleman gave him a stinging box on the ear, which brought his teeth rather sharply together on the tip of his tongue, which was bitten in consequence.

"It's no use *speaking*," said the hot-tempered gentleman, driving his hands through his hair.

Children are like dogs: they are very good judges of their real friends. Harry did not like the hot-tempered gentleman a bit the less because he was obliged to respect and obey him; and all the children welcomed him boisterously when he arrived that Christmas which we have spoken of in connection with his attack on Snap.

It was on the morning of Christmas Eve that the china punch-bowl was broken. Mr. Skratdj had a warm dispute with Mrs. Skratdj as to whether it

had been kept in a safe place; after which both had
a brisk encounter with the housemaid, who did not
know how it happened; and she, flouncing down
the back passage, kicked Snap, who forthwith flew
at the gardener as he was bringing in the horse-
radish for the beef; who, stepping backwards, trod
upon the cat; who spit and swore, and went up the
pump with her tail as big as a fox's brush.

To avoid this domestic scene, the hot-tempered
gentleman withdrew to the breakfast-room and
took up a newspaper. By and by, Harry and
Polly came in, and they were soon snapping comfortably over their own affairs in a corner.

The hot-tempered gentleman's umber eyes had
been looking over the top of his newspaper at them
for some time, before he called, "Harry, my boy!"

And Harry came up to him.

"Show me your tongue, Harry," said he.

"What for?" said Harry; "you're not a doctor."

"Do as I tell you," said the hot-tempered gentleman; and as Harry saw his hand moving, he
put his tongue out with all possible haste. The hot-
tempered gentleman sighed. "Ah!" he said in de-
pressed tones; "I thought so!—Polly, come and let
me look at yours."

Polly, who had crept up during this process, now
put out hers. But the hot-tempered gentleman
looked gloomier still, and shook his head.

"What is it?" cried both the children, "What
do you mean?" And they seized the tips of their
tongues in their fingers, to feel for themselves.

But the hot-tempered gentleman went slowly out
of the room without answering; passing his hands

through his hair, and saying, "Ah! hum!" and nodding with an air of grave foreboding.

Just as he crossed the threshold, he turned back, and put his head into the room. "Have you ever noticed that your tongues are growing pointed?" he asked.

"No!" cried the children with alarm. "Are they?"

"If ever you find them becoming forked," said the gentleman in solemn tones, "let me know."

With which he departed, gravely shaking his head.

In the afternoon the children attacked him again.

"*Do* tell us what's the matter with our tongues."

"You were snapping and squabbling just as usual this morning," said the hot-tempered gentleman.

"Well, we forgot," said Polly. "We don't mean anything, you know. But never mind that now, please. Tell us about our tongues. What is going to happen to them?"

"I'm very much afraid," said the hot-tempered gentleman, in solemn, measured tones, "that you are both of you—fast—going—to—the—"

"Dogs?" suggested Harry, who was learned in cant expressions.

"Dogs!" said the hot-tempered gentleman, driving his hands through his hair. "Bless your life, no! Nothing half so pleasant! (That is, unless all dogs were like Snap, which mercifully they are not.) No, my sad fear is, that you are both of you—rapidly—going—*to the Snap-Dragons!*"

And not another word would the hot-tempered gentleman say on the subject.

In the course of a few hours Mr. and Mrs. Skratdj recovered their equanimity. The punch was brewed in a jug, and tasted quite as good as usual. The evening was very lively. There were a Christmas tree, Yule cakes, log, and candles, furmety, and snap-dragon after supper. When the company were tired of the tree, and had gained an appetite by the hard exercise of stretching to high branches, blowing out "dangerous" tapers, and cutting ribbon and pack-threads in all directions, supper came, with its welcome cakes, and furmety, and punch. And when furmety somewhat palled upon the taste (and it must be admitted to boast more sentiment than flavor as a Christmas dish), the Yule candles were blown out and both the spirits and the palates of the party were stimulated by the mysterious and pungent pleasures of snap-dragon.

Then, as the hot-tempered gentleman warmed his coat tails at the Yule log, a grim smile stole over his features as he listened to the sounds in the room. In the darkness the blue flames leaped and danced, the raisins were snapped and snatched from hand to hand, scattering fragments of flame hither and thither. The children shouted as the fiery sweetmeats burnt away the mawkish taste of the furmety. Mr. Skratdj cried that they were spoiling the carpet; Mrs. Skratdj complained that he had spilled some brandy on her dress. Mr. Skratdj retorted that she should not wear dresses so susceptible of damage in the family circle. Mrs.

Skratdj recalled an old speech of Mr. Skratdj on the subject of wearing one's nice things for the benefit of one's family and not reserving them for visitors. Mr. Skratdj remembered that Mrs. Skratdj's excuse for buying that particular dress when she did not need it, was her intention of keeping it for the next year. The children disputed as to the credit for courage and the amount of raisins due to each. Snap barked furiously at the flames; and the maids hustled each other for good places in the doorway, and would not have allowed the man servant to see at all, but he looked over their heads.

"St! St! At it! At it!" chuckled the hot-tempered gentleman in undertones. And when he said this, it seemed as if the voices of Mr. and Mrs. Skratdj rose higher in matrimonial repartee, and the children's squabbles became louder, and the dog yelped as if he were mad, and the maids' contest was sharper; whilst the snap-dragon flames leaped up and up, and blue fire flew about the room like foam.

At last the raisins were finished, the flames were all put out, and the company withdrew to the drawing-room. Only Harry lingered.

"Come along, Harry," said the hot-tempered gentleman.

"Wait a minute," said Harry.

"You had better come," said the gentleman.

"Why?" said Harry.

"There's nothing to stop for. The raisins are eaten, the brandy is burnt out."

"No, it's not," said Harry.

"Well, almost. It would be better if it were

quite out. Now come. It's dangerous for a boy like you to be alone with the Snap-Dragons to-night."

"Fiddlesticks!" said Harry.

"Go your own way, then!" said the hot-tempered gentleman; and he bounced out of the room, and Harry was left alone.

He crept up to the table, where one little pale blue flame flickered in the snap-dragon dish.

"What a pity it should go out!" said Harry. At this moment the brandy bottle on the sideboard caught his eye.

"Just a little more," murmured Harry to himself; and he uncorked the bottle, and poured a little brandy on to the flame.

Now, of course, as soon as the brandy touched the fire, all the brandy in the bottle blazed up at once, and the bottle split to pieces; and it was very fortunate for Harry that he did not get seriously hurt. A little of the hot brandy did get into his eyes, and made them smart, so that he had to shut them for a few seconds.

But when he opened them again what a sight he saw! All over the room the blue flames leaped and danced as they had leaped and danced in the soup-plate with the raisins. And Harry saw that each successive flame was the fold in the long body of a bright-blue Dragon, which moved like the body of a snake. And the room was full of these Dragons. In the face they were like the dragons one sees made of very old blue and white china; and they had forked tongues like the tongues of serpents. They were most beautiful in color, being sky-blue. Lobsters who have just changed their coats are very handsome, but the violet and indigo of a lobster's coat is nothing to the brilliant sky-blue of a Snap-Dragon.

How they leaped about! They were forever leaping over each other like seals at play. But if it was "play" at all with them, it was of a very rough kind; for as they jumped, they snapped and barked at each other, and their barking was like that of the barking Gnu in the Zoölogical Gardens; and from time to time they tore the hair out of each other's heads with their claws, and scattered it about the floor. And as it dropped it was like the flecks of flame people shake from their fingers when they are eating snap-dragon raisins.

Harry stood aghast.

"What fun!" said a voice close by him; and he saw that one of the Dragons was lying near, and not joining in the game. He had lost one of the forks of his tongue by accident, and could not bark for a while.

"I'm glad you think it funny," said Harry; "I don't."

"That's right. Snap away!" sneered the Dragon. "You're a perfect treasure. They'll take you in with them the third round."

"Not those creatures?" cried Harry.

"Yes, those creatures. And if I hadn't lost my bark, I'd be the first to lead you off," said the Dragon. "Oh, the game will exactly suit you."

"What is it, please?" Harry asked.

"You'd better not say 'please' to the others," said

the Dragon, "if you don't want to have all your hair pulled out. The game is this: You have always to be jumping over somebody else, and you must either talk or bark. If anybody speaks to you, you must snap in return. I need not explain what *snapping* is. You *know*. If any one by accident gives a civil answer, a clawful of hair is torn out of his head to stimulate his brain. Nothing can be funnier."

"I dare say it suits you capitally," said Harry; "but I'm sure we shouldn't like it. I mean men and women and children. It wouldn't do for us at all."

"Wouldn't it?" said the Dragon. "You don't know how many human beings dance with Dragons on Christmas Eve. If we are kept going in a house till after midnight, we can pull people out of their beds, and take them to dance in Vesuvius."

"Vesuvius!" cried Harry.

"Yes, Vesuvius. We come from Italy originally, you know. Our skins are the color of the Bay of Naples. We live on dry grapes and ardent spirits. We have glorious fun in the mountain sometimes. Oh! what snapping, and scratching, and tearing! Delicious! There are times when the squabbling becomes too great, and Mother Mountain won't stand it, and spits us all out, and throws cinders after us. But this is only at times. We had a charming meeting last year. So many human beings, and how they *can* snap! It was a choice party. So very select. We always have plenty of saucy children, and servants. Husbands and wives, too, and quite as many of the former as the latter, if not more. But besides these, we had two vestry-men, a country postmaster, who devoted his talents to insulting the public instead of to learning the postal regulations, three cabmen and two 'fares,' two young shop-girls from a Berlin wool shop in a town where there was no competition, four commercial travellers, six landladies, six Old Bailey lawyers, several widows from almshouses, seven single gentlemen, and nine cats, who swore at everything; a dozen sulphur-colored screaming cockatoos; a lot of street children from a town; a pack of mongrel curs from the colonies, who snapped at the human beings' heels, and five elderly ladies in their Sunday bonnets, with prayer-books, who had been fighting for good seats in church."

"Dear me!" said Harry.

"If you can find nothing sharper to say than 'Dear me,'" said the Dragon, "you will fare badly, I can tell you. Why, I thought you'd a sharp tongue, but it's not forked yet, I see. Here they are, however. Off with you! And if you value your curls—snap!"

And before Harry could reply, the Snap-Dragons come on their third round, and as they passed they swept Harry with them.

He shuddered as he looked at his companions. They were as transparent as shrimps, but of this lovely cerulean blue. And as they leaped they barked—"Howf! Howf!"—like barking Gnus; and when they leaped Harry had to leap with them. Besides barking, they snapped and wrangled with each other; and in this Harry must join also.

"Pleasant, isn't it?" said one of the blue Dragons.

"Not at all," snapped Harry.

"That's your bad taste," snapped the blue Dragon.

"No, it's not!" snapped Harry.

"Then it's pride and perverseness. You want your hair combing."

"Oh, please don't!" shrieked Harry, forgetting himself. On which the Dragon clawed a handful of hair out of his head, and Harry screamed, and the blue Dragons barked and danced.

"That made your hair curl, didn't it?" asked another Dragon, leaping over Harry.

"That's no business of yours," Harry snapped, as well as he could for crying.

"It's more my pleasure than business," retorted the Dragon.

"Keep it to yourself, then," snapped Harry.

"I mean to share it with you, when I get hold of your hair," snapped the Dragon.

"Wait till you get the chance," Harry snapped, with desperate presence of mind.

"Do you know whom you're talking to?" roared the Dragon; and he opened his mouth from ear to ear, and shot out his forked tongue in Harry's face; and the boy was so frightened that he forgot to snap, and cried piteously:

"Oh, I beg your pardon, please don't!"

On which the blue Dragon clawed another handful of hair out of his head, and all the Dragons barked as before.

How long the dreadful game went on Harry never exactly knew. Well practised as he was in snapping in the nursery, he often failed to think of a retort, and paid for his unreadiness by the loss of his hair. Oh, how foolish and wearisome all this rudeness and snapping now seemed to him! But on he had to go, wondering all the time how near it was to twelve o'clock, and whether the Snap-Dragons would stay till midnight and take him with them to Vesuvius.

At last, to his joy, it became evident that the brandy was coming to an end. The Dragons moved slower, they could not leap so high, and at last one after another they began to go out.

"Oh, if they only all of them get away before twelve!" thought poor Harry.

At last there was only one. He and Harry jumped about and snapped and barked, and Harry was thinking with joy that he was the last, when the clock in the hall gave that whirring sound which clocks do before they strike, as if it were clearing its throat.

"Oh, *please* go!" screamed Harry, in despair.

The blue Dragon leaped up, and took such a clawful of hair out of the boy's head, that it seemed as if part of the skin went, too. But that leap was his last. He went out at once, vanishing before the first stroke of twelve. And Harry was left on his face in the darkness.

When his friends found him there was blood on his forehead. Harry thought it was where the Dragon had clawed him, but they said it was a cut from a fragment of the broken brandy bottle. The Dragons had disappeared as completely as the brandy.

Harry was cured of snapping. He had had quite enough of it for a lifetime, and the catch contradictions of the household now made him shudder. Polly had not had the benefit of his experiences, and yet she improved also.

In the first place, snapping, like other kinds of quarrelling, requires two parties to it, and Harry would never be a party to snapping any more. And when he gave civil and kind answers to Polly's smart speeches, she felt ashamed of herself, and did not repeat them.

In the second place, she heard about the Snap-Dragons. Harry told all about it to her and to the hot-tempered gentleman.

"Now do you think it's true?" Polly asked the hot-tempered gentleman.

"Hum! Ha!" said he, driving his hands through his hair. You know I warned you you were going to the Snap-Dragons."

Harry and Polly snubbed "the little ones" when they snapped, and utterly discountenanced snapping in the nursery. The example and admonitions of elder children are a powerful instrument of nursery discipline, and before long there was not a "sharp tongue" among all the little Skratdjs.

But I doubt if the parents ever were cured. I don't know if they heard the story. Besides, bad habits are not easily cured when one is old.

I fear Mr. and Mrs. Skratdj have yet got to dance with the Dragons.

UNCLE JACK'S STORY

By Mrs. E. M. Field

"ONCE upon a time," began Uncle Jack, "since we know no fairy stories are worth hearing unless they begin with 'once upon a time.'

"Once upon a time there was a country ruled over by a king and queen who had no children. Having no children of their own, these sovereigns thought other people's children a nuisance. I am afraid they were like the fox, who said the grapes were sour because he could not reach them, for it was well-known that they wanted some of these 'torments' very badly themselves."

"Don't call us torments, Uncle Jack," interrupted his little niece.

"Well, you see, madam, historians must be truthful. I am bound to say that the king and queen passed a law in which the children were described as 'pickles, torments, plagues, bothers, nuisances, worries,' and by twenty-four other titles of respect which I have forgotten. This law enacted:

"First—That the children were to be seen and not heard. Wherefore all children under the age of sixteen were to speak in a whisper and laugh in a whisper."

"They couldn't, Uncle Jack," broke in Bryda, "they could only smile!"

"Or grin," said Uncle Jack. "So you think that a cruel law, Bryda?

"Secondly—As the sight of a child set the royal teeth on edge, no child was to be allowed to set foot

241

out of doors, unless between the hours of twelve and one on any night when there was neither moon or stars."

"At that rate they would *never* go out," said Bryda.

"Well, you see this was a law for the abolition of children; so they were to be suppressed as much as possible, of course.

"Then thirdly, the law declared—That, as little pitchers have long ears, no child should ever hear the conversation of grown-up people. Therefore children were never to be admitted into any sitting-room used by the elders of the family, nor into any kitchen or room occupied by servants."

"O-o-oh!" said Bryda; "did they keep them in the coal-cellar?"

"In some houses, perhaps.

"Fourthly—Forasmuch as play was not a profitable occupation, and led to noise and laughter, all play-time and holidays should at once be abolished."

"That was a very bad law," said Bryda warmly.

"Well, the law was passed, and was soon carried out; and any one coming to the city would have thought there were no children, so carefully were they kept out of sight. All the toy-shops were closed, and confectioners were ordered, under pain of death, neither to make nor sell goodies. But one thing the king had forgotten, and that was that, after all, there were *more* children than grown people in the country. One family had nine children, another six, and so on; so that, counting the boarding-schools, there were just three times as many children as grown people in the capital. Well, after about a week of this treatment (for the parents were compelled under threat of instant execution to carry it out), it happened that there came a night when at twelve o'clock, though it was not raining, there was neither moon nor star to be seen. So all the children in the city rushed forth into the park with Chinese lanterns in their hands, making quite a fairy gathering under the trees. Oh, how delicious it was! They ran and shouted, and played games and laughed, till suddenly one o'clock struck; and all the king's horses, and all the king's men, came to drive them to their homes again. But there were hundreds and hundreds of children, and only a few soldiers with wooden swords; for this was a very peaceable nation, and armed even its police with only birch rods. So one of the biggest boys blew a tin trumpet, and called all the children to him.

"'I vote we rebel,' he said. 'We will not stand this any more; let us drive away all the grown-ups, and have the town altogether to ourselves.'

"Now it so happened that a fairy had been watching all that went on in the town, and was not at all pleased. So when she heard this bold boy speak she thought it would be a good thing to let this rebellion be carried out. 'Serve 'em right,' she said; 'young and old shall all learn a lesson.'

"So she collected a few thousand fairies, and they flew to all the king's men, and whispered in their left ears dreadful things, which frightened them terribly and made them believe an immense army, instead of the troops of children, was coming to crush them all. Then the fairies whispered in their right ears that it would be wise to fly to a neighboring mountain where there was a large old fort, and there take refuge. So they galloped off as fast as the king's horses would carry them. Then the fairies flew all over the town and whispered the same things to all the grown-up people—fathers and mothers, old maids and old bachelors—till they, too, tumbled out of bed, dressed in a terrible hurry, and fled to the mountain. Even the king jumped out of bed, tied up his crown in his pocket-handkerchief, and ran for his life in his dressing-gown, while two lords in waiting, or gentlemen of the bedchamber, rushed after him with the royal mantle of ermine, and the scepter and golden ball. The lord chancellor filled his pockets with new sovereigns from the mint (for he slept there to look after the money) and then he too ran, but rather slowly, for he had the woolsack on his back, and it was pretty heavy. When they asked him why he took the trouble he answered that he thought the ground might be damp, and he already had a cold in his head.

"Well, all the elders being gone, the children were left in possession of the city, at which you may well suppose they were greatly astonished. They went on with their games for a while; but then the lanterns began to go out, and one after another they grew very sleepy. So the boy with the tin trumpet blew it again, and commanded that every one should now go to bed, and that a meeting should be held at twelve o'clock next day in the park, at which every child should appear.

"Appear they did, in their Sunday clothes, those

of them at least who cared for finery; there were no mothers or nurses to object. All were in great delight at having no one to rule them.

" 'I shall never go to bed at eight!' said one.

" 'I shall never eat rice pudding—horrid stuff!'

" 'I shall never take any more doses!'

" 'I shall never do any more lessons!'

" 'Nor I! nor I! nor I!' shouted one after another; 'we shall all do only what we like! How happy we shall be!'

"Only one little maid whispered, with a tear trembling on the long lashes of her blue eyes, 'Dottie wants mother!' But Dottie was soon comforted, and ran about as merrily as ever.

"Meantime the elder boys and girls held a very noisy parliament, in which there were never less than five speaking at once. After a great deal of chatter they determined to set up a queen; and a very pretty little girl called May was chosen, and crowned with a crown of flowers.

"Next, Queen May and her council of six, three boys and three girls, ordered that a big bonfire should be made of all lesson-books and pinafores, for they thought pinafores were signs of an inferior state, of being under command, as servants sometimes think their caps are.

"The next law was that all the raspberry jam in the city should be set aside for the use of the queen and her court, and for those who were invited to the royal tea parties. There was a little grumbling about this, but finally the grumblers gave in. All this time troops of children came pouring in from the neighboring villages with pinafores on the end of broomsticks as flags of rebellion. Being pretty hungry, they dispersed for dinner, which in most of the houses was a very curious meal, as, of course, no one could cook, so they had to forage in the kitchens and storerooms, while bands of hungry young folks stormed the confectioners' shops, and dined off ices and wedding-cakes.

"Then they opened the toy-shops and put them in charge of parties of children and gradually the other shops were treated in the same way, for buying and selling is always a game children like, and it was such a treat to have real things to sell. Only money was such a trouble: they were always forgetting to bring any, and the young shopkeepers never were sure if a shilling or a sovereign was the right price for a thing. Therefore they concluded to do without it; and costly things were bought for kisses, while cheap ones were to be had for saying, 'If you please,' or, if they were very small, as a penny bun, for instance, then 'please' was enough."

"How nice!" said Bryda.

"Well, for a whole week there never was such happiness as the children enjoyed. Games from morning to night, bread and jam three times a day, no lessons, no forbidden things, and a queen of their own age in place of the tyrant king.

"But when a week was over some little murmurs began to arise. Every morning, I ought to say, the queen sat on her throne in the royal palace, to receive any of her subjects who liked playing at being courtiers, and she and her council then settled any difficulty that arose about rules of games, about the way to make the best toffee and any other important question.

"On this particular morning, then, rather more than a week after the establishment of the Children's Kingdom, a very large throng entered the queen's presence. Foremost came a troop of boys and girls, who led in a pale, serious-looking boy as a prisoner, and brought him to Queen May's feet.

" 'What is the charge against this prisoner?' asked the queen, with dignity. 'Don't all speak at once,' she added, so hastily that several courtiers giggled.

" 'Please your majesty,' said a boy, stepping forward, 'we caught him in the act—the very act—of learning lessons!'

" 'Lessons!' cried the whole court, in every tone of disgust, anger, grief and dismay.

" 'Lessons!' screamed the queen, and at once fainted away."

"She didn't!" said Bryda indignantly.

"Don't you think the shock was great enough?" asked Uncle Jack. "Besides, she felt it part of her royal duty, perhaps.

"Anyhow, they tickled her with feathers, and put burned cork to her nose till she had a black mustache; and one boy brought a red-hot poker, which he said he had heard was a good thing, though he did not quite know how it was applied.

"It was the best remedy, certainly, for on its appearance the queen jumped up shrieking, and declared she was perfectly well.

"Then the queen proceeded to try the prisoner, and requested the whole court to act as jury. It was a very sad case of youthful depravity—the criminal had carefully kept this one book, 'Somebody's Arithmetic,' or 'Mangnall's Questions,' to gloat over in secret; and even now was not at all penitent, but declared, when asked what he had to say for himself, that it was 'stupid, and a bore,' to play games all day long, and he was sick of them.

"The jury could not agree as to what was to be done with such an offender, and so he was allowed to go, and bidden 'not to do it again,' and the queen went on to the next difficulty. Here the throneroom became quite full of children, all in great perplexity; for the matter was this, that the food supply was running short. The confectioners' shops were nearly empty; there was plenty of jam, but very little bread; and one or two boys, who had breakfasted on jam out of a pot, eaten with a spoon, said, 'They didn't know how it could be, but somehow they thought it did not quite agree with them.'

"This was really very serious. Could no one cook?

"Well several had tried to make puddings; but somehow, though they ought to have been quite right, *something* was wrong, and no one would eat them. One girl had bravely made some appledumplings, and baked them quite brown; but then she could not find out how to get the apple in, so they were no more than hard balls, and not real apple-dumplings at all.

" 'What are we going to do?' said Queen May sorrowfully.

"A dead silence reigned.

" 'I know!' said a boy called Eric, starting forward suddenly, and all eyes turned to this owner of a bright idea. 'I know!' he said, brandishing a many-bladed knife; 'I'll kill a pig!'

"A murmur of horror arose from the girls.

" 'Oh, no!' said Queen May politely; 'my faithful subject, we will not let you make yourself so miserable.'

" 'Oh, *I* don't mind!' cried Eric; 'really, you know, I should *like* it!'

" 'I'll hold him for you!' cried several boys at once.

" 'Quite as if they liked it,' whispered the girls.

"But Queen May interposed, and said the court should break up and go to blind-man's-buff. At the same hour next day any one who had a bright idea should come and tell it. For the rest of the day she, at least, did not mean to bother her head. If a pig were killed, it would have to be cooked. And shaking her curls, which were like a crown of gold, Queen May jumped off her throne and ran out into the park.

"Presently the Fairy Set-'em-right came flying over the town, and saw all the children running about and shrieking with laughter.

" 'Bless my broomstick!' she said, for she had borrowed one from a witch to fly upon, saying she had rheumatism in her left wing. 'Bless my broomstick! this won't do at all!'

"She did not notice that a great many children were standing about in groups, whispering—what they dared not say aloud—that they were getting tired of games all day, and of nothing to eat but sweet cakes and jam at meals.

" 'I should really, really and truly, like some boiled mutton,' said Master Archie, who was known to have had a special dislike to that dish.

" 'I know what I shall do,' said the fairy; 'I shall make these children feel like grown-ups, and then I shall fly off to the mountains, and make the grown-ups feel like children; and if *that* doesn't bring them to their senses, I am sure I don't know what will.'

"So the Fairy Set-'em-right waved her hand over the troop of children. 'You shall all feel like grown-up people,' she said.

"In a few minutes a strange change began to come over them all. A great game of 'blind-man's-buff' was going on, when suddenly several of the girls put themselves into very stiff, solemn attitudes, just like old maids, and said, 'Really, they thought they were almost afraid they could not play any more. Such games, especially at their time of life, were hardly quite proper.' So they would not go on.

"Others, again, declared that there was nothing they so thoroughly enjoyed as watching people playing at these kind of amusements; but for themselves—well, if the others did not mind, they would like just to sit quietly and watch. So they did, and presently some of the boys began stroking that part of their faces where a mustache might some day grow, and remarking that 'Haw! don't know, you know—a—this sort of thing was all very well for schoolboys, but really—a—we could not, you know.' "

This sentence Uncle Jack brought out with a

very funny drawl, the boys being turned into dreadfully fashionable fellows.

"The crowning point," continued Uncle Jack, "was reached when the blind man, pushing down his bandage, stood still, and addressed this altered crowd very seriously indeed. 'What miserable folly is this?' he asked. 'Shall we mortals waste our precious flying moments in—in what, my brethren?'

"You see he had turned into a preacher," explained Uncle Jack.

" 'In what a miserable, frivolous occupation! catching each other!—nay, only *trying* to catch each other! Poor fools and blind! let us cease, I say—' But he had no one to say it to, for the whole audience had gone off in different directions, and the preacher had only his little brother of five left to listen to his wise words. 'Come along, Tommy,' said he, 'I will try and find some one for you to play with, little man.'

" 'Play with!' answered the little brother in a tone of utter surprise. 'My dear sir, I have no time to play. Letters, telegrams, appointments by scores fill my time. Let me tell you, sir, there is no busier man than your humble servant in the whole country.'

"With which he turned about and strode off with the longest strides his little legs in their blue sailor trousers could take; for he had become a man of business.

" 'This is too absurd,' muttered the elder, and went off to look for the church of which he was vicar.

"The same remarkable change came over all the

children. One little brat who was busy teasing an
unfortunate kitten stopped suddenly, and rushed
off in search of pen and paper, with which he returned, and began at once to compose an ode 'To
Tabitha.'

> " 'Fairest pussy ever seen!
>   With thine eyes of clearest green,
>   Fly me not.'

That was how it began, for he had become a poet."

"I thought poets wrote about knights and ladies,
and green fields and the moon," remonstrated
Bryda.

"So they do. But sometimes they want a new
subject, and this young genius thought he had
found one.

"Well, all the children, without losing their child
faces and figures, turned into the sort of people
they would be when they were grown up. So of
course their games seemed very dull, and they
wanted grown-up occupations. But not knowing
quite how to set to work, they were all lounging
vaguely about, when the clear notes of a bugle
sounded through the city.

"This was the well-known signal for the assem-
bling of the whole population in the park, and off
went all these queer grown-up children to the place
of meeting. Here they were met by Queen May,
who sat on a garden-chair with her court around
her, all looking very solemn.

" 'My faithful subjects,' said the queen, 'I have
sent for you to consider a very grave question. I
regret to state that the affairs of this kingdom are

in a condition which will, perhaps, be best described as unsatisfactory.'

" 'Hear, hear!' said a gentleman of four, bowing gravely.

" 'Hear, hear!' echoed many voices.

" 'Perhaps the most unsatisfactory point is,' went on Queen May, who, you see, talked in very grown-up language, 'is, I say, the banishment of a large portion of the population; that portion, in fact, which we were formerly accustomed to call our elders and betters.'

"Cries of 'No, no!'

"Queen May went on to explain that after all they got on badly without these elders. With all their efforts the young folks had not strength or skill to do a variety of things, without which the round of life seemed likely soon to come to a standstill. So she proposed that she and all who would go should start at once for the mountain and fetch home the exiles.

"There was some murmuring at this. The old law might be carried out, and the children made wretched again.

" 'And—why, bless me,' said an elderly person of nine, as he fixed on a double eyeglass with gold rims, 'they might actually want to send me, me! to bed at eight o'clock!'

" 'Proper conditions would be made,' the queen said.

"One after another all the objections were overcome, and a long procession started, with Queen May, mounted on a white pony, at its head.

"On arriving at the mountain they were greatly

surprised to meet the king, that stern tyrant who wanted to stop all fun, running as hard as his legs could carry his fat body, with his crown on the back of his head, and a green net-bag tied on to the end of his scepter, chasing a white butterfly.

"'Please, your majesty,' began Queen May shyly; but the king only looked round for a moment, and ran on, then tumbled over a furzebush, so that his crown rolled far away, and the butterfly escaped, while he lay there kicking.

"The children were very much surprised at this, and thought the king must have gone mad, and, in fact, they felt very penitent, for they supposed his hurried flight must have been too much for the brain, so they were to blame for this terrible alteration.

"A little further on, however, they were still more surprised to see a circle of the most serious old maids in the whole capital, ladies whose time was mostly spent in making flannel garments for the poor, or sitting at neat tea tables with neat curls on each side of their faces, and a neat cat, curled on a neat cushion, in a neat chair, close at hand, and these old ladies were all screaming and laughing like children.

"These very respectable old ladies now looked anything but neat! Their curls were flying in all directions, and they were screaming with laughter, pinching each other, and making all sorts of silly jokes over a furious game of 'hunt the slipper.' For you see they had gone back to what they used to like when they were children.

"Queen May looked at them gravely.

" 'Dear friends,' she said, 'at your age, is this decorous? Is it proper? Is it even ladylike?'

" 'There it is! Catch it! Catch it!' cried one of the old ladies.

" 'Come and play with us!' cried another.

"None of the rest paid any attention to the serious looks of the grown-up children who went sadly on toward the fort, hoping to find some one more reasonable.

"The next person they saw was the lord chancellor, a bald, stout old gentleman, who was sitting on the woolsack, which, you remember, he had carried away on his back. He was very busy with a pipe, and the children thought he was smoking, and grew more hopeful. He might have some trace of good sense left, they thought, if he could care for such a grown-up pursuit."

Here Uncle Jack offered his cigar to Bryda politely; but she made a face and turned her head away.

"I don't want to be so grown-up as *that*," she said.

"Oh!" said Uncle Jack, with his funny face, that he always put on to tease Bryda. "Oh, I thought you wanted to grow up all of a sudden."

"Well—only for some things," answered she, feeling that Uncle Jack was taking a mean advantage in remembering her sayings, and bringing them up again. "Please go on," she added hastily.

Uncle Jack winked at her very slowly and solemnly; then took a good puff at his cigar, and went on:

"When they came up he was found to be blowing soap-bubbles!

" 'A-ah!' he spluttered, trying to talk with the pipe in his mouth. 'D-don't break it, please! There!' as the bubble burst and vanished; 'it's too bad, I declare! Directly I got a really good one, big and bright, that always happens. Have a try,' he added, offering Queen May the pipe.

" 'I say, my lord,' said the major-general commanding the royal army, coming up at the moment, 'can you tell me how to mend lead soldiers? I've tried gum and glue, and one of the maids of honor tried to sew one, but somehow they don't join properly. It's a horrid bore, and that fellow, the speaker, won't let me have a ride on his rocking-horse. I'd punch him, only he's six feet three, and as broad as he's long. So I don't know what to play at.'

" 'It *is* slow,' answered the lord chancellor, pityingly. 'Never mind, old chap, come up to the fort and we'll make some toffee.'

"So the elderly gentlemen went off arm-in-arm, and Queen May shook her head sadly.

" 'They are all mad, poor things! What are we to do?'

" 'Hi! hi!' cried a voice, and looking round they saw that tall, handsome nobleman, the master of the horse, running toward them as fast as he could. At last, perhaps, they had found some one to speak sensibly to.

" 'Hi! you fellows,' he cried breathlessly; 'stop a minute, will you? Is that a circus pony? and can he do tricks? Sit up with a hat on, and drink out of teacups, I mean.'

" 'Certainly not,' replied Queen May, with her utmost dignity. 'I hardly understand, Lord Moyers, how you can ask such a strange question. Did you ever see a lady, especially if she were a crowned queen, riding a circus pony?'

"Lord Moyers giggled, and turned head-over-heels on the spot, after which he rushed off again to join the rest of the House of Lords, who were playing 'hi! cockalorum,' close by.

"The procession went on very sorrowfully toward the fort. It grieved them to see this frivolity in those to whom they had been taught to look up.

" 'Alas, my country!' sighed Eric, the boy who, you remember, had proposed to kill the pig before he was touched with the fairy wand.

"Perhaps it was on arriving at the gates of the fort that the very strangest sight was seen. The queen was a very stout and middle-aged person, of rather stern countenance, and here she was busy with a skipping rope—her hair loose, her royal robes tucked up, and her crown on one side.

" 'It's the best fun and the finest exercise in the world,' she gasped. 'If I could only skip twice to one turn of the rope!'

"And on she went, while the children watched. But there was something so utterly ridiculous about the sight that Queen May and her followers, after various vain efforts to suppress their mirth, burst into one peal of laughter, which rang merrily through the old fort, and over the hillside.

"It broke the charm, and in a moment the children became children again, and the grown people became as they were before.

"There was a large flat field on the mountain top, in front of the gates of the old fort, and here all the exiles were in a few minutes assembled.

"The king was about to address them, when in a moment, no one knowing how she came there, the Fairy Set-'em-right stood among them, close beside his majesty.

" 'You have all learned a lesson, and I will put it into words for you,' she said."

"Oh, dear!" interrupted Bryda, "here comes the moral! Don't make a very hard one, Uncle Jack, please!"

He laughed. "I must finish this truthful story truthfully, miss.

"She said, turning to the king and queen:

" 'Your fault was that you forgot you once were young yourselves.' "

Bryda nodded her head very wisely.

" 'And you, children, forgot that you could not do without old people. That wicked law is at once repealed.'

" 'Certainly, ma'am,' said the king, bowing.

" 'Children are to be children, and behave as such, and be treated as such. Parents are parents, the children are not to forget that. Now go home all of you, and don't forget this one caution, *I've got my eye on you.*'

"With these awful words the fairy vanished. And that's the end of the story."

"And a very nice ending, too!" said Bryda.

 "IS THERE A PECULIAR FLAVOR IN WHAT YOU
SPRINKLE FROM YOUR TORCH?" ASKED SCROOGE
—page 271

From the drawing by T. Leech

BRYDA'S DREADFUL SCRAPE

By Mrs. E. M. Field

BRYDA was awakened from her pleasant morning sleep by a strange sound. Her window was partly open, but something struck against the upper sash; it was not a bird that had lost its way, nor a wasp come to look for jam, for as Bryda raised her head something that could only be a handful of light gravel or shot struck the window again, and at the same time a clear, shrill whistle sounded outside.

Bryda hastily sprang up. One does not care much about dress at nine years old, so in white nightdress and dark twisted hair she fearlessly put her head out of the window, and saw, to her delight, her cousin, Maurice Gray, a boy some two years younger than herself, with his queer, ugly little Scotch terrier, Toby, standing on the lawn. She need not be sad for want of a playmate to-day.

"Get up and dress!" cried Maurice. "Aren't you ashamed, my Lady Lie-in-bed? Come out directly!"

Bryda did not need a second invitation. A very short time indeed passed before she was by Maurice's side.

His father had brought him over, he said; his father wanted to see grandfather about some business, so he had started off very early. Maurice was dreadfully hungry, and, as the grannies never breakfasted till ten, he and Bryda each got a thick slice of bread and jam from the good-natured cook, and then went off to the garden, Bryda running races with Toby, who mostly had the best of it. You see he had four legs to Bryda's two.

They went to the vinery, and acted a little play, which, however, wanted a few more actors sadly. It was so puzzling for Bryda to be both the imprisoned princess and the ogre at once; and when Maurice, the valiant knight, slew Toby for a dragon, and stepped over his corpse (or would have done, if Toby had been a little more dead, and not run away every other minute), it got really puzzling, and it was well that the breakfast-bell rang at that moment.

Breakfast was rather a long, dull affair. Uncle James, Maurice's father, explained to grandfather a great deal about a drainage scheme; and grandmother, every five minutes, asked her maid Martha, who stood behind her chair, to tell her what it was all about, which Martha had to do in very loud whispers over and over again.

Maurice and Bryda were very glad to run out again, with special directions from grandmother to keep off wet grass, and not get into mischief. This, they thought, could not possibly happen. This time they rambled into the farmyard. Bryda would not look for more kittens, but tried to make friends with some small balls of fluff, which meant some day to be turkeys. At one corner of the yard was a deep tank, or little pond, full of a dark brown, rather thick fluid, which was used in the fields, and had a great effect in the way things grow. Bryda and her cousin ng at it.

BRYDA'S DREADFUL SCRAPE

"I declare," said Bryda, "it's like the Styx!"

"I don't see any sticks," said ignorant Maurice, who had never learned that the old heathens believed the souls of dead people went in a ferryboat across a dark river called the Styx, and that the old man who rowed the boat was called Charon.

Bryda thought it would be capital fun to act this little scene. Certainly the treacle-colored stuff in the pool looked nasty enough to do very well for this dark river.

As to Maurice, he was younger than his cousin, and when they were together she always invented the games, although he had been to school already, and thought girls generally were very little use.

So when Bryda explained what she wanted to do, he only said that he did not know how to act a story that he had never heard; to which Bryda only answered quietly, and as if it were a fact no one could think of doubting for a moment, "You don't know anything about anything, Maurice. Sit down there—no! not on a cabbage, but on the wheelbarrow—and I will tell you all about it."

So she told him the story, in the middle of which the wheelbarrow upset, because Maurice laughed. So he sat on a log of wood, and Bryda picked up the wheelbarrow, got into it, and began in the words of one of her lesson-books, with a little alteration to suit the occasion.

"Friend! Roman! Countryman! lend me your ears! I am Charon—"

"What?" asked Maurice.

"Don't spoil my speech! You may only say 'Hear, hear!' as they do in Parliament."

"But suppose I don't want to hear?"

Bryda had no notion of what they would do under such unlikely circumstances; so, after thinking a little, she merely said, "Don't be silly, Maurice!" And that sort of answer puts an end to any argument quite easily.

"This is my dog Cerberus, with three heads," went on Bryda, pointing to Toby.

"My! what a lot of bones he would eat!" said his master.

Bryda suddenly jumped down from her rather unsteady pulpit.

"Oh, we *will* have fun! Here, Maurice, put on my white pinafore. You shall be a ghost, and I will get into the tub with my dog Cerberus, and ferry you over the river," she said.

"It won't hold two," said Maurice, looking rather doubtfully at the rotten tub which Bryda pushed into the filthy waters, making a splash and a most horrible smell as it went in.

"Oh, ghosts don't want much room! Now, Cerberus, in you go!" and in the poor dog went, hastily and ungracefully; being, in fact, thrown in head foremost.

After one howl he resigned himself, and lay down at the bottom of the tub, into which unsteady boat Bryda, armed with her own small spade, followed with Maurice's help.

Having balanced herself by crouching down, so as to bring the center of gravity to the right place, she proceeded to paddle, or, as she called it, to row with the little wooden spade, splashing a good deal, and, of course, making the tub turn round and

round, and wriggle very uncomfortably in the pool.
"Well, it doesn't matter," said Charon, giving up
in despair, and looking very red in the face. "We
can pretend I crossed the Styx to fetch you. Now
I must speak to the soul in Latin, because, of course,
Charon and Cerberus talked Latin always."

"I suppose Cerberus barked in Latin—all three
mouths at once," said Maurice; "what a horrid row
it must have been!"

"Now talk away," said Bryda.

"But we don't know Latin; I've only just begun
at *hic, haec, hoc.*"

"*That* doesn't matter; we must make it up, of
course. If we put 'us' or 'o' at the end of every
word it will sound exactly like the stuff Cousin
Ronald learns. Now: Poor-us soul-us, do-us you-
us want-o to cross over-o?"

"Yes-o," replied Maurice promptly.

"Then-us come-o—oh! oh!" screamed Bryda,
making the last word very long indeed; for she trod
on the *one* tail of the dog Cerberus, causing that remarkable animal to jump up howling. Charon's
ferryboat was not built to allow of athletic sports
on board, so it went over, and Bryda went in.

Oh, dear! what word can describe the filthy mess
into which Bryda was plunged up to her waist! the
smell of it, and the chill, horrible feeling! Fortunately, she had just taken Maurice's hand, to
help in "the soul," who indeed felt very lucky to
escape such a voyage! Maurice was able to help
her, but, soaked to the waist and ready to cry, she
scrambled up to dry land.

By way of mending matters, the dog Cerberus,

who may be supposed to have become Toby again, had gone in altogether, and was rather pleased with himself. So he came and had a good shake close to Bryda, so as to splash all the rest of her small person, and then ran round and round, expressing his delight by all sorts of queer noises.

But, oh! here was a mess! And this after the trouble of yesterday, and all Bryda's good resolutions! It was too dreadful, and tears came fast to her eyes.

But kind Maurice, instead of laughing, pitied her. "Don't cry," he said; "can't you *wash?*"

"I might *run*," said Bryda dolefully, remembering what dreadful things happened to frocks that "ran."

"That stuff might run off," said Maurice; "come on."

And she followed meekly to the nearest greenhouse, where was a large tub of fresh water, and beside it a big squirt or syringe used for watering plants high up in the greenhouse.

"Oh, Maurice dear, I never will call you stupid again!" cried Bryda, delighted, as Maurice filled the syringe and set to work upon her. What fun that was! It was almost worth the fright of that horrid splash, and almost—not quite, perhaps— worth the disgrace Bryda would certainly be in with nurse. Such peals of laughter followed each shower that the quiet cows in the fields beyond lifted up their great heavy heads, and stared with brown eyes of mild astonishment.

Can you imagine the sort of figure Bryda was when grandmother came out in her wheel-chair to take a turn in the sunshine? Soaked from head to foot; streams of clean water, and others of the horribly smelling stuff into which she had plunged, pouring off her in all directions! She did indeed look a miserable little guilty thing, hanging her head while grandmother looked at her through her gold eyeglass, evidently so surprised and shocked that she could find no words for a few minutes, and at last could only tell her she must never! never! never! do such dreadful things again. If she did, the consequences would be

* * * * * * *

This row of stars must stand for those dreadful consequences, for Bryda never heard them! Uncle James and grandfather had come up by this time, and she fled, as fast as wet, clinging clothes would let her, to the house. It was "out of the frying-pan into the fire," though, for nurse's wrath was really something too dreadful; and the way in which she ended, by saying that she supposed Miss Bryda would like better to make mud pies in the streets than to play with other Christians, hurt the child's feelings dreadfully. I am sorry to say she walked out of the nursery with damp, smooth hair and a clean frock, but with her head so very much in the air that her namesake, Saint Bride, or Bridget, or Bryda, would have been quite shocked.

"You see, Cousin Salome," she said afterwards, "it was such a dose of disgraces, and I meant to be so wise, and clever, and useful."

"Did you ask to be made wise, and clever, and useful?" asked Salome gently.

Bryda hung her head. She had forgotten that,

I am afraid she dressed so quickly in the morning to join Maurice that she never remembered to ask the Helper of the helpless to make her what she would like to be.

"I have been so miserable, Cousin Salome," she added; "I don't believe Mary, Queen of Scots, could have been more wretched if she had had her head cut off three times running."

How this was to be managed did not seem to strike Bryda as puzzling. She and Maurice had so often acted the execution of Mary of Scotland, with an armchair for the block, and an umbrella for an ax, that they were quite used to the queen having her head cut off very often without minding it in the least, or being any the worse for it afterward.

But, certainly, it is very tiresome when our most amusing games end in some mischief that we never dreamed of doing! It was not so very long before this dreadful accident in the tub that Bryda, who had been reading English history, told Maurice they would act King Canute and his courtiers on the seashore.

So she put two chairs, and collected all the water she could from every jug and water-bottle she could find, so as nearly to fill a bath placed in front of the two chairs on which she and Maurice sat.

"So they put chairs close by the seashore as the tide came in," related Bryda, "and the little waves came nearer and nearer. And the courtiers said, 'Oh king, let us move a little higher up.' But Canute said, 'Why should we? Did you not say I was such a great king that no doubt even the sea would obey me?' And the courtiers held their stupid tongues, for they knew very well that they had said so. But the tide kept on coming, and presently the courtiers got up and ran away, for the water was halfway up the legs of their chairs, and they had already been sitting with their knees up to their noses."

But here Bryda, trying to get herself into this graceful position, lost her balance, and rolled off her chair, falling on the edge of the bath; which, of course, upset, and made a higher tide in the nursery than had ever been seen there before, for the water flowed in every direction, and the children, ashamed and frightened though they were, could not help laughing at the way in which a pair of Bryda's shoes floated about like little canoes, till one that had a hole at the side turned over and went down.

This happened at Bryda's own home, before her father and mother went away. Mother was not pleased, of course; but still she was not quite so dreadfully shocked as the grannies were at the adventure in the old tub.

THE CRATCHITS' CHRISTMAS DINNER

By Charles Dickens

SCROOGE stood with the Ghost of Christmas Present in the city streets on Christmas morning, where (for the weather was severe) the people made a rough, but brisk and not unpleasant kind of music, in scraping the snow from the pave-

ment in front of their dwellings, and from the tops
of their houses: whence it was mad delight to the
boys to see it come plumping down into the road
below, and splitting into artificial little snow-
storms.

The house fronts looked black enough, and the
windows blacker, contrasting with the smooth
white sheet of snow upon the roofs, and with the
dirtier snow upon the ground; which last deposit
had been plowed up in deep furrows by the heavy
wheels of carts and wagons; furrows that crossed
and recrossed each other hundreds of times where
the great streets branched off, and made intricate
channels, hard to trace, in the thick yellow mud
and icy water. The sky was gloomy, and the
shortest streets were choked up with a dingy mist,
half thawed half frozen, whose heavier particles descended in a shower of sooty atoms, as if all the
chimneys in Great Britain had, by one consent,
caught fire, and were blazing away to their dear
hearts' content. There was nothing very cheerful
in the climate or the town, and yet was there an air
of cheerfulness abroad that the clearest summer
air and brightest summer sun might have en-
deavored to diffuse in vain.

For, the people who were shovelling away on the
house-tops were jovial and full of glee; calling out
to one another from the parapets, and now and then
exchanging a facetious snowball—better-natured
missile far than many a wordy jest—laughing
heartily if it went right and not less heartily if it
went wrong. The poulterers' shops were still half
open, and the fruiterers' were radiant in their glory.

THE CHRISTMAS DINNER

There were great, round, pot-bellied baskets of chestnuts, shaped like the waistcoats of jolly old gentlemen, lolling at the doors, and tumbling out into the street in their apoplectic opulence. There were ruddy, brown-faced, broad-girthed Spanish onions, shining in the fatness of their growth like Spanish friars; and winking from their shelves in wanton slyness at the girls as they went by, and glanced demurely at the hung-up mistletoe. There were pears and apples, clustered high in blooming pyramids; there were bunches of grapes, made, in the shopkeepers' benevolence, to dangle from conspicuous hooks, that people's mouths might water gratis as they passed; there were piles of filberts, mossy and brown, recalling, in their fragrance, ancient walks among the woods, and pleasant shufflings ankle-deep through withered leaves; there were Norfolk Biffins, squab, and swarthy, setting off the yellow of the oranges and lemons, and, in the great compactness of their juicy persons, urgently entreating and beseeching to be carried home in paper bags and eaten after dinner. The very gold and silver fish, set forth among these choice fruits in a bowl, though members of a dull and stagnant-blooded race, appeared to know that there was something going on; and, to a fish, went gasping round and round their little world in slow and passionless excitement.

The grocers'! oh, the grocers'! nearly closed, with perhaps two shutters down, or one; but through those gaps such glimpses! It was not alone that the scales descending on the counter made a merry sound, or that the twine and roller parted company so briskly, or that the canisters were rattled up and down like juggling tricks, or even that the blended scents of tea and coffee were so grateful to the nose, or even that the raisins were so plentiful and rare, the almonds so extremely white, the sticks of cinnamon so long and straight, the other spices so delicious, the candied fruits so caked and spotted with molten sugar as to make the coldest lookers-on feel faint and subsequently bilious. Nor was it that the figs were moist and pulpy, or that the French plums blushed in modest tartness from their highly-decorated boxes, or that everything was good to eat and in its Christmas dress: but the customers were all so hurried and so eager in the hopeful promise of the day, that they tumbled up against each other at the door, clashing their wicker baskets wildly, and left their purchases upon the counter, and came running back to fetch them, and committed hundreds of the like mistakes in the best humor possible; while the grocer and his people were so frank and fresh that the polished hearts with which they fastened their aprons behind might have been their own, worn outside for general inspection, and for Christmas daws to peck at if they chose.

But soon the steeples called good people all, to church and chapel, and away they came, flocking through the streets in their best clothes, and with their gayest faces. And at the same time there emerged from scores of by-streets, lanes, and nameless turnings, innumerable people, carrying their dinners to the bakers' shops. The sight of these poor revellers appeared to interest the Spirit very much, for he stood with Scrooge beside him in a baker's doorway, and taking off the covers as their bearers passed, sprinkled incense on their dinners from his torch. And it was a very uncommon kind of torch, for once or twice when there were angry words between some dinner-carriers who had jostled with each other, he shed a few drops of water on them from it, and their good humor was restored directly.

For they said, it was a shame to quarrel upon Christmas Day. And so it was! God love it, so it was!

In time the bells ceased, and the bakers' were shut up; and yet there was a genial shadowing forth of all these dinners and the progress of their cooking, in the thawed blotch of wet above each baker's oven; where the pavements smoked as if its stones were cooking too.

"Is there a peculiar flavor in what you sprinkle from your torch?" asked Scrooge.

"There is. My own."

"Would it apply to any kind of dinner on this day?" asked Scrooge.

"To any kindly given. To a poor one most."

"Why to a poor one most?" asked Scrooge.

"Because it needs it most."

"Spirit," said Scrooge, after a moment's thought, "I wonder you, of all the beings in the many worlds about us, should desire to cramp these people's opportunities of innocent enjoyment."

"I!" cried the Spirit.

"You would deprive them of their means of dining every seventh day, often the only day on which they can be said to dine at all," said Scrooge. "Wouldn't you?"

"I!" cried the Spirit.

"You seek to close these places on the Seventh Day?" said Scrooge. "And it comes to the same thing."

"*I* seek!" exclaimed the Spirit.

"Forgive me if I am wrong. It has been done in your name, or at least in that of your family," said Scrooge.

"There are some upon this earth of yours," returned the Spirit, "who lay claim to know us, and who do their deeds of passion, pride, ill-will, hatred, envy, bigotry, and selfishness in our name, who are as strange to us and all our kith and kin, as if they had never lived. Remember that, and charge their doings on themselves, not us."

Scrooge promised that he would; and they went on, invisible, as they had been before, into the suburbs of the town. It was a remarkable quality of the Ghost (which Scrooge had observed at the baker's), that notwithstanding his gigantic size, he could accommodate himself to any place with ease; and that he stood beneath a low roof quite as gracefully and like a supernatural creature, as it was possible he could have done in any lofty hall.

And perhaps it was the pleasure the good Spirit had in showing off this power of his, or else it was his own kind, generous, hearty nature, and his sympathy with all poor men, that led him straight to Scrooge's clerk's; for there he went, and took Scrooge with him, holding to his robe; and on the threshold of the door the Spirit smiled, and stopped to bless Bob Cratchit's dwelling with the sprinklings of his torch. Think of that! Bob had but fifteen "Bob" a week himself; he pocketed on Saturdays but fifteen copies of his Christian name; and yet the Ghost of Christmas Present blessed his four-roomed house!

Then up rose Mrs. Cratchit, Cratchit's wife, dressed out but poorly in a twice-turned gown, but brave in ribbons, which are cheap and make a goodly show for sixpence; and she laid the cloth, assisted by Belinda Cratchit, second of her daughters, also brave in ribbons; while Master Peter Cratchit plunged a fork into the saucepan of potatoes, and getting the corners of his monstrous shirt collar (Bob's private property, conferred upon his son and heir in honor of the day) into his mouth, rejoiced to find himself so gallantly attired, and yearned to show his linen in the fashionable parks. And now two smaller Cratchits, boy and girl, came tearing in, screaming that outside the baker's they had smelled the goose, and known it for their own; and basking in luxurious thoughts of sage-and-onion, these young Cratchits danced about the table, and exalted Master Peter Cratchit to the skies, while he (not proud, although his collars nearly choked him) blew the fire, until the slow potatoes bubbling up, knocked loudly at the saucepan-lid to be let out and peeled.

"What has ever got your precious father then?" said Mrs. Cratchit. "And your brother, Tiny Tim! And Martha warn't as late last Christmas Day by half-an-hour!"

"Here's Martha, mother!" said a girl, appearing as she spoke.

"Here's Martha, mother!" cried the two young Cratchits. "Hurrah! There's *such* a goose, Martha!"

"Why, bless your heart alive, my dear, how late you are!" said Mrs. Cratchit, kissing her a dozen times, and taking off her shawl and bonnet for her with officious zeal.

"We'd a deal of work to finish up last night," replied the girl, "and had to clear away this morning, mother!"

"Well! Never mind so long as you are come," said Mrs. Cratchit. "Sit ye down before the fire, my dear, and have a warm, Lord bless ye!"

"No, no! There's father coming," cried the two young Cratchits, who were everywhere at once. "Hide, Martha, hide!"

So Martha hid herself, and in came little Bob, the father, with at least three feet of comforter, exclusive of the fringe, hanging down before him; and his threadbare clothes darned up and brushed, to look seasonable; and Tiny Tim upon his shoulder. Alas for Tiny Tim, he bore a little crutch, and had his limbs supported by an iron frame!

"Why, where's our Martha?" cried Bob Cratchit, looking round.

"Not coming," said Mrs. Cratchit.

"Not coming!" said Bob, with a sudden declension in his high spirits; for he had been Tim's blood horse all the way from church, and had come home rampant. "Not coming upon Christmas Day!"

Martha didn't like to see him disappointed, if it

were only in joke; so she came out prematurely from behind the closet door, and ran into his arms, while the two young Cratchits hustled Tiny Tim, and bore him off into the wash-house, that he might hear the pudding singing in the copper.

"And how did little Tim behave?" asked Mrs. Cratchit, when she had rallied Bob on his credulity, and Bob had hugged his daughter to his heart's content.

"As good as gold," said Bob, "and better. Somehow he gets thoughtful, sitting by himself so much, and thinks the strangest things you ever heard. He told me, coming home, that he hoped the people saw him in the church, because he was a cripple, and it might be pleasant to them to remember upon Christmas Day, who made lame beggars walk and blind men see."

Bob's voice was tremulous when he told them this, and trembled more when he said that Tiny Tim was growing strong and hearty.

His active little crutch was heard upon the floor, and back came Tiny Tim before another word was spoken, escorted by his brother and sister to his stool before the fire; and while Bob, turning up his cuffs—as if, poor fellow, they were capable of being made more shabby—compounded some hot mixture in a jug with gin and lemons, and stirred it round and round and put it on the hob to simmer; Master Peter, and the two ubiquitous young Cratchits went to fetch the goose, with which they soon returned in high procession.

Such a bustle ensued that you might have thought a goose the rarest of all birds; a feathered phenomenon, to which a black swan was a matter of course—and in truth it was something very like it in that house. Mrs. Cratchit made the gravy (ready beforehand in a little saucepan) hissing hot; Master Peter mashed the potatoes with incredible vigor; Miss Belinda sweetened up the apple-sauce; Martha dusted the hot plates; Bob took Tiny Tim beside him in a tiny corner at the table; the two young Cratchits set chairs for everybody, not forgetting themselves, and mounting guard upon their posts, crammed spoons into their mouths, lest they should shriek for goose before their turn came to be helped. At last the dishes were set on, and grace was said. It was succeeded by a breathless pause, as Mrs. Cratchit, looking slowly all along the carving-knife, prepared to plunge it in the breast; but when she did, and when the long expected gush of stuffing issued forth, one murmur of delight arose all round the board, and even Tiny Tim, excited by the two young Cratchits, beat on the table with the handle of his knife, and feebly cried Hurrah!

There never was such a goose. Bob said he didn't believe there ever was such a goose cooked. Its tenderness and flavor, size and cheapness, were the themes of universal admiration. Eked out by the apple-sauce and mashed potatoes, it was a sufficient dinner for the whole family; indeed, as Mrs. Cratchit said with great delight (surveying one small atom of a bone upon the dish), they hadn't ate it all at last! Yet every one had had enough, and the younger Cratchits in particular, were steeped in sage and onion to the eyebrows! But now, the plates being changed by Miss Belinda, Mrs. Cratchit left the room alone—too nervous to bear witness—to take the pudding up and bring it in.

Suppose it should not be done enough! Suppose it should break in turning out! Suppose somebody should have got over the wall of the backyard, and stolen it, while they were merry with the goose—a supposition at which the two young Cratchits became livid! All sorts of horrors were supposed.

Hallo! A great deal of steam! The pudding was out of the copper. A smell like a washing-day! That was the cloth. A smell like an eating-house and a pastrycook's next door to each other, with a laundress's next door to that! That was the pudding! In half a minute Mrs. Cratchit entered—flushed, but smiling proudly—with the pudding, like a speckled cannon-ball, so hard and firm, blazing in half of half-a-quartern of ignited brandy, and bedight with Christmas holly stuck into the top.

Oh, a wonderful pudding! Bob Cratchit said, and calmly too, that he regarded it as the greatest success achieved by Mrs. Cratchit since their marriage. Mrs. Cratchit said that now the weight was off her mind, she would confess she had had her doubts about the quantity of flour. Everybody had something to say about it, but nobody said or thought it was at all a small pudding for a large family. It would have been flat heresy to do so. Any Cratchit would have blushed to hint at such a thing.

EMBELLISHMENT

At last the dinner was all done, the cloth was cleared, the hearth swept, and the fire made up. The compound in the jug being tasted, and considered perfect, apples and oranges were put upon the table, and a shovelful of chestnuts on the fire. Then all the Cratchit family drew round the hearth, in what Bob Cratchit called a circle, meaning half a one; and at Bob Cratchit's elbow stood the family display of glass. Two tumblers, and a custard-cup without a handle.

These held the hot stuff from the jug, however, as well as golden goblets would have done; and Bob served it out with beaming looks, while the chestnuts on the fire sputtered and cracked noisily. Then Bob proposed:

"A Merry Christmas to us all, my dears. God bless us!"

Which all the family re-echoed.

"God bless us every one!" said Tiny Tim, the last of all.

EMBELLISHMENT

By Jacob Abbott

ONE day Beechnut, who had been ill, was taken by Phonny and Madeline for a drive. When Phonny and Madeline found themselves riding quietly along in the waggon in Beechnut's company, the first thought which occurred to them, after the interest and excitement awakened by the setting out had passed in some measure away, was that they would ask him to tell them a story. This was a request which they almost always made in similar circumstances. In all their rides and rambles Beechnut's stories were an unfailing resource, furnishing them with an inexhaustible fund of amusement sometimes, and sometimes of instruction.

"Well," said Beechnut, in answer to their request, "I will tell you now about my voyage across the Atlantic Ocean."

"Yes," exclaimed Madeline, "I should like to hear about that very much indeed."

"Shall I tell the story to you just as it was," asked Beechnut, "as a sober matter of fact, or shall I embellish it a little?"

"I don't know what you mean by embellishing it," said Madeline.

"Why, not telling exactly what is true," said Beechnut, "but inventing something to add to it, to make it interesting."

"I want to have it true," said Madeline, "and interesting, too."

"But sometimes," replied Beechnut, "interesting things don't happen, and in such cases, if we should only relate what actually does happen, the story would be likely to be dull."

"I think you had better embellish the story a little," said Phonny—"just a *little,* you know."

"I don't think I can do that very well," replied Beechnut. "If I attempt to relate the actual facts, I depend simply on my memory, and I can confine myself to what my memory teaches; but if I undertake to follow my invention, I must go wherever it leads me."

EMBELLISHMENT

"Well," said Phonny, "I think you had better embellish the story, at any rate, for I want it to be interesting."

"So do I," said Madeline.

"Then," said Beechnut, "I will give you an embellished account of my voyage across the Atlantic. But, in the first place, I must tell you how it happened that my father decided to leave Paris and come to America. It was mainly on my account. My father was well enough contented with his situation so far as he himself was concerned, and he was able to save a large part of his salary, so as to lay up a considerable sum of money every year; but he was anxious about me.

"There seemed to be nothing," continued Beechnut, "for me to do, and nothing desirable for me to look forward to, when I should become a man. My father thought, therefore, that, though it would perhaps be better for *him* to remain in France, it would probably be better for *me* if he should come to America, where he said people might rise in the world, according to their talents, thrift, and industry. He was sure, he said, that I should rise, for, you must understand, he considered me an extraordinary boy."

"Well," said Phonny, "*I* think you were an extraordinary boy."

"Yes, but my father thought," rejoined Beechnut, "that I was something very extraordinary indeed. He thought I was a genius."

"So do I," said Phonny.

"He said," continued Beechnut, "he thought it would in the end be a great deal better for him to come to America, where I might become a man of some consequence in the world, and he said that he should enjoy his own old age a great deal better, even in a strange land, if he could see me going on prosperously in life, than to remain all his days in that porter's lodge.

"All the money that my father had saved," Beechnut continued, "he got changed into gold at an office in the Boulevards; but then he was very much perplexed to decide how it was best to carry it."

"Why did he not pack it up in his chest?" asked Phonny.

"He was afraid," replied Beechnut, "that his chest might be broken open, or unlocked by false keys, on the voyage, and that the money might be thus stolen away; so he thought that he would try to hide it somewhere in some small thing that he could keep with him all the voyage."

"Could not he keep his chest with him all the voyage?" asked Phonny.

"No," said Beechnut; "the chests, and all large parcels of baggage belonging to the passengers, must be sent down into the hold of the ship out of the way. It is only a very little baggage that the people are allowed to keep with them between the decks. My father wished very much to keep his gold with him, and yet he was afraid to keep it in a bag, or in any other similar package, in his little trunk, for then whoever saw it would know that it was gold, and so perhaps form some plan to rob him of it.

"While we were considering what plan it would

be best to adopt for the gold, Arielle, who was the daughter of a friend of ours, proposed to hide it in my *top*. I had a very large top which my father had made for me. It was painted yellow outside, with four stripes of bright blue passing down over it from the stem to the point. When the top was in motion, both the yellow ground and the blue stripes entirely disappeared, and the top appeared to be of a uniform green colour. Then, when it came to its rest again, the original colours would reappear."

"How curious!" said Madeline. "Why would it do so?"

"Why, when it was revolving," said Beechnut, "the yellow and the blue were blended together in the eye, and that made green. Yellow and blue always make green. Arielle coloured my top, after my father had made it, and then my father varnished it over the colours, and that fixed them.

"This top of mine was a monstrous large one, and being hollow, Arielle thought that the gold could all be put inside. She said she thought that that would be a very safe hiding-place, too, since nobody would think of looking into a top for gold. But my father said that he thought that the space would not be quite large enough, and then if anybody should happen to see the top, and should touch it, the weight of it would immediately reveal the secret.

"At last my father thought of a plan which he believed would answer the purpose very perfectly. We had a very curious old clock. It was made by my grandfather, who was a clockmaker in Geneva.

EMBELLISHMENT

There was a little door in the face of the clock, and whenever the time came for striking the hours, this door would open, and a little platform would come out with a tree upon it. There was a beautiful little bird upon the tree, and when the clock had done striking, the bird would flap its wings and sing. Then the platform would slide back into its place, the door would shut, and the clock go on ticking quietly for another hour.

"This clock was made to go," continued Beechnut, "as many other clocks are, by two heavy weights, which were hung to the wheel-work by strong cords. The cords were wound round some of the wheels, and as they slowly descended by their weight, they made the wheels go round. There was a contrivance inside the clock to make the wheels go slowly and regularly, and not spin round too fast, as they would have done if the weights had been left to themselves. This is the way that clocks are often made.

"Now, my father," continued Beechnut, "had intended to take this old family clock with him to America, and he now conceived the idea of hiding his treasure in the weights. The weights were formed of two round tin canisters filled with something very heavy. My father said he did not know whether it was shot or sand. He unsoldered the bottom from these canisters, and found that the filling was shot. He poured out the shot, put his gold pieces in in place of it, and then filled up all the interstices between and around the gold pieces with sand, to prevent the money from jingling. Then he soldered the bottom of the canisters on again, and no one would have known that the weights were anything more than ordinary clock-weights. He then packed the clock in a box, and put the box in his trunk. It did not take up a great deal of room, for he did not take the case of the clock, but only the face and the works and the two weights, which last he packed carefully and securely in the box, one on each side of the clock itself.

"When we got to Havre, all our baggage was examined at the custom-house, and the officers allowed it all to pass. When they came to the clock, my father showed them the little door and the bird inside, and they said it was very curious. They did not pay any attention to the weights at all.

"When we went on board of the vessel our chests were put by the side of an immense heap of baggage upon the deck, where some seamen were at work lowering it down into the hold through a square opening in the deck of the ship. As for the trunk, my father took that with him to the place where he was going to be himself during the voyage. This place was called the steerage. It was crowded full of men, women, and children, all going to America. Some talked French, some German, some Dutch, and there were ever so many babies that were too little to talk at all. Pretty soon the vessel sailed.

"We did not meet with anything remarkable on the voyage, except that once we saw an iceberg."

"What is that?" asked Madeline.

"It is a great mountain of ice," replied Beechnut, "floating about in the sea on the top of the water. I don't know how it comes to be there."

"I should not think it would float upon the top of the water," said Phonny. "All the ice that I ever saw in the water sinks into it."

"It does not sink to the bottom," said Madeline.

"No," replied Phonny, "but it sinks down until the top of the ice is just level with the water. But Beechnut says that his iceberg rose up like a mountain."

"Yes," said Beechnut, "it was several hundred feet high above the water, all glittering in the sun. And I think that if you look at any small piece of ice floating in the water, you will see that a small part of it rises above the surface."

"Yes," said Phonny, "a very little."

"It is a certain proportion of the whole mass," rejoined Beechnut. "They told us on board our vessel that about one-tenth part of the iceberg was above the water; the rest—that is, nine-tenths—was under it; so you see what an enormous big piece of ice it must have been to have only one-tenth part of it tower up so high.

"There was one thing very curious and beautiful about our iceberg," said Beechnut. "We came in sight of it one day about sunset, just after a shower. The cloud, which was very large and black, had passed off into the west, and there was a splendid rainbow upon it. It happened, too, that when we were nearest to the iceberg it lay toward the west, and, of course, toward the cloud, and it appeared directly under the rainbow, and the iceberg and the rainbow made a most magnificent spectacle. The iceberg, which was very bright and dazzling in the evening sun, looked like an enormous diamond, with the rainbow for the setting."

"How curious!" said Phonny.

"Yes," said Beechnut, "and to make it more remarkable still, a whale just then came along directly before the iceberg, and spouted there two or three times; and as the sun shone very brilliantly upon the jet of water which the whale threw into the air, it made a sort of silver rainbow below in the centre of the picture."

"How beautiful it must have been!" said Phonny.

"Yes," rejoined Beechnut, "very beautiful indeed. We saw a great many beautiful spectacles on the sea; but then, on the other hand, we saw some that were dreadful."

"Did you?" asked Phonny. "What?"

"Why, we had a terrible storm and shipwreck at the end," said Beechnut. "For three days and three nights the wind blew almost a hurricane. They took in all the sails, and let the ship drive before the gale under bare poles. She went on over the seas for five hundred miles, howling all the way like a frightened dog."

"Were you frightened?" asked Phonny.

"Yes," said Beechnut. "When the storm first came on, several of the passengers came up the hatchways and got up on the deck to see it; and then we could not get down again, for the ship gave a sudden pitch just after we came up, and knocked away the step-ladder. We were terribly frightened. The seas were breaking over the forecastle and sweeping along the decks, and the shouts and outcries of the captain and the sailors made a dreadful din. At last they put the step-ladder in its place again, and we got down. Then they put the hatches on, and we could not come out any more."

"The hatches?" said Phonny. "What are they?"

"The hatches," replied Beechnut, "are a sort of scuttle-doors that cover over the square openings in the deck of a ship. They always have to put them on and fasten them down in a great storm."

Just at this time the party happened to arrive at a place where two roads met, and as there was a broad and level space of ground at the junction, where it would be easy to turn the waggon, Beechnut said that he thought it would be better to make that the end of their ride, and so turn round and go home. Phonny and Madeline were quite desirous of going a little farther, but Beechnut thought that he should be tired by the time he reached the house again.

"But you will not have time to finish the story," said Phonny.

"Yes," replied Beechnut; "there is very little more to tell. It is only to give an account of our shipwreck."

"Why, did you have a shipwreck?" exclaimed Phonny.

"Yes," said Beechnut. "When you have turned the waggon, I will tell you about it."

So Phonny, taking a great sweep, turned the waggon round, and the party set their faces toward home. The Marshal was immediately going to set out upon a trot, but Phonny held him back by pulling upon the reins and saying:

"Steady, Marshal! steady! You have got to walk all the way home."

"The storm drove us upon the Nova Scotia coast," said Beechnut, resuming his story. "We did not know anything about the great danger that we were in until just before the ship went ashore. When we got near the shore the sailors put down all the anchors; but they would not hold, and at length the ship struck. Then there followed a dreadful scene of consternation and confusion. Some jumped into the sea in their terror, and were drowned. Some cried and screamed, and acted as if they were insane. Some were calm, and behaved rationally. The sailors opened the hatches and let the passengers come up, and we got into the most sheltered places that we could find about the decks and rigging and tied ourselves to whatever was nearest at hand. My father opened his trunk and took out his two clock-weights, and gave me one of them; the other he kept himself. He told me that we might as well try to save them, though he did not suppose that we should be able to do so.

"Pretty soon after we struck the storm seemed to abate a little. The people of the country came down to the shore and stood upon the rocks to see if they could do anything to save us. We were very near the shore, but the breakers and the boiling surf were so violent between us and the land that whoever took to the water was sure to be dashed in pieces. So everybody clung to the ship, waiting for the captain to contrive some way to get us to the shore."

"And what did he do?" asked Phonny.

"He first got a long line and a cask, and he fastened the end of the long line to the cask, and then threw the cask overboard. The other end of the line was kept on board the ship. The cask was tossed about upon the waves, every successive surge driving it in nearer and nearer to the shore, until at last it was thrown up high upon the rocks. The men upon the shore ran to seize it, but before they could get hold of it the receding wave carried it back again among the breakers, where it was tossed about as if it had been a feather, and overwhelmed with the spray. Presently away it went again up upon the shore, and the men again attempted to seize it. This was repeated two or three times. At last they succeeded in grasping hold of it, and they ran up with it upon the rocks, out of the reach of the seas.

"The captain then made signs to the men to pull the line in toward the shore. He was obliged to use signs, because the roaring and thundering of the seas made such a noise that nothing could be heard. The sailors had before this, under the captain's direction, fastened a much stronger line—a small cable, in fact—to the end of the line which had been attached to the barrel. Thus, by pulling upon the smaller line, the men drew one end of the cable to the shore. The other end remained on board the ship, while the middle of it lay tossing among the breakers between the ship and the shore.

"The seamen then carried that part of the cable

which was on shipboard up to the masthead, while the men on shore made their end fast to a very strong post which they set in the ground. The seamen drew the cable as tight as they could, and fastened their end very strongly to the masthead. Thus the line of the cable passed in a gentle slope from the top of the mast to the land, high above all the surges and spray. The captain then rigged what he called a sling, which was a sort of loop of ropes that a person could be put into and made to slide down in it on the cable to the shore. A great many of the passengers were afraid to go in this way, but they were still more afraid to remain on board the ship."

"What were they afraid of?" asked Phonny.

"They were afraid," replied Beechnut, "that the shocks of the seas would soon break the ship to pieces, and then they would all be thrown into the sea together. In this case they would certainly be destroyed, for if they were not drowned, they would be dashed to pieces on the rocks which lined the shore.

"Sliding down the line seemed thus a very dangerous attempt, but they consented one after another to make the trial, and thus we all escaped safe to land."

"And did you get the clock-weights safe to the shore?" asked Phonny.

"Yes," replied Beechnut, "and as soon as we landed we hid them in the sand. My father took me to a little cove close by, where there was not much surf, as the place was protected by a rocky point of land which bounded it on one side. Behind this point of land the waves rolled up quietly upon a sandy beach. My father went down upon the slope of this beach, to a place a little below where the highest waves came, and began to dig a hole in the sand. He called me to come and help him. The waves impeded our work a little, but we persevered until we had dug a hole about a foot deep. We put our clock-weights into this hole and covered them over. We then ran back up upon the beach. The waves that came up every moment over the place soon smoothed the surface of the sand again, and made it look as if nothing had been done there. My father measured the distance from the place where he had deposited his treasure up to a certain great white rock upon the shore exactly opposite to it, so as to be able to find the place again, and then we went back to our company. They were collected on the rocks in little groups, wet and tired, and in great confusion, but rejoiced at having escaped with their lives. Some of the last of the sailors were then coming over in the sling. The captain himself came last of all.

"There were some huts near the place on the shore, where the men made good fires, and we warmed and dried ourselves. The storm abated a great deal in a few hours, and the tide went down, so that we could go off to the ship before night to get some provisions. The next morning the men could work at the ship very easily, and they brought all the passengers' baggage on shore. My father got his trunk with the clock in it. A day or two afterward some sloops came to the place, and took us all away to carry us to Quebec. Just before we embarked on board the sloops, my father and I, watching a good opportunity, dug up our weights out of the sand, and put them back safely in their places in the clock-box."

"Is that the end?" asked Phonny, when Beech-nut paused.

"Yes," replied Beechnut, "I believe I had better make that the end."

"I think it is a very interesting and well-told story," said Madeline. "And do you feel very tired?"

"No," said Beechnut. "On the contrary, I feel all the better for my ride. I believe I will sit up a little while."

So saying, he raised himself in the waggon and sat up, and began to look about him.

"What a wonderful voyage you had, Beechnut!" said Phonny. "But I never knew before that you were shipwrecked."

"Well, in point of fact," replied Beechnut, "I never was shipwrecked."

"Never was!" exclaimed Phonny. "Why, what is all this story that you have been telling us, then?"

"Embellishment," said Beechnut quietly.

"Embellishment!" repeated Phonny, more and more amazed.

"Yes," said Beechnut.

"Then you were not wrecked at all?" said Phonny.

"No," replied Beechnut.

"And how did you get to the land?" asked Phonny.

"Why, we sailed quietly up the St. Lawrence,"

replied Beechnut, "and landed safely at Quebec, as other vessels do."

"And the clock-weights?" asked Phonny.

"All embellishment," said Beechnut. "My father had no such clock, in point of fact. He put his money in a bag, his bag in his chest, and his chest in the hold, and it came as safe as the captain's sextant."

"And the iceberg and the rainbow?" said Madeline.

"Embellishment, all embellishment," said Beechnut.

"Dear me!" said Phonny, "I thought it was all true."

"Did you?" said Beechnut. "I am sorry that you were so deceived, and I am sure it was not my fault, for I gave you your choice of a true story or an invention, and you chose the invention."

"Yes," said Phonny, "so we did."

THE GREAT STONE FACE

By Nathaniel Hawthorne

ONE afternoon, when the sun was going down, a mother and her little boy sat at the door of their cottage, talking about the Great Stone Face. They had but to lift their eyes, and there it was plainly to be seen, though miles away, with the sunshine brightening all its features.

And what was the Great Stone Face?

Embosomed among a family of lofty mountains,

there was a valley so spacious that it contained many thousand inhabitants. Some of these good people dwelt in log huts, with the black forest all around them, on the steep and difficult hillsides. Others had their homes in comfortable farmhouses, and cultivated the rich soil on the gentle slopes or level surfaces of the valley. Others, again, were congregated into populous villages, where some wild, highland rivulet, tumbling down from its birthplace in the upper mountain region, had been caught and tamed by human cunning, and compelled to turn the machinery of cotton factories. The inhabitants of this valley, in short, were numerous, and of many modes of life. But all of them, grown people and children, had a kind of familiarity with the Great Stone Face, although some possessed the gift of distinguishing this grand natural phenomenon more perfectly than many of their neighbors.

The Great Stone Face, then, was a work of Nature in her mood of majestic playfulness, formed on the perpendicular side of a mountain by some immense rocks, which had been thrown together in such a position as, when viewed at a proper distance, precisely to resemble the features of the human countenance. It seemed as if an enormous giant, or a Titan, had sculptured his own likeness on the precipice. There was the broad arch of the forehead, a hundred feet in height; the nose, with its long bridge; and the vast lips, which, if they could have spoken, would have rolled their thunder accents from one end of the valley to the other. True it is, that if the spectator approached too near, he lost the outline of the gigantic visage, and could discern only a heap of ponderous and gigantic rocks, piled in chaotic ruin one upon another. Retracing his steps, however, the wondrous features would again be seen; and the further he withdrew from them, the more like a human face, with all its original divinity intact, did they appear; until, as it grew dim in the distance, with the clouds and glorified vapor of the mountains clustering about it, the Great Stone Face seemed positively to be alive.

It was a happy lot for children to grow up to manhood or womanhood with the Great Stone Face before their eyes, for all the features were noble, and the expression was at once grand and sweet, as if it were the glow of a vast, warm heart, that embraced all mankind in its affections, and had room for more. It was an education only to look at it. According to the belief of many people, the valley owed much of its fertility to this benign aspect that was continually beaming over it, illuminating the clouds, and infusing its tenderness into the sunshine.

As we began with saying, a mother and her little boy sat at their cottage-door, gazing at the Great Stone Face, and talking about it. The child's name was Ernest.

"Mother," said he, while the Titanic visage smiled on him, "I wish that it could speak, for it looks so very kindly that its voice must needs be pleasant. If I were to see a man with such a face, I should love him dearly."

"If an old prophecy should come to pass," answered his mother, "we may see a man, some time or other, with exactly such a face as that."

"What prophecy do you mean, dear mother?" eagerly inquired Ernest. "Pray tell me all about it!"

So his mother told him a story that her own mother had told to her, when she herself was younger than little Ernest; a story, not of things that were past, but of what was yet to come; a story, nevertheless, so very old, that even the Indians, who formerly inhabited this valley, had heard it from their forefathers, to whom, as they affirmed, it had been murmured by the mountain streams, and whispered by the wind among the tree-tops. The purport was that, at some future day, a child should be born hereabouts, who was destined to become the greatest and noblest personage of his time, and whose countenance, in manhood, should bear an exact resemblance to the Great Stone Face. Not a few old-fashioned people, and young ones likewise, in the ardor of their hopes, still cherished an enduring faith in this old prophecy. But others, who had seen more of the world, had watched and waited till they were weary, and had beheld no man with such a face, nor any man that proved to be much greater or nobler than his neighbors, concluded it to be nothing but an idle tale. At all events, the great man of the prophecy had not yet appeared.

"O mother, dear mother!" cried Ernest, clapping his hands above his head, "I do hope that I shall live to see him!"

His mother was an affectionate and thoughtful

woman, and felt that it was wisest not to discourage the generous hopes of her little boy. So she only said to him, "Perhaps you may."

And Ernest never forgot the story that his mother told him. It was always in his mind, whenever he looked upon the Great Stone Face. He spent his childhood in the log-cottage where he was born, and was dutiful to his mother, and helpful to her in many things, assisting her much with his little hands, and more with his loving heart. In this manner, from a happy yet often pensive child, he grew up to be a mild, quiet, unobtrusive boy, and sunbrowned with labor in the fields, but with more intelligence brightening his aspect than is seen in many lads who have been taught at famous schools. Yet Ernest had had no teacher, save only that the Great Stone Face became one to him. When the toil of day was over, he would gaze at it for hours, until he began to imagine that those vast features recognized him, and gave him a smile of kindness and encouragement, responsive to his own look of veneration. We must not take upon us to affirm that this was a mistake, although the Face may have looked no more kindly at Ernest than at all the world besides. But the secret was, that the boy's tender and confiding simplicity discerned what other people could not see; and thus the love, which was meant for all, became his peculiar portion.

About this time, there went a rumor throughout the valley, that the great man, foretold from ages ago, who was to bear a resemblance to the Great Stone Face, had appeared at last. It seems that, many years before, a young man had migrated from the valley and settled at a distant seaport, where, after getting together a little money, he had set up as a shopkeeper. His name—but I could never learn whether it was his real one, or a nickname that had grown out of his habits and success in life—was Gathergold. Being shrewd and active, and endowed by Providence with that inscrutable faculty which develops itself in what the world calls luck, he became an exceedingly rich merchant, and owner of a whole fleet of bulky-bottomed ships. All the countries of the globe appeared to join hands for the mere purpose of adding heap after heap to the mountainous accumulation of this one man's wealth. The cold regions of the north, almost within the gloom and shadow of the Arctic Circle, sent him their tribute in the shape of furs; hot Africa sifted for him the golden sands of her rivers, and gathered up the ivory tusks of her great elephants out of the forests; the East came bringing him the rich shawls, and spices, and teas, and the effulgence of diamonds, and the gleaming purity of large pearls. The ocean, not to be behindhand with the earth, yielded up her mighty whales, that Mr. Gathergold might sell their oil, and make a profit on it. Be the original commodity what it might, it was gold within his grasp. It might be said of him, as of Midas in the fable, that whatever he touched with his finger immediately glistened, and grew yellow, and was changed at once into sterling metal, or, which suited him still better, into piles of coin. And, when Mr. Gathergold had become so very rich that it would have taken him a hundred years only to count his wealth, he bethought himself of his native valley, and resolved to go back thither, and end his days where he was born. With this purpose in view, he sent a skilful architect to build him such a palace as should be fit for a man of his vast wealth to live in.

As I have said above, it had already been rumored in the valley that Mr. Gathergold had turned out to be the prophetic personage so long and vainly looked for, and that his visage was the perfect and undeniable similitude of the Great Stone Face. People were the more ready to believe that this must needs be the fact, when they beheld the splendid edifice that rose, as if by enchantment, on the site of his father's old weather-beaten farm-house. The exterior was of marble, so dazzlingly white that it seemed as though the whole structure might melt away in the sunshine, like those humbler ones which Mr. Gathergold, in his young play-days, before his fingers were gifted with the touch of transmutation, had been accustomed to build of snow. It had a richly ornamented portico, supported by tall pillars, beneath which was a lofty door, studded with silver knobs, and made of a kind of variegated wood that had been brought from beyond the sea. The windows, from the floor to the ceiling of each stately apartment, were composed, respectively, of but one enormous pane of glass, so transparently pure that it was said to be a finer medium than even the vacant atmosphere. Hardly anybody had been permitted to see the interior of this palace; but it was reported, and with good semblance of truth, to be far more gorgeous than the outside, insomuch that whatever was iron or brass in other houses was silver or gold in this;

and Mr. Gathergold's bedchamber, especially, made such a glittering appearance that no ordinary man would have been able to close his eyes there. But, on the other hand, Mr. Gathergold was now so inured to wealth, that perhaps he could not have closed his eyes unless where the gleam of it was certain to find its way beneath his eyelids.

In due time, the mansion was finished; next came the upholsterers, with magnificent furniture; then a whole troop of black and white servants, the harbingers of Mr. Gathergold, who, in his own majestic person, was expected to arrive at sunset. Our friend Ernest, meanwhile, had been deeply stirred by the idea that the great man, the noble man, the man of prophecy, after so many ages of delay, was at length to be made manifest to his native valley. He knew, boy as he was, that there were a thousand ways in which Mr. Gathergold, with his vast wealth, might transform himself into an angel of beneficence, and assume a control over human affairs as wide and benignant as the smile of the Great Stone Face. Full of faith and hope, Ernest doubted not that what the people said was true, and that now he was to behold the living likeness of those wondrous features on the mountain side. While the boy was still gazing up the valley, and fancying, as he always did, that the Great Stone Face returned his gaze and looked kindly at him, the rumbling of wheels was heard, approaching swiftly along the winding road.

"Here he comes!" cried the group of people who were assembled to witness the arrival. "Here comes the great Mr. Gathergold!"

THE GREAT STONE FACE

A carriage, drawn by four horses, dashed round the turn of the road. Within it, thrust partly out of the window, appeared the physiognomy of a little old man, with a skin as yellow as if his own Midas-hand had transmuted it. He had a low forehead, small, sharp eyes, puckered about with innumerable wrinkles, and very thin lips, which he made still thinner by pressing them forcibly together.

"The very image of the Great Stone Face!" shouted the people. "Sure enough, the old prophecy is true; and here we have the great man come, at last!"

And, what greatly perplexed Ernest, they seemed actually to believe that here was the likeness which they spoke of. By the roadside there chanced to be an old beggar-woman and two little beggar-children, stragglers from some far-off region, who, as the carriage rolled onward, held out their hands and lifted up their doleful voices, most piteously beseeching charity. A yellow claw—the very same that had clawed together so much wealth—poked itself out of the coach window, and dropped some copper coins upon the ground; so that, though the great man's name seems to have been Gathergold, he might just as suitably have been nicknamed Scattercopper. Still, nevertheless, with an earnest shout, and evidently with as much good faith as ever, the people bellowed—

"He is the very image of the Great Stone Face!"

But Ernest turned sadly from the wrinkled shrewdness of that sordid visage, and gazed up the valley, where, amid a gathering mist, gilded by the last sunbeams, he could still distinguish those glorious features which had impressed themselves into his soul. Their aspect cheered him. What did the benign lips seem to say?

"He will come! Fear not, Ernest; the man will come!"

The years went on, and Ernest ceased to be a boy. He had grown to be a young man now. He attracted little notice from the other inhabitants of the valley; for they saw nothing remarkable in his way of life, save that, when the labor of the day was over, he still loved to go apart and gaze and meditate upon the Great Stone Face. According to their idea of the matter, it was a folly, indeed, but pardonable, inasmuch as Ernest was industrious, kind, and neighborly, and neglected no duty for the sake of indulging this idle habit. They knew not that the Great Stone Face had become a teacher to him, and that the sentiment which was expressed in it would enlarge the young man's heart, and fill it with wider and deeper sympathies than other hearts. They knew not that thence would come a better wisdom than could be learned from books, and a better life than could be molded on the defaced example of other human lives. Neither did Ernest know that the thoughts and affections which came to him so naturally, in the fields and at the fireside, and wherever he communed with himself, were of a higher tone than those which all men shared with him. A simple soul—simple as when his mother first taught him the old prophecy—he beheld the marvellous features beaming adown the valley, and still wondered that their human counterpart was so long in making his appearance.

THE GREAT STONE FACE

By this time poor Mr. Gathergold was dead and buried; and the oddest part of the matter was, that his wealth, which was the body and spirit of his existence, had disappeared before his death, leaving nothing of him but a living skeleton, covered over with a wrinkled, yellow skin. Since the melting away of his gold, it had been very generally conceded that there was no such striking resemblance, after all, between the ignoble features of the ruined merchant and that majestic face upon the mountain-side. So the people ceased to honor him during his lifetime, and quietly consigned him to forgetfulness after his decease. Once in a while, it is true, his memory was brought up in connection with the magnificent palace which he had built, and which had long ago been turned into a hotel for the accommodation of strangers, multitudes of whom came, every summer, to visit that famous natural curiosity, the Great Stone Face. Thus, Mr. Gathergold being discredited and thrown into the shade, the man of prophecy was yet to come.

It so happened that a native-born son of the valley, many years before, had enlisted as a soldier, and, after a great deal of hard fighting, had now become an illustrious commander. Whatever he may be called in history, he was known in camps and on the battle-field under the nickname of Old Blood-and-Thunder. This war-worn veteran, being now infirm with age and wounds, and weary of the turmoil of a military life, and of the roll of the drum and the clangor of the trumpet, that had so long been ringing in his ears, had lately signified a purpose of returning to his native valley, hoping to

find repose where he remembered to have left it.
The inhabitants, his old neighbors and their grown-
up children, were resolved to welcome the re-
nowned warrior with a salute of cannon and a
public dinner; and all the more enthusiastically, it
being affirmed that now, at last, the likeness of the
Great Stone Face had actually appeared. An aid-
de-camp of Old Blood-and-Thunder, travelling
through the valley, was said to have been struck
with the resemblance. Moreover the schoolmates
and early acquaintances of the general were ready
to testify, on oath, that, to the best of their recol-
lection, the aforesaid general had been exceedingly
like the majestic image, even when a boy, only that
the idea had never occurred to them at that period.
Great, therefore, was the excitement throughout
the valley; and many people, who had never once
thought of glancing at the Great Stone Face for
years before, now spent their time in gazing at it,
for the sake of knowing exactly how General Blood-
and-Thunder looked.

On the day of the great festival, Ernest, with
all the other people of the valley, left their work,
and proceeded to the spot where the sylvan banquet
was prepared. As he approached, the loud voice
of the Rev. Dr. Battleblast was heard, beseeching
a blessing on the good things set before them, and
on the distinguished friend of peace in whose honor
they were assembled. The tables were arranged in
a cleared space of the woods, shut in by the sur-
rounding trees, except where a vista opened east-
ward, and afforded a distant view of the Great
Stone Face. Over the general's chair, which was a

relic from the home of Washington, there was an arch of verdant boughs, with the laurel profusely intermixed, and surmounted by his country's banner, beneath which he had won his victories. Our friend Ernest raised himself on his tip-toes, in hopes to get a glimpse of the celebrated guest; but there was a mighty crowd about the tables anxious to hear the toasts and speeches, and to catch any word that might fall from the general in reply; and a volunteer company, doing duty as a guard, pricked ruthlessly with their bayonets at any particularly quiet person among the throng. So Ernest, being of an unobtrusive character, was thrust quite into the background, where he could see no more of Old Blood-and-Thunder's physiognomy than if it had been still blazing on the battle-field. To console himself, he turned toward the Great Stone Face, which, like a faithful and long-remembered friend, looked back and smiled upon him through the vista of the forest. Meantime, however, he could overhear the remarks of various individuals, who were comparing the features of the hero with the face on the distant mountain-side.

"'Tis the same face, to a hair!" cried one man, cutting a caper for joy.

"Wonderfully like, that's a fact!" responded another.

"Like! why, I call it Old Blood-and-Thunder himself, in a monstrous looking-glass!" cried a third. "And why not? He's the greatest man of this or any other age, beyond a doubt."

And then all three of the speakers gave a great shout, which communicated electricity to the crowd,

and called forth a roar from a thousand voices, that
went reverberating for miles among the mountains,
until you might have supposed that the Great Stone
Face had poured its thunder-breath into the cry.
All these comments, and this vast enthusiasm,
served the more to interest our friend; nor did he
think of questioning that now, at length, the moun-
tain-visage had found its human counterpart. It is
true, Ernest had imagined that this long-looked-for
personage would appear in the character of a man
of peace, uttering wisdom, and doing good, and
making people happy. But, taking an habitual
breadth of view, with all his simplicity, he contended
that Providence should choose its own method of
blessing mankind, and could conceive that this great
end might be effected even by a warrior and a
bloody sword, should inscrutable wisdom see fit to
order matters so.

"The general! the general!" was now the cry.
"Hush! silence! Old Blood-and-Thunder's going
to make a speech."

Even so; for, the cloth being removed, the general's health had been drunk amid shouts of applause, and he now stood upon his feet to thank the
company. Ernest saw him. There he was, over the
shoulders of the crowd, from the two glittering epau-
lets and embroidered collar upward, beneath the
arch of green boughs with intertwined laurel, and
the banner drooping as if to shade his brow! And
there, too, visible in the same glance, through the
vista of the forest, appeared the Great Stone Face!
And was there, indeed, such a resemblance as the
crowd had testified? Alas, Ernest could not recog-

nize it! He beheld a war-worn and weather-beaten countenance, full of energy, and expressive of an iron will; but the gentle wisdom, the deep, broad, tender sympathies, were altogether wanting in Old Blood-and-Thunder's visage; and even if the Great Stone Face had assumed his look of stern command, the milder traits would still have tempered it.

"This is not the man of prophecy," sighed Ernest, to himself, as he made his way out of the throng. "And must the world wait longer yet?"

The mists had congregated about the distant mountain-side, and there were seen the grand and awful features of the Great Stone Face, awful but benignant, as if a mighty angel were sitting among the hills, and enrobing himself in a cloud-vesture of gold and purple. As he looked, Ernest could hardly believe but that a smile beamed over the whole visage, with a radiance still brightening, although without motion of the lips. It was probably the effect of the western sunshine, melting through the thinly diffused vapors that had swept between him and the object that he gazed at. But—as it always did—the aspect of his marvellous friend made Ernest as hopeful as if he had never hoped in vain.

"Fear not, Ernest," said his heart, even as if the Great Face were whispering him—"fear not, Ernest; he will come."

More years sped swiftly and tranquilly away. Ernest still dwelt in his native valley, and was now a man of middle age. By imperceptible degrees, he had become known among the people. Now, as heretofore, he labored for his bread, and was the same simple-hearted man that he had always been. But he had thought and felt so much, he had given so many of the best hours of his life to unworldly hopes for some great good to mankind, that it seemed as though he had been talking with the angels, and had imbibed a portion of their wisdom unawares. It was visible in the calm and well-considered beneficence of his daily life, the quiet stream of which had made a wide green margin all along its course. Not a day passed by, that the world was not the better because this man, humble as he was, had lived. He never stepped aside from his own path, yet would always reach a blessing to his neighbor. Almost involuntarily, too, he had become a preacher. The pure and high simplicity of his thought, which, as one of its manifestations, took shape in the good deeds that dropped silently from his hand, flowed also forth in speech. He uttered truths that wrought upon and molded the lives of those who heard him. His auditors, it may be, never suspected that Ernest, their own neighbor and familiar friend, was more than an ordinary man; least of all did Ernest himself suspect it; but, inevitably as the murmur of a rivulet, came thoughts out of his mouth that no other human lips had spoken.

When the people's minds had had a little time to cool, they were ready enough to acknowledge their mistake in imagining a similarity between General Blood-and-Thunder's truculent physiognomy and the benign visage on the mountain-side. But now, again, there were reports and many paragraphs in the newspapers, affirming that the likeness of the

Great Stone Face had appeared upon the broad shoulders of a certain eminent statesman. He, like Mr. Gathergold and Old Blood-and-Thunder, was a native of the valley, but had left it in his early days, and taken up the trades of law and politics. Instead of the rich man's wealth and the warrior's sword, he had but a tongue, and it was mightier than both together. So wonderfully eloquent was he, that whatever he might choose to say, his auditors had no choice but to believe him; wrong looked like right, and right like wrong; for when it pleased him, he could make a kind of illuminated fog with his mere breath, and obscure the natural daylight with it. His tongue, indeed, was a magic instrument: sometimes it rumbled like the thunder; sometimes it warbled like the sweetest music. It was the blast of war—the song of peace; and it seemed to have a heart in it, when there was no such matter. In good truth, he was a wondrous man; and when his tongue had acquired him all other imaginable success—when it had been heard in halls of state, and in the courts of princes and potentates—after it had made him known all over the world, even as a voice crying from shore to shore— it finally persuaded his countrymen to select him for the presidency. Before this time—indeed, as soon as he began to grow celebrated—his admirers had found out the resemblance between him and the Great Stone Face; and so much were they struck by it, that throughout the country this distinguished gentleman was known by the name of Old Stony Phiz. The phrase was considered as giving a highly favorable aspect to his political prospects; for, as is likewise the case with the Popedom, nobody ever becomes president without taking a name other than his own.

While his friends were doing their best to make him president, Old Stony Phiz, as he was called, set out on a visit to the valley where he was born. Of course, he had no other object than to shake hands with his fellow-citizens, and neither thought nor cared about any effect which his progress through the country might have upon the election. Magnificent preparations were made to receive the illustrious statesman; a cavalcade of horsemen set forth to meet him at the boundary line of the State, and all the people left their business and gathered along the wayside to see him pass. Among these was Ernest. Though more than once disappointed, as we have seen, he had such a hopeful and confiding nature, that he was always ready to believe in whatever seemed beautiful and good. He kept his heart continually open, and thus was sure to catch the blessing from on high, when it should come. So now again, as buoyantly as ever, he went forth to behold the likeness of the Great Stone Face.

The cavalcade came prancing along the road, with a great clattering of hoofs and a mighty cloud of dust, which rose up so dense and high that the visage of the mountain-side was completely hidden from Ernest's eyes. All the great men of the neighborhood were there on horseback: militia officers, in uniform; the member of Congress; the sheriff of the county; the editors of newspapers; and many a farmer, too, had mounted his patient steed, with his Sunday coat upon his back. It really was a very brilliant spectacle, especially as there were numerous banners flaunting over the cavalcade, on some of which were gorgeous portraits of the illustrious statesman and the Great Stone Face, smiling familiarly at one another, like two brothers. If the pictures were to be trusted, the mutual resemblance, it must be confessed, was marvellous. We must not forget to mention that there was a band of music, which made the echoes of the mountains ring and reverberate with the loud triumph of its strains; so that airy and soul-thrilling melodies broke out among all the heights and hollows, as if every nook of his native valley had found a voice, to welcome the distinguished guest. But the grandest effect was when the far-off mountain precipice flung back the music; for then the Great Stone Face itself seemed to be swelling the triumphant chorus, in acknowledgment that, at length, the man of prophecy was come.

All this while the people were throwing up their hats and shouting, with enthusiasm so contagious that the heart of Ernest kindled up, and he likewise threw up his hat, and shouted, as loudly as the loudest, "Huzza for the great man! Huzza for Old Stony Phiz!" But as yet he had not seen him.

"Here he is, now!" cried those who stood near Ernest. "There! There! Look at Old Stony Phiz and then at the Old Man of the Mountain, and see if they are not as like as two twin-brothers!"

In the midst of all this gallant array, came an open barouche, drawn by four white horses; and in the barouche, with his massive head uncovered, sat the illustrious statesman, Old Stony Phiz himself.

"Confess it," said one of Ernest's neighbors to him, "the Great Stone Face has met its match at last!"

Now, it must be owned that, at his first glimpse of the countenance which was bowing and smiling from the barouche, Ernest did fancy that there was a resemblance between it and the old familiar face upon the mountain-side. The brow, with its massive depth and loftiness, and all the other features, indeed, were boldly and strongly hewn, as if in emulation of a more than heroic, of a Titanic model. But the sublimity and stateliness, the grand expression of a divine sympathy, that illuminated the mountain visage, and etherealized its ponderous granite substance into spirit, might here be sought in vain. Something had been originally left out, or had departed. And therefore the marvellously gifted statesman had always a weary gloom in the deep caverns of his eyes, as of a child that has outgrown its playthings, or a man of mighty faculties and little aims, whose life, with all its high performances, was vague and empty, because no high purpose had endowed it with reality.

Still, Ernest's neighbor was thrusting his elbow into his side, and pressing him for an answer.

"Confess! confess! Is not he the very picture of your Old Man of the Mountain?"

"No!" said Ernest, bluntly, "I see little or no likeness."

"Then so much the worse for the Great Stone Face!" answered his neighbor; and again he set up a shout for Old Stony Phiz.

But Ernest turned away, melancholy, and al-

old sea, even the deep immensity of its dread bosom seemed to swell the higher, as if moved by the emotions of the song. Thus the world assumed another and a better aspect from the hour that the poet blessed it with his happy eyes. The Creator had bestowed him, as the last best touch to his own handiwork. Creation was not finished till the poet came to interpret, and so complete it.

The effect was no less high and beautiful, when his human brethren were the subject of his verse. The man or woman, sordid with the common dust of life, who crossed his daily path, and the little child who played in it, were glorified if he beheld them in his mood of poetic faith. He showed the golden links of the great chain that intertwined them with an angelic kindred; he brought out the hidden traits of a celestial birth that made them worthy of such kin. Some, indeed, there were, who thought to show the soundness of their judgment by affirming that all the beauty and dignity of the natural world existed only in the poet's fancy. Let such men speak for themselves, who undoubtedly appear to have been spawned forth by Nature with a contemptuous bitterness; she having plastered them up out of her refuse stuff, after all the swine were made.

As respects all things else, the poet's ideal was the truest truth.

The songs of this poet found their way to Ernest. He read them after his customary toil, seated on the bench before his cottage-door, where for such a length of time he had filled his repose with thought, by gazing at the Great Stone Face. And now as he read stanzas that caused the soul to thrill within him, he lifted his eyes to the vast countenance beaming on him so benignantly.

"O majestic friend," he murmured, addressing the Great Stone Face, "is not this man worthy to resemble thee?"

The Face seemed to smile, but answered not a word.

Now it happened that the poet, though he dwelt so far away, had not only heard of Ernest, but had meditated much upon his character, until he deemed nothing so desirable as to meet this man, whose untaught wisdom walked hand in hand with the noble simplicity of his life. One summer morning, therefore, he took passage by the railroad, and in the decline of the afternoon, alighted from the cars at no great distance from Ernest's cottage. The great hotel, which had formerly been the palace of Mr. Gathergold, was close at hand, but the poet, with his carpet-bag on his arm, inquired at once where Ernest dwelt, and was resolved to be accepted as his guest.

Approaching the door, he there found the good old man, holding a volume in his hand, which alternately he read, and then, with a finger between the leaves, looked lovingly at the Great Stone Face.

"Good evening," said the poet. "Can you give a traveller a night's lodging?"

"Willingly," answered Ernest; and then he added, smiling, "Methinks I never saw the Great Stone Face look so hospitably at a stranger."

The poet sat down on the bench beside him, and

he and Ernest talked t   Often had the poet
held intercourse with   mo tiest and the wisest,
but never before wi   disa like Ernest, whose
thoughts and feeling   fulfi p with such a natural
freedom, and who m   Mea truths so familiar by
his simple utterance   and t Angels, as had been
so often said, seem   erous wrought with him at
his labor in the fi   angels seemed to have sat
with him by the fir   e; and, dwelling with angels
as friend with fri   , he had imbibed the sublimity of their ideas,   imbued it with the sweet and
lowly charm of h   sehold words. So thought the
poet. And Ern   on the other hand, was moved
and agitated by ae living images which the poet
flung out of hi mind, and which peopled all the
air about the cottage-door with shapes of beauty,
both gay and pensive. The sympathies of these two
men instructed them with a profounder sense than
either could have attained alone. Their minds accorded into one strain, and made delightful music
which neither of them could have claimed as all his
own, nor distinguished his own share from the
other's. They led one another, as it were, into a
high pavilion of their thoughts, so remote, and
hitherto so dim, that they had never entered it before, and so beautiful that they desired to be there
always.

As Ernest listened to the poet, he imagined that
the Great Stone Face was bending forward to
listen too. He gazed earnestly into the poet's glowing eyes.

"Who are you, my strangely gifted guest?" he
said.

The poet laid his finger on the volume that Ernest had been reading.

"You have read these poems," said he. "You know me, then—for I wrote them."

Again, and still more earnestly than before, Ernest examined the poet's features; then turned toward the Great Stone Face; then back, with an uncertain aspect, to his guest. But his countenance fell; he shook his head, and sighed.

"Wherefore are you sad?" inquired the poet.

"Because," replied Ernest, "all through life I have awaited the fulfilment of a prophecy; and, when I read these poems, I hoped that it might be fulfilled in you."

"You hoped," answered the poet, faintly smiling, "to find in me the likeness of the Great Stone Face. And you are disappointed, as formerly with Mr. Gathergold, and Old Blood-and-Thunder, and Old Stony Phiz. Yes, Ernest, it is my doom. You must add my name to the illustrious three, and record another failure of your hopes. For—in shame and sadness do I speak it, Ernest—I am not worthy to be typified by yonder benign and majestic image."

"And why?" asked Ernest. He pointed to the volume. "Are not those thoughts divine?"

"They have a strain of the Divinity," replied the poet. "You can hear in them the far-off echo of a heavenly song. But my life, dear Ernest, has not corresponded with my thought. I have had grand dreams, but they have been only dreams, because I have lived—and that, too, by my own choice—among poor and mean realities. Sometimes even—shall I dare to say it?—I lack faith in the grandeur, the beauty, and the goodness, which my own works are said to have made more evident in nature and in human life. Why, then, pure seeker of the good and true, shouldst thou hope to find me, in yonder image of the divine?"

The poet spoke sadly, and his eyes were dim with tears. So, likewise, were those of Ernest.

At the hour of sunset, as had long been his frequent custom, Ernest was to discourse to an assemblage of the neighboring inhabitants in the open air.

He and the poet, arm in arm, still talking together as they went along, proceeded to the spot. It was a small nook among the hills, with a gray precipice behind, the stern front of which was relieved by the pleasant foliage of many creeping plants, that made a tapestry for the naked rock, by hanging their festoons from all its rugged angles. At a small elevation above the ground, set in a rich framework of verdure, there appeared a niche, spacious enough to admit a human figure, with freedom for such gestures as spontaneously accompany earnest thought and genuine emotion. Into this natural pulpit Ernest ascended, and threw a look of familiar kindness around upon his audience. They stood, or sat, or reclined upon the grass, as seemed good to each, with the departing sunshine falling obliquely over them, and mingling its subdued cheerfulness with the solemnity of a grove of ancient trees, beneath and amid the boughs of which the golden rays were constrained to pass. In another direction was seen the Great Stone Face, with the same cheer, combined with the same solemnity, in its benignant aspect.

Ernest began to speak, giving to the people of what was in his heart and mind. His words had power, because they accorded with his thoughts; and his thoughts had reality and depth, because they harmonized with the life which he had always lived. It was not mere breath that this preacher uttered; they were the words of life, because a life of good deeds and holy love was melted into them. Pearls, pure and rich, had been dissolved into this precious draught. The poet, as he listened, felt that the being and character of Ernest were a nobler strain of poetry than he had ever written. His eyes glistening with tears, he gazed reverentially at the venerable man, and said within himself that never was there an aspect so worthy of a prophet and a sage as that mild, sweet, thoughtful countenance, with the glory of white hair diffused about it. At a distance, but distinctly to be seen, high up in the golden light of the setting sun, appeared the Great Stone Face, with hoary mists around it, like the white hairs around the brow of Ernest. Its look of grand beneficence seemed to embrace the world.

At that moment, in sympathy with a thought which he was about to utter, the face of Ernest assumed a grandeur of expression, so imbued with benevolence, that the poet, by an irresistible impulse, threw his arms aloft, and shouted:

"Behold! Behold! Ernest is himself the likeness of the Great Stone Face!"

Then all the people looked, and saw that what

the deep-sighted poet said was true. The prophecy was fulfilled. But Ernest, having finished what he had to say, took the poet's arm, and walked slowly homeward, still hoping that some wiser and better man than himself would by and by appear, bearing a resemblance to the GREAT STONE FACE.

THE KING OF THE GOLDEN RIVER

By John Ruskin

IN a secluded and mountainous part of Stiria there was, in old time, a valley of the most surprising and luxuriant fertility. It was surrounded, on all sides, by steep and rocky mountains, rising into peaks, which were always covered with snow, and from which a number of torrents descended in constant cataracts. One of these fell westward, over the face of a crag so high, that, when the sun had set to everything else, and all below was darkness, his beams still shone full upon this waterfall, so that it looked like a shower of gold. It was therefore, called by the people of the neighbourhood, the Golden River. It was strange that none of these streams fell into the valley itself. They all descended on the other side of the mountains, and wound away through broad plains and by populous cities. But the clouds were drawn so constantly to the snowy hills, and rested so softly in the circular hollow, that in time of drought and heat, when all the country round was burnt up, there was still rain in the little valley; and its crops

were so heavy, and its hay so high, and its apples
so red, and its grapes so blue, and its wine so rich,
and its honey so sweet, that it was a marvel to
every one who beheld it, and was commonly called
the Treasure Valley.

The whole of this little valley belonged to three
brothers, called Schwartz, Hans, and Gluck.
Schwartz and Hans, the two elder brothers, were
very ugly men, with over-hanging eyebrows and
small dull eyes, which were always half shut, so
that you couldn't see into *them,* and always fancied
they saw very far into *you.* They lived by farming the Treasure Valley, and very good farmers
they were. They killed everything that did not
pay for its eating. They shot the blackbirds, because they pecked the fruit; and killed the hedgehogs, lest they should suck the cows; they poisoned
the crickets for eating the crumbs in the kitchen;
and smothered the cicadas, which used to sing all
summer in the lime trees. They worked their servants without any wages, till they would not work
any more, and then quarrelled with them, and
turned them out of doors without paying them.
It would have been very odd, if with such a farm,
and such a system of farming, they hadn't got very
rich; and very rich they *did* get. They genera'ly
contrived to keep their corn by them till it was very
dear, and then sell it for twice its value; they had
heaps of gold lying about on their floors, yet it was
never known that they had given so much as a
penny or a crust in charity; they never went to
mass; grumbled perpetually at paying tithes; and
were, in a word, of so cruel and grinding a temper,

as to receive from all those with whom they had any dealings, the nickname of the "Black Brothers."

The youngest brother, Gluck, was as completely opposed, in both appearance and character, to his seniors as could possibly be imagined or desired. He was not above twelve years old, fair, blue-eyed, and kind in temper to every living thing. He did not, of course, agree particularly well with his brothers, or rather, they did not agree with *him*. He was usually appointed to the honourable office of turnspit, when there was anything to roast, which was not often; for, to do the brothers justice, they were hardly less sparing upon themselves than upon other people.

At other times he used to clean the shoes, floors, and sometimes the plates, occasionally getting what was left on them, by way of encouragement, and a wholesome quantity of dry blows, by way of education.

Things went on in this manner for a long time. At last came a very wet summer, and everything went wrong in the country around. The hay had hardly been got in, when the haystacks were floated bodily down to the sea by an inundation; the vines were cut to pieces with the hail; the corn was all killed by a black blight; only in the Treasure Valley, as usual, all was safe. As it had rain when there was rain nowhere else, so it had sun when there was sun nowhere else. Everybody came to buy corn at the farm, and went away pouring maledictions on the Black Brothers. They asked what they liked, and got it, except from the poor people, who could only beg, and several of whom were starved at their very door, without the slightest regard or notice.

It was drawing towards winter, and very cold weather, when one day the two elder brothers had gone out, with their usual warning to little Gluck, who was left to mind the roast, that he was to let nobody in, and give nothing out. Gluck sat down quite close to the fire, for it was raining very hard, and the kitchen walls were by no means dry or comfortable looking. He turned and turned, and the roast got nice and brown. "What a pity," thought Gluck, "my brothers never ask anybody to dinner. I'm sure, when they've got such a nice piece of mutton as this, and nobody else has got so much as a piece of dry bread, it would do their hearts good to have somebody to eat it with them."

Just as he spoke, there came a double knock at the house door, yet heavy and dull, as though the knocker had been tied up—more like a puff than a knock.

"It must be the wind," said Gluck; "nobody else would venture to knock double knocks at our door."

No; it wasn't the wind: there it came again very hard, and what was particularly astounding, the knocker seemed to be in a hurry, and not to be in the least afraid of the consequences. Gluck went to the window, opened it, and put his head out to see who it was.

It was the most extraordinary looking little gentleman he had ever seen in his life. He had a very large nose, slightly brass-coloured; his cheeks were very round, and very red, and might have warranted a supposition that he had been blowing a refractory fire for the last eight-and-forty hours; his eyes twinkled merrily through long silky eyelashes, his moustaches curled twice round like a corkscrew on each side of his mouth, and his hair, of a curious mixed pepper-and-salt colour, descended far over his shoulders. He was about four feet six in height, and wore a conical pointed cap of nearly the same altitude, decorated with a black feather some three feet long. His doublet was prolonged behind into something resembling a violent exaggeration of what is now termed a "swallow tail," but was much obscured by the swelling folds of an enormous black, glossy-looking cloak, which must have been very much too long in calm weather, as the wind, whistling round the old house, carried it clear out from the wearer's shoulders to about four times his own length.

Gluck was so perfectly paralyzed by the singular appearance of his visitor, that he remained fixed without uttering a word, until the old gentleman, having performed another, and a more energetic concerto on the knocker, turned round to look after his fly-away cloak. In so doing he caught sight of Gluck's little yellow head jammed in the window, with its mouth and eyes very wide open indeed.

"Hullo!" said the little gentleman, "that's not the way to answer the door: I'm wet, let me in."

To do the little gentleman justice, he *was* wet. His feather hung down between his legs like a beaten puppy's tail, dripping like an umbrella; and from the ends of his moustaches the water was running into his waistcoat pockets, and out again like a mill stream.

"I beg pardon, sir," said Gluck, "I'm **very sorry.** but I really can't."

"Can't what!" said the old gentleman.

"I can't let you in, sir,—I can't, indeed; my brothers would beat me to death, sir, if I thought of such a thing. What do you want, sir?"

"Want?" said the old gentleman, petulantly. "I want fire, and shelter; and there's your great fire there blazing, cracking, and dancing on the walls, with nobody to feel it. Let me in, I say; I only want to warm myself."

Gluck had had his head, by this time, so long out of the window, that he began to feel it was really unpleasantly cold, and when he turned, and saw the beautiful fire rustling and roaring, and throwing long bright tongues up the chimney, as if it were licking its chops at the savoury smell of the leg of mutton, his heart melted within him that it should be burning away for nothing. "He does look *very* wet," said little Gluck; "I'll just let him in for a quarter of an hour." Round he went to the door, and opened it; and as the little gentleman walked in, there came a gust of wind through the house that made the old chimneys totter.

"That's a good boy," said the little gentleman. "Never mind your brothers. I'll talk to them."

"Pray, sir, don't do any such thing," said Gluck. "I can't let you stay till they come; they'd be the death of me."

"Dear me," said the old gentleman, "I'm very sorry to hear that. How long may I stay?"

"Only till the mutton's done, sir," replied Gluck, "and it's very brown."

Then the old gentleman walked into the kitchen, and sat himself down on the hob, with the top of his cap accommodated up the chimney, for it was a great deal too high for the roof.

"You'll soon dry there, sir," said Gluck, and sat down again to turn the mutton. But the old gentleman did *not* dry there, but went on drip, drip, dripping among the cinders, and the fire fizzed, and sputtered, and began to look very black, and uncomfortable: never was such a cloak; every fold in it ran like a gutter.

"I beg pardon, sir," said Gluck at length, after watching the water spreading in long quicksilver-like streams over the floor for a quarter of an hour; "mayn't I take your cloak?"

"No, thank you," said the old gentleman.

"Your cap, sir?"

"I am all right, thank you," said the old gentleman rather gruffly.

"But,—sir,—I'm very sorry," said Gluck, hesitatingly; "but—really, sir,—you're—putting the fire out."

"It'll take longer to do the mutton, then," replied his visitor drily.

Gluck was very much puzzled by the behaviour of his guest; it was such a strange mixture of coolness and humility.

He turned away at the string meditatively for another five minutes.

"That mutton looks very nice," said the old gentleman at length. "Can't you give me a little bit?"

"Impossible, sir," said Gluck.

"I'm very hungry," continued the old gentleman:

"I've had nothing to eat yesterday, nor to-day. They surely couldn't miss a bit from the knuckle!"

He spoke in so very melancholy a tone, that it quite melted Gluck's heart. "They promised me one slice to-day, sir," said he; "I can give you that, but not a bit more."

"That's a good boy," said the old gentleman again.

Then Gluck warmed a plate, and sharpened a knife. "I don't care if I do get beaten for it," thought he. Just as he had cut a large slice out of the mutton, there came a tremendous rap at the door. The old gentleman jumped off the hob, as if it had suddenly become inconveniently warm. Gluck fitted the slice into the mutton again, with desperate efforts at exactitude, and ran to open the door.

"What did you keep us waiting in the rain for?" said Schwartz, as he walked in, throwing his umbrella in Gluck's face. "Ay! what for, indeed, you little vagabond?" said Hans, administering an educational box on the ear, as he followed his brother into the kitchen.

"Bless my soul!" said Schwartz when he opened the door.

"Amen," said the little gentleman, who had taken his cap off, and was standing in the middle of the kitchen, bowing with the utmost possible velocity.

"Who's that?" said Schwartz, catching up a rolling-pin, and turning to Gluck with a fierce frown.

"I don't know, indeed, brother," said Gluck in great terror.

THE GOLDEN RIVER

"How did he get in?" roared Schwartz.

"My dear brother," said Gluck, deprecatingly, "he was so *very* wet!"

The rolling-pin was descending on Gluck's head; but, at the instant, the old gentleman interposed his conical cap, on which it crashed with a shock that shook the water out of it all over the room. What was very odd, the rolling-pin no sooner touched the cap, than it flew out of Schwartz's hand, spinning like a straw in a high wind, and fell into the corner at the further end of the room.

"Who are you, sir?" demanded Schwartz, turning upon him.

"What's your business?" snarled Hans.

"I'm a poor old man, sir," the little gentleman began very modestly, "and I saw your fire through the window, and begged shelter for a quarter of an hour."

"Have the goodness to walk out again, then," said Schwartz. "We've quite enough water in our kitchen, without making it a drying house."

"It is a cold day to turn an old man out in, sir; look at my grey hairs." They hung down to his shoulders, as I told you before.

"Ay!" said Hans, "there are enough of them to keep you warm. Walk!"

"I'm very, very hungry, sir; couldn't you spare me a bit of bread before I go?"

"Bread, indeed!" said Schwartz; "do you suppose we've nothing to do with our bread, but to give it to such red-nosed fellows as you?"

"Why don't you sell your feather?" said Hans, sneeringly. "Out with you."

"A little bit," said the old gentleman.

"Be off!" said Schwartz.

"Pray, gentlemen."

"Off, and be hanged!" cried Hans, seizing him by the collar. But he had no sooner touched the old gentleman's collar, than away he went after the rolling-pin, spinning round and round, till he fell into the corner on top of it. Then Schwartz was very angry, and ran at the old gentleman to turn him out; but he also had hardly touched him, when away he went after Hans and the rolling-pin, and hit his head against the wall as he tumbled into the corner.

And so there they lay, all three.

Then the old gentleman spun himself round with velocity in the opposite direction; continued to spin until his long cloak was all wound neatly about him; clapped his cap on his head, very much on one side (for it could not stand upright without going through the ceiling), gave an additional twist to his corkscrew moustaches, and replied with perfect coolness: "Gentlemen, I wish you a very good morning. At twelve o'clock to-night I'll call again; after such a refusal of hospitality as I have just experienced, you will not be surprised if that visit is the last I ever pay you."

"If ever I catch you here again," muttered Schwartz, coming, half frightened, out of the corner—but, before he could finish his sentence, the old gentleman had shut the house door behind him with a great bang: and there drove past the window, at the same instant, a wreath of ragged cloud, that whirled and rolled away down the valley in all manner of shapes; turning over and over in the air; and melting away at last in a gush of rain.

"A very pretty business, indeed, Mr. Gluck!" said Schwartz. "Dish the mutton, sir. If ever I catch you at such a trick again—bless me, why, the mutton's been cut!"

"You promised me one slice, brother, you know," said Gluck.

"Oh! and you were cutting it hot, I suppose, and going to catch all the gravy. It'll be long before I promise you such a thing again. Leave the room, sir; and have the kindness to wait in the coal-cellar till I call you."

Gluck left the room melancholy enough. The brothers ate as much mutton as they could, locked the rest in the cupboard, and proceeded to get very drunk after dinner.

Such a night as it was! Howling wind, and rushing rain, without intermission. The brothers had just sense enough left to put up all the shutters, and double bar the door, before they went to bed. They usually slept in the same room. As the clock struck twelve, they were both awakened by a tremendous crash. Their door burst open with a violence that shook the house from top to bottom.

"What's that?" cried Schwartz, starting up in his bed.

"Only I," said the little gentleman.

The two brothers sat up on their bolster, and stared into the darkness. The room was full of water, and by a misty moon-beam, which found its way through a hole in the shutter, they could see in the midst of it an enormous foam globe, spinning round, and bobbing up and down like a cork, on which, as on a most luxurious cushion, reclined the little old gentleman, cap and all. There was plenty of room for it now, for the roof was off.

"Sorry to incommode you," said their visitor, ironically. "I'm afraid your beds are dampish; perhaps you had better go to your brother's room: I've left the ceiling on, there."

They required no second admonition, but rushed into Gluck's room, wet through, and in an agony of terror.

"You'll find my card on the kitchen table," the old gentleman called after them. "Remember, the *last* visit."

"Pray Heaven it may!" said Schwartz, shuddering. And the foam globe disappeared.

Dawn came at last, and the two brothers looked out of Gluck's little window in the morning. The Treasure Valley was one mass of ruin and desolation. The inundation had swept away trees, crops, and cattle, and left in their stead a waste of red sand and grey mud. The two brothers crept shivering and horror-struck into the kitchen. The water had gutted the whole first floor; corn, money, almost every movable thing had been swept away, and there was left only a small white card on the kitchen table. On it, in large, breezy, long-legged letters, were engraved the words:—

SOUTH-WEST WIND, ESQUIRE

South-West Wind, Esquire, was as good as his word. After the momentous visit above related,

he entered the Treasure Valley no more; and, what
was worse, he had so much influence with his relations, the West Winds in general, and used it so
effectually, that they all adopted a similar line of
conduct. So no rain fell in the valley from one
year's end to another. Though everything remained green and flourishing in the plains below,
the inheritance of the three brothers was a desert.
What had once been the richest soil in the kingdom, became a shifting heap of red sand; and the
brothers, unable longer to contend with the adverse
skies, abandoned their valueless patrimony in despair, to seek some means of gaining a livelihood
among the cities and people of the plains.

All their money was gone, and they had nothing left but some curious old-fashioned pieces of
gold plate, the last remnants of their ill-gotten
wealth.

"Suppose we turn goldsmiths?" said Schwartz
to Hans, as they entered the large city. "It is a
good knave's trade; we can put a great deal of
copper into the gold, without any one's finding it
out."

The thought was agreed to be a very good one;
they hired a furnace, and turned goldsmiths. But
two slight circumstances affected their trade: the
first, that people did not approve of the coppered
gold; the second, that the two elder brothers, whenever they had sold anything, used to leave little
Gluck to mind the furnace, and go and drink out
the money in the ale-house next door. So they
melted all their gold, without making money enough
to buy more, and were at last reduced to one large

drinking mug, which an uncle of his had given to little Gluck, and which he was very fond of, and would not have parted with for the world; though he never drank anything out of it but milk and water. The mug was a very odd mug to look at. The handle was formed of two wreaths of flowing golden hair, so finely spun that it looked more like silk than metal, and these wreaths descended into, and mixed with, a beard and whiskers of the same exquisite workmanship, which surrounded and decorated a very fierce little face, of the reddest gold imaginable, right in the front of the mug, with a pair of eyes in it which seemed to command its whole circumference. It was impossible to drink out of the mug without being subjected to an intense gaze out of the side of these eyes; and Schwartz positively averred, that once, after emptying it, full of Rhenish, seventeen times, he had seen them wink! When it came to the mug's turn to be made into spoons, it half broke poor little Gluck's heart; but the brothers only laughed at him, tossed the mug into the melting-pot, and staggered out to the ale-house: leaving him, as usual, to pour the gold into bars, when it was all ready.

When they were gone, Gluck took a farewell look at his old friend in the melting-pot. The flowing hair was all gone; nothing remained but the red nose, and the sparkling eyes, which looked more malicious than ever. "And no wonder," thought Gluck, "after being treated in that way." He sauntered disconsolately to the window, and sat himself down to catch the fresh evening air, and escape the hot breath of the furnace. Now this window commanded a direct view of the range of mountains, which, as I told you before, overhung the Treasure Valley, and more especially of the peak from which fell the Golden River. It was just at the close of the day, and, when Gluck sat down at the window, he saw the rocks of the mountain tops, all crimson and purple with the sunset; and there were bright tongues of fiery cloud burning and quivering about them; and the river, brighter than all, fell, in a waving column of pure gold, from precipice to precipice, with the double arch of a broad purple rainbow stretched across it, flushing and fading alternately in the wreaths of spray.

"Ah!" said Gluck aloud, after he had looked at it for a while, "if that river were really all gold, what a nice thing it would be."

"No, it wouldn't, Gluck," said a clear, metallic voice, close at his ear.

"Bless me, what's that?" exclaimed Gluck, jumping up. There was nobody there. He looked round the room, and under the table, and a great many times behind him, but there was certainly nobody there, and he sat down again at the window.

This time he didn't speak, but he couldn't help thinking again that it would be very convenient if the river were really all gold.

"Not at all, my boy," said the same voice, louder than before.

"Bless me!" said Gluck again, "what *is* that?" He looked again into all the corners and cupboards, and then began turning round and round as fast as he could in the middle of the room, thinking there was somebody behind him, when the same voice struck again on his ear. It was singing now, very merrily, "Lala-lira-la;" no words, only a soft running effervescent melody, something like that of a kettle on the boil. Gluck looked out of the window. No, it was certainly in the house. Up stairs, and down stairs. No, it was certainly in that very room, coming in quicker time and clearer notes every moment. "Lala-lira-la." All at once it struck Gluck that it sounded louder near the furnace. He ran to the opening and looked in; yes, he saw right, it seemed to be coming, not only out of the furnace, but out of the pot. He uncovered it, and ran back in a great fright, for the pot was certainly singing! He stood in the farthest corner of the room, with his hands up and his mouth open, for a minute or two, when the singing stopped, and the voice became clear and pronunciative.

"Hullo!" said the voice.

Gluck made no answer.

"Hullo! Gluck, my boy," said the pot again.

Gluck summoned all his energies, walked straight up to the crucible, drew it out of the furnace, and looked in. The gold was all melted, and its surface as smooth and polished as a river; but instead of reflecting little Gluck's head, as he looked in he saw meeting his glance from beneath the gold, the red nose and sharp eyes of his old friend of the mug, a thousand times redder and sharper than ever he had seen them in his life.

"Come, Gluck, my boy," said the voice out of the pot again, "I'm all right; pour me out."

But Gluck was too much astonished to do anything of the kind.

"Pour me out, I say," said the voice, rather gruffly. Still Gluck couldn't move.

"*Will* you pour me out?" said the voice, passionately. "I'm too hot."

By a violent effort, Gluck recovered the use of his limbs, took hold of the crucible and sloped it, so as to pour out the gold. But, instead of a liquid stream, there came out, first a pair of pretty little yellow legs, then some coat tails, then a pair of arms stuck a-kimbo, and finally the well-known head of his friend the mug; all which articles, uniting as they rolled out, stood up energetically on the floor, in the shape of a little golden dwarf, about a foot and a half high.

"That's right!" said the dwarf, stretching out first his legs, and then his arms, and then shaking his head up and down, and as far round as it would go, for five minutes without stopping, apparently with the view of ascertaining if he were quite correctly put together, while Gluck stood contemplating him in speechless amazement. He was dressed in a slashed doublet of spun gold, so fine in its texture, that the prismatic colours gleamed over it as if on a surface of mother of pearl; and, over this brilliant doublet, his hair and beard fell full half way to the ground in waving curls, so exquisitely delicate, that Gluck could hardly tell where they ended; they seemed to melt into air. The features of the face, however, were by no means finished with the same delicacy; they were rather coarse, slightly inclining to coppery in complexion, and indicative, in expression, of a very pertinacious and intractable disposition in their small proprietor. When the dwarf had finished his self-examination, he turned his small sharp eyes full on Gluck, and stared at him deliberately for a minute or two. "No, it wouldn't, Gluck, my boy," said the little man.

This was certainly rather an abrupt and unconnected mode of commencing conversation. It might indeed be supposed to refer to the course of Gluck's thoughts, which had first produced the dwarf's observations out of the pot; but whatever it referred to, Gluck had no inclination to dispute the dictum.

"Wouldn't it, sir?" said Gluck, very mildly and submissively indeed.

"No," said the dwarf, conclusively, "no, it wouldn't." And with that the dwarf pulled his cap hard over his brows, and took two turns, of three feet long, up and down the room, lifting his legs up very high, and setting them down very hard. This pause gave time for Gluck to collect his thoughts a little, and, seeing no great reason to view his diminutive visitor with dread, and feeling his curiosity overcome his amazement, he ventured on a question of peculiar delicacy.

"Pray, sir," said Gluck, rather hesitatingly, "were you my mug?"

On which the little man turned sharp round, walked straight up to Gluck, and drew himself up to his full height. "I," said the little man, "am the King of the Golden River." Whereupon he turned about again, and took two more turns, some six feet long, in order to allow time for the consternation which this announcement produced in his auditor to evaporate.

After which, he again walked up to Gluck and stood still, as if expecting some comment on his communication.

Gluck determined to say something at all events. "I hope your majesty is very well," said Gluck.

"Listen!" said the little man, deigning no reply to this polite inquiry. "I am the King of what you mortals call the Golden River. The shape you saw me in, was owing to the malice of a stronger king, from whose enchantments you have this instant freed me. What I have seen of you, and your conduct to your wicked brothers, renders me willing to serve you; therefore, attend to what I tell you. Whoever shall climb to the top of that mountain from which you see the Golden River issue, and shall cast into the stream at its source, three drops of holy water, for him, and for him only, the river shall turn to gold. But no one failing in his first, can succeed in a second attempt; and if any one shall cast unholy water into the river, it will overwhelm him, and he will become a black stone." So saying, the King of the Golden River turned away and deliberately walked into the centre of the hottest flame of the furnace. His figure became red, white, transparent, dazzling,—a blaze of intense light,—rose, trembled, and disappeared. The King of the Golden River had evaporated.

"Oh!" cried poor Gluck, running to look up the chimney after him; "Oh, dear, dear, dear me! My mug! my mug! my mug!"

THE GOLDEN RIVER

The King of the Golden River had hardly made the extraordinary exit related in the last chapter, before Hans and Schwartz came roaring into the house, very savagely drunk. The discovery of the total loss of their last piece of plate had the effect of sobering them just enough to enable them to stand over Gluck, beating him very steadily for a quarter of an hour; at the expiration of which period they dropped into a couple of chairs, and requested to know what he had got to say for himself. Gluck told them his story, of which, of course, they did not believe a word. They beat him again, till their arms were tired, and staggered to bed. In the morning, however, the steadiness with which he adhered to his story obtained him some degree of credence; the immediate consequence of which was, that the two brothers, after wrangling a long time on the knotty question, which of them should try his fortune first, drew their swords and began fighting. The noise of the fray alarmed the neighbours, who, finding they could not pacify the combatants, sent for the constable.

Hans, on hearing this, contrived to escape, and hid himself; but Schwartz was taken before the magistrate, fined for breaking the peace, and, having drunk out his last penny the evening before, was thrown into prison till he should pay.

When Hans heard this, he was much delighted, and determined to set out immediately for the Golden River. How to get the holy water, was the question. He went to the priest, but the priest could not give any holy water to so abandoned a character. So Hans went to vespers in the evening for the first time in his life, and, under pretence of crossing himself, stole a cupful, and returned home in triumph.

Next morning he got up before the sun rose, put the holy water into a strong flask, and two bottles of wine and some meat in a basket, slung them over his back, took his alpine staff in his hand, and set off for the mountains.

On his way out of the town he had to pass the prison, and as he looked in at the windows, whom should he see but Schwartz himself peeping out of the bars, and looking very disconsolate.

"Good morning, brother," said Hans; "have you any message for the King of the Golden River?"

Schwartz gnashed his teeth with rage, and shook the bars with all his strength; but Hans only laughed at him, and advising him to make himself comfortable till he came back again, shouldered his basket, shook the bottle of holy water in Schwartz's face till it frothed again, and marched off in the highest spirits in the world.

It was, indeed, a morning that might have made any one happy, even with no Golden River to seek for. Level lines of dewy mist lay stretched along the valley, out of which rose the massy mountains —their lower cliffs in pale grey shadow, hardly distinguishable from the floating vapour, but gradually ascending till they caught the sunlight, which ran in sharp touches of ruddy colour, along the angular crags, and pierced, in long level rays, through their fringes of spear-like pine. Far above, shot up red splintered masses of castellated rock, jagged and shivered into myriads of fantastic forms, with here and there a streak of sunlit snow, traced down their chasms like a line of forked lightning; and, far beyond, and far above all these, fainter than the morning cloud, but purer and changeless, slept, in the blue sky, the utmost peaks of the eternal snow.

The Golden River, which sprang from one of the lower and snowless elevations, was now nearly in shadow; all but the uppermost jets of spray, which rose like slow smoke above the undulating line of the cataract, and floated away in feeble wreaths upon the morning wind.

On this object, and on this alone, Hans' eyes and thoughts were fixed; forgetting the distance he had to traverse, he set off at an imprudent rate of walking, which greatly exhausted him before he had scaled the first range of the green and low hills. He was, moreover, surprised, on surmounting them, to find that a large glacier, of whose existence, notwithstanding his previous knowledge of the mountains, he had been absolutely ignorant, lay between him and the source of the Golden River. He entered on it with the boldness of a practised mountaineer; yet he thought he had never traversed so strange or so dangerous a glacier in his life. The ice was excessively slippery, and out of all its chasms came wild sounds of gushing water; not monotonous or low, but changeful and loud, rising occasionally into drifting passages of wild melody, then breaking off into short melancholy tones, or sudden shrieks, resembling those of human voices in distress or pain. The ice was broken into thousands of confused shapes, but none, Hans thought, like the ordinary forms of splintered ice. There seemed a curious *expression* about all their outlines —a perpetual resemblance to living features, distorted and scornful. Myriads of deceitful shadows, and lurid lights, played and floated about and through the pale blue pinnacles, dazzling and confusing the sight of the traveller; while his ears grew dull and his head giddy with the constant gush and roar of the concealed waters. These painful circumstances increased upon him as he advanced; the ice crashed and yawned into fresh chasms at his feet, tottering spires nodded around him, and fell thundering across his path; and though he had repeatedly faced these dangers on the most terrific glaciers, and in the wildest weather, it was with a new and oppressive feeling of panic terror that he leaped the last chasm, and flung himself, exhausted and shuddering, on the firm turf of the mountain.

He had been compelled to abandon his basket of food, which became a perilous incumbrance on the glacier, and had now no means of refreshing himself but by breaking off and eating some of the pieces of ice. This, however, relieved his thirst; an hour's repose recruited his hardy frame, and with the indomitable spirit of avarice, he resumed his laborious journey.

His way now lay straight up a ridge of bare red rocks, without a blade of grass to ease the foot, or a projecting angle to afford an inch of shade from the south sun. It was past noon, and the rays beat intensely upon the steep path, while the whole atmosphere was motionless, and penetrated with heat. Intense thirst was soon added to the bodily fatigue with which Hans was now afflicted; glance after glance he cast on the flask of water which hung at his belt. "Three drops are enough," at last thought he; "I may, at least, cool my lips with it."

He opened the flask, and was raising it to his lips, when his eye fell on an object lying on the rock beside him; he thought it moved. It was a small dog, apparently in the last agony of death from thirst. Its tongue was out, its jaws dry, its limbs extended lifelessly, and a swarm of black ants were crawling about its lips and throat. Its eye moved to the bottle which Hans held in his hand. He raised it, drank, spurned the animal with his foot, and passed on. And he did not know how it was, but he thought that a strange shadow had suddenly come across the blue sky.

The path became steeper and more rugged every moment; and the high hill air, instead of refreshing him, seemed to throw his blood into a fever. The noise of the hill cataracts sounded like mockery in his ears; they were all distant, and his thirst increased every moment. Another hour passed, and he again looked down to the flask at his side; it was half empty; but there was much more than three drops in it. He stopped to open it, and again, as he did so, something moved in the path above him.

It was a fair child, stretched nearly lifeless on the rock, its breast heaving with thirst, its eyes closed, and its lips parched and burning. Hans eyed it deliberately, drank, and passed on. And a dark grey cloud came over the sun, and long, snake-like shadows crept up along the mountain sides. Hans struggled on. The sun was sinking, but its descent seemed to bring no coolness; the leaden weight of the dead air pressed upon his brow and heart, but the goal was near. He saw the cataract of the Golden River springing from the hill-side, scarcely five hundred feet above him. He paused for a moment to breathe, and sprang on to complete his task.

At this instant a faint cry fell on his ear. He turned and saw a grey-haired old man extended on the rocks. His eyes were sunk, his features deadly pale, and gathered into an expression of despair. "Water!" he stretched his arms to Hans, and cried feebly, "Water! I am dying."

"I have none," replied Hans; "thou hast had thy share of life." He strode over the prostrate body, and darted on. And a flash of blue lightning rose out of the East, shaped like a sword; it shook thrice over the whole heaven, and left it dark with one heavy, impenetrable shade. The sun was setting; it plunged towards the horizon like a red-hot ball.

The roar of the Golden River rose on Hans' ear. He stood at the brink of the chasm through which it ran.

Its waves were filled with the red glory of the sunset: they shook their crests like tongues of fire, and flashes of bloody light gleamed along their foam. Their sound came mightier and mightier on his senses; his brain grew giddy with the prolonged thunder. Shuddering he drew the flask from his girdle, and hurled it into the center of the torrent.

As he did so, an icy chill shot through his limbs: he staggered, shrieked, and fell. The waters closed over his cry. And the moaning of the river rose wildly into the night, as it gushed over

THE BLACK STONE

Poor little Gluck waited very anxiously alone in the house, for Hans' return. Finding he did not come back, he was terribly frightened, and went and told Schwartz in the prison, all that had happened. Then Schwartz was very much pleased, and said that Hans must certainly have been turned into a black stone, and he should have all the gold to himself. But Gluck was very sorry, and cried all night. When he got up in the morning, there was no bread in the house, nor any money; so Gluck went, and hired himself to another goldsmith, and he worked so hard, and so neatly, and so long every day, that he soon got money enough together to pay his brother's fine; and he went, and gave it all to Schwartz, and Schwartz got out of prison. Then Schwartz was quite pleased, and said he should have some of the gold of the river. But Gluck only begged he would go and see what had become of Hans.

Now when Schwartz had heard that Hans had stolen the holy water, he thought to himself that such a proceeding might not be considered altogether correct by the King of the Golden River, and determined to manage matters better. So he took some more of Gluck's money, and went to a bad man, who gave him some holy water very

readily for it. Then Schwartz was sure it was all
quite right. So Schwartz got up early in the morning before the sun rose, and took some bread and
wine, in a basket, and put his holy water in a flask,
and set off for the mountains. Like his brother he
was much surprised at the sight of the glacier, and
had great difficulty in crossing it, even after leaving his basket behind him. The day was cloudless,
but not bright: there was a heavy purple haze hanging over the sky, and the hills looked lowering and
gloomy. And as Schwartz climbed the steep rock
path, the thirst came upon him, as it had upon his
brother, until he lifted his flask to his lips to drink.
Then he saw the fair child lying near him on the
rocks, and it cried to him, and moaned for water.
Water, indeed," said Schwartz; "I haven't half
enough for myself," and passed on. And as he
went he thought the sunbeams grew more dim, and
he saw a low bank of black cloud rising out of the
West; and, when he had climbed for another hour,
the thirst overcame him again, and he would have
drunk.

Then he saw the old man lying before him
on the path, and heard him cry out for water.
"Water, indeed," said Schwartz, "I haven't half
enough for myself," and on he went.

Then again the light seemed to fade from before
his eyes, and he looked up, and, behold, a mist, of
the colour of blood, had come over the sun; and the
bank of black cloud had risen very high, and its
edges were tossing and tumbling like the waves of
the angry sea. And they cast long shadows, which
flickered over Schwartz's path.

Then Schwartz climbed for another hour, and again his thirst returned; and as lifted his flask to his lips, he thought he saw his brother Hans lying exhausted on the path before him, and, as he gazed, the figure stretched its arms to him, and cried for water. "Ha, ha," laughed Schwartz, "are you there? Remember the prison bars, my boy. Water, indeed! Do you suppose I carried it all the way up here for *you?*"

And he strode over the figure; yet, as he passed, he thought he saw a strange expression of mockery about its lips. And, when he had gone a few yards farther, he looked back; but the figure was not there.

And a sudden horror came over Schwartz, he knew not why; but the thirst for gold prevailed over his fear, and he rushed on. And the bank of black cloud rose to the zenith, and out of it came bursts of spiry lightning, and waves of darkness seemed to heave and float between their flashes, over the whole heavens. And the sky where the sun was setting was all level, and like a lake of blood; and a strong wind came out of that sky, tearing its crimson clouds into fragments, and scattering them far into the darkness. And when Schwartz stood by the brink of the Golden River, its waves were black, like thunder clouds, but their foam was like fire; and the roar of the waters below, and the thunder above met, as he cast the flask into the stream.

And, as he did so, the lightning glared in his eyes, and the earth gave way beneath him, and the waters closed over his cry. And the moaning of the river rose wildly into the night, as it gushed over the

TWO BLACK STONES

When Gluck found that Schwartz did not come back, he was very sorry, and did not know what to do. He had no money, and was obliged to go and hire himself again to the goldsmith, who worked him very hard, and gave him very little money. So, after a month or two Gluck grew tired, and made up his mind to go and try his fortune with the Golden River. "The little king looked very kind," thought he. "I don't think he will turn me into a black stone." So he went to the priest, and the priest gave him some holy water as soon as he asked for it. Then Gluck took some bread in his basket, and the bottle of water, and set off very early for the mountains.

If the glacier had occasioned a great deal of fatigue to his brothers, it was twenty times worse for him, who was neither so strong nor so practised on the mountains. He had several very bad falls, lost his basket and bread, and was very much frightened at the strange noises under the ice. He lay a long time to rest on the grass, after he had got over, and began to climb the hill just in the hottest part of the day. When he had climbed for an hour, he got dreadfully thirsty, and was going to drink like his brothers, when he saw an old man coming down the path above him, looking very feeble, and leaning on a staff. "My son," said the old man, "I am faint with thirst; give me some of

that water." Then Gluck looked at him, and when
he saw that he was pale and weary, he gave him the
water; "Only pray don't drink it all," said Gluck.
But the old man drank a great deal, and gave him
back the bottle two-thirds empty. Then he bade
him good speed, and Gluck went on again merrily.
And the path became easier to his feet, and two
or three blades of grass appeared upon it, and some
grasshoppers began singing on the bank beside it;
and Gluck thought he had never heard such merry
singing.

Then he went on for another hour, and the thirst
increased on him so that he thought he should be
forced to drink. But, as he raised the flask, he saw
a little child lying panting by the road-side, and
it cried out piteously for water. Then Gluck
struggled with himself, and determined to bear the
thirst a little longer; and he put the bottle to the
child's lips, and it drank it all but a few drops.
Then it smiled on him, and got up, and ran down
the hill; and Gluck looked after it, till it became as
small as a little star, and then turned and began
climbing again. And then there were all kinds
of sweet flowers growing on the rocks, bright green
moss, with pale pink starry flowers, and soft belled
gentians, more blue than the sky at its deepest, and
pure white transparent lilies. And crimson and
purple butterflies darted hither and thither, and
the sky sent down such pure light, that Gluck had
never felt so happy in his life.

Yet, when he had climbed for another hour, his
thirst became intolerable again; and, when he
looked at his bottle, he saw that there were only

five or six drops left in it, and he could not venture
to drink. And, as he was hanging the flask to his
belt again, he saw a little dog lying on the rocks,
gasping for breath—just as Hans had seen it on the
day of his ascent. And Gluck stopped and looked
at it, and then at the Golden River, not five hundred yards above him; and he thought of the
dwarf's words, "that no one could succeed, except
in his first attempt"; and he tried to pass the dog,
but it whined piteously, and Gluck stopped again.
"Poor beastie," said Gluck, "it'll be dead when I
come down again, if I don't help it." Then he
looked closer and closer at it, and its eye turned
on him so mournfully, that he could not stand it.
"Confound the king and his gold too," said Gluck;
and he opened the flask, and poured all the water
into the dog's mouth.

The dog sprang up and stood on its hind legs.
Its tail disappeared, its ears became long, longer,
silky, golden; its nose became very red, its eyes
became very twinkling; in three seconds the dog
was gone, and before Gluck stood his old acquaintance, the King of the Golden River.

"Thank you," said the monarch; "but don't be
frightened, it's all right;" for Gluck showed manifest symptoms of consternation at this unlooked-for
reply to his last observation. "Why didn't you
come before," continued the dwarf, "instead of
sending me those rascally brothers of yours, for
me to have the trouble of turning into stones?
Very hard stones they make too."

"Oh dear me!" said Gluck, "have you really
been so cruel?"

THE GOLDEN RIVER

"Cruel!" said the dwarf, "they poured unholy water into my stream: do you suppose I'm going to allow that?"

"Why," said Gluck, "I am sure, sir—your majesty, I mean—they got the water out of the church font."

"Very probably," replied the dwarf; "but," and his countenance grew stern as he spoke, "the water which has been refused to the cry of the weary and dying, is unholy, though it had been blessed by every saint in heaven; and the water which is found in the vessel of mercy is holy, though it had been defiled with corpses."

So saying, the dwarf stooped and plucked a lily that grew at his feet. On its white leaves there hung three drops of clear dew. And the dwarf shook them into the flask which Gluck held in his hand. "Cast these into the river," he said, "and descend on the other side of the mountains into the Treasure Valley. And so good speed."

As he spoke, the figure of the dwarf became indistinct. The playing colours of his robe formed themselves into a prismatic mist of dewy light: he stood for an instant veiled with them as with the belt of a broad rainbow. The colours grew faint, the mist rose into the air; the monarch had evaporated.

And Gluck climbed to the brink of the Golden River, and its waves were as clear as crystal, and as brilliant as the sun. And, when he cast the three drops of dew into the stream, there opened where they fell, a small circular whirlpool, into which the waters descended with a musical noise.

Gluck stood watching it for some time, very

much disappointed, because not only the river was not turned into gold, but its waters seemed much diminished in quantity. Yet he obeyed his friend the dwarf, and descended the other side of the mountains, towards the Treasure Valley; and, as he went, he thought he heard the noise of water working its way under the ground. And, when he came in sight of the Treasure Valley, behold, a river, like the Golden River, was springing from a new cleft of the rocks above it, and was flowing in innumerable streams among the dry heaps of red sand.

And as Gluck gazed, fresh grass sprang beside the new streams, and creeping plants grew, and climbed among the moistening soil. Young flowers opened suddenly along the river sides, as stars leap out when twilight is deepening, and thickets of myrtle, and tendrils of vine, cast lengthening shadows over the valley as they grew. And thus the Treasure Valley became a garden again, and the inheritance, which had been lost by cruelty, was regained by love.

And Gluck went, and dwelt in the valley, and the poor were never driven from his door: so that his barns became full of corn, and his house of treasure. And, for him, the river had, according to the dwarf's promise, become a River of Gold.

And, to this day, the inhabitants of the valley point out the place where the three drops of holy dew were cast into the stream, and trace the course of the Golden River under the ground, until it emerges in the Treasure Valley. And at the top of the cataract of the Golden River, are still to be

seen TWO BLACK STONES, round which the waters
howl mournfully every day at sunset; and these
stones are still called by the people of the valley

THE BLACK BROTHERS

THE TWO GIFTS

By Lillian M. Gask

A HEAVY snow-storm was raging, and great
soft flakes fell through the air like feathers
shaken from the wings of an innumerable host of
angels. By the side of the roadway sat a poor old
woman, her scanty clothing affording but poor
protection from the icy blast of the wind. She was
very hungry, for she had tasted no food that day,
but her faded eyes were calm and patient, telling
of an unwavering trust in Providence. Perhaps,
she thought, some traveller might come that way
who would take compassion on her, and give her
alms; then she could return to the garret that she
called "home," with bread to eat, and fuel to kindle
a fire.

The day drew in, and still she sat and waited.
At last a traveller approached. The thick snow
muffled every sound, and she was not aware of his
coming until his burly figure loomed before her.
Her plaintive voice made him turn with a start.

"Poor woman," he cried, pausing to look at her
very pityingly. "It is hard for you to be out in
such weather as this." Then he passed on, without
giving her anything; his conscience told him that

he ought to have relieved her, but he did not feel inclined to take off his thick glove in that bitter cold, and without doing this he could not have found a coin.

The poor woman was naturally disappointed, but she was grateful for his kind words. By-and-by another traveller appeared. This one was driving in a splendid carriage, warmly wrapped in a great fur cloak. As he caught sight of the poor creature by the roadside, he felt vaguely touched by the contrast of his own comfort with her misery. Obeying a sudden impulse, with one hand he let down the carriage window and signed to his coachman to stop, and with the other felt in his pocket. The poor old woman hurried up to the carriage, a thrill of hope bringing a tinge of colour to her pale and withered cheeks.

"How terribly cold it is!" exclaimed the rich man, and as he took his hand from his pocket, and held out a coin to her, he noticed that instead of silver he was about to give her a piece of gold.

"Dear me! That is far too much," he cried, but before he could return it to his pocket, the coin slipped through his fingers, and fell in the snow. A rough blast of wind made his teeth chatter, and pulling up the window in a great hurry, with a little shiver he drew the fur rug closely round him.

"It certainly was too much," he murmured philosophically, as the carriage rolled on, "but then I am very rich, and can afford to do a generous action now and then."

When his comfortable dinner was over, and he

12-Jun. Cl-6

was sitting in front of a blazing fire, he thought once more of the poor old woman.

"It is not nearly so cold as I thought," he remarked as he settled himself more comfortably in his deep arm-chair. "I certainly gave that old creature too much. However, what's done, is done, and I hope she will make good use of it. I was generous, very generous indeed, and no doubt God will reward me."

Meanwhile the other traveller had also reached his journey's end; and he too had found a blazing fire and good dinner awaiting him. He could not enjoy it, however, for he was haunted by the remembrance of that bent and shrunken figure in the waste of snow, and felt very remorseful for not having stopped to help her. At last he could bear it no longer.

"Bring another plate," he said, calling the servant to him. "There will be two to dine instead of one. I shall be back soon."

Saying this, he hurried through the darkness to the spot where he had left the old woman; she was still there, feebly searching amongst the snow.

"What are you looking for?" he asked.

"I am trying to find a piece of money, which a gentleman threw me from his carriage window," she told him falteringly, scarcely able to speak from cold and hunger. It was no wonder, he thought, that she had not found it, for her hands were numbed and half frozen, and she was not only old, but nearly blind.

"I am afraid you will never find it now," he said. "But come with me," he added consolingly. "I will take you to my inn, where there is a bright fire and a good dinner waiting for both of us. You shall be my guest, and I will see that you have a comfortable night's lodging."

The poor old woman could scarcely believe her good fortune, as she tremblingly prepared to follow her new friend. Noticing that she was lame as well as nearly blind, he took her arm, and with slow and patient steps led her to the hotel.

When the recording angel wrote that night in the Book of Heaven, he made no mention of the piece of gold which the wealthy traveller had given by mistake, for only a worthy motive gains credit in that Book; but amidst the good deeds that had been wrought that day, he gave a foremost place to that of the man who had repented of his hardness, and faced once more the bitter cold that he might share his comforts with a fellow-creature so much less fortunate than himself.

THE BAR OF GOLD

By Lillian M. Gask

LONG years ago there lived a poor labouring man who never knew what it was to sleep in peace. Whether the times were good or bad, he was haunted by fears for the morrow, and this constant worrying caused him to look so thin and worn that the neighbouring farmers hesitated to give him work. He was steady and frugal, and had never been known to waste his time in the village inn, or indulge in foolish pleasures—in fact, a worthier man could not be found, and his friends agreed in saying that he certainly deserved success, though this never came his way.

One day as he sat by the roadside with his head on his hands, a kindly and charitable doctor from the town close by stopped his carriage to ask him what was the matter.

"You seem in trouble, my good man," he said. "Tell me what I can do to help you."

Encouraged by the sympathy in his voice, "Weeping John," as he was called, poured out his woes, to which the doctor listened with much attention.

"If I should fall sick," the poor man finished by saying, "what would happen to my little children, and the wife whom I love more dearly than life itself? They would surely starve, for even as it is they often go hungry to bed. Surely a more unfortunate man has never been born—I toil early and late, and this is my reward." And once more he buried his face in his hands, while bitter sobs shook his ill-clad shoulders.

"Come, come!" said the doctor briskly. "Get up at once, man, and I will do my best for you. I can see that if you do not kill worry, worry will kill you." Helping the poor fellow into his carriage, he told the coachman to drive straight home, and when they arrived at his comfortable mansion, he led him into his surgery.

"See here," he cried, pointing to a shining bar in a glass case, "that bar of gold was bequeathed to me by my father, who was once as poor as you are now. By means of the strictest economy, and hard work, he managed to save sufficient money to purchase this safeguard against want. When it came to me, I, too, was poor, but by following his example, and keeping a brave heart, in cloud and storm as well as sunshine, I have now amassed a fortune that is more than sufficient for my needs. Therefore, I will now hand over to you the bar of gold, since I no longer require it. Its possession will give you confidence for the future. Do not break into it if you can avoid it, and remember that sighing and weeping should be left to weak women and girls."

The labourer thanked him with much fervour, and hiding the bar of gold beneath his coat, sped joyfully homeward.

As he and his wife sat over the fire, which they were now no longer afraid to replenish, he told her all that the good doctor had said, and they agreed that unless the worst came to the worst, they would never touch that bar of gold.

"The knowledge that we have it, safely hidden in the cellar," said his wife, "will keep from us all anxiety. And now, John, you must do your best to make a fortune, so that we may be able to hand it on to our dear children."

From that day John was a changed man. He sang and whistled merrily as he went about his work, and bore himself like a prosperous citizen. His cheeks filled out, and his eye grew bright; no longer did he waste his leisure in lamentations, but dug and planted his little garden until it yielded him richly of the fruits of the earth, and the proceeds helped to swell the silver coins in his good wife's stocking. The farmer who had before employed him when short of hands, was so impressed with his altered looks that he took him permanently into his service, and with regular food and sufficient clothing John's delicate children grew strong and hardy.

"That bar of gold has brought us luck," he would sometimes say blithely to his wife, who held her tongue like a wise woman, although she was tempted to remind him that the "luck" had come since he had given up weeping and lamentations concerning the future.

One summer's evening, long afterwards, as they sat in the wide porch, while their grandchildren played in the meadow beyond, and the lowing of the cows on their peaceful farm mingled with the little people's merry shouts, a stranger came up the pathway and begged for alms. Though torn and tattered, and gaunt with hunger, he had an air of gentleness and refinement, and, full of compassion, the worthy couple invited him in to rest. They set before him the best they had, and when he tried to express his gratitude, John laid his hand on his shoulder.

"My friend," he said, "Providence has been good to us, and blessed the labour of our hands. In times gone by, however, I was as wretched as you appeared to be when you crossed the road, and it is owing to a stranger's kindness that I am in my present position." He went on to tell him of the bar of gold, and, after a long look at his wife, who nodded her head as if well pleased, he went and fetched it from the cellar, where it had lain hidden all these years.

"There!" he exclaimed. "I am going to give it to you. I shall not want it now, and my children are all well settled. It is fitting that you should have it, since your need is very great."

Now the stranger understood the science of metals, for he was a learned man who had fallen on evil times. As he took the gleaming bar in his hands, while murmuring his astonished thanks, he knew by its weight that it was not gold.

"You have made a mistake, my friends," he cried. "This bar is not what you think it, though I own that most men would be deceived."

Greatly surprised, the old woman took it from him, and polished it with her apron in order to show him how brightly it gleamed. As she did so, an inscription appeared, which neither she nor her husband had noticed before. Both listened with great interest as the stranger read it out for them.

"It is less a matter of actual want," it ran, "than the fear of what the morrow will bring, which causes the unhappiness of the poor. Then tread the path of life with courage, for it is clear that at last you will reach the end of your journey."

When the stranger paused there was a dead silence, for the old man and woman were thinking many things, and words do not come quickly when one is deeply moved. At last John offered the stranger a tremulous apology for the disappointment he must now be suffering through their innocent mistake.

"On the contrary," he replied warmly, "the lesson that bar has taught me is worth far more than any money that you could give me. I shall make a new start in life, and, remembering that we fail through fear, will henceforth bear myself as a brave man should."

So saying, he bade them adieu, and passed out into the fragrant twilight.

UNCLE DAVID'S NONSENSICAL STORY

By Catherine Sinclair

IN the days of yore children were not all such clever, good, sensible people as they are now. Lessons were then considered rather a plague, sugar-plums were still in demand, holidays continued yet in fashion, and toys were not then made to teach mathematics, nor story-books to give instruction in chemistry and navigation. These were very strange times, and there existed at that period a very idle, greedy, naughty boy, such as we never hear of in the present day. His father and mother were—no matter who, and he lived—no matter where. His name was Master No-book, and he seemed to think his eyes were made for nothing but to stare out of the windows, and his mouth for no other purpose but to eat. This young gentleman hated lessons like mustard, both of which brought tears into his eyes, and during school hours he sat gazing at his books, pretending to be busy, while his mind wandered away to wish impatiently for dinner, and to consider where he could get the nicest pies, pastry, ices, and jellies, while he smacked his lips at the very thoughts of them.

Whenever Master No-book spoke it was always to ask for something, and you might continually hear him say in a whining tone of voice: "Father, may I take this piece of cake?" "Aunt Sarah, will you give me an apple?" "Mother, do send me the whole of that plum-pudding." Indeed, very frequently, when he did not get permission to gormandize, this naughty glutton helped himself without leave. Even his dreams were like his waking hours, for he had often a horrible nightmare about lessons, thinking he was smothered with Greek lexicons or pelted out of the school with a shower of English grammars, while one night he fancied himself sitting down to devour an enormous plum-cake, and all on a sudden it became transformed into a Latin dictionary.

One afternoon Master No-book, having played truant all day from school, was lolling on his mother's best sofa in the drawing-room with his leather boots tucked up on the satin cushions, and nothing to do but to suck a few oranges, and nothing to think of but how much sugar to put upon them, when suddenly an event took place which filled him with astonishment.

A sound of soft music stole into the room, becoming louder and louder the longer he listened, till at length, in a few moments afterwards, a large hole burst open in the wall of his room, and there stepped into his presence two magnificent fairies, just arrived from their castles in the air, to pay him a visit. They had travelled all the way on purpose to have some conversation with Master No-book, and immediately introduced themselves in a very ceremonious manner.

The fairy Do-nothing was gorgeously dressed with a wreath of flaming gas round her head, a robe of gold tissue, a necklace of rubies, and a bouquet in her hand of glittering diamonds. Her cheeks were rouged to the very eyes, her teeth were set in gold, and her hair was of a most brilliant purple; in short, so fine and fashionable-looking a fairy was never seen in a drawing-room before. The fairy Teach-all, who followed next, was simply dressed in white muslin, with bunches of natural flowers in her light-brown hair, and she carried in her hand a few neat small volumes, which Master No-book looked at with a shudder of aversion.

The two fairies now informed him that they very often invited large parties of children to spend some time at their palaces, but as they lived in quite an opposite direction, it was necessary for their young guests to choose which it would be best to visit first; therefore they had now come to inquire of Master No-book whom he thought it would be most agreeable to accompany on the present occasion.

"In my house," said the fairy Teach-all, speaking with a very sweet smile and a soft, pleasing voice, "you shall be taught to find pleasure in every sort of exertion, for I delight in activity and diligence. My young friends rise at seven every morning, and amuse themselves with working in a beautiful garden of flowers, rearing whatever fruit they wish to eat, visiting among the poor, associating pleasantly together, studying the arts and sciences, and learning to know the world in which they live, and to fulfil the purposes for which they have been brought into it. In short, all our amusements tend to some useful object, either for our own improvement or the good of others, and you will grow wiser, better, and happier every day you remain in the palace of Knowledge."

"But in Castle Needless, where I live," interrupted the fairy Do-nothing, rudely pushing her companion aside with an angry, contemptuous look, "we never think of exerting ourselves for anything. You may put your head in your pocket and your hands in your sides as long as you choose to stay. No one is ever even asked a question, that he may be spared the trouble of answering. We lead the most fashionable life imaginable, for nobody speaks to anybody. Each of my visitors is quite an exclusive, and sits with his back to as many of the company as possible, in the most comfortable arm-chair that can be contrived. There, if you are only so good as to take the trouble of wishing for anything, it is yours without even turning an eye round to look where it comes from. Dresses are provided of the most magnificent kind, which go on themselves, without your having the smallest annoyance with either buttons or strings; games which you can play without an effort of thought; and dishes dressed by a French cook, smoking hot under your nose, from morning till night; while any rain we have is either made of lemonade or lavender-water, and in winter it generally snows iced punch for an hour during the forenoon."

Nobody need be told which fairy Master No-book preferred, and quite charmed at his own good fortune in receiving so agreeable an invitation, he eagerly gave his hand to the splendid new acquaintance who promised him so much pleasure and ease, and gladly proceeded in a carriage lined with velvet, stuffed with downy pillows, and drawn by milk-white swans, to that magnificent residence, Castle Needless, which was lighted by a thousand windows during the day, and by a million of lamps every night.

Here Master No-book enjoyed a constant holiday and a constant feast, while a beautiful lady covered with jewels was ready to tell him stories from morning till night, and servants waited to pick up his playthings if they fell, or to draw out his purse or his pocket-handkerchief when he wished to use them.

Thus Master No-book lay dozing for hours and days on rich embroidered cushions, never stirring from his place, but admiring the view of trees covered with the richest burnt almonds, grottoes of sugar-candy, a *jet d'eau* of champagne, a wide sea which tasted of sugar instead of salt, and a bright, clear pond, filled with gold fish that let themselves be caught whenever he pleased. Nothing could be more complete, and yet, very strange to say, Master No-book did not seem particularly happy. This appears exceedingly unreasonable, when so much trouble was taken to please him; but the truth is that every day he became more fretful and peevish. No sweetmeats were worth the trouble of eating, nothing was pleasant to play at, and in the end he wished it were possible to sleep all day, as well as all night.

Not a hundred miles from the fairy Do-nothing's palace there lived a most cruel monster called the giant Snap-'em-up, who looked, when he stood up, like the tall steeple of a great church, raising his head so high that he could peep over the loftiest mountains, and was obliged to climb up a ladder to comb his own hair.

Every morning regularly this prodigiously great giant walked round the world before breakfast for an appetite, after which he made tea in a large lake, used the sea as a slop-basin, and boiled his kettle on Mount Vesuvius. He lived in great style, and his dinners were most magnificent, consisting very often of an elephant roasted whole, ostrich patties, a tiger smothered in onions, stewed lions, and whale soup; but for a side-dish his greatest favourite consisted of little boys, as fat as possible, fried in crumbs of bread, with plenty of pepper and salt.

No children were so well fed or in such good condition for eating as those in the fairy Do-nothing's garden, who was a very particular friend of the giant Snap-'em-up, and who sometimes laughingly said she would give him a license, and call her own garden his "preserve," because she always allowed him to help himself, whenever he pleased, to as many of her visitors as he chose, without taking the trouble even to count them; and in return for such extreme civility, the giant very frequently invited her to dinner.

Snap-'em-up's favourite sport was to see how many brace of little boys he could bag in a morning; so, in passing along the streets, he peeped into all the drawing-rooms, without having occasion to get upon tiptoe, and picked up every young gentleman who was idly looking out of the windows, and even a few occasionally who were playing truant from school; but busy children seemed always somehow quite out of his reach.

One day, when Master No-book felt even more lazy, more idle, and more miserable than ever, he lay beside a perfect mountain of toys and cakes, wondering what to wish for next, and hating the very sight of everything and everybody. At last he gave so loud a yawn of weariness and disgust that his jaw very nearly fell out of joint, and then he sighed so deeply that the giant Snap-'em-up heard the sound as he passed along the road after breakfast, and instantly stepped into the garden, with his glass at his eye, to see what was the matter. Immediately, on observing a large, fat, overgrown boy, as round as a dumpling, lying on a bed of roses, he gave a cry of delight, followed by a gigantic peal of laughter, which was heard three miles off, and picking up Master No-book between his finger and thumb, with a pinch that very nearly broke his ribs, he carried him rapidly towards his own castle, while the fairy Do-nothing laughingly shook her head as he passed, saying:

"That little man does me a great credit. He has

only been fed for a week, and is as fat already as a prize ox. What a dainty morsel he will be! When do you dine to-day, in case I should have time to look in upon you?"

On reaching home the giant immediately hung up Master No-book by the hair of his head, on a prodigious hook in the larder, having first taken some large lumps of nasty suet, forcing them down his throat to make him become still fatter, and then stirring the fire, that he might be almost melted with heat, to make his liver grow larger. On a shelf quite near Master No-book perceived the bodies of six other boys, whom he remembered to have seen fattening in the fairy Do-nothing's garden, while he recollected how some of them had rejoiced at the thoughts of leading a long, useless, idle life, with no one to please but themselves.

The enormous cook now seized hold of Master No-book, brandishing her knife with an aspect of horrible determination, intending to kill him, while he took the trouble of screaming and kicking in the most desperate manner, when the giant turned gravely round, and said that, as pigs were considered a much greater dainty when whipped to death than killed in any other way, he meant to see whether children might not be improved by it also; therefore she might leave that great hog of a boy till he had time to try the experiment, especially as his own appetite would be improved by the exercise. This was a dreadful prospect for the unhappy prisoner, but meantime it prolonged his life a few hours, as he was immediately hung up in the larder and left to himself. There, in torture of mind and body, like a fish upon a hook, the wretched boy began at last to reflect seriously upon his former ways, and to consider what a happy home he might have had, if he could only have been satisfied with business and pleasure succeeding each other, like day and night, while lessons might have come in as a pleasant sauce to his play-hours, and his play-hours as a sauce to his lessons.

In the midst of many reflections, which were all very sensible, though rather too late, Master No-book's attention became attracted by the sound of many voices laughing, talking, and singing, which caused him to turn his eyes in a new direction, when, for the first time, he observed that the fairy Teach-all's garden lay upon a beautiful sloping bank not far off. There a crowd of merry, noisy, rosy-cheeked boys were busily employed, and seemed happier than the day was long, while poor Master No-book watched them during his own miserable hours, envying the enjoyment with which they raked the flower-borders, gathered the fruit, carried baskets of vegetables to the poor, worked with carpenter's tools, drew pictures, shot with bows-and-arrows, played at cricket, and then sat in the sunny arbours learning their tasks, or talking agreeably together, till at length, a dinner-bell having been rung, the whole party sat merrily down with hearty appetites and cheerful good-humour, to an entertainment of plain roast meat and pudding, where the fairy Teach-all presided herself, and helped her guests moderately to as much as was good for each.

Large tears rolled down the cheeks of Master

No-book while watching this scene, and remembering that if he had known what was best for him, he might have been as happy as the happiest of these excellent boys, instead of suffering ennui and weariness, as he had done at the fairy Do-nothing's, ending in a miserable death. But his attention was soon after most alarmingly roused by hearing the giant Snap-'em-up again in conversation with his cook, who said that, if he wished for a good large dish of scalloped children at dinner, it would be necessary to catch a few more, as those he had already provided would scarcely be a mouthful.

As the giant kept very fashionable hours, and always waited dinner for himself till nine o'clock, there was still plenty of time; so, with a loud grumble about the trouble, he seized a large basket in his hand, and set off at a rapid pace towards the fairy Teach-all's garden. It was very seldom that Snap-'em-up ventured to think of foraging in this direction, as he never once succeeded in carrying off a single captive from the enclosure, it was so well fortified and so bravely defended; but on this occasion, being desperately hungry, he felt as bold as a lion, and walked, with outstretched hands, straight towards the fairy Teach-all's dinner-table, taking such prodigious strides that he seemed almost as if he would trample on himself.

A cry of consternation arose the instant this tremendous giant appeared, and, as usual on such occasions, when he had made the same attempt before, a dreadful battle took place. Fifty active little boys bravely flew upon the enemy, armed with their dinner-knives, and looked like a nest of hornets, stinging him in every direction, till he roared with pain, and would have run away; but the fairy Teach-all, seeing his intention, rushed forward with the carving-knife, and brandishing it high over her head, she most courageously stabbed him to the heart.

If a great mountain had fallen to the earth it would have seemed like nothing in comparison with the giant Snap-'em-up, who crushed two or three houses to powder beneath him, and upset several fine monuments that were to have made people remembered for ever. But all this would have seemed scarcely worth mentioning had it not been for a still greater event which occurred on the occasion, no less than the death of the fairy Do-nothing, who had been indolently looking on at this great battle without taking the trouble to interfere, or even to care who was victorious; but being also lazy about running away, when the giant fell, his sword came with so violent a stroke on her head that she instantly expired.

Thus, luckily for the whole world, the fairy Teach-all got possession of immense property, which she proceeded without delay to make the best use of in her power.

In the first place, however, she lost no time in liberating Master No-book from his hook in the larder, and gave him a lecture on activity, moderation, and good conduct, which he never afterwards forgot; and it was astonishing to see the change that took place immediately in his whole thoughts and actions. From this very hour Master No-book became the most diligent, active, happy boy in the fairy Teach-all's garden; and on returning home a month afterwards, he astonished all the masters at school by his extraordinary reformation. The most difficult lessons were a pleasure to him, he scarcely ever stirred without a book in his hand, never lay on a sofa again, would scarcely even sit on a chair with a back to it, but preferred a three-legged stool, detested holidays, never thought any exertion a trouble, preferred climbing over the top of a hill to creeping round the bottom, always ate the plainest food in very small quantities, joined a temperance society, and never tasted a morsel till he had worked very hard and got an appetite.

Not long after this an old uncle, who had formerly been ashamed of Master No-book's indolence and gluttony, became so pleased at the wonderful change that on his death he left him a magnificent estate, desiring that he should take his name; therefore, instead of being any longer one of the No-book family, he is now called Sir Timothy Blue-stocking, a pattern to the whole country around for the good he does to everyone, and especially for his extraordinary activity, appearing as if he could do twenty things at once. Though generally very good-natured and agreeable, Sir Timothy is occasionally observed in a violent passion, laying about him with his walking-stick in the most terrific manner, and beating little boys within an inch of their lives; but on inquiry it invariably appears that he has found them out to be lazy, idle, or greedy; for all the industrious boys in the parish are sent to get employment from him, while he assures them that they are far happier breaking stones on the road than if they were sitting idly in a drawing-room with nothing to do.

THE GRAND FEAST

By Catherine Sinclair

LADY HARRIET GRAHAM was an extremely thin, delicate, old lady, with a very pale face and a sweet, gentle voice, which the children delighted to hear; for it always spoke kindly to them, and sounded like music, after the loud, rough tones of Mrs. Crabtree. She wore her own gray hair, which had become almost as white as the widow's cap which covered her head. The rest of her dress was generally black velvet, and she usually sat in a comfortable arm-chair by the fireside, watching her grandchildren at play, with a large work-bag by her side, and a prodigious Bible open on the table before her. Lady Harriet often said that it made her young again to see the joyous gambols of Harry and Laura; and when unable any longer to bear their noise, she sometimes kept them quiet by telling them the most delightful stories about what happened to herself when she was young.

Once upon a time, however, Lady Harriet suddenly became so very ill, that Dr. Bell said she must spend a few days in the country, for change of air, and accordingly she determined on passing a quiet week at Holiday House with her relations,

THE GRAND FEAST

Lord and Lady Rockville. Meanwhile, Harry and Laura were to be left under the sole care of Mrs. Crabtree, so it might have been expected that they would both feel more frightened of her, now that she was reigning monarch of the house, than ever. Harry would obey those he loved, if they only held up a little finger; but all the terrors of Mrs. Crabtree, and her cat-o'-nine-tails, were generally forgotten soon after she left the room; therefore he thought little at first about the many threats she held out, if he behaved ill, but he listened most seriously when his dear, sick grandmamma told him, in a faint, weak voice, on the day of her departure from home, how very well he ought to behave in her absence, as no one remained but the maids to keep him in order, and that she hoped Mrs. Crabtree would write her a letter full of good news about his excellent conduct.

Harry felt as if he would gladly sit still without stirring till his grandmamma came back, if that could only please her; and there never was any one more determined to be a good boy than he, at the moment when Lady Harriet's carriage came round to the door. Laura, Frank, and Harry helped to carry all the pillows, boxes, books, and baskets which were necessary for the journey, of which there seemed to be about fifty; then they arranged the cushions as comfortably as possible, and watched very sorrowfully when their grandmamma, after kindly embracing them both, was carefully supported by Major Graham and her own maid Harrison into the chariot. Uncle

375

THE GRAND FEAST

David gave each of the children a pretty picture-book before taking leave, and said, as he was stepping into the carriage, "Now, children, I have only one piece of serious, important advice to give you all, so attend to me! Never crack nuts with your teeth."

When the carriage had driven off, Mrs. Crabtree became so busy scolding Betty, and storming at Jack the footboy, for not cleaning her shoes well enough, that she left Harry and Laura standing in the passage, not knowing exactly what they ought to do first, and Frank, seeing them looking rather melancholy and bewildered at the loss of their grandmamma, stopped a moment as he passed on the way to school, and said in a very kind, affectionate voice:

"Now, Harry and Laura, listen both of you— here is a grand opportunity to show everybody that we can be trusted to ourselves, without getting into any scrapes, so that if grandmamma is ever ill again and obliged to go away, she need not feel so sad and anxious as she did to-day. I mean to become nine times more attentive to my lessons than usual this morning, to show how trustworthy we are, and if you are wise, pray march straight up to the nursery yourselves. I have arranged a gown and cap of Mrs. Crabtree's on the large arm-chair, to look as like herself as possible, that you may be reminded how soon she will come back, and you must not behave like the mice when the cat is out. Good-bye! Say the alphabet backwards, and count your fingers for half an hour; but when Mrs. Crabtree appears again, pray do not jump out of the window for joy."

Harry and Laura were proceeding directly towards the nursery, as Frank had recommended, when unluckily they observed, in passing the drawing-room door, that it was wide open; so Harry peeped in, and they began idly wandering round the tables and cabinets. Not ten minutes elapsed before they both commenced racing about as if they were mad, perfectly screaming with joy, and laughing so loudly at their own funny tricks that an old gentleman who lived next door very nearly sent in a message to ask what the joke was.

Presently Harry and Laura ran up and down stairs till the housemaid was quite fatigued with running after them. They jumped upon the fine damask sofas in the drawing-room, stirred the fire till it was in a blaze, and rushed out on the balcony upsetting one or two geraniums and a myrtle. They spilt Lady Harriet's perfumes over their handkerchiefs,—they looked into all the beautiful books of pictures,—they tumbled many of the pretty Dresden china figures on the floor,—they wound up the little French clock till it was broken,—they made the musical work-box play its tunes, and set the Chinese mandarins a-nodding, till they very nearly nodded their heads off. In short, so much mischief has seldom been done in so short a time, till at last Harry, perfectly worn out with laughing and running, threw himself into a large arm-chair, and Laura, with her ringlets tumbling in frightful confusion over her face, and the beads of her coral necklace rolling on the floor, tossed herself into a sofa beside him.

"Oh what fun!" cried Harry, in an ecstasy of delight. "I wish Frank had been here, and crowds of little boys and girls, to play with us all day! It would be a good joke, Laura, to write and ask all our little cousins and companions to drink tea here to-morrow evening! Their mammas could never guess we had not leave from grandmamma to invite everybody, so I daresay we might gather quite a large party! Oh how enchanting!"

Laura laughed heartily when she heard this proposal of Harry's; and without hesitating a moment about it, she joyously placed herself before Lady Harriet's writing-table, and scribbled a multitude of little notes, in large text, to more than twenty young friends, all of whom had at other times been asked by Lady Harriet to spend the evening with her.

Laura felt very much puzzled to know what was usually said in a card of invitation; but after many consultations, she and Harry thought at last that it was very nicely expressed, for they wrote these words upon a large sheet of paper to each of their friends:

"Master Harry Graham and Miss Laura wish you to have the honor of drinking tea with us to-morrow at six o'clock.
      (Signed)   HARRY and LAURA."

Laura afterwards singed a hole in her muslin frock while lighting one of the vesta matches to seal these numerous notes, and Harry dropped some burning sealing-wax on his hand in the hurry of assisting her; but he thought that little accident no matter, and ran away to see if the cards could be sent off immediately.

Now there lived in the house a very old footman, called Andrew, who remembered Harry and Laura since they were quite little babies; and he often looked exceedingly sad and sorry when they suffered punishment from Mrs. Crabtree. He was ready to do anything in the world when it pleased the children, and would have carried a message to the moon, if they had only shown him the way. Many odd jobs and private messages he had already been employed in by Harry, who now called Andrew upstairs, entreating him to carry out all those absurd notes as fast as possible, and to deliver them immediately, as they were of the greatest consequence. Upon hearing this, old Andrew lost not a moment, but threw on his hat, and instantly started off, looking like the twopenny postman, he carried such a prodigious parcel of invitations; while Harry and Laura stood at the drawing-room window, almost screaming with joy when they saw him set out, and when they observed that, to oblige them, he actually ran along the street at a sort of trot, which was as fast as he could possibly go. Presently, however, he certainly did stop for a single minute, and Laura saw that it was in order to take a peep into one of the notes, that he might ascertain what they were all about; but as he never carried any letters without doing so, she thought that quite natural, and was only very glad when he had finished, and rapidly pursued his way again.

Next morning, Mrs. Crabtree and Betty became very much surprised to observe what a number of smart livery-servants knocked at the street door, and gave in cards; but their astonishment became still greater when old Andrew brought up a whole parcel of them to Harry and Laura, who immediately broke the seals, and read the contents in a corner together.

"What are you about there, Master Graham?" cried Mrs. Crabtree, angrily. "How dare anybody venture to touch your grandmamma's letters?"

"They are not for grandmamma!—they are all for us! every one of them!" answered Harry, dancing about the room with joy, and waving the notes over his head! "Look at this direction! For Master and Miss Graham! put on your spectacles, and read it yourself, Mrs. Crabtree! What delightful fun! the house will be as full as an egg!"

Mrs. Crabtree seemed completely puzzled what to think of all this, and looked so much as if she did not know exactly what to be angry at, and so ready to be in a passion if possible, that Harry burst out a-laughing, while he said, "Only think, Mrs. Crabtree! here is everybody coming to tea with us!—all my cousins, besides Peter Grey, John Stewart, Charles Forrester, Anna Perceval, Diana Wentworth, John Fordyce, Edmund Ashford, Frank Abercromby, Ned Russell, and Tom——"

"The boy is distracted!" exclaimed Betty, staring with astonishment. "What does all this mean, Master Harry?"

"And who gave you leave to invite company into your grandmamma's house?" cried Mrs. Crabtree, snatching up all the notes, and angrily thrusting them into the fire. "I never heard of such doings in all my life before, Master Harry! but as sure as eggs are eggs you shall repent of this, for not one morsel of cake or anything else shall you have to give any of the party; no, not so much as a crust of bread, or a thimbleful of tea!"

Harry and Laura had never thought of such a catastrophe as this before; they always saw a great table covered with everything that could be named for tea, whenever their little friends came to visit them, and whether it rose out of the floor, or was brought by Aladdin's lamp, they never considered it possible that the table would not be provided as usual on such occasions; so this terrible speech of Mrs. Crabtree's frightened them out of their wits. What was to be done? They both knew by experience that she always did what she threatened, or something a great deal worse, so they began by bursting into tears, and begging Mrs. Crabtree for this once to excuse them and to give some cakes and tea to their little visitors; but they might as well have spoken to one of the Chinese mandarins, for she only shook her head with a positive look, declaring over and over again that nothing should appear upon the table except what was always brought up for their own supper—two biscuits and two cups of milk.

THE GRAND FEAST

"Therefore say no more about it!" added she, sternly. "I am your best friend, Master Harry, trying to teach you and Miss Laura your duty; so save your breath to cool your porridge."

Poor Harry and Laura looked perfectly ill with fright and vexation when they thought of what was to happen next, while Mrs. Crabtree sat down to her knitting, grumbling to herself, and dropping her stitches every minute, with rage and irritation. Old Andrew felt exceedingly sorry after he heard what distress and difficulty Harry was in; and when the hour for the party approached, he very good-naturedly spread out a large table in the dining-room, where he put down as many cups, saucers, plates, and spoons as Laura chose to direct; but in spite of all his trouble, though it looked very grand, there was nothing whatever to eat or drink except the two dry biscuits, and the two miserable cups of milk, which seemed to become smaller every time that Harry looked at them.

Presently the clock struck six, and Harry listened to the hour very much as a prisoner would do in the condemned cell in Newgate, feeling that the dreaded time was at last arrived. Soon afterwards several handsome carriages drove up to the door, filled with little masters and misses, who hurried joyfully into the house, talking and laughing all the way upstairs, while poor Harry and Laura almost wished the floor would open and swallow them up; so they shrunk into a distant corner of the room, quite ashamed to show their faces.

THE GRAND FEAST

The young ladies were all dressed in their best frocks, with pink sashes and pink shoes; while the little boys appeared in their holiday clothes, with their hair newly brushed and their faces washed. The whole party had dined at two o'clock, so they were as hungry as hawks, looking eagerly round, whenever they entered, to see what was on the tea-table, and evidently surprised that nothing had yet been put down. Laura and Harry soon afterwards heard their visitors whispering to each other about Norwich buns, rice-cakes, sponge-biscuits, and macaroons; while Peter Grey was loud in praise of a party at George Lorraine's the night before, where an immense plum-cake had been sugared over like a snowstorm, and covered with crowds of beautiful amusing mottoes; not to mention a quantity of noisy crackers that exploded like pistols; besides which, a glass of hot jelly had been handed to each little guest before he was sent home.

Every time the door opened, all eyes were anxiously turned round, expecting a grand feast to be brought in; but quite the contrary—it was only Andrew showing up more hungry visitors; while Harry felt so unspeakably wretched, that, if some kind fairy could only have turned him into a Norwich bun at the moment, he would gladly have consented to be cut in pieces, that his ravenous guests might be satisfied.

Charles Forrester was a particularly good-natured boy, so Harry at last took courage and beckoned him into a remote corner of the room, where he confessed, in whispers, the real state of affairs about tea, and how sadly distressed he and

Laura felt, because they had nothing whatever to give among so many visitors, seeing that Mrs. Crabtree kept her determination of affording them no provisions.

"What is to be done?" said Charles, very anxiously, as he felt extremely sorry for his little friends. "If mamma had been at home, she would gladly have sent whatever you liked for tea, but unluckily she is dining out! I saw a loaf of bread lying on a table at home this evening, which she would make you quite welcome to! Shall I run home, as fast as possible, to fetch it? That would, at any rate, be better than nothing!"

Poor Charles Forrester was very lame; therefore while he talked of running, he could hardly walk; but Lady Forrester's house stood so near that he soon reached home, when, snatching up the loaf, he hurried back towards the street with his prize, quite delighted to see how large and substantial it looked. Scarcely had he reached the door, however, before the housekeeper ran hastily out, saying:

"Stop, Master Charles! stop! sure you are not running away with the loaf for my tea; and the parrot must have her supper too. What do you want with that there bread?"

"Never mind, Mrs. Comfit!" answered Charles, hastening on faster than ever, while he grasped the precious loaf more firmly in his hand, and limped along at a prodigious rate: "Polly is getting too fat, so she will be the better of fasting for one day."

Mrs. Comfit, being enormously fat herself, became very angry at this remark, so she seemed quite desperate to recover the loaf, and hurried forward to overtake Charles; but the old housekeeper was so heavy and breathless, while the young gentleman was so lame, that it seemed an even chance which won the race. Harry stood at his own door, impatiently hoping to receive the prize, and eagerly stretched out his arms to encourage his friend, while it was impossible to say which of the runners might arrive first. Harry had sometimes heard of a race between two old women tied up in sacks, and he thought they could scarcely move with more difficulty; but at the very moment when Charles had reached the door, he stumbled over a stone, and fell on the ground. Mrs. Comfit then instantly rushed up, and, seizing the loaf, she carried it off in triumph, leaving the two little friends ready to cry with vexation, and quite at a loss what plan to attempt next.

Meantime a sad riot had arisen in the diningroom, where the boys called loudly for their tea; and the young ladies drew their chairs all round the table, to wait till it was ready. Still nothing appeared; so everybody wondered more and more how long they were to wait for all the nice cakes and sweetmeats which must, of course, be coming; for the longer they were delayed, the more was expected.

The last at a feast, and the first at a fray, was generally Peter Grey, who now lost patience, and seized one of the two biscuits, which he was in the middle of greedily devouring, when Laura returned with Harry to the dining-room, and observed what he had done.

"Peter Grey," said she, holding up her head, and trying to look very dignified, "you are an exceedingly naughty boy, to help yourself! As a punishment for being so rude, you shall have nothing more to eat all this evening."

"If I do not help myself, nobody else seems likely to give me any supper! I appear to be the only person who is to taste anything to-night," answered Peter, laughing; while the impudent boy took a cup of milk, and drunk it off, saying, "Here's to your very good health, Miss Laura, and an excellent appetite to everybody!"

Upon hearing this absurd speech all the other boys began laughing, and made signs, as if they were eating their fingers off with hunger. Then Peter called Lady Harriet's house "Famine Castle," and pretended he would swallow the knives, like an Indian juggler.

"We must learn to live upon air, and here are some spoons to eat it with," said John Fordyce. "Harry! shall I help you to a mouthful of moonshine?"

"Peter, would you like a roasted fly?" asked Frank Abercromby, catching one on the window. "I daresay it is excellent for hungry people,—or a slice of buttered wall?"

"Or a stewed spider?" asked Peter. "Shall we all be cannibals, and eat one another?"

"What is the use of all those forks, when there is nothing to stick upon them?" asked George Maxwell, throwing them about on the floor. "No buns!—no rruit!—no cakes!—no nothing!"

"What are we to do with those tea-cups, when

there is no tea?" cried Frank Abercromby, pulling the table-cloth, till the whole affair fell prostrate on the floor. After this, these riotous boys tossed the plates in the air, and caught them, becoming at last so outrageous that poor old Andrew called them a "meal mob!" Never was there so much broken china seen in a dining-room before. It all lay scattered on the floor in countless fragments, looking as if there had been a bull in a china-shop, when suddenly Mrs. Crabtree herself opened the door and walked in, with an aspect of rage enough to petrify a milestone. Now old Andrew had long been trying all in his power to render the boys quiet and contented. He had made them a speech,—he had chased the ringleaders all round the room,—and he had thrown his stick at Peter, who seemed the most riotous,—but all in vain; they became worse and worse, laughing into fits, and calling Andrew "the police officer and the bailiff." It was a very different story, however, when Mrs. Crabtree appeared, so flaming with fury she might have blown up a powder-mill.

Nobody could help being afraid of her. Even Peter himself stood stock still, and seemed withering away to nothing when she looked at him; and when she began to scold in her most furious manner, not a boy ventured to look off the ground. A large pair of tawse then became visible in her hand, so every heart sunk with fright, and the riotous visitors began to get behind each other, and to huddle out of sight as much as possible, whispering, and pushing, and fighting, in a desperate scuffle to escape.

"What is all this?" cried she at the full pitch of her voice; "has bedlam broke loose? Who smashed these cups! I'll break his head for him, let me tell you that! Master Peter, you should be hissed out of the world for your misconduct; but I shall certainly whip you round the room like a whipping-top."

At this moment Peter observed that the dining-room window, which was only about six feet from the ground, had been left wide open; so instantly seizing the opportunity, he threw himself out with a single bound, and ran laughing away. All the other boys immediately followed his example, and disappeared by the same road; after which, Mrs. Crabtree leaned far out of the window and scolded loudly, as long as they remained in sight, till her face became red, and her voice perfectly hoarse.

Meantime the little misses sat soberly down before the empty table, and talked in whispers to each other, waiting, till their maids came to take them home, after which they all hurried away as fast as possible, hardly waiting to say "Good-bye!" and intending to ask for some supper at home.

During that night, long after Harry and Laura had been scolded, whipped, and put to bed, they were each heard in different rooms sobbing and crying as if their very hearts would break, while Mrs. Crabtree grumbled and scolded to herself, saying she must do her duty, and make them good children, though she were to flay them alive first.

When Lady Harriet returned home some days afterwards, she heard an account of Harry and Laura's misconduct from Mrs. Crabtree, and the whole story was such a terrible case against them, that their poor grandmamma became perfectly astonished and shocked, while even Uncle David was preparing to be very angry; but before the culprits appeared, Frank most kindly stepped forward, and begged that they might be pardoned for this once, adding all in his power to excuse Harry and Laura, by describing how very penitent they had become, and how very severely they had already been punished.

Frank then mentioned all that Harry had told him about the starving party, which he related with so much humor and drollery that Lady Harriet could not help laughing; so then he saw that a victory had been gained, and ran to the nursery for the two little prisoners.

Uncle David shook his walking-stick at them, and made a terrible face, when they entered; but Harry jumped upon his knee with joy at seeing him again while Laura forgot all her distress, and rushed up to Lady Harriet, who folded her in her arms and kissed her most affectionately.

Not a word was said that day about the tea-party, but next morning Major Graham asked Harry very gravely, "if he had read in the newspaper the melancholy accounts about several of his little companions, who were ill and confined to bed from having eaten too much at a certain tea-party on Saturday last. Poor Peter Grey has been given over; and Charles Forrester, it is feared, may be not able to eat another loaf of bread for a fortnight!"

"Oh, Uncle David, it makes me ill whenever I

think of that party!" said Harry, coloring perfectly scarlet; "that was the most miserable evening of my life!"

"I must say it was not quite fair in Mrs. Crabtree to starve all the strange little boys and girls who came as visitors to my house, without knowing who had invited them," observed Lady Harriet. "Probably those unlucky children will never forget, as long as they live, that scanty supper in our dining-room."

And it turned out exactly as Lady Harriet had predicted; for though they were all asked to tea, in proper form, the very next Saturday, when Major Graham showered torrents of sugar-plums on the table, while the children scrambled to pick them up, and the sideboard almost broke down afterwards under the weight of buns, cakes, cheese-cakes, biscuits, fruit, and preserves, which were heaped upon each other—yet, for years afterwards, Peter Grey, whenever he ate a particularly enormous dinner, always observed, that he must make up for having once been starved at Harry Graham's; and whenever any one of those little boys or girls again happened to meet Harry or Laura, they were sure to laugh and say, "When are you going to give us another

GRAND FEAST?"

THE STORY OF FAIRYFOOT

By Frances Browne

ONCE upon a time there stood far away in
the west country a town called Stumpinghame. It contained seven windmills, a royal palace,
a market place, and a prison, with every other
convenience befitting the capital of a kingdom.
A capital city was Stumpinghame, and its inhabitants thought it the only one in the world. It
stood in the midst of a great plain, which for three
leagues round its walls was covered with corn, flax,
and orchards. Beyond that lay a great circle of
pasture land, seven leagues in breadth, and it was
bounded on all sides by a forest so thick and old
that no man in Stumpinghame knew its extent.

Whether it was the nature of the place or the
people, I cannot tell, but great feet had been the
fashion there time immemorial, and the higher the
family the larger were they. It was, therefore, the
aim of everybody above the degree of shepherds,
and such-like rustics, to swell out and enlarge their
feet by way of gentility; and so successful were
they in these undertakings that, on a pinch, respectable people's slippers would have served for
panniers.

Stumpinghame had a king of its own, and his
name was Stiffstep; his family was very ancient
and large-footed. His subjects called him Lord
of the World, and he made a speech to them every
year concerning the grandeur of his mighty
empire. His queen, Hammerheel, was the greatest

beauty in Stumpinghame. Her majesty's shoe was not much less than a fishing-boat; their six children promised to be quite as handsome, and all went well till the birth of their seventh son.

For a long time nobody about the palace could understand what was the matter — the ladies-in-waiting looked so astonished, and the king so vexed; but at last it was whispered through the city that the queen's seventh child had been born with such miserably small feet that they resembled nothing ever seen or heard of in Stumpinghame, except the feet of the fairies.

The chronicles furnished no example of such an affliction ever before happening in the royal family.

The common people thought it portended some great calamity to the city; the learned men began to write books about it; and all the relations of the king and queen assembled at the palace to mourn with them over their singular misfortune. The whole court and most of the citizens helped in this mourning, but when it had lasted seven days they all found out it was of no use. So the relations went to their homes, and the people took to their work. If the learned men's books were written, nobody ever read them; and to cheer up the queen's spirits, the young prince was sent privately out to the pasture lands, to be nursed among the shepherds.

The chief man there was called Fleecefold, and his wife's name was Rough Ruddy. They lived in a snug cottage with their son Blackthorn and their daughter Brownberry, and were thought great people, because they kept the king's sheep.

Moreover, Fleecefold's family were known to be ancient; and Rough Ruddy boasted that she had the largest feet in all the pastures. The shepherds held them in high respect, and it grew still higher when the news spread that the king's seventh son had been sent to their cottage. People came from all quarters to see the young prince, and great were the lamentations over his misfortune in having such small feet.

The king and queen had given him fourteen names, beginning with Augustus—such being the fashion in that royal family; but the honest country people could not remember so many; besides, his feet were the most remarkable thing about the child, so with one accord they called him Fairyfoot. At first it was feared this might be high treason, but when no notice was taken by the king or his ministers, the shepherds concluded it was no harm, and the boy never had another name throughout the pastures. At court it was not thought polite to speak of him at all. They did not keep his birthday, and he was never sent for at Christmas, because the queen and her ladies could not bear the sight. Once a year the undermost scullion was sent to see how he did, with a bundle of his next brother's cast-off clothes; and, as the king grew old and cross, it was said he had thoughts of disowning him.

So Fairyfoot grew in Fleecefold's cottage. Perhaps the country air made him fair and rosy—for all agreed that he would have been a handsome boy but for his small feet, with which nevertheless he learned to walk, and in time to run and to jump, thereby amazing everybody, for such doings were not known among the children of Stumpinghame. The news of court, however, travelled to the shepherds, and Fairyfoot was despised among them. The old people thought him unlucky; the children refused to play with him. Fleecefold was ashamed to have him in his cottage, but he durst not disobey the king's orders. Moreover, Blackthorn wore most of the clothes brought by the scullion. At last, Rough Ruddy found out that the sight of such horrid jumping would make her children vulgar; and, as soon as he was old enough, she sent Fairyfoot every day to watch some sickly sheep that grazed on a wild, weedy pasture, hard by the forest.

Poor Fairyfoot was often lonely and sorrowful; many a time he wished his feet would grow larger, or that people wouldn't notice them so much; and all the comfort he had was running and jumping by himself in the wild pasture, and thinking that none of the shepherds' children could do the like, for all their pride of their great feet.

Tired of this sport, he was lying in the shadow of a mossy rock one warm summer's noon, with the sheep feeding around, when a robin, pursued by a great hawk, flew into the old velvet cap which lay on the ground beside him. Fairyfoot covered it up, and the hawk, frightened by his shout, flew away.

"Now you may go, poor robin!" he said, opening the cap: but instead of the bird, out sprang a little man dressed in russet-brown, and looking as if he were an hundred years old. Fairyfoot could not speak for astonishment, but the little man said—

"Thank you for your shelter, and be sure I will do as much for you. Call on me if you are ever in trouble; my name is Robin Goodfellow;" and darting off, he was out of sight in an instant. For days the boy wondered who that little man could be, but he told nobody, for the little man's feet were as small as his own, and it was clear he would be no favourite in Stumpinghame. Fairyfoot kept the story to himself, and at last midsummer came. That evening was a feast among the shepherds. There were bonfires on the hills, and fun in the villages. But Fairyfoot sat alone beside his sheepfold, for the children of his village had refused to let him dance with them about the bonfire, and he had gone there to bewail the size of his feet, which came between him and so many good things. Fairyfoot had never felt so lonely in all his life, and remembering the little man, he plucked up spirit, and cried—

"Ho! Robin Goodfellow!"

"Here I am," said a shrill voice at his elbow; and there stood the little man himself.

"I am very lonely, and no one will play with me, because my feet are not large enough," said Fairyfoot.

"Come then and play with us," said the little man. "We lead the merriest lives in the world, and care for nobody's feet; but all companies have their own manners, and there are two things you must mind among us; first, do as you see the rest doing; and secondly, never speak of anything you may hear or see, for we and the people of this country have had no friendship ever since large feet came in fashion."

"I will do that, and anything more you like," said Fairyfoot; and the little man taking his hand, led him over the pasture into the forest, and along a mossy path among old trees wreathed with ivy (he never knew how far), till they heard the sound of music, and came upon a meadow where the moon shone as bright as day, and all the flowers of the year—snowdrops, violets, primroses, and cowslips —bloomed together in the thick grass. There were a crowd of little men and women, some clad in russet colour, but far more in green, dancing round a little well as clear as crystal. And under great rose-trees which grew here and there in the meadow, companies were sitting round low tables covered with cups of milk, dishes of honey, and carved wooden flagons filled with clear red wine. The little man led Fairyfoot up to the nearest table, handed him one of the flagons, and said—

"Drink to the good company!"

Wine was not very common among the shepherds of Stumpinghame, and the boy had never tasted such drink as that before; for scarcely had it gone down, when he forgot all his troubles—how Blackthorn and Brownberry wore his clothes, how Rough Ruddy sent him to keep the sickly sheep, and the children would not dance with him: in short, he forgot the whole misfortune of his feet, and it seemed to his mind that he was a king's son, and all was well with him. All the little people about the well cried—

"Welcome! welcome!" and every one said—
"Come and dance with me!" So Fairyfoot was as
happy as a prince, and drank milk and ate honey
till the moon was low in the sky.

Next morning Fairyfoot was not tired for all his
dancing. Nobody in the cottage had missed him,
and he went out with the sheep as usual; but every
night all that summer, when the shepherds were
safe in bed, the little man came and took him away
to dance in the forest. Now he did not care to play
with the shepherds' children, nor grieve that his
father and mother had forgotten him, but watched
the sheep all day, singing to himself or plaiting
rushes.

The wonder was that he was never tired nor
sleepy, as people are apt to be who dance all night;
but before the summer was ended Fairyfoot found
out the reason. One night, when the moon was full,
and the last of the ripe corn rustling in the fields,
Robin Goodfellow came for him as usual, and away
they went to the flowery green. The fun there was
high, and Robin was in haste. So he only pointed
to the carved cup from which Fairyfoot every night
drank the clear red wine.

"I am not thirsty, and there is no use losing time,"
thought the boy to himself, and he joined the dance;
but never in all his life did Fairyfoot find such hard
work as to keep pace with the company. Their feet
seemed to move like lightning; the swallows did not
fly so fast or turn so quickly. Fairyfoot did his
best, for he never gave in easily, but at length, his
breath and strength being spent, the boy was glad
to steal away, and sit down behind a mossy oak,

where his eyes closed for very weariness. When he awoke the dance was nearly over, but two little ladies clad in green talked close beside him.

"What a beautiful boy!" said one of them. "He is worthy to be a king's son. Only see what handsome feet he has!"

"Yes," said the other, with a laugh that sounded spiteful; "they are just like the feet Princess Maybloom had before she washed them in the Growing Well. Her father has sent far and wide throughout the whole country searching for a doctor to make them small again, but nothing in this world can do it except the water of the Fair Fountain, and none but I and the nightingales know where it is."

"One would not care to let the like be known," said the first little lady: "there would come such crowds of these great coarse creatures of mankind, nobody would have peace for leagues round. But you will surely send word to the sweet princess!— she was so kind to our birds and butterflies, and danced so like one of ourselves!"

"Not I, indeed!" said the spiteful fairy. "Her old skinflint of a father cut down the cedar which I loved best in the whole forest, and made a chest of it to hold his money in; besides, I never liked the princess—everybody praised her so. But come, we shall be too late for the last dance."

When they were gone, Fairyfoot could sleep no more with astonishment. He did not wonder at the fairies admiring his feet, because their own were much the same; but it amazed him that Princess Maybloom's father should be troubled at hers growing large. Moreover, he wished to see that same princess and her country, since there were really other places in the world than Stumpinghame.

When Robin Goodfellow came to take him home as usual he durst not let him know that he had overheard anything; but never was the boy so unwilling to get up as on that morning, and all day he was so weary that in the afternoon Fairyfoot fell asleep, with his head on a clump of rushes. It was seldom that any one thought of looking after him and the sickly sheep; but it so happened that towards evening the old shepherd, Fleecefold, thought he would see how things went on in the pastures. The shepherd had a bad temper and a thick staff, and no sooner did he catch sight of Fairyfoot sleeping, and his flock straying away, than shouting all the ill names he could remember, in a voice which woke up the boy, he ran after him as fast as his great feet would allow; while Fairyfoot, seeing no other shelter from his fury, fled into the forest, and never stopped nor stayed till he reached the banks of a little stream.

Thinking it might lead him to the fairies' dancing-ground, he followed that stream for many an hour, but it wound away into the heart of the forest, flowing through dells, falling over mossy rocks and at last leading Fairyfoot, when he was tired and the night had fallen, to a grove of great rose-trees, with the moon shining on it as bright as day, and thousands of nightingales singing in the branches. In the midst of that grove was a clear spring, bordered with banks of lilies, and Fairyfoot sat down by it to rest himself and listen. The singing was so sweet he could have listened for ever, but as he sat the nightingales left off their songs, and began to talk together in the silence of the night—

"What boy is that," said one on a branch above him, "who sits so lonely by the Fair Fountain? He cannot have come from Stumpinghame with such small and handsome feet."

"No, I'll warrant you," said another, "he has come from the west country. How in the world did he find the way?"

"How simple you are!" said a third nightingale. "What had he to do but follow the ground-ivy which grows over height and hollow, bank and bush, from the lowest gate of the king's kitchen garden to the root of this rose-tree? He looks a wise boy, and I hope he will keep the secret, or we shall have all the west country here, dabbling in our fountain, and leaving us no rest to either talk or sing."

Fairyfoot sat in great astonishment at this discourse, but by and by, when the talk ceased and the songs began, he thought it might be as well for him to follow the ground-ivy, and see the Princess Maybloom, not to speak of getting rid of Rough Ruddy, the sickly sheep, and the crusty old shepherd. It was a long journey; but he went on, eating wild berries by day, sleeping in the hollows of old trees by night, and never losing sight of the ground-ivy, which led him over height and hollow, bank and bush, out of the forest, and along a noble high road, with fields and villages on every side, to a great city, and a low old-fashioned gate of the king's kitchen-garden, which was thought too mean for the scullions, and had not been opened for seven years.

There was no use knocking—the gate was overgrown with tall weeds and moss; so, being an active boy, he climbed over, and walked through the garden, till a white fawn came frisking by, and he heard a soft voice saying sorrowfully—

"Come back, come back, my fawn! I cannot run and play with you now, my feet have grown so heavy;" and looking round he saw the loveliest young princess in the world, dressed in snow-white, and wearing a wreath of roses on her golden hair; but walking slowly, as the great people did in Stumpinghame, for her feet were as large as the best of them.

After her came six young ladies, dressed in white and walking slowly, for they could not go before the princess; but Fairyfoot was amazed to see that their feet were as small as his own. At once he guessed that this must be the Princess Maybloom, and made her an humble bow, saying—

"Royal princess, I have heard of your trouble because your feet have grown large: in my country that's all the fashion. For seven years past I have been wondering what would make mine grow, to no purpose; but I know of a certain fountain that will make yours smaller and finer than ever they were, if the king, your father, gives you leave to come with me, accompanied by two of your maids that are the least given to talking, and the most prudent officer in all his household; for it would grievously offend the fairies and the nightingales to make that fountain known."

When the princess heard that, she danced for joy
in spite of her large feet, and she and her six maids
brought Fairyfoot before the king and queen,
where they sat in their palace hall, with all the
courtiers paying their morning compliments. The
lords were very much astonished to see a ragged,
bare-footed boy brought in among them, and the
ladies thought Princess Maybloom must have gone
mad; but Fairyfoot, making an humble reverence,
told his message to the king and queen, and offered
to set out with the princess that very day. At first
the king would not believe that there could be any
use in his offer, because so many great physicians
had failed to give any relief. The courtiers laughed
Fairyfoot to scorn, the pages wanted to turn him
out for an impudent impostor, and the prime-
minister said he ought to be put to death for high-
treason.

Fairyfoot wished himself safe in the forest again,
or even keeping the sickly sheep; but the queen,
being a prudent woman, said—

"I pray your majesty to notice what fine feet
this boy has. There may be some truth in his story.
For the sake of our only daughter, I will choose two
maids who talk the least of all our train, and my
chamberlain, who is the most discreet officer in our
household. Let them go with the princess: who
knows but our sorrow may be lessened?"

After some persuasion the king consented, though
all his councillors advised the contrary. So the
two silent maids, the discreet chamberlain, and her
fawn, which would not stay behind, were sent with
Princess Maybloom, and they all set out after din-

ner. Fairyfoot had hard work guiding them along
the track of the ground-ivy. The maids and the
chamberlain did not like the brambles and rough
roots of the forest—they thought it hard to eat
berries and sleep in hollow trees; but the princess
went on with good courage, and at last they reached
the grove of rose-trees, and the spring bordered
with lilies.

The chamberlain washed—and though his hair
had been grey, and his face wrinkled, the young
courtiers envied his beauty for years after. The
maids washed—and from that day they were
esteemed the fairest in all the palace. Lastly, the
princess washed also—it could make her no fairer,
but the moment her feet touched the water they
grew less, and when she had washed and dried them
three times, they were as small and finely-shaped
as Fairyfoot's own. There was great joy among
them, but the boy said sorrowfully—

"Oh! if there had been a well in the world to
make my feet large, my father and mother would
not have cast me off, nor sent me to live among the
shepherds."

"Cheer up your heart," said the Princess Maybloom; "if you want large feet, there is a well in this
forest that will do it. Last summer time, I came
with my father and his foresters to see a great cedar
cut down, of which he meant to make a money
chest. While they were busy with the cedar, I saw
a bramble branch covered with berries. Some were
ripe and some were green, but it was the longest
bramble that ever grew; for the sake of the berries,
I went on and on to its root, which grew hard by

a muddy-looking well, with banks of dark green moss, in the deepest part of the forest. The day was warm and dry, and my feet were sore with the rough ground, so I took off my scarlet shoes, and washed my feet in the well; but as I washed they grew larger every minute, and nothing could ever make them less again. I have seen the bramble this day; it is not far off, and as you have shown me the Fair Fountain, I will show you the Growing Well."

Up rose Fairyfoot and Princess Maybloom, and went together till they found the bramble, and came to where its root grew, hard by the muddy-looking well with banks of dark green moss, in the deepest dell of the forest. Fairyfoot sat down to wash, but at that minute he heard a sound of music, and knew it was the fairies going to their dancing ground.

"If my feet grow large," said the boy to himself, "how shall I dance with them?" So, rising quickly, he took the Princess Maybloom by the hand. The fawn followed them; the maids and the chamberlain followed it, and all followed the music through the forest. At last they came to the flowery green. Robin Goodfellow welcomed the company for Fairyfoot's sake, and gave every one a drink of the fairies' wine. So they danced there from sunset till the grey morning, and nobody was tired; but before the lark sang, Robin Goodfellow took them all safe home, as he used to take Fairyfoot.

There was great joy that day in the palace because Princess Maybloom's feet were made small again. The king gave Fairyfoot all manner of fine clothes and rich jewels; and when they heard his wonderful story, he and the queen asked him to live with them and be their son. In process of time Fairyfoot and Princess Maybloom were married, and still live happily. When they go to visit at Stumpinghame, they always wash their feet in the Growing Well, lest the royal family might think them a disgrace, but when they come back, they make haste to the Fair Fountain; and the fairies and the nightingales are great friends to them, as well as to the maids and the chamberlain, because they have told nobody about it, and there is peace and quiet yet in the grove of rose-trees.

ALICE IN WONDERLAND

Few books have given more real pleasure to young people than "Alice in Wonderland," by Charles L. Dodgson, a professor of mathematics in Oxford University, who signed his stories Lewis Carroll. He was always a great favorite with the children, from the time he began acting little plays in a little theatre for his nine brothers and sisters, and up to the time of his death in 1898 there were hundreds of happy boys and girls, but mostly girls, who delighted to call him friend.

"Through the Looking-Glass" is a continuation of "Alice in Wonderland."

DOWN THE RABBIT-HOLE

By Lewis Carroll

ALICE was beginning to get very tired of sitting by her sister on the bank, and of having nothing to do: once or twice she had peeped into the book her sister was reading, but it had no pictures or conversations in it, "and what is the use of a book," thought Alice, "without pictures or conversations?"

So she was considering, in her own mind (as well as she could, for the hot day made her feel very sleepy and stupid), whether the pleasure of making a daisy-chain would be worth the trouble of getting up and picking the daisies, when suddenly a White Rabbit with pink eyes ran close by her.

There was nothing so *very* remarkable in that; nor did Alice think it so *very* much out of the way to hear the Rabbit say to itself, "Oh dear! Oh dear! I shall be too late!" (when she thought it over afterward, it occurred to her that she ought to have wondered at this, but at the time it all seemed quite natural); but, when the Rabbit actually *took a watch out of its waistcoat-pocket,* and looked at it, and then hurried on, Alice started to her feet, for it flashed across her mind that she had never before seen a rabbit with either a waistcoat-pocket, or a watch to take out of it, and, burning with curiosity, she ran across the field after it, and was just in time to see it pop down a large rabbit-hole under the hedge.

In another moment down went Alice after it, never once considering how in the world she was to get out again.

The rabbit-hole went straight on like a tunnel for some way, and then dipped suddenly down, so suddenly that Alice had not a moment to think about stopping herself before she found herself falling down what seemed to be a very deep well.

Either the well was very deep, or she fell very slowly, for she had plenty of time as she went down to look about her, and to wonder what was going to happen next. First, she tried to look down and make out what she was coming to, but it was too dark to see anything: then she looked at the sides of the well, and noticed that they were filled with cupboards and book-shelves: here and there she saw maps and pictures hung upon pegs. She took down a jar from one of the shelves as she passed: it was labeled "ORANGE MARMALADE," but to her great disappointment it was empty: she did not like to drop the jar, for fear of killing somebody underneath, so managed to put it into one of the cupboards as she fell past it.

"Well!" thought Alice to herself. "After such a fall as this, I shall think nothing of tumbling downstairs! How brave they'll all think me at home! Why, I wouldn't say anything about it, even if I fell off the top of the house!" (Which was very likely true.)

Down, down, down. Would the fall *never* come

to an end? "I wonder how many miles I've fallen by this time?" she said aloud. "I must be getting somewhere near the centre of the earth. Let me see: that would be four thousand miles down, I think—" (for, you see, Alice had learned several things of this sort in her lessons in the school-room, and though this was not a *very* good opportunity for showing off her knowledge, as there was no one to listen to her, still it was good practice to say it over) "—yes, that's about the right distance—but then I wonder what Latitude or Longitude I've got to?" (Alice had not the slightest idea what Latitude was, or Longitude either, but she thought they were nice grand words to say).

Presently she began again. "I wonder if I shall fall right *through* the earth! How funny it'll seem to come out among the people that walk with their heads downward! The antipathies, I think—" (she was rather glad there *was* no one listening, this time, as it didn't sound at all the right word) "—but I shall have to ask them what the name of the country is, you know. Please, Ma'am, is this New Zealand? Or Australia?" (and she tried to curtsey as she spoke—fancy, *curtseying* as you're falling through the air! Do you think you could manage it?) "And what an ignorant little girl she'll think me for asking! No, it'll never do to ask: perhaps I shall see it written up somewhere."

Down, down, down. There was nothing else to do, so Alice soon began talking again. "Dinah'll miss me very much to-night, I should think!" (Dinah was the cat.) "I hope they'll remember her saucer of milk at tea-time. Dinah, my dear! I wish you were down here with me! There are no mice in the air, I'm afraid, but you might catch a bat, and that's very like a mouse, you know. But do cats eat bats, I wonder?" And here Alice began to get rather sleepy, and went on saying to herself, in a dreamy sort of way, "Do cats eat bats? Do cats eat bats?" and sometimes, "Do bats eat cats?" for, you see, as she couldn't answer either question, it didn't much matter which way she put it. She felt that she was dozing off, and had just begun to dream that she was walking hand in hand with Dinah, and was saying to her, very earnestly, "Now, Dinah, tell me the truth: did you ever eat a bat?" when suddenly, thump! thump! down she came upon a heap of sticks and dry leaves, and the fall was over.

Alice was not a bit hurt, and she jumped up on to her feet in a moment: she looked up, but it was all dark overhead: before her was another long passage, and the White Rabbit was still in sight, hurrying down it. There was not a moment to be lost: away went Alice like the wind, and was just in time to hear it say, as it turned a corner, "Oh my ears and whiskers, how late it's getting!" She was close behind it when she turned the corner, but the Rabbit was no longer to be seen: she found herself in a long, low hall, which was lit up by a row of lamps hanging from the roof.

There were doors all round the hall, but they were all locked; and when Alice had been all the way down one side and up the other, trying every door, she walked sadly down the middle, wondering how she was ever to get out again.

DOWN THE RABBIT-HOLE

Suddenly she came upon a little three-legged table, all made of solid glass: there was nothing on it but a tiny golden key, and Alice's first idea was that this might belong to one of the doors of the hall; but alas! either the locks were too large, or the key was too small, but at any rate it would not open any of them. However, on the second time round, she came upon a low curtain she had not noticed before, and behind it was a little door about fifteen inches high: she tried the little golden key in the lock, and to her great delight it fitted!

Alice opened the door and found that it led into a small passage, not much larger than a rat-hole: she knelt down and looked along the passage into the loveliest garden you ever saw. How she longed to get out of that dark hall, and wander about among those beds of bright flowers and those cool fountains, but she could not even get her head through the doorway; "and even if my head *would* go through," thought poor Alice, "it would be of very little use without my shoulders. Oh, how I wish I could shut up like a telescope! I think I could, if I only knew how to begin." For, you see, so many out-of-the-way things had happened lately, that Alice had begun to think that very few things indeed were really impossible.

There seemed to be no use in waiting by the little door, so she went back to the table, half hoping she might find another key on it, or at any rate a book of rules for shutting people up like telescopes: this time she found a little bottle on it ("which certainly was not here before," said Alice), and tied round the neck of the bottle was a paper label, with the

413

words "DRINK ME" beautifully printed on it in large letters.

It was all very well to say "Drink me," but the wise little Alice was not going to do *that* in a hurry. "No, I'll look first," she said, "and see whether it's marked '*poison*' or not"; for she had read several nice little stories about children who had got burned, and eaten up by wild beasts, and other unpleasant things, all because they *would* not remember the simple rules their friends had taught them: such as, that a red-hot poker will burn you if you hold it too long; and that, if you cut your finger *very* deeply with a knife, it usually bleeds; and she had never forgotten that, if you drink much from a bottle marked "poison," it is almost certain to disagree with you, sooner or later.

However, this bottle was *not* marked "poison," so Alice ventured to taste it, and, finding it very nice (it had, in fact, a sort of mixed flavor of cherry-tart, custard, pine-apple, roast turkey, toffy, and hot buttered toast), she very soon finished it off.

*　　*　　*　　*　　*　　*

"What a curious feeling!" said Alice. "I must be shutting up like a telescope!"

And so it was indeed: she was now only ten inches high, and her face brightened up at the thought that she was now the right size for going through the little door into that lovely garden. First, however, she waited for a few minutes to see if she was going to shrink any further: she felt a little nervous about this; "for it might end, you know," said Alice to herself, "in my going out altogether, like a candle. I wonder what I should be like then?" And she tried to fancy what the flame of a candle looks like after the candle is blown out, for she could not remember ever having seen such a thing.

After a while, finding that nothing more happened, she decided on going into the garden at once; but, alas for poor Alice! when she got to the door, she found she had forgotten the little golden key, and when she went back to the table for it, she found she could not possibly reach it: she could see it quite plainly through the glass, and she tried her best to climb up one of the legs of the table, but it was too slippery; and when she had tired herself out with trying, the poor little thing sat down and cried.

"Come, there's no use in crying like that!" said Alice to herself rather sharply. "I advise you to leave off this minute!" She generally gave herself very good advice (though she very seldom followed it), and sometimes she scolded herself so severely as to bring tears into her eyes; and once she remembered trying to box her own ears for having cheated herself in a game of croquet she was playing against herself, for this curious child was very fond of pretending to be two people. "But it's no use now," thought poor Alice, "to pretend to be two people! Why, there's hardly enough of me left to make *one* respectable person!"

Soon her eye fell on a little glass box that was lying under the table: she opened it, and found in it a very small cake, on which the words "EAT ME" were beautifully marked in currants. "Well, I'll eat it," said Alice, "and if it makes me grow larger, I can reach the key; and if it makes me grow smaller, I can creep under the door: so either way I'll get into the garden, and I don't care which happens!"

She ate a little bit, and said anxiously to herself, "Which way? Which way?" holding her hand on the top of her head to feel which way it was growing; and she was quite surprised to find that she remained the same size. To be sure, this is what generally happens when one eats cake; but Alice had got so much into the way of expecting nothing but out-of-the-way things to happen, that it seemed quite dull and stupid for life to go on in the common way.

So she set to work, and very soon finished off the cake.

* * * * * *

THE POOL OF TEARS

By Lewis Carroll

"CURIOUSER and curiouser!" cried Alice (she was so much surprised, that for the moment she quite forgot how to speak good English). "Now I'm opening out like the largest telescope that ever was! Good-by, feet!" (for when she looked down at her feet, they seemed to be almost out of sight, they were getting so far off). "Oh, my poor little feet, I wonder who will put on your shoes and stockings for you now, dears? I'm sure *I* shan't be able! I shall be a great deal too far off to trouble myself about you: you must manage the best way you can—but I must be kind to them," thought Alice, "or perhaps they won't walk the way I want to go! Let me see. I'll give them a new pair of boots every Christmas."

And she went on planning to herself how she would manage it. "They must go by the carrier," she thought; "and how funny it'll seem, sending presents to one's own feet! And how odd the directions will look!

> *Alice's Right Foot, Esq.,*
> *Hearthrug,*
> *near the Fender,*
> *(with Alice's love).*

Oh dear, what nonsense I'm talking!"

Just at this moment her head struck against the roof of the hall: in fact she was now rather more than nine feet high, and she at once took up the little golden key and hurried off to the garden door.

Poor Alice! It was as much as she could do, lying down on one side, to look through into the garden with one eye; but to get through was more hopeless than ever: she sat down and began to cry again.

"You ought to be ashamed of yourself," said Alice, "a great girl like you" (she might well say this), "to go on crying in this way! Stop this moment, I tell you!"

But she went on all the same, shedding gallons of tears, until there was a large pool all round her, about four inches deep, and reaching half down the hall.

After a time she heard a little pattering of feet

in the distance, and she hastily dried her eyes to see
what was coming. It was the White Rabbit returning, splendidly dressed, with a pair of white
kid-gloves in one hand and a large fan in the other:
he came trotting along in a great hurry, muttering
to himself, as he came, "Oh! The Duchess, the
Duchess! Oh! *Won't* she be savage if I've kept
her waiting!"

Alice felt so desperate that she was ready to
ask help of any one: so, when the Rabbit came
near her, she began, in a low, timid voice, "If
you please, Sir—" The Rabbit started violently,
dropped the white kid-gloves and the fan, and
skurried away into the darkness as hard as he
could go.

Alice took up the fan and gloves, and, as the hall
was very hot, she kept fanning herself all the time
she went on talking. "Dear, dear! How queer
everything is to-day! And yesterday things went
on just as usual. I wonder if I've been changed
in the night? Let me think: *was* I the same when
I got up this morning? I almost think I can remember feeling a little different. But if I'm not
the same, the next question is, 'Who in the world
am I?' Ah, *that's* the great puzzle!"

And she began thinking over all the children
she knew that were of the same age as herself,
to see if she could have been changed for any of
them.

"I'm sure I'm not Ada," she said, "for her hair
goes in such long ringlets, and mine doesn't go in
ringlets at all; and I'm sure I can't be Mabel, for
I know all sorts of things, and she, oh, she knows

such a very little! Besides, *she's* she, and *I'm* I, and—oh dear, how puzzling it all is! I'll try if I know all the things I used to know. Let me see: four times five is twelve, and four times six is thirteen, and four times seven is—oh dear! I shall never get to twenty at that rate! However, the Multiplication-Table doesn't signify: let's try Geography. London is the capital of Paris, and Paris is the capital of Rome, and Rome—no, *that's* all wrong, I'm certain! I must have been changed for Mabel! I'll try and say '*How doth the little—,*' " and she crossed her hands on her lap, as if she were saying lessons, and began to repeat it, but her voice sounded hoarse and strange, and the words did not come the same as they used to do:—

> "How doth the little crocodile
>   Improve his shining tail,
> And pour the waters of the Nile
>   On every golden scale!
>
> "How cheerfully he seems to grin,
>   How neatly spreads his claws,
> And welcomes little fishes in
>   With gently smiling jaws!"

"I'm sure those are not the right words," said poor Alice, and her eyes filled with tears again as she went on, "I must be Mabel after all, and I shall have to go and live in that poky little house, and have next to no toys to play with, and oh, ever so many lessons to learn! No, I've made up my mind about it: if I'm Mabel, I'll stay down here! It'll be no use their putting their heads down and saying, 'Come up again, dear!' I shall only look up

14-Jun. Cl-6

and say, 'Who am I, then? Tell me that first, and then, if I like being that person, I'll come up: if not, I'll stay down here till I am somebody else'— but, oh dear!" cried Alice, with a sudden burst of tears, "I do wish they *would* put their heads down! I am so *very* tired of being all alone here!"

As she said this she looked down at her hands, and was surprised to see that she had put on one of the Rabbit's little white kid-gloves while she was talking.

"How *can* I have done that?" she thought. "I must be growing small again." She got up and went to the table to measure herself by it, and found that, as nearly as she could guess, she was now about two feet high, and was going on shrinking rapidly: she soon found out that the cause of this was the fan she was holding, and she dropped it hastily, just in time to save herself from shrinking away altogether.

"That *was* a narrow escape!" said Alice, a good deal frightened at the sudden change, but very glad to find herself still in existence. "And now for the garden!" And she ran with all speed back to the little door; but, alas! the little door was shut again, and the little golden key was lying on the glass table as before, "and things are worse than ever," thought the poor child, "for I never was so small as this before, never! And I declare it's too bad, that it is!"

As she said these words her foot slipped, and in another moment, splash! she was up to her chin in salt-water.

Her first idea was that she had somehow

fallen into the sea, "and in that case I can go back by railway," she said to herself. (Alice had been to the seaside once in her life, and had come to the general conclusion that, wherever you go to on the English coast, you find a number of bathing machines in the sea, some children digging in the sand with wooden spades, then a row of lodging-houses, and behind them a railway station.) However, she soon made out that she was in the pool of tears which she had wept when she was nine feet high.

"I wish I hadn't cried so much!" said Alice, as she swam about, trying to find her way out. "I shall be punished for it now, I suppose, by being drowned in my own tears! That *will* be a queer thing, to be sure! However, everything is queer to-day."

Just then she heard something splashing about in the pool a little way off, and she swam nearer to make out what it was: at first she thought it must be a walrus or hippopotamus, but then she remembered how small she was now, and she soon made out that it was only a mouse that had slipped in like herself.

"Would it be of any use, now," thought Alice, "to speak to this mouse? Everything is so out-of-the-way down here, that I should think very likely it can talk: at any rate, there's no harm in trying." So she began: "O Mouse, do you know the way out of this pool? I am very tired of swimming about here, O Mouse!" (Alice thought this must be the right way of speaking to a mouse: she had never done such a thing before, but she remembered having seen, in her brother's Latin Grammar, "A mouse—of a mouse—to a mouse—a mouse—O mouse!"

The Mouse looked at her rather inquisitively, and seemed to her to wink with one of its little eyes, but it said nothing.

"Perhaps it doesn't understand English," thought Alice. "I dare say it's a French mouse, come over with William the Conqueror." (For with all her knowledge of history, Alice had no very clear notion how long ago anything had happened.)

So she began again: "Où est ma chatte?" which was the first sentence in her French lesson-book.

The Mouse gave a sudden leap out of the water, and seemed to quiver all over with fright. "Oh, I beg your pardon!" cried Alice hastily, afraid that she had hurt the poor animal's feelings. "I quite forgot you didn't like cats."

"Not like cats!" cried the Mouse in a shrill, passionate voice. "Would you like cats if you were me?"

"Well, perhaps not," said Alice in a soothing tone: "don't be angry about it. And yet I wish I could show you our cat Dinah. I think you'd take a fancy to cats, if you could only see her. She is such a dear quiet thing," Alice went on, half to herself, as she swam lazily about in the pool, "and she sits purring so nicely by the fire, licking her paws and washing her face—and she is such a nice soft thing to nurse—and she's such a capital one for catching mice—oh, I beg your pardon!" cried

Alice again, for this time the Mouse was bristling all over, and she felt certain it must be really offended. "We won't talk about her any more, if you'd rather not."

"We, indeed!" cried the Mouse, who was trembling down to the end of its tail. "As if *I* would talk on such a subject! Our family always *hated* cats: nasty, low, vulgar things! Don't let me hear the name again!"

"I won't indeed!" said Alice, in a great hurry to change the subject of conversation. "Are you— are you fond—of—of dogs?" The Mouse did not answer, so Alice went on eagerly: "There is such a nice little dog, near our house, I should like to show you! A little bright-eyed terrier, you know, with oh, such long curly brown hair! And it'll fetch things when you throw them, and it'll sit up and beg for its dinner, and all sorts of things—I can't remember half of them—and it belongs to a farmer, you know, and he says it's so useful, it's worth a hundred pounds! He says it kills all the rats, and—oh dear!" cried Alice in a sorrowful tone, "I'm afraid I've offended it again!" For the Mouse was swimming away from her as hard as it could go, and making quite a commotion in the pool as it went.

So she called softly after it, "Mouse dear! Do come back again, and we won't talk about cats, or dogs either, if you don't like them!" When the Mouse heard this, it turned round and swam slowly back to her: its face was quite pale (with passion, Alice thought), and it said, in a low trembling voice, "Let us get to the shore, and then I'll tell you my history, and you'll understand why it is I hate cats and dogs."

It was high time to go, for the pool was getting quite crowded with the birds and animals that had fallen into it: there was a Duck and a Dodo, a Lory and an Eaglet, and several other curious creatures.

Alice led the way, and the whole party swam to the shore.

A CAUCUS-RACE AND A LONG TALE

By Lewis Carroll

THEY were, indeed, a queer-looking party that assembled on the bank—the birds with draggled feathers, the animals with their fur clinging close to them, and all dripping wet, cross, and uncomfortable.

The first question of course was, how to get dry again: they had a consultation about this, and after a few minutes it seemed quite natural to Alice to find herself talking familiarly with them, as if she had known them all her life. Indeed, she had quite a long argument with the Lory, who at last turned sulky, and would only say, "I'm older than you, and must know better."

And this Alice would not allow, without knowing how old it was, and, as the Lory positively refused to tell its age, there was no more to be said.

A CAUCUS-RACE

At last the Mouse, who seemed to be a person of some authority among them, called out, "Sit down, all of you, and listen to me! *I'll* soon make you dry enough!" They all sat down at once, in a large ring, with the Mouse in the middle. Alice kept her eyes anxiously fixed on it, for she felt sure she would catch a bad cold if she did not get dry very soon.

"Ahem!" said the Mouse with an important air. "Are you all ready? This is the driest thing I know. Silence all round, if you please! 'William the Conqueror, whose cause was favored by the pope, was soon submitted to by the English, who wanted leaders, and had been of late much accustomed to usurpation and conquest. Edwin and Morcar, the earls of Mercia and Northumbria—'"

"Ugh!" said the Lory, with a shiver.

"I beg your pardon!" said the Mouse, frowning, but very politely. "Did you speak?"

"Not I!" said the Lory, hastily.

"I thought you did," said the Mouse. "I proceed. 'Edwin and Morcar, the earls of Mercia and Northumbria, declared for him; and even Stigand, the patriotic archbishop of Canterbury, found it advisable—'"

"Found *what?*" said the Duck.

"Found *it,*" the Mouse replied, rather crossly: "of course you know what 'it' means."

"I know what 'it' means well enough, when *I* find a thing," said the Duck; "it's generally a frog, or a worm. The question is, what did the archbishop find?"

The Mouse did not notice this question, but hurriedly went on, " '—found it advisable to go with Edgar Atheling to meet William and offer him the crown. William's conduct at first was moderate. But the insolence of his Normans—' How are you getting on now, my dear?" it continued, turning to Alice as it spoke.

"As wet as ever," said Alice, in a melancholy tone: "it doesn't seem to dry me at all."

"In that case," said the Dodo, solemnly, rising to its feet, "I move that the meeting adjourn, for the immediate adoption of more energetic remedies—"

"Speak English!" said Eaglet. "I don't know the meaning of half those long words, and, what's more, I don't believe you do either!" And the Eaglet bent down its head to hide a smile: some of the other birds tittered audibly.

"What I was going to say," said the Dodo in an offended tone, "was, that the best thing to get us dry would be a Caucus-race."

"What *is* a Caucus-race?" said Alice; not that she much wanted to know, but the Dodo had paused as if it thought that *somebody* ought to speak, and no one else seemed inclined to say anything.

"Why," said the Dodo, "the best way to explain it is to do it." (And, as you might like to try the thing yourself, some winter day, I will tell you how the Dodo managed it.)

First it marked out a race-course, in a sort of circle ("the exact shape doesn't matter," it said), and then all the party were placed along the course, here and there.

There was no "One, two, three, and away!" but they began running when they liked, and left off when they liked, so that it was not easy to know when the race was over. However, when they had been running half an hour or so, and were quite dry again, the Dodo suddenly called out "The race is over!" and they all crowded round it, panting, and asking, "But who has won?"

This question the Dodo could not answer without a great deal of thought, and it stood for a long time with one finger pressed upon its forehead (the position in which you usually see Shakespeare, in the pictures of him), while the rest waited in silence.

At last the Dodo said, *"Everybody* has won, and *all* must have prizes."

"But who is to give the prizes?" quite a chorus of voices asked.

"Why, *she,* of course," said the Dodo, pointing to Alice with one finger; and the whole party at once crowded round her, calling out, in a confused way, "Prizes! Prizes!"

Alice had no idea what to do, and in despair she put her hand in her pocket, and pulled out a box of comfits (luckily the salt water had not got into it), and handed them round as prizes. There was exactly one a-piece, all round.

"But she must have a prize herself, you know," said the Mouse.

"Of course," the Dodo replied very gravely.

"What else have you got in your pocket?" it went on, turning to Alice.

"Only a thimble," said Alice sadly.

"Hand it over here," said the Dodo.

Then they all crowded round her once more, while the Dodo solemnly presented the thimble, saying:

"We beg your acceptance of this elegant thimble"; and, when it had finished this short speech, they all cheered.

Alice thought the whole thing very absurd, but they all looked so grave that she did not dare to laugh; and, as she could not think of anything to say, she simply bowed, and took the thimble, looking as solemn as she could.

The next thing was to eat the comfits: this caused some noise and confusion, as the large birds complained that they could not taste theirs, and the small ones choked and had to be patted on the back.

However, it was over at last, and they sat down again in a ring, and begged the Mouse to tell them something more.

"You promised to tell me your history, you know," said Alice, "and why it is you hate—C and D," she added in a whisper, half afraid that it would be offended again.

"Mine is a long and a sad tale!" said the Mouse, turning to Alice, and sighing.

"It *is* a long tail, certainly," said Alice, looking down with wonder at the Mouse's tail; "but why do you call it sad?" And she kept on puzzling about it while the Mouse was speaking, so that her

A CAUCUS-RACE

so that her idea of the tale was something like this:

"Fury said to
a mouse, That
he met in the
house, 'Let
us both go
to law: *I*
will prose-
cute *you*.—
Come, I'll
take no de-
nial: We
must have
the trial;
For really
this morn-
ing I've
nothing
to do.'
Said the
mouse to
the cur,
'Such a
trial, dear
sir. With
no jury
or judge,
would
be wast-
ing our
breath.'
'I'll be
judge,
I'll be
jury,'
said
cun-
ning
old
Fury:
'I'll
try
the
whole
cause,
and
con-
demn
you to
death.'"

"You are not attending!" said the Mouse to Alice, severely. "What are you thinking of?"

"I beg your pardon," said Alice very humbly: "you had got to the fifth bend, I think?"

"I had *not!*" cried the Mouse, sharply and very angrily.

"A knot!" said Alice, always ready to make herself useful, and looking anxiously about her. "Oh, do let me help to undo it!"

"I shall do nothing of the sort," said the Mouse, getting up and walking away. "You insult me by talking such nonsense!"

"I didn't mean it!" pleaded poor Alice. "But you're so easily offended, you know!"

The Mouse only growled in reply.

"Please come back, and finish your story!" Alice called after it. And the others all joined in chorus, "Yes, please do!" But the Mouse only shook its head impatiently, and walked a little quicker.

"What a pity it wouldn't stay!" sighed the Lory, as soon as it was quite out of sight. And an old Crab took the opportunity of saying to her daughter, "Ah, my dear! Let this be a lesson to you never to lose *your* temper!" "Hold your tongue, Ma!" said the young Crab, a little snappishly. "You're enough to try the patience of an oyster!"

"I wish I had our Dinah here, I know I do!" said Alice aloud, addressing nobody in particular. *"She'd* soon fetch it back!"

"And who is Dinah, if I might venture to ask the question?" said the Lory.

Alice replied eagerly, for she was always ready to talk about her pet: "Dinah's our cat. And she's such a capital one for catching mice, you can't think! And oh, I wish you could see her after the birds! Why, she'll eat a little bird as soon as look at it!"

This speech caused a remarkable sensation among the party. Some of the birds hurried off at once: one old Magpie began wrapping itself up very carefully, remarking, "I really must be getting home: the night-air doesn't suit my throat!" And a Canary called out in a trembling voice to its children, "Come away, my dears! It's high time you were all in bed!" On various pretexts they all moved off, and Alice was soon left alone.

"I wish I hadn't mentioned Dinah!" she said to herself in a melancholy tone. "Nobody seems to like her down here, and I'm sure she's the best cat in the world! Oh, my dear Dinah! I wonder if I shall ever see you any more!" And here poor Alice began to cry again, for she felt very lonely and low-spirited. In a little while, however, she again heard a little pattering of footsteps in the distance, and she looked up eagerly, half hoping that the Mouse had changed his mind, and was coming back to finish his story.

THE RABBIT SENDS IN A LITTLE BILL

By Lewis Carroll

IT was the White Rabbit, trotting slowly back again, and looking anxiously about as it went, as if it had lost something; and she heard it muttering to itself, "The Duchess! The Duchess! Oh my dear paws! Oh my fur and whiskers! She'll get me executed, as sure as ferrets are ferrets! Where *can* I have dropped them, I wonder?" Alice guessed in a moment that it was looking for the fan and the pair of white kid-gloves, and she very good-naturedly began hunting about for them, but they were nowhere to be seen—everything seemed to have changed since her swim in the pool; and the great hall, with the glass table and the little door, had vanished completely.

Very soon the Rabbit noticed Alice, as she went hunting about, and called out to her, in an angry tone, "Why, Mary Ann, what *are* you doing out here? Run home this moment, and fetch me a pair of gloves and a fan! Quick, now!" And Alice was so much frightened that she ran off at once in the direction it pointed to, without trying to explain the mistake that it had made.

"He took me for his housemaid," she said to herself as she ran. "How surprised he'll be when he finds out who I am! But I'd better take him his fan and gloves—that is, if I can find them." As she said this, she came upon a neat little house, on the door of which was a bright brass plate with the name "w. RABBIT" engraved upon it. She went in without knocking, and hurried upstairs, in great fear lest she should meet the real Mary Ann, and be turned out of the house before she had found the fan and gloves.

"How queer it seems," Alice said to herself, "to be going messages for a rabbit! I suppose Dinah'll be sending me on messages next!" And she began fancying the sort of thing that would happen: "'Miss Alice! Come here directly, and get ready for your walk!' 'Coming in a minute, nurse! But I've got to watch this mouse-hole till Dinah comes back, and see that the mouse doesn't get out.' Only I don't think," Alice went on, "that they'd let Dinah stop in the house if it began ordering people about like that!"

By this time she had found her way into a tidy little room with a table in the window, and on it (as she had hoped) a fan and two or three pairs of tiny white kid-gloves: she took up the fan and a pair of the gloves, and was just going to leave the room, when her eye fell upon a little bottle that stood near the looking glass. There was no label this time with the words, "DRINK ME," but nevertheless she uncorked it and put it to her lips.

"I know *something* interesting is sure to happen," she said to herself, "whenever I eat or drink anything: so I'll just see what this bottle does. I do hope it'll make me grow large again, for really I'm quite tired of being such a tiny little thing!"

It did so indeed, and much sooner than she had

expected: before she had drunk half the bottle she found her head pressing against the ceiling, and had to stoop to save her neck from being broken. She hastily put down the bottle, saying to herself "That's quite enough—I hope I shan't grow any more—As it is, I can't get out at the door—I do wish I hadn't drunk quite so much!"

Alas! It was too late to wish that! She went on growing, and growing, and very soon had to kneel down on the floor: in another minute there was not even room for this, and she tried the effect of lying down with one elbow against the door and the other arm curled round her head. Still she went on growing, and, as a last resource, she put one arm out of the window, and one foot up the chimney, and said to herself, "Now I can do no more, whatever happens. What *will* become of me?"

Luckily for Alice, the little magic bottle had now had its full effect, and she grew no larger: still it was very uncomfortable, and, as there seemed to be no sort of chance of her ever getting out of the room again, no wonder she felt unhappy.

"It was much pleasanter at home," thought poor Alice, "when one wasn't always growing larger and smaller, and being ordered about by mice and rabbits. I almost wish I hadn't gone down that rabbit-hole—and yet—and yet—it's rather curious, you know, this sort of life! I do wonder what *can* have happened to me! When I used to read fairy tales, I fancied that kind of thing never happened, and now here I am in the middle of one! There ought to be a book written about me, that there ought! And when I grow up I'll write one—but I'm grown up now," she added in a sorrowful tone: "at least there's no room to grow up any more *here*."

"But then," thought Alice, "shall I *never* get any older than I am now? That'll be a comfort, one way—never to be an old woman—but then— always to have lessons to learn! Oh, I shouldn't like *that!*"

"Oh, you foolish Alice!" she answered herself. "How can you learn lessons in here? Why, there's hardly room for *you,* and no room at all for any lesson books!"

And so she went on, taking first one side and then the other, and making quite a conversation of it altogether; but after a few minutes she heard a voice outside, and stopped to listen.

"Mary Ann! Mary Ann!" said the voice. "Fetch me my gloves this moment!" Then came a little pattering of feet on the stairs. Alice knew it was the Rabbit coming to look for her, and she trembled till she shook the house, quite forgetting that she was now about a thousand times as large as the Rabbit, and had no reason to be afraid of it.

Presently the Rabbit came up to the door, and tried to open it; but, as the door opened inward, and Alice's elbow was pressed hard against it, that attempt proved a failure. Alice heard it say to itself, "Then I'll go round and get in at the window."

"*That* you won't!" thought Alice, and, after waiting till she fancied she heard the Rabbit just under the window, she suddenly spread out her hand, and made a snatch in the air. She did not get hold of anything, but she heard a little shriek and a fall, and a crash of broken glass, from which she concluded that it was just possible it had fallen into a cucum ber-frame, or something of the sort.

Next came an angry voice—the Rabbit's—"Pat! Pat! Where are you?" And then a voice she had never heard before, "Sure then I'm here! Digging for apples, yer honor!"

"Digging for apples, indeed!" said the Rabbit, angrily. "Here! Come and help me out of *this!*" (Sounds of more broken glass.)

"Now tell me, Pat, what's that in the window?"

"Sure, it's an arm, yer honor!" (He pronounced it "arrum.")

"An arm, you goose! Who ever saw one that size? Why, it fills the whole window!"

"Sure, it does, yer honor: but it's an arm for all that."

"Well, it's got no business there, at any rate: go and take it away!"

There was a long silence after this, and Alice could only hear whispers now and then; such as "Sure, I don't like it, yer honor, at all, at all!" "Do as I tell you, you coward!" and at last she spread out her hand again, and made another snatch in the air. This time there were *two* little shrieks, and more sounds of broken glass. "What a number of cucumber-frames there must be!" thought Alice. "I wonder what they'll do next! As for pulling me out of the window, I only wish they *could!* I'm sure *I* don't want to stay in here any longer!"

She waited for some time without hearing anything more: at last came a rumbling of little cartwheels, and the sound of a good many voices all

talking together: she made out the words:
"Where's the other ladder?—Why, I hadn't to
bring but one. Bill's got the other—Bill! Fetch
it here, lad!—Here, put 'em up at this corner—No,
tie 'em together first—they don't reach half high
enough yet—Oh, they'll do well enough. Don't
be particular—Here, Bill! Catch hold of this
rope—Will the roof bear?—Mind that loose slate
—Oh, it's coming down! Heads below!" (a loud
crash)—"Now, who did that?—It was Bill, I fancy
—Who's to go down the chimney?—Nay, *I* shan't!
You do it!—*That* I won't, then!—Bill's got to go
down—Here, Bill! The master says you've got
to go down the chimney!"

"Oh! So Bill's got to come down the chimney,
has he?" said Alice to herself. "Why, they seem
to put everything upon Bill! I wouldn't be in
Bill's place for a good deal: this fireplace is narrow,
to be sure; but I *think* I can kick a little!"

She drew her foot as far down the chimney as she
could, and waited till she heard a little animal (she
couldn't guess of what sort it was) scratching and
scrambling about in the chimney close above her:
then, saying to herself, "This is Bill," she gave one
sharp kick, and waited to see what would happen
next.

The first thing she heard was a general chorus of,
"There goes Bill!" then the Rabbit's voice alone—
"Catch him, you by the hedge!" then silence, and
then another confusion of voices—"Hold up his
head—Brandy now—Don't choke him—How was
it, old fellow? What happened to you? Tell us
all about it!"

Last came a little feeble, squeaking voice ("That's Bill," thought Alice), "Well, I hardly know—No more, thank ye; I'm better now—but I'm a deal too flustered to tell you—all I know is, something comes at me like a Jack-in-the-box, and up I goes like a sky-rocket!"

"So you did, old fellow!" said the others.

"We must burn the house down!" said the Rabbit's voice. And Alice called out, as loud as she could, "If you do, I'll set Dinah at you!"

There was a dead silence instantly, and Alice thought to herself, "I wonder what they *will* do next! If they had any sense, they'd take the roof off." After a minute or two, they began moving about again, and Alice heard the Rabbit say, "A barrowful will do, to begin with."

"A barrowful of *what?*" thought Alice. But she had not long to doubt, for the next moment a shower of little pebbles came rattling in at the window, and some of them hit her in the face. "I'll put a stop to this," she said to herself, and shouted out, "You'd better not do that again!" which produced another dead silence.

Alice noticed, with some surprise, that the pebbles were all turning into little cakes as they lay on the floor, and a bright idea came into her head. "If I eat one of these cakes," she thought, "it's sure to make *some* change in my size; and, as it can't possibly make me larger, it must make me smaller, I suppose."

So she swallowed one of the cakes, and was delighted to find that she began shrinking directly. As soon as she was small enough to get through the door, she ran out of the house, and found quite a crowd of little animals and birds waiting outside. The poor little Lizard, Bill, was in the middle, being held up by two guinea-pigs, who were giving it something out of a bottle. They all made a rush at Alice the moment she appeared; but she ran off as hard as she could, and soon found herself safe in a thick wood.

"The first thing I've got to do," said Alice to herself, as she wandered about in the wood, "is to grow to my right size again; and the second thing is to find my way into that lovely garden. I think that will be the best plan."

It sounded an excellent plan, no doubt, and very neatly and simply arranged: the only difficulty was, that she had not the smallest idea how to set about it; and, while she was peering about anxiously among the trees, a little sharp bark just over her head made her look up in a great hurry.

An enormous puppy was looking down at her with large round eyes, and feebly stretching out one paw, trying to touch her. "Poor little thing!" said Alice, in a coaxing tone, and she tried hard to whistle to it; but she was terribly frightened all the time at the thought that it might be hungry, in which case it would be very likely to eat her up in spite of all her coaxing.

Hardly knowing what she did, she picked up a little bit of stick, and held it out to the puppy: whereupon the puppy jumped into the air off all its feet at once, with a yelp of delight, and rushed at the stick, and made believe to worry it: then Alice dodged behind a great thistle, to keep herself from being run over; and, the moment she appeared on the other side, the puppy made another rush at the stick, and tumbled head over heels in its hurry to get hold of it: then Alice, thinking it was very like having a game of play with a cart-horse, and expecting every moment to be trampled under its feet, ran round the thistle again: then the puppy began a series of short charges at the stick, running a very little way forward each time and a long way back, and barking hoarsely all the while, till at last it sat down a good way off, panting, with its tongue hanging out of its mouth, and its great eyes half shut.

This seemed to Alice a good opportunity for making her escape: so she set off at once, and ran till she was quite tired and out of breath, and till the puppy's bark sounded quite faint in the distance.

"And yet what a dear little puppy it was!" said Alice, as she leaned against a buttercup to rest herself, and fanned herself with one of the leaves. "I should have liked teaching it tricks very much, if— if I'd only been the right size to do it! Oh dear! I'd nearly forgotten that I've got to grow up again! Let me see—how *is* it to be managed? I suppose I ought to eat or drink something or other; but the great question is, 'What?'"

The great qustion certainly was "What?" Alice looked all round her at the flowers and the blades of grass, but she could not see anything that looked like the right thing to eat or drink under the circumstances. There was a large mushroom growing near her, about the same height as herself; and, when she had looked under it, and on both sides of it, and behind it, it occurred to her that she might as well look and see what was on the top of it.

She stretched herself up on tiptoe, and peeped over the edge of the mushroom, and her eyes immediately met those of a large blue caterpillar, that was sitting on the top, with his arms folded, quietly smoking a long hookah, and taking not the smallest notice of her or of anything else.

ADVICE FROM A CATERPILLAR

By Lewis Carroll

THE Caterpillar and Alice looked at each other for some time in silence: at last the Caterpillar took the hookah out of its mouth, and addressed her in a languid, sleepy voice.

"Who are *you?*" said the Caterpillar.

This was not an encouraging opening for a conversation. Alice replied, rather shyly, "I—I hardly know, Sir, just at present—at least I know who I *was* when I got up this morning, but I think I must have changed several times since then."

"What do you mean by that?" said the Caterpillar, sternly. "Explain yourself!"

"I can't explain *myself*, I'm afraid, Sir," said Alice, "because I'm not myself, you see."

"I don't see," said the Caterpillar.

"I'm afraid I can't put it more clearly," Alice replied, very politely, "for I can't understand it myself, to begin with; and being so many different sizes in a day is very confusing."

"It isn't," said the Caterpillar.

"Well, perhaps you haven't found it so yet," said Alice; "but when you have to turn into a chrysalis —you will some day, you know—and then after that into a butterfly, I should think you'll feel it a little queer, won't you?"

"Not a bit," said the Caterpillar.

"Well, perhaps *your* feelings may be different," said Alice: "all I know is, it would feel very queer to *me*."

"You!" said the Caterpillar contemptuously. "Who are *you?*"

Which brought them back again to the beginning of the conversation.

Alice felt a little irritated at the Caterpillar's making such *very* short remarks, and she drew herself up and said, very gravely, "I think you ought to tell me who *you* are, first."

"Why?" said the Caterpillar.

Here was another puzzling question; and, as Alice could not think of any good reason, and the Caterpillar seemed to be in a *very* unpleasant state of mind, she turned away.

"Come back!" the Caterpillar called after her. "I've something important to say!"

This sounded promising, certainly. Alice turned and came back again.

"Keep your temper," said the Caterpillar.

"Is that all?" said Alice, swallowing down her anger as well as she could.

"No," said the Caterpillar.

Alice thought she might as well wait, as she had nothing else to do, and perhaps after all it might tell her something worth hearing. For some minutes it puffed away without speaking; but at last it unfolded its arms, took the hookah out of its mouth again, and said, "So you think you're changed, do you?"

"I'm afraid I am, Sir," said Alice. "I can't remember things as I used—and I don't keep the same size for ten minutes together!"

"Can't remember *what* things?" said the Caterpillar.

"Well, I've tried to say, '*How doth the little busy bee,*' but it all came different!" Alice replied in a very melancholy voice.

"Repeat, '*You are old, Father William,*'" said the Caterpillar.

Alice folded her hands, and began:

"You are old, Father William," the young man said,
  "And your hair has become very white;
And yet you incessantly stand on your head—
  Do you think, at your age, it is right?"

"In my youth," Father William replied to his son,
  "I feared it might injure the brain;
But, now that I'm perfectly sure I have none,
  Why, I do it again and again."

"You are old," said the youth, "as I mentioned before,
  And have grown most uncommonly fat;
Yet you turned a back-somersault in at the door—
  Pray, what is the reason of that?"

"In my youth," said the sage, as he shook his gray locks,
  "I kept all my limbs very supple
By the use of this ointment—one shilling the box—
  Allow me to sell you a couple?"

ADVICE FROM A CATERPILLAR

"You are old," said the youth, "and your jaws are too weak
  For anything tougher than suet;
Yet you finished the goose, with the bones and the beak—
  Pray, how did you manage to do it?"

"In my youth," said his father, "I took to the law,
  And argued each case with my wife;
And the muscular strength which it gave to my jaw
  Has lasted the rest of my life."

"You are old," said the youth, "one would hardly suppose
  That your eye was as steady as ever;
Yet you balanced an eel on the end of your nose—
  What made you so awfully clever?"

"I have answered three questions, and that is enough,"
  Said his father. "Don't give yourself airs!
Do you think I can listen all day to such stuff?
  Be off, or I'll kick you down-stairs!"

"That is not said right," said the Caterpillar.

"Not *quite* right, I'm afraid," said Alice, timidly: "some of the words have got altered."

"It is wrong from beginning to end," said the Caterpillar, decidedly; and there was silence for some minutes.

The Caterpillar was the first to speak.

"What size do you want to be?" it asked.

"Oh, I'm not particular as to size," Alice hastily replied; "only one doesn't like changing so often, you know."

"I *don't* know," said the Caterpillar.

Alice said nothing: she had never been so much contradicted in all her life before, and she felt that she was losing her temper.

"Are you content now?" said the Caterpillar.

444

ADVICE FROM A CATERPILLAR

"Well, I should like to be a *little* larger, Sir, if you wouldn't mind," said Alice: "three inches is such a wretched height to be."

"It is a very good height indeed!" said the Caterpillar angrily, rearing itself upright as it spoke (it was exactly three inches high).

"But I'm not used to it!" pleaded poor Alice in a piteous tone. And she thought to herself, "I wish the creature wouldn't be so easily offended!"

"You'll get used to it in time," said the Caterpillar; and it put the hookah into its mouth, and began smoking again.

This time Alice waited patiently until it chose to speak again. In a minute or two the Caterpillar took the hookah out of its mouth, and yawned once or twice, and shook itself. Then it got down off the mushroom, and crawled away into the grass, merely remarking, as it went, "One side will make you grow taller, and the other side will make you grow shorter."

"One side of *what?* The other side of *what?*" thought Alice to herself.

"Of the mushroom," said the Caterpillar, just as if she had asked it aloud; and in another moment it was out of sight.

Alice remained looking thoughtfully at the mushroom for a minute, trying to make out which were the two sides of it; and, as it was perfectly round, she found this a very difficult question. However, at last she stretched her arms round it as far as they would go, and broke off a bit of the edge with each hand.

"And now which is which?" she said to herself,

and nibbled a little of the right-hand bit to try the effect.

The next moment she felt a violent blow underneath her chin: it had struck her foot!

She was a good deal frightened by this very sudden change, but she felt that there was no time to be lost, as she was shrinking rapidly: so she set to work at once to eat some of the other bit. Her chin was pressed so closely against her foot, that there was hardly room to open her mouth; but she did it at last, and managed to swallow a morsel of the left-hand bit.

* * * * * *

"Come, my head's free at last!" said Alice in a tone of delight, which changed into alarm in another moment, when she found that her shoulders were nowhere to be found: all she could see, when she looked down, was an immense length of neck, which seemed to rise like a stalk out a sea of green leaves that lay far below her.

"What *can* all that green stuff be?" said Alice. "And where *have* my shoulders got to? And oh, my poor hands, how is it I can't see you?" She was moving them about, as she spoke, but no result seemed to follow, except a little shaking among the distant green leaves.

As there seemed to be no chance of getting her hands up to her head, she tried to get her head down to *them,* and was delighted to find that her neck would bend about easily in any direction, like a serpent. She had just succeeded in curving it down into a graceful zigzag, and was going to dive in among the leaves, which she found to be nothing but the tops of the trees under which she had been wandering, when a sharp hiss made her draw back in a hurry: a large pigeon had flown into her face, and was beating her violently with its wings.

"Serpent!" screamed the Pigeon.

"I'm *not* a serpent!" said Alice indignantly. "Let me alone!"

"Serpent, I say again!" repeated the Pigeon, but in a more subdued tone, and added, with a kind of sob, "I've tried every way, but nothing seems to suit them!"

"I haven't the least idea what you're talking about," said Alice.

"I've tried the roots of trees, and I've tried banks, and I've tried hedges," the Pigeon went on, without attending to her; "but those serpents! There's no pleasing them!"

Alice was more and more puzzled, but she thought there was no use in saying anything more till the Pigeon had finished.

"As if it wasn't trouble enough hatching the eggs," said the Pigeon; "but I must be on the look-out for serpents, night and day! Why, I haven't had a wink of sleep these three weeks!"

"I'm very sorry you've been annoyed," said Alice, who was beginning to see its meaning.

"And just as I'd taken the highest tree in the wood," continued the Pigeon, raising its voice to a shriek, "and just as I was thinking I should be free of them at last, they must needs come wriggling down from the sky! Ugh, Serpent!"

"But I'm *not* a serpent, I tell you!" said Alice. "I'm a— I'm a—"

"Well! *What* are you?" said the Pigeon. "I can see you're trying to invent something!"

"I—I'm a little girl," said Alice, rather doubtfully, as she remembered the number of changes she had gone through that day.

"A likely story indeed!" said the Pigeon, in a tone of the deepest contempt. "I've seen a good many little girls in my time, but never *one* with such a neck as that! No, no! You're a serpent; and there's no use denying it. I suppose you'll be telling me next that you never tasted an egg!"

"I *have* tasted eggs, certainly," said Alice, who was a very truthful child; "but little girls eat eggs quite as much as serpents do, you know."

"I don't believe it," said the Pigeon; "but if they do, why, then they're a kind of serpent: that's all I can say."

This was such a new idea to Alice that she was quite silent for a minute or two, which gave the Pigeon the opportunity of adding, "You're looking for eggs, I know *that* well enough; and what does it matter to me whether you're a little girl or a serpent?"

"It matters a good deal to *me*," said Alice, hastily; "but I'm not looking for eggs, as it happens; and, if I was, I shouldn't want *yours*: I don't like them raw."

"Well, be off, then!" said the Pigeon in a sulky tone, as it settled down again into its nest. Alice crouched down among the trees as well as she could, for her neck kept getting entangled among the branches, and every now and then she had to stop and untwist it. After a while she remembered that she still held the pieces of mushroom in her hands, and she set to work very carefully, nibbling first at one and then at the other, and growing sometimes taller, and sometimes shorter, until she had succeeded in bringing herself down to her usual height.

It was so long since she had been anything near the right size that it felt quite strange at first; but she got used to it in a few minutes, and began talking to herself, as usual, "Come, there's half my plan done now! How puzzling all these changes are! I'm never sure what I'm going to be, from one minute to another! However, I've got back to my right size: the next thing is, to get into that beautiful garden—how *is* that to be done, I wonder?" As she said this, she came suddenly upon an open place, with a little house in it about four feet high. "Whoever lives there," thought Alice, "it'll never do to come upon them *this* size: why, I should frighten them out of their wits!" So she began nibbling at the right-hand bit again, and did not venture to go near the house till she had brought herself down to nine inches high.

PIG AND PEPPER

By Lewis Carroll

FOR a minute or two she stood looking at the house, and wondering what to do next, when suddenly a footman in livery came running out of the wood—(she considered him to be a footman because he was in livery: otherwise, judging by his face only, she would have called him a fish)—and rapped loudly at the door with his knuckles. It was opened by another footman in livery, with a round face, and large eyes like a frog; and both footmen, Alice noticed, had powdered hair that curled all over their heads. She felt very curious to know what it was all about, and crept a little way out of the wood to listen.

The Fish-Footman began by producing from under his arm a great letter, nearly as large as himself, and this he handed over to the other, saying, in a solemn tone, "For the Duchess. An invitation from the Queen to play croquet." The Frog-Footman repeated, in the same solemn tone, only changing the order of the words a little, "From the Queen. An invitation for the Duchess to play croquet."

Then they both bowed low, and their curls got entangled together.

Alice laughed so much at this, that she had to run back into the wood for fear of their hearing her; and, when she next peeped out, the Fish-Footman was gone, and the other was sitting on the ground near the door, staring stupidly up into the sky.

Alice went timidly up to the door, and knocked.

"There's no sort of use in knocking," said the Footman, "and that for two reasons. First, because I'm on the same side of the door as you are: secondly, because they're making such a noise inside, no one could possibly hear you." And certainly there *was* a most extraordinary noise going on within—a constant howling and sneezing, and every now and then a great crash, as if a dish or kettle had been broken to pieces.

PIG AND PEPPER

"Please, then," said Alice, "how am I to get in?"

"There might be some sense in your knocking," the Footman went on, without attending to her, "if we had the door between us. For instance, if you were *inside,* you might knock, and I could let you out, you know." He was looking up into the sky all the time he was speaking, and this Alice thought decidedly uncivil. "But perhaps he can't help it," she said to herself; "his eyes are so *very* nearly at the top of his head. But at any rate he might answer questions—How am I to get in?" she repeated, aloud.

"I shall sit here," the Footman remarked, "till to-morrow—"

At this moment the door of the house opened, and a large plate came skimming out, straight at the Footman's head: it just grazed his nose, and broke to pieces against one of the trees behind him.

"—or next day, maybe," the Footman continued in the same tone, exactly as if nothing had happened.

"How am I to get in?" asked Alice again, in a louder tone.

"*Are* you to get in at all?" said the Footman. "That's the first question, you know."

It was, no doubt: only Alice did not like to be told so. "It's really dreadful," she muttered to herself, "the way all the creatures argue. It's enough to drive one crazy!"

The Footman seemed to think this a good opportunity for repeating his remark, with variations. "I shall sit here," he said, "on and off, for days and days."

"But what am *I* to do?" said Alice.

"Anything you like," said the Footman, and began whistling.

"Oh, there's no use in talking to him," said Alice desperately: "he's perfectly idiotic!" And she opened the door and went in.

The door led right into a large kitchen, which was full of smoke from one end to the other; the Duchess was sitting on a three-legged stool in the middle, nursing a baby: the cook was leaning over the fire, stirring a large caldron which seemed to be full of soup.

"There's certainly too much pepper in that soup!" Alice said to herself, as well as she could for sneezing.

There was certainly too much of it in the *air*. Even the Duchess sneezed occasionally; and as for the baby, it was sneezing and howling alternately without a moment's pause. The only two creatures in the kitchen, that did *not* sneeze, were the cook, and a large cat, which was lying on the hearth and grinning from ear to ear.

"Please would you tell me," said Alice, a little timidly, for she was not quite sure whether it was good manners for her to speak first, "why your cat grins like that?"

"It's a Cheshire-Cat," said the Duchess, "and that's why. Pig!"

She said the last word with such sudden violence that Alice quite jumped; but she saw in another moment that it was addressed to the baby, and not to her, so she took courage, and went on again:

"I didn't know that Cheshire-Cats always

grinned; in fact, I didn't know that cats *could* grin."

"They all can," said the Duchess; "and most of 'em do."

"I don't know of any that do," Alice said, very politely, feeling quite pleased to have got into a conversation.

"You don't know much," said the Duchess; "and that's a fact."

Alice did not at all like the tone of this remark, and thought it would be as well to introduce some other subject of conversation. While she was trying to fix on one, the cook took the caldron of soup off the fire, and at once set to work throwing everything within her reach at the Duchess and the baby —the fire-irons came first; then followed a shower of saucepans, plates, and dishes. The Duchess took no notice of them even when they hit her; and the baby was howling so much already, that it was quite impossible to say whether the blows hurt it or not.

"Oh, *please* mind what you're doing!" cried Alice, jumping up and down in an agony of terror. "Oh, there goes his *precious* nose!" as an unusually large saucepan flew close by it, and very nearly carried it off.

"If everybody minded their own business," the Duchess said, in a hoarse growl, "the world would go round a deal faster than it does."

"Which would *not* be an advantage," said Alice, who felt very glad to get an opportunity of showing off a little of her knowledge. "Just think what work it would make with the day and night! You

see the earth takes twenty-four hours to turn round
on its axis—"

"Talking of axes," said the Duchess, "chop off
her head!"

Alice glanced rather anxiously at the cook, to see
if she meant to take the hint; but the cook was
busily stirring the soup, and seemed not to be listening, so she went on again: "Twenty-four hours,
I *think;* or is it twelve? I—"

"Oh, don't bother *me!*" said the Duchess. "I
never could abide figures!" And with that she began nursing her child again, singing a sort of lullaby
to it as she did so, and giving it a violent shake at
the end of every line:—

> "Speak roughly to your little boy,
>   And beat him when he sneezes:
> He only does it to annoy,
>   Because he knows it teases."

Chorus

(in which the cook and the baby joined):

> "Wow! wow! wow!"

While the Duchess sang the second verse of the
song, she kept tossing the baby violently up and
down, and the poor little thing howled so, that Alice
could hardly hear the words:

> "I speak severely to my boy,
>   I beat him when he sneezes;
> For he can thoroughly enjoy
>   The pepper when he pleases!"

Chorus

> "Wow! wow! wow!"

"Here! You may nurse it a bit, if you like!" the Duchess said to Alice, flinging the baby at her as she spoke. "I must go and get ready to play croquet with the Queen," and she hurried out of the room. The cook threw a frying-pan after her as she went, but it just missed her.

Alice caught the baby with some difficulty, as it was a queer-shaped little creature, and held out its arms and legs in all directions, "just like a star fish," thought Alice. The poor little thing was snorting like a steam-engine when she caught it, and kept doubling itself up and straightening itself out again, so that altogether, for the first minute or two, it was as much as she could do to hold it.

As soon as she had made out the proper way of nursing it (which was to twist it up into a sort of knot, and then keep tight hold of its right ear and left foot, so as to prevent its undoing itself), she carried it out into the open air. "If I don't take this child away with me," thought Alice, "they're sure to kill it in a day or two. Wouldn't it be murder to leave it behind?" She said the last words out loud, and the little thing grunted in reply (it had left off sneezing by this time). "Don't grunt," said Alice; "that's not at all a proper way of expressing yourself."

The baby grunted again, and Alice looked very anxiously into its face to see what was the matter with it. There could be no doubt that it had a *very* turn-up nose, much more like a snout than a real nose: also its eyes were getting extremely small for a baby: altogether Alice did not like the look of the thing at all. "But perhaps it was only sobbing," she thought, and looked into its eyes again, to see if there were any tears.

No, there were no tears. "If you're going to turn into a pig, my dear," said Alice, seriously, "I'll have nothing more to do with you. Mind now!" The poor little thing sobbed again (or grunted, it was impossible to say which), and they went on for some while in silence.

Alice was just beginning to think to herself, "Now, what am I to do with this creature, when I get it home?" when it grunted again, so violently, that she looked down into its face in some alarm. This time there could be *no* mistake about it: it was neither more nor less than a pig, and she felt that it would be quite absurd for her to carry it any further.

So she set the little creature down, and felt quite relieved to see it trot away quietly into the wood. "If it had grown up," she said to herself, "it would have made a dreadfully ugly child: but it makes rather a handsome pig, I think." And she began thinking over other children she knew, who might do very well as pigs, and was just saying to herself, "if one only knew the right way to change them—" when she was a little startled by seeing the Cheshire-Cat sitting on a bough of a tree a few yards off.

The Cat only grinned when it saw Alice. It looked good-natured, she thought: still it had *very* long claws and a great many teeth, so she felt that it ought to be treated with respect.

"Cheshire-Puss," she began, rather timidly, as she did not at all know whether it would like the name: however, it only grinned a little wider. "Come, it's pleased so far," thought Alice, and she went on: "Would you tell me, please, which way I ought to go from here?"

"That depends a good deal on where you want to get to," said the Cat.

"I don't much care where—" said Alice.

"Then it doesn't matter which way you go," said the Cat.

"—so long as I get *somewhere*," Alice added as an explanation.

"Oh, you're sure to do that," said the Cat, "if you only walk long enough."

Alice felt that this could not be denied, so she tried another question. "What sort of people live about here?"

"In *that* direction," the Cat said, waving its right paw round, "lives a Hatter: and in *that* direction," waving the other paw, "lives a March Hare. Visit either you like: they're both mad."

"But I don't want to go among mad people," Alice remarked.

"Oh, you can't help that," said the Cat: "we're all mad here. I'm mad. You're mad."

"How do you know I'm mad?" said Alice.

"You must be," said the Cat, "or you wouldn't have come here."

Alice didn't think that proved it at all: however, she went on: "And how do you know that you're mad?"

"To begin with," said the Cat, "a dog's not mad. You grant that?"

"I suppose so," said Alice.

"Well, then," the Cat went on, "you see a dog

growls when it's angry, and wags its tail when it's pleased. Now *I* growl when I'm pleased, and wag my tail when I'm angry. Therefore I'm mad."

"*I* call it purring, not growling," said Alice.

"Call it what you like," said the Cat. "Do you play croquet with the Queen to-day?"

"I should like it very much," said Alice, "but I haven't been invited yet."

"You'll see me there," said the Cat, and vanished.

Alice was not much surprised at this, she was getting so well used to queer things happening. While she was still looking at the place where it had been, it suddenly appeared again.

"By the by, what became of the baby?" said the Cat. "I'd nearly forgotten to ask."

"It turned into a pig," Alice answered very quietly, just is if the Cat had come back in a natural way.

"I thought it would," said the Cat, and vanished again.

Alice waited a little, half expecting to see it again, but it did not appear, and after a minute or two she walked on in the direction in which the March Hare was said to live. "I've seen hatters before," she said to herself: "the March Hare will be much the most interesting, and perhaps, as this is May, it won't be raving mad—at least not so mad as it was in March." As she said this, she looked up, and there was the Cat again sitting on a branch of a tree.

"Did you say 'pig,' or 'fig'?" said the Cat.

"I said 'pig'," replied Alice; "and I wish you wouldn't keep appearing and vanishing so suddenly: you make one quite giddy!"

A MAD TEA-PARTY

"All right," said the Cat; and this time it vanished quite slowly, beginning with the end of the tail, and ending with the grin, which remained some time after the rest of it had gone.

"Well! I've often seen a cat without a grin," thought Alice; "but a grin without a cat! It's the most curious thing I ever saw in all my life!"

She had not gone much further before she came in sight of the house of the March Hare: she thought it must be the right house, because the chimneys were shaped like ears and the roof was thatched with fur. It was so large a house, that she did not like to go nearer till she had nibbled some more of the left-hand bit of mushroom, and raised herself to about two feet high: even then she walked up toward it rather timidly, saying to herself, "Suppose it should be raving mad after all! I almost wish I'd gone to see the Hatter instead!"

A MAD TEA-PARTY

By Lewis Carroll

THERE was a table set out under a tree in front of the house, and the March Hare and the Hatter were having tea at it: a Dormouse was sitting between them, fast asleep, and the other two were using it as a cushion, resting their elbows on it, and talking over its head. "Very uncomfortable for the Dormouse," thought Alice; "only as it's asleep, I suppose it doesn't mind."

The table was a large one, but the three were all

crowded together at one corner of it. "No room! No room!" they cried out when they saw Alice coming.

"There's *plenty* of room!" said Alice indignantly, and she sat down in a large arm-chair at one end of the table.

"Have some wine," the March Hare said in an encouraging tone.

Alice looked all round the table, but there was nothing on it but tea. "I don't see any wine," she remarked.

"There isn't any," said the March Hare.

"Then it wasn't very civil of you to offer it," said Alice, angrily.

"It wasn't very civil of you to sit down without being invited," said the March Hare.

"I didn't know it was *your* table," said Alice: "it's laid for a great many more than three."

"Your hair wants cutting," said the Hatter. He had been looking at Alice for some time with great curiosity, and this was his first speech.

"You should learn not to make personal remarks," Alice said with some severity: "it's very rude."

The Hatter opened his eyes very wide on hearing this; but all he *said* was, "Why is a raven like a writing-desk?"

"Come, we shall have some fun now!" thought Alice. "I'm glad they've begun asking riddles—I believe I can guess that," she added, aloud.

"Do you mean that you think you can find out the answer to it?" said the March Hare.

"Exactly so," said Alice.

"Then you should say what you mean," the March Hare went on.

"I do," Alice hastily replied; "at least—at least I mean what I say—that's the same thing, you know."

"Not the same thing a bit!" said the Hatter. "Why, you might just as well say that 'I see what I eat' is the same thing as 'I eat what I see'!"

"You might just as well say," added the March Hare, "that 'I like what I get' is the same thing as 'I get what I like'!"

"You might just as well say," added the Dormouse, which seemed to be talking in its sleep, "that 'I breathe when I sleep' is the same thing as 'I sleep when I breathe'!"

"It *is* the same thing with you," said the Hatter, and here the conversation dropped, and the party sat silent for a minute, while Alice thought over all she could remember about ravens and writing-desks, which wasn't much.

The Hatter was the first to break the silence. "What day of the month is it?" he said, turning to Alice: he had taken his watch out of his pocket, and was looking at it uneasily, shaking it every now and then, and holding it to his ear.

Alice considered a little, and then said, "The fourth."

"Two days wrong!" sighed the Hatter. "I told you butter wouldn't suit the works!" he added, looking angrily at the March Hare.

"It was the *best* butter," the March Hare meekly replied.

"Yes, but some crumbs must have got in as well,"

461

the Hatter grumbled: "you shouldn't have put it in with the bread-knife."

The March Hare took the watch and looked at it gloomily: then he dipped it into his cup of tea, and looked at it again: but he could think of nothing better to say than his first remark, "It was the *best* butter, you know."

Alice had been looking over his shoulder with some curiosity. "What a funny watch!" she remarked. "It tells the day of the month, and doesn't tell what o'clock it is!"

"Why should it?" muttered the Hatter. "Does *your* watch tell you what year it is?"

"Of course not," Alice replied very readily: "but that's because it stays the same year for such a long time together."

"Which is just the case with *mine*," said the Hatter.

Alice felt dreadfully puzzled. The Hatter's remark seemed to her to have no sort of meaning in it, and yet it was certainly English. "I don't quite understand you," she said, as politely as she could.

"The Dormouse is asleep again," said the Hatter, and he poured a little hot tea upon its nose.

The Dormouse shook its head impatiently, and said, without opening its eyes, "Of course, of course: just what I was going to remark myself."

"Have you guessed the riddle yet?" the Hatter said, turning to Alice again.

"No, I give it up," Alice replied. "What's the answer?"

"I haven't the slightest idea," said the Hatter.

"Nor I," said the March Hare.

Alice sighed wearily. "I think you might do something better with the time," she said, "than wasting it in asking riddles that have no answers."

"If you knew Time as well as I do," said the Hatter, "you wouldn't talk about wasting *it*. It's *him*."

"I don't know what you mean," said Alice.

"Of course you don't!" the Hatter said, tossing his head contemptuously. "I dare say you never even spoke to Time!"

"Perhaps not," Alice cautiously replied; "but I know I have to beat time when I learn music."

"Ah! That accounts for it," said the Hatter. "He won't stand beating. Now, if you only kept on good terms with him, he'd do almost anything you liked with the clock. For instance, suppose it were nine o'clock in the morning, just time to begin lessons: you'd only have to whisper a hint to Time, and round goes the clock in a twinkling! Half-past one, time for dinner!"

("I only wish it was," the March Hare said to itself in a whisper.)

"That would be grand, certainly," said Alice thoughtfully; "but then—I shouldn't be hungry for it, you know."

"Not at first, perhaps," said the Hatter: "but you could keep it to half-past one as long as you liked."

"Is that the way *you* manage?" Alice asked.

The Hatter shook his head mournfully. "Not I!" he replied. "We quarrelled last March—just before *he* went mad, you know—" (pointing with

his teaspoon at the March Hare), "—it was at the
great concert given by the Queen of Hearts, and
I had to sing:

> 'Twinkle, twinkle, little bat!
> How I wonder what you're at!'

You know the song, perhaps?"

"I've heard something like it," said Alice.

"It goes on, you know," the Hatter continued,
"in this way:—

> 'Up above the world you fly,
> Like a tea-tray in the sky.
> Twinkle, twinkle—' "

Here the Dormouse shook itself, and began
singing in its sleep, *"Twinkle, twinkle, twinkle,
twinkle—"* and went on so long that they had to
pinch it to make it stop.

"Well, I'd hardly finished the first verse," said
the Hatter, "when the Queen bawled out 'He's
murdering the time! Off with his head!' "

"How dreadfully savage!" exclaimed Alice.

"And ever since that," the Hatter went on in a
mournful tone, "he won't do a thing I ask! It's
always six o'clock now."

A bright idea came into Alice's head. "Is that
the reason so many tea-things are put out here?"
she asked.

"Yes, that's it," said the Hatter with a sigh:
"it's always tea-time, and we've no time to wash
the things between whiles."

"Then you keep moving round, I suppose?" said
Alice.

"Exactly so," said the Hatter: "as the things get used up."

"But what happens when you come to the beginning again?" Alice ventured to ask.

"Suppose we change the subject," the March Hare interrupted, yawning. "I'm getting tired of this. I vote the young lady tells us a story."

"I'm afraid I don't know one," said Alice, rather alarmed at the proposal.

"Then the Dormouse shall!" they both cried. "Wake up, Dormouse!" And they pinched it on both sides at once.

The Dormouse slowly opened its eyes. "I wasn't asleep," it said in a hoarse, feeble voice, "I heard every word you fellows were saying."

"Tell us a story!" said the March Hare.

"Yes, please do!" pleaded Alice.

"And be quick about it," added the Hatter, "or you'll be asleep again before it's done."

"Once upon a time there were three little sisters," the Dormouse began in a great hurry; "and their names were Elsie, Lacie, and Tillie; and they lived at the bottom of a well—"

"What did they live on?" said Alice, who always took a great interest in questions of eating and drinking.

"They lived on treacle," said the Dormouse, after thinking a minute or two.

"They couldn't have done that, you know," Alice gently remarked. "They'd have been ill."

"So they were," said the Dormouse; "*very* ill."

Alice tried a little to fancy to herself what

such an extraordinary way of living would be like, but it puzzled her too much: so she went on:

"But why did they live at the bottom of a well?"

"Take some more tea," the March Hare said to Alice, very earnestly.

"I've had nothing yet," Alice replied in an offended tone: "so I can't take more."

"You mean you can't take *less*," said the Hatter: "it's very easy to take *more* than nothing."

"Nobody asked *your* opinion," said Alice.

"Who's making personal remarks now?" the Hatter asked triumphantly.

Alice did not quite know what to say to this: so she helped herself to some tea and bread-and-butter, and then turned to the Dormouse, and repeated her question. "Why did they live at the bottom of a well?"

The Dormouse again took a minute or two to think about it, and then said, "It was a treacle-well."

"There's no such thing!" Alice was beginning very angrily, but the Hatter and the March Hare went, "Sh! Sh!" and the Dormouse sulkily remarked, "If you can't be civil, you'd better finish the story for yourself."

"No, please go on!" Alice said very humbly. "I won't interrupt you again. I dare say there may be *one*."

"One, indeed!" said the Dormouse indignantly. However, he consented to go on. "And so these three little sisters—they were learning to draw, you know—"

"What did they draw?" said Alice, quite forgetting her promise.

"Treacle," said the Dormouse, without considering at all, this time.

"I want a clean cup," interrupted the Hatter: "let's all move one place on."

He moved on as he spoke, and the Dormouse followed him: the March Hare moved into the Dormouse's place, and Alice rather unwillingly took the place of the March Hare. The Hatter was the only one who got any advantage from the change; and Alice was a good deal worse off than before, as the March Hare had just upset the milk-jug into his plate.

Alice did not wish to offend the Dormouse again, so she began very cautiously: "But I don't understand. Where did they draw the treacle from?"

"You can draw water out of a water-well," said the Hatter; "so I should think you could draw treacle out of a treacle-well—eh, stupid?"

"But they were *in* the well," Alice said to the Dormouse, not choosing to notice this last remark.

"Of course they were," said the Dormouse: "well in."

This answer so confused poor Alice, that she let the Dormouse go on for some time without interrupting it.

"They were learning to draw," the Dormouse went on, yawning and rubbing its eyes, for it was getting very sleepy; "and they drew all manner of things—everything that begins with an M—"

"Why with an M?" said Alice.

"Why not?" said the March Hare.

Alice was silent.

The Dormouse had closed its eyes by this time, and was going off into a doze; but, on being pinched by the Hatter, it woke up again with a little shriek, and went on: "—that begins with an M, such as mouse-traps, and the moon, and memory, and muchness—you know you say things are 'much of a muchness'—did you ever see such a thing as a drawing of a muchness?"

"Really, now you ask me," said Alice, very much confused, "I don't think—"

"Then you shouldn't talk," said the Hatter.

This piece of rudeness was more than Alice could bear: she got up in great disgust, and walked off: the Dormouse fell asleep instantly, and neither of the others took the least notice of her going, though she looked back once or twice, half hoping that they would call after her; the last time she saw them, they were trying to put the Dormouse into the tea-pot.

"At any rate I'll never go *there* again!" said Alice, as she picked her way through the wood. "It's the stupidest tea-party I ever was at in all my life!"

Just as she said this, she noticed that one of the trees had a door leading right into it. "That's very curious!" she thought. "But everything's curious to-day. I think I may as well go in at once." And in she went.

Once more she found herself in the long hall, and close to the little glass table. "Now, I'll manage better this time," she said to herself, and began by taking the little golden key, and unlocking the door that led into the garden. Then she set to work nibbling at the mushroom (she had kept a piece of it in her pocket) till she was about a foot high: then she walked down the little passage: and *then* —she found herself at last in the beautiful garden among the bright flower-beds and the cool fountains.

THE QUEEN'S CROQUET GROUND

By Lewis Carroll

A LARGE rose-tree stood near the entrance of the garden: the roses growing on it were white, but there were three gardeners at it, busily painting them red. Alice thought this a very curious thing, and she went nearer to watch them, and, just as she came up to them, she heard one of them say "Look out, now, Five! Don't go splashing paint over me like that!"

"I couldn't help it," said Five, in a sulky tone. "Seven jogged my elbow."

On which Seven looked up and said, "That's right, Five! Always lay the blame on others!"

"*You'd* better not talk!" said Five. "I heard the Queen say only yesterday you deserved to be beheaded."

"What for?" said the one who had spoken first.

"That's none of *your* business, Two!" said Seven.

"Yes, it *is* his business!" said Five. "And I'll tell him—it was for bringing the cook tulip-roots instead of onions."

Seven flung down his brush, and had just begun,

"Well, of all the unjust things—" when his eye chanced to fall upon Alice, as she stood watching them, and he checked himself suddenly: the others looked round also, and all of them bowed low.

"Would you tell me, please," said Alice, a little timidly, "why you are painting those roses?"

Five and Seven said nothing, but looked at Two. Two began, in a low voice, "Why, the fact is, you see, Miss, this here ought to have been a *red* rosetree, and we put a white one in by mistake; and, if the Queen was to find it out, we should all have our heads cut off, you know. So you see, Miss, we're doing out best, afore she comes, to—" At this moment, Five, who had been anxiously looking across the garden, called out, "The Queen! The Queen!" and the three gardeners instantly threw themselves flat upon their faces. There was a sound of many footsteps, and Alice looked round, eager to see the Queen.

First came ten soldiers carrying clubs: these were all shaped like the three gardeners, oblong and flat, with their hands and feet at the corners: next the ten courtiers: these were ornamented all over with diamonds, and walked two and two, as the soldiers did. After these came the royal children: there were ten of them, and the little dears came jumping merrily along, hand in hand, in couples: they were all ornamented with hearts. Next came the guests, mostly Kings and Queens, and among them Alice recognized the White Rabbit: it was talking in a hurried nervous manner, smiling at everything that was said, and went by without noticing her. Then followed the Knave of Hearts, carrying the

King's crown on a crimson velvet cushion; and, last of all this grand procession, came THE KING AND THE QUEEN OF HEARTS.

Alice was rather doubtful whether she ought not to lie down on her face like the three gardeners, but she could not remember ever having heard of such a rule at processions; "and besides, what would be the use of a procession," thought she, "if people had all to lie down on their faces, so that they couldn't see it?" So she stood where she was, and waited.

When the procession came opposite to Alice, they all stopped and looked at her, and the Queen said, severely, "Who is this?"

She said it to the Knave of Hearts, who only bowed and smiled in reply.

"Idiot!" said the Queen, tossing her head impatiently: and, turning to Alice, she went on: "What's your name, child?"

"My name is Alice, so please your Majesty," said Alice very politely; but she added, to herself, "Why, they're only a pack of cards after all. I needn't be afraid of them!"

"And who are *these?*" said the Queen, pointing to the three gardeners who were lying round the rose-tree; for, you see, as they were lying on their faces, and the pattern on their backs was the same as the rest of the pack, she could not tell whether they were gardeners, or soldiers, or courtiers, or three of her own children.

"How should *I* know!" said Alice, surprised at her own courage. "It's no business of mine."

The Queen turned crimson with fury, and, after

471

glaring at her for a moment like a wild beast, began screaming, "Off with her head! Off with—"

"Nonsense!" said Alice, very loudly and decidedly, and the Queen was silent.

The King laid his hand upon her arm, and timidly said, "Consider, my dear: she is only a child!"

The Queen turned angrily away from him, and said to the Knave, "Turn them over!"

The Knave did so, very carefully, with one foot.

"Get up!" said the Queen in a shrill, loud voice, and the three gardeners instantly jumped up, and began bowing to the King, Queen, the royal children, and everybody else.

"Leave off that!" screamed the Queen. "You make me giddy." And then, turning to the rose-tree, she went on "What *have* you been doing here?"

"May it please your Majesty," said Two, in a very humble tone, going down on one knee as he spoke, "we were trying—"

"*I* see!" said the Queen, who had meanwhile been examining the roses. "Off with their heads!" and the procession moved on, three of the soldiers remaining behind to execute the unfortunate gardeners, who ran to Alice for protection.

"You shan't be beheaded!" said Alice, and she put them into a large flower-pot that stood near. The three soldiers wandered about for a minute or two, looking for them, and then quietly marched off after the others.

"Are their heads off?" shouted the Queen.

"Their heads are gone, if it please your Majesty!" the soldiers shouted in reply.

"That's right!" shouted the Queen. "Can you play croquet?"

The soldiers were silent, and looked at Alice, as the question was evidently meant for her.

"Yes!" shouted Alice.

"Come on, then!" roared the Queen, and Alice joined the procession, wondering very much what would happen next.

"It's—it's a very fine day!" said a timid voice at her side. She was walking by the White Rabbit, who was peeping anxiously into her face.

"Very," said Alice. "Where's the Duchess?"

"Hush! Hush!" said the Rabbit in a low hurried tone. He looked anxiously over his shoulder as he spoke, and then raised himself upon tiptoe, put his mouth close to her ear, and whispered, "She's under sentence of execution."

"What for?" said Alice.

"Did you say, 'What a pity!'?" the Rabbit asked.

"No, I didn't," said Alice. "I don't think it's at all a pity. I said 'What for?'"

"She boxed the Queen's ears—" the Rabbit began. Alice gave a little scream of laughter. "Oh, hush!" the Rabbit whispered in a frightened tone. "The Queen will hear you! You see she came rather late, and the Queen said—"

"Get to your places!" shouted the Queen in a voice of thunder, and people began running about in all directions, tumbling up against each other: however, they got settled down in a minute or two, and the game began.

Alice thought she had never seen such a curious croquet-ground in her life: it was all ridges and furrows: the croquet balls were live hedgehogs, and the mallets live flamingoes, and the soldiers had to double themselves up and stand on their hands and feet, to make the arches.

The chief difficulty Alice found at first was in managing her flamingo: she succeeded in getting its body tucked away comfortably enough under her arm, with its legs hanging down, but generally, just as she had got its neck nicely straightened out, and was going to give the hedgehog a blow with its head, it *would* twist itself round and look up in her face, with such a puzzled expression that she could not help bursting out laughing; and, when she had got its head down, and was going to begin again, it was very provoking to find that the hedgehog had unrolled itself, and was in the act of crawling away: besides all this, there was generally a ridge or a furrow in the way wherever she wanted to send the hedgehog to, and, as the doubled-up soldiers were always getting up and walking off to other parts of the ground, Alice soon came to the conclusion that it was a very difficult game indeed.

The players all played at once, without waiting for turns, quarrelling all the while, and fighting for the hedgehogs; and in a very short time the Queen was in a furious passion, and went stamping about and shouting, "Off with his head!" or "Off with her head!" about once in a minute.

Alice began to feel very uneasy: to be sure she had not as yet had any dispute with the Queen, but she knew that it might happen any minute, "and then," thought she, "what would become of me?

They're dreadfully fond of beheading people here: the great wonder is that there's any one left alive!"

She was looking about for some way of escape, and wondering whether she could get away without being seen when she noticed a curious appearance in the air: it puzzled her very much at first, but after watching it a minute or two she made it out to be a grin, and she said to herself, "It's the Cheshire-Cat: now I shall have somebody to talk to."

"How are you getting on?" said the Cat, as soon as there was mouth enough for it to speak with.

Alice waited till the eyes appeared, and then nodded. "It's no use speaking to it," she thought, "till its ears have come, or at least one of them." In another minute the whole head appeared, and then Alice put down her flamingo, and began an account of the game, feeling very glad she had some one to listen to her. The Cat seemed to think that there was enough of it now in sight, and no more of it appeared.

"I don't think they play at all fairly," Alice began, in rather a complaining tone, "and they all quarrel so dreadfully one can't hear one's self speak—and they don't seem to have any rules in particular: at least, if there are, nobody attends to them—and you've no idea how confusing it is all the things being alive: for instance, there's the arch I've got to go through next walking about at the other end of the ground—and I should have croqueted the Queen's hedgehog just now, only it ran away when it saw mine coming!"

"How do you like the Queen?" said the Cat in a low voice.

"Not at all," said Alice: "she's so extremely—" Just then she noticed that the Queen was close behind her, listening: so she went on "—likely to win, that it's hardly worth while finishing the game."

The Queen smiled and passed on.

"Who *are* you talking to?" said the King, coming up to Alice, and looking at the Cat's head with great curiosity.

"It's a friend of mine—a Cheshire-Cat," said Alice: "allow me to introduce it."

"I don't like the look of it at all," said the King: "however, it may kiss my hand, if it likes."

"I'd rather not," the Cat remarked.

"Don't be impertinent," said the King, "and don't look at me like that!" He got behind Alice as he spoke.

"A cat may look at a king," said Alice. "I've read that in some book, but I don't remember where."

"Well, it must be removed," said the King very decidedly; and he called to the Queen, who was passing at the moment, "My dear! I wish you would have this Cat removed!"

The Queen had only one way of settling all difficulties, great or small. "Off with his head!" she said without even looking round.

"I'll fetch the executioner myself," said the King eagerly, and he hurried off.

Alice thought she might as well go back and see how the game was going on, as she heard the

Queen's voice in the distance, screaming with passion. She had already heard her sentence three of the players to be executed for having missed their turns, and she did not like the look of things at all, as the game was in such confusion that she never knew whether it was her turn or not. So she went off in search of her hedgehog.

The hedgehog was engaged in a fight with another hedgehog, which seemed to Alice an excellent opportunity for croqueting one of them with the other: the only difficulty was, that her flamingo was gone across to the other side of the garden, where Alice could see it trying in a helpless sort of way to fly up into a tree.

By the time she had caught the flamingo and brought it back, the fight was over, and both the hedgehogs were out of sight: "but it doesn't matter much," thought Alice, "as all the arches are gone from this side of the ground." So she tucked it away under her arm, that it might not escape again, and went back to have a little more conversation with her friend.

When she got back to the Cheshire-Cat, she was surprised to find quite a large crowd collected round it: there was a dispute going on between the executioner, the King, and the Queen, who were all talking at once, while all the rest were quite silent, and looked very uncomfortable.

The moment Alice appeared, she was appealed to by all three to settle the question, and they repeated their arguments to her, though, as they all spoke at once, she found it very hard to make out exactly what they said.

The executioner's argument was, that you couldn't cut off a head unless there was a body to cut it off from: that he had never had to do such a thing before, and he wasn't going to begin at *his* time of life.

The King's argument was that anything that had a head could be beheaded, and that you weren't to talk nonsense.

The Queen's argument was that, if something wasn't done about it in less than no time, she'd have everybody executed, all round. (It was this last remark that had made the whole party look so grave and anxious.)

Alice could think of nothing else to say but "It belongs to the Duchess: you'd better ask *her* about it."

"She's in prison," the Queen said to the executioner: "fetch her here." And the executioner went off like an arrow.

The Cat's head began fading away the moment he was gone, and, by the time he had come back with the Duchess, it had entirely disappeared: so the King and the executioner ran wildly up and down, looking for it, while the rest of the party went back to the game.

THE MOCK TURTLE'S STORY

By Lewis Carroll

"YOU can't think how glad I am to see you, again, you dear old thing!" said the Duchess, as she tucked her arm affectionately into Alice's, and they walked off together.

Alice was very glad to find her in such a pleasant temper, and thought to herself that perhaps it was only the pepper that had made her so savage when they met in the kitchen.

"When *I'm* a Duchess," she said to herself (not in a very hopeful tone, though), "I won't have any pepper in my kitchen *at all*. Soup does very well without—Maybe it's always pepper that makes people hot-tempered," she went on, very much pleased at having found out a new kind of rule, "and vinegar that makes them sour—and camomile that makes them bitter—and—and barley-sugar and such things that make children sweet-tempered. I only wish people knew *that*: then they wouldn't be so stingy about it, you know—"

She had quite forgotten the Duchess by this time, and was a little startled when she heard her voice close to her ear. "You're thinking about something, my dear, and that makes you forget to talk. I can't tell you just now what the moral of that is, but I shall remember it in a bit."

"Perhaps it hasn't one," Alice ventured to remark.

"Tut, tut, child!" said the Duchess. "Everything's got a moral, if only you can find it." And she squeezed herself up closer to Alice's side as she spoke.

Alice did not much like her keeping so close to her: first, because the Duchess was *very* ugly; and secondly, because she was exactly the right height to rest her chin on Alice's shoulder, and it was an uncomfortably sharp chin. However, she did not like to be rude: so she bore it as well as she could.

"The game's going on rather better now," she said, by way of keeping up the conversation a little.

" 'Tis so," said the Duchess: "and the moral of that is—'Oh, 'tis love, 'tis love, that makes the world go round!' "

"Somebody said," Alice whispered, "that it's done by everybody minding their own business!"

"Ah, well! It means much the same thing," said the Duchess, digging her sharp little chin into Alice's shoulder as she added, "and the moral of *that* is—'Take care of the sense, and the sounds will take care of themselves.' "

"How fond she is of finding morals in things!" Alice thought to herself.

"I dare say you're wondering why I don't put my arm round your waist," the Duchess said, after a pause: "the reason is, that I'm doubtful about the temper of your flamingo. Shall I try the experiment?"

"He might bite," Alice cautiously replied, not feeling at all anxious to have the experiment tried.

"Very true," said the Duchess: "flamingoes and mustard both bite. And the moral of that is— 'Birds of a feather flock together.' "

"Only mustard isn't a bird," Alice remarked.

"Right, as usual," said the Duchess: "what a clear way you have of putting things!"

"It's a mineral, I *think*," said Alice.

"Of course it is," said the Duchess, who seemed ready to agree to everything that Alice said: "there's a large mustard mine near here. And the moral of that is—'The more there is of mine, the less there is of yours.'"

"Oh, I know!" exclaimed Alice, who had not attended to this last remark. "It's a vegetable. It doesn't look like one, but it is."

"I quite agree with you," said the Duchess; "and the moral of that is—'Be what you would seem to be'—or, if you'd like it put more simply—'Never imagine yourself not to be otherwise than what it might appear to others that what you were or might have been was not otherwise than what you had been would have appeared to them to be otherwise.'"

"I think I should understand that better," Alice said very politely, "if I had it written down: but I can't quite follow it as you say it."

"That's nothing to what I could say if I chose," the Duchess replied, in a pleased tone.

"Pray don't trouble yourself to say it any longer than that," said Alice.

"Oh, don't talk about trouble!" said the Duchess. "I make you a present of everything I've said as yet."

"A cheap sort of present," thought Alice. "I'm glad people don't give birthday presents like that!" But she did not venture to say it out loud.

"Thinking again?" the Duchess asked, with another dig of her sharp little chin.

"I've a right to think," said Alice sharply, for she was beginning to feel a little worried.

"Just about as much right," said the Duchess, "as pigs have to fly; and the m—"

But here, to Alice's great surprise, the Duchess's voice died away, even in the middle of her favorite word "moral," and the arm that was linked into hers began to tremble.

Alice looked up, and there stood the Queen in front of them, with her arms folded, frowning like a thunderstorm.

"A fine day, your Majesty!" the Duchess began in a low, weak voice.

"Now, I give you fair warning," shouted the Queen, stamping on the ground as she spoke; "either you or your head must be off, and that in about half no time! Take your choice!"

The Duchess took her choice, and was gone in a moment.

"Let's go on with the game," the Queen said to Alice; and Alice was too much frightened to say a word, but slowly followed her back to the croquet ground.

The other guests had taken advantage of the Queen's absence, and were resting in the shade: however, the moment they saw her they hurried back to the game, the Queen merely remarking that a moment's delay would cost them their lives.

All the time they were playing the Queen never

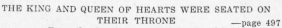

THE KING AND QUEEN OF HEARTS WERE SEATED ON
THEIR THRONE   —page 497
From the drawing by Sir John Tenniel

left off quarrelling with the other players and shouting, "Off with his head!" or "Off with her head!"

Those whom she sentenced were taken into custody by the soldiers, who of course had to leave off being arches to do this, so that, by the end of half an hour or so, there were no arches left, and all the players, except the King, the Queen, and Alice, were in custody and under sentence of execution.

Then the Queen left off, quite out of breath, and said to Alice:

"Have you seen the Mock Turtle yet?"

"No," said Alice. "I don't even know what a Mock Turtle is."

"It's the thing Mock Turtle soup is made from," said the Queen.

"I never saw one, or heard of one," said Alice.

"Come on, then," said the Queen, "and he shall tell you his history."

As they walked off together, Alice heard the King say in a low voice, to the company generally, "You are all pardoned." "Come, *that's* a good thing!" she said to herself, for she had felt quite unhappy at the number of executions the Queen had ordered.

They very soon came upon a Gryphon, lying fast asleep in the sun. "Up, lazy thing!" said the Queen, "and take this young lady to see the Mock Turtle, and to hear his history. I must go back and see after some executions I have ordered;" and she walked off, leaving Alice alone with the Gryphon.

Alice did not quite like the look of the creature, but on the whole she thought it would be quite as safe to stay with it as to go after that savage Queen: so she waited.

The Gryphon sat up and rubbed its eyes: then it watched the Queen till she was out of sight: then it chuckled.

"What fun!" said the Gryphon, half to itself, half to Alice.

"What *is* the fun?" said Alice.

"Why, *she,*" said the Gryphon. "It's all her fancy, that: they never executes nobody, you know. Come on!"

"Everybody says 'come on!' here," thought Alice, as she went slowly after it: "I never was so ordered about before, in all my life, never!"

They had not gone far before they saw the Mock Turtle in the distance, sitting sad and lonely on a little ledge of rock, and, as they came nearer, Alice could hear him sighing as if his heart would break.

She pitied him deeply. "What is his sorrow?" she asked the Gryphon. And the Gryphon answered, very nearly in the same words as before, "It's all his fancy, that: he hasn't got no sorrow, you know. Come on!"

So they went up to the Mock Turtle, who looked at them with large eyes full of tears, but said nothing.

"This here young lady," said the Gryphon, "she wants for to know your history, she do."

"I'll tell it her," said the Mock Turtle in a deep,

hollow tone. "Sit down, both of you, and don't speak a word till I've finished."

So they sat down, and nobody spoke for some minutes. Alice thought to herself "I don't see how he can *ever* finish, if he doesn't begin." But she waited patiently.

"Once," said the Mock Turtle at last, with a deep sigh, "I was a real Turtle."

These words were followed by a very long silence, broken only by an occasional exclamation of "Hjckrrh!" from the Gryphon, and the constant heavy sobbing of the Mock Turtle. Alice was very nearly getting up and saying, "Thank you, Sir, for your interesting story," but she could not help thinking there *must* be more to come, so she sat still and said nothing.

"When we were little," the Mock Turtle went on at last, more calmly, though still sobbing a little now and then, "we went to school in the sea. The master was an old Turtle—we used to call him Tortoise—"

"Why did you call him Tortoise, if he wasn't one?" Alice asked.

"We called him Tortoise because he taught us," said the Mock Turtle angrily. "Really you are very dull!"

"You ought to be ashamed of yourself for asking such a simple question," added the Gryphon; and then they both sat silent and looked at poor Alice, who felt ready to sink into the earth. At last the Gryphon said to the Mock Turtle, "Drive on, old fellow! Don't be all day about it!" and he went on in these words:

"Yes, we went to school in the sea, though you mayn't believe it—"

"I never said I didn't!" interrupted Alice.

"You did," said the Mock Turtle.

"Hold your tongue!" added the Gryphon, before Alice could speak again. The Mock Turtle went on:

"We had the best of educations—in fact, we went to school every day—"

"*I've* been to a day-school, too," said Alice. "You needn't be so proud as all that."

"With extras?" asked the Mock Turtle, a little anxiously.

"Yes," said Alice; "we learned French and music."

"And washing?" said the Mock Turtle.

"Certainly not!" said Alice indignantly.

"Ah! Then yours wasn't a really good school," said the Mock Turtle in a tone of great relief. "Now, at *ours*, they had, at the end of the bill, 'French, music, *and washing*—extra.'"

"You couldn't have wanted it much," said Alice; "living at the bottom of the sea."

"I couldn't afford to learn it," said the Mock Turtle with a sigh. "I only took the regular course."

"What was that?" inquired Alice.

"Reeling and Writhing, of course, to begin with," the Mock Turtle replied; "and then the different branches of Arithmetic—Ambition, Distraction, Uglification, and Derision."

"I never heard of 'Uglification,'" Alice ventured to say. "What is it?"

The Gryphon lifted up both its paws in surprise. "Never heard of uglifying!" it exclaimed. "You know what to beautify is, I suppose?"

"Yes," said Alice doubtfully: "it means—to—make—anything—prettier."

"Well, then," the Gryphon went on, "if you don't know what to uglify is, you *are* a simpleton."

Alice did not feel encouraged to ask any more questions about it: so she turned to the Mock Turtle, and said, "What else had you to learn?"

"Well, there was Mystery," the Mock Turtle replied, counting off the subjects on his flappers—"Mystery, ancient and modern, with Seaography: then Drawling—the Drawling-master was an old conger-eel, that used to come once a week: *he* taught us Drawling, Stretching, and Fainting in Coils."

"What was *that* like?" said Alice.

"Well, I can't show it you, myself," the Mock Turtle said: "I'm too stiff. And the Gryphon never learned it."

"Hadn't time," said the Gryphon: "I went to the Classical master, though. He was an old crab, *he* was."

"I never went to him," the Mock Turtle said with a sigh. "He taught Laughing and Grief, they used to say."

"So he did, so he did," said the Gryphon, sighing in his turn; and both creatures hid their faces in their paws.

"And how many hours a day did you do lessons?" said Alice, in a hurry to change the subject.

"Ten hours the first day," said the Mock Turtle: "nine the next, and so on."

"What a curious plan!" exclaimed Alice.

"That's the reason they're called lessons," the Gryphon remarked: "because they lessen from day to day."

This was quite a new idea to Alice, and she thought it over a little before she made her next remark. "Then the eleventh day must have been a holiday?"

"Of course it was," said the Mock Turtle.

"And how did you manage on the twelfth?" Alice went on eagerly.

"That's enough about lessons," the Gryphon interrupted in a very decided tone. "Tell her something about the games now."

THE LOBSTER-QUADRILLE

By Lewis Carroll

THE Mock Turtle sighed deeply, and drew the back of one flapper across his eyes. He looked at Alice and tried to speak, but, for a minute or two, sobs choked his voice. "Same as if he had a bone in his throat," said the Gryphon; and it set to work shaking him and punching him in the back. At last the Mock Turtle recovered his voice, and, with tears running down his cheeks, he went on again:

"You may not have lived much under the sea—" ("I haven't," said Alice)—"and perhaps you were never even introduced to a lobster—" (Alice began to say, "I once tasted—" but checked herself hastily, and said, "No, never") "—so you can have no idea what a delightful thing a Lobster-Quadrille is!"

"No, indeed," said Alice. "What sort of a dance is it?"

"Why," said the Gryphon, "you first form into a line along the sea-shore—"

"Two lines!" cried the Mock Turtle. "Seals, turtles, salmon, and so on: then, when you've cleared all the jelly-fish out of the way—"

"*That* generally takes some time," interrupted the Gryphon.

"—you advance twice—"

"Each with a lobster as a partner!" cried the Gryphon.

"Of course," the Mock Turtle said: "advance twice, set to partners—"

"—change lobsters, and retire in same order," continued the Gryphon.

"Then, you know," the Mock Turtle went on, "you throw the—"

"The lobsters!" shouted the Gryphon, with a bound into the air.

"—as far out to sea as you can—"

"Swim after them!" screamed the Gryphon.

"Turn a somersault in the sea!" cried the Mock Turtle, capering wildly about.

"Change lobsters again!" yelled the Gryphon at the top of its voice.

"Back to land again, and—that's all the first figure," said the Mock Turtle, suddenly dropping his voice; and the two creatures, who had been jumping about like mad things all this time, sat down again very sadly and quietly and looked at Alice.

"It must be a very pretty dance," said Alice timidly.

"Would you like to see a little of it?" said the Mock Turtle.

"Very much indeed," said Alice.

"Come, let's try the first figure!" said the Mock Turtle to the Gryphon. "We can do it without lobsters, you know. Which shall sing?"

"Oh, *you* sing," said the Gryphon. "I've forgotten the words."

So they began solemnly dancing round and round Alice, every now and then treading on her toes when they passed too close, and waving their fore-paws to mark the time, while the Mock Turtle sang this, very slowly and sadly:

"Will you walk a little faster?" said a whiting to a snail,
"There's a porpoise close behind us, and he's treading on my tail.
See how eagerly the lobsters and the turtles all advance!
They are waiting on the shingle—will you come and join the dance?
Will you, won't you, will you, won't you, will you join the dance?
Will you, won't you, will you, won't you, won't you join the dance?

"You can really have no notion how delightful it will be
When they take us up and throw us, with the lobsters, out to sea!"
But the snail replied, "Too far, too far!" and gave a look askance—

Said he thanked the whiting kindly, but he would not join
the dance.
Would not, could not, would not, could not, would not join
the dance.
Would not, could not, would not, could not, could not join
the dance.

"What matters it how far we go?" his scaly friend replied.
"There is another shore, you know, upon the other side.
The further off from England the nearer is to France—
Then turn not pale, beloved snail, but come and join the
dance.
Will you, won't you, will you, won't you, will you join the
dance?
Will you, won't you, will you, won't you, won't you join the
dance?"

"Thank you, it's a very interesting dance to watch," said Alice, feeling very glad that it was over at last: "and I do so like that curious song about the whiting!"

"Oh, as to the whiting," said the Mock Turtle, "they—you've seen them, of course?"

"Yes," said Alice, "I've often seen them at dinn—" she checked herself hastily.

"I don't know where Dinn may be," said the Mock Turtle; "but, if you've seen them so often, of course you know what they're like?"

"I believe so," Alice replied thoughtfully. "They have their tails in their mouths—and they're all over crumbs."

"You're wrong about the crumbs," said the Mock Turtle: "crumbs would all wash off in the sea. But they *have* their tails in their mouths; and the reason is—" here the Mock Turtle yawned and shut his eyes.

"Tell her about the reason and all that," he said to the Gryphon.

"The reason is," said the Gryphon, "that they *would* go with the lobsters to the dance. So they got thrown out to sea. So they had to fall a long way. So they got their tails fast in their mouths. So they couldn't get them out again. That's all."

"Thank you," said Alice, "it's very interesting. I never knew so much about a whiting before."

"I can tell you more than that, if you like," said the Gryphon. "Do you know why it's called a whiting?"

"I never thought about it," said Alice. "Why?"

"It does the boots and shoes," the Gryphon replied very solemnly.

Alice was thoroughly puzzled. "Does the boots and shoes!" she repeated in a wondering tone.

"Why, what are *your* shoes done with?" said the Gryphon. "I mean, what makes them so shiny?"

Alice looked down at them, and considered a little before she gave her answer. "They're done with blacking, I believe."

"Boots and shoes under the sea," the Gryphon went on in a deep voice, "are done with whiting. Now you know."

"And what are they made of?" Alice asked in a tone of great curiosity.

"Soles and eels, of course," the Gryphon replied, rather impatiently: "any shrimp could have told you that."

THE LOBSTER-QUADRILLE

"If I'd been the whiting," said Alice, whose thoughts were still running on the song, "I'd have said to the porpoise, 'Keep back, please! We don't want *you* with us!'"

"They were obliged to have him with them," the Mock Turtle said. "No wise fish would go anywhere without a porpoise."

"Wouldn't it really?" said Alice, in a tone of great surprise.

"Of course not," said the Mock Turtle. "Why, if a fish came to *me* and told me he was going a journey, I should say, 'With what porpoise?'"

"Don't you mean 'purpose'?" said Alice.

"I mean what I say," the Mock Turtle replied, in an offended tone. And the Gryphon added, "Come, let's hear some of *your* adventures."

"I could tell you my adventures—beginning from this morning," said Alice a little timidly; "but it's no use going back to yesterday, because I was a different person then."

"Explain all that," said the Mock Turtle.

"No, no! The adventures first," said the Gryphon in an impatient tone: "explanations take such a dreadful time."

So Alice began telling them her adventures from the time when she first saw the White Rabbit. She was a little nervous about it, just at first, the two creatures got so close to her, one on each side, and opened their eyes and mouths so *very* wide; but she gained courage as she went on. Her listeners were perfectly quiet till she got to the part about her repeating, *"You are old, Father William,"* to the Caterpillar, and the words all coming different, and then the Mock Turtle drew a long breath, and said, "That's very curious!"

"It's all about as curious as it can be," said the Gryphon.

"It all came different!" the Mock Turtle repeated thoughtfully. "I should like to hear her try and repeat something now. Tell her to begin." He looked at the Gryphon as if he thought it had some kind of authority over Alice.

"Stand up and repeat, ' *'Tis the voice of the slug-gard,*'" said the Gryphon.

"How the creatures order one about, and make one repeat lessons!" thought Alice. "I might just as well be at school at once." However, she got up, and began to repeat it, but her head was so full of the Lobster-Quadrille, that she hardly knew what she was saying; and the words came very queer indeed:

"'Tis the voice of the Lobster: I heard him declare
'You have baked me too brown, I must sugar my hair.'
As a duck with its eyelids, so he with his nose
Trims his belt and his buttons, and turns out his toes.
When the sands are all dry, he is gay as a lark,
And will talk in contemptuous tones of the shark:
But, when the tide rises and sharks are around,
His voice has a timid and tremulous sound."

"That's different from what *I* used to say when I was a child," said the Gryphon.

"Well, *I* never heard it before," said the Mock Turtle, "but it sounds uncommon nonsense."

Alice said nothing: she had sat down with her face in her hands, wondering if anything would *ever* happen in a natural way again.

"I should like to have it explained," said the Mock Turtle.

"She can't explain it," said the Gryphon hastily. "Go on with the next verse."

"But about his toes?" the Mock Turtle persisted. "How *could* he turn them out with his nose, you know?"

"It's the first position in dancing," Alice said; but she was dreadfully puzzled by the whole thing, and longed to change the subject.

"Go on with the next verse," the Gryphon repeated: "it begins, '*I passed by his garden.*'"

Alice did not dare to disobey, though she felt sure it would all come wrong, and she went on in a trembling voice:—

"I passed by his garden and marked, with one eye,
How the Owl and the Panther were sharing a pie:
The Panther took pie-crust, and gravy, and meat,
While the Owl had the dish as its share of the treat.
When the pie was all finished, the Owl, as a boon,
Was kindly permitted to pocket the spoon:
While the Panther received knife and fork with a growl,
And concluded the banquet by—"

"What *is* the use of repeating all that stuff?" the Mock Turtle interrupted, "if you don't explain it as you go on? It's by far the most confusing thing *I* ever heard!"

"Yes, I think you'd better leave off," said the Gryphon, and Alice was only too glad to do so.

THE LOBSTER-QUADRILLE

"Shall we try another figure of the Lobster-Quadrille?" the Gryphon went on. "Or would you like the Mock Turtle to sing you another song?"

"Oh, a song, please, if the Mock Turtle would be so kind," Alice replied, so eagerly that the Gryphon said, in a rather offended tone, "Hm! No accounting for tastes! Sing her '*Turtle Soup*,' will you, old fellow?"

The Mock Turtle sighed deeply, and began, in a voice choked with sobs, to sing this:—

> "Beautiful Soup, so rich and green,
>   Waiting in a hot tureen!
>   Who for such dainties would not stoop?
>   Soup of the evening, beautiful Soup!
>   Soup of the evening, beautiful Soup!
>   Beau—ootiful Soo—oop!
>   Beau—ootiful Soo—oop!
>   Soo—oop of the e—e—evening,
>   Beautiful, beautiful Soup!
>
> "Beautiful Soup! Who cares for fish,
>   Game, or any other dish?
>   Who would not give all else for two p
>   ennyworth only of beautiful Soup?
>   Pennyworth only of beautiful Soup?
>   Beau—ootiful Soo—oop!
>   Beau—ootiful Soo—oop!
>   Soo—oop of the e—e—evening,
>   Beautiful, beauti—FUL SOUP!"

"Chorus again!" cried the Gryphon, and the Mock Turtle had just begun to repeat it, when a cry of "The trial's beginning!" was heard in the distance.

WHO STOLE THE TARTS?

"Come on!" cried the Gryphon, and, taking Alice by the hand, it hurried off without waiting for the end of the song.

"What trial is it?" Alice panted as she ran; but the Gryphon only answered, "Come on!" and ran the faster, while more and more faintly came, carried on the breeze that followed them, the melancholy words:

> "Soo—oop of the e—e—evening,
> Beautiful, beautiful Soup!"

WHO STOLE THE TARTS?

By Lewis Carroll

THE King and Queen of Hearts were seated on their throne when they arrived, with a great crowd assembled about them—all sorts of little birds and beasts, as well as the whole pack of cards: the Knave was standing before them, in chains, with a soldier on each side to guard him; and near the King was the White Rabbit, with a trumpet in one hand, and a scroll of parchment in the other.

In the very middle of the court was a table with a large dish of tarts upon it: they looked so good, that it made Alice quite hungry to look at them—"I wish they'd get the trial done," she thought, "and hand round the refreshments!" But there seemed to be no chance of this; so she began looking at everything about her to pass away the time.

Alice had never been in a court of justice before, but she had read about them in books, and she was quite pleased to find that she knew the name of nearly everything there.

"That's the judge," she said to herself, "because of his great wig."

The judge, by the way, was the King; and, as he wore his crown over the wig, he did not look at all comfortable, and it was certainly not becoming.

"And that's the jury-box," thought Alice; "and those twelve creatures" (she was obliged to say "creatures," you see, because some of them were animals, and some were birds), "I suppose they are the jurors." She said this last word two or three times over to herself, being rather proud of it: for she thought, and rightly too, that very few little girls of her age knew the meaning of it at all. However, "jurymen" would have done just as well.

The twelve jurors were all writing very busily on slates.

"What are they doing?" Alice whispered to the Gryphon. "They can't have anything to put down yet, before the trial's begun."

"They're putting down their names," the Gryphon whispered in reply, "for fear they should forget them before the end of the trial."

"Stupid things!" Alice began in a loud indignant voice; but she stopped herself hastily, for the White Rabbit cried out, "Silence in the court!" and the King put on his spectacles and looked anxiously round, to make out who was talking.

WHO STOLE THE TARTS?

Alice could see, as well as if she were looking over their shoulders, that all the jurors were writing down "Stupid things!" on their slates, and she could even make out that one of them didn't know how to spell "stupid," and that he had to ask his neighbor to tell him.

"A nice muddle their slates'll be in, before the trial's over!" thought Alice.

One of the jurors had a pencil that squeaked. This, of course, Alice could *not* stand, and she went round the court and got behind him, and very soon found an opportunity of taking it away. She did it so quickly that the poor little juror (it was Bill, the Lizard) could not make out at all what had become of it; so, after hunting all about for it, he was obliged to write with one finger for the rest of the day; and this was of very little use as it left no mark on the slate.

"Herald, read the accusation!" said the King.

On this the White Rabbit blew three blasts on the trumpet, and then unrolled the parchment-scroll, and read as follows:

"The Queen of Hearts, she made some tarts,
　All on a summer day:
The Knave of Hearts, he stole those tarts
　And took them quite away!"

"Consider your verdict," the King said to the jury.

"Not yet, not yet!" the Rabbit hastily interrupted. "There's a great deal to come before that!"

"Call the first witness," said the King; and the

WHO STOLE THE TARTS?

White Rabbit blew three blasts on the trumpet, and called out "First witness!"

The first witness was the Hatter. He came in with a teacup in one hand and a piece of bread-and-butter in the other.

"I beg pardon, your Majesty," he began, "for bringing these in; but I hadn't quite finished my tea when I was sent for."

"You ought to have finished," said the King. "When did you begin?"

The Hatter looked at the March Hare, who had followed him into the court, arm-in-arm with the Dormouse. "Fourteenth of March, I *think* it was," he said.

"Fifteenth," said the March Hare.

"Sixteenth," said the Dormouse.

"Write that down," the King said to the jury; and the jury eagerly wrote down all three dates on their slates, and then added them up, and reduced the answer to shillings and pence.

"Take off your hat," the King said to the Hatter.

"It isn't mine," said the Hatter.

"*Stolen!*" the King exclaimed, turning to the jury, who instantly made a memorandum of the fact.

"I keep them to sell," the Hatter added as an explanation. "I've none of my own. I'm a hatter."

Here the Queen put on her spectacles, and began staring hard at the Hatter, who turned pale and fidgeted.

"Give your evidence," said the King; "and don't be nervous, or I'll have you executed on the spot."

This did not seem to encourage the witness at all: he kept shifting from one foot to the other, looking uneasily at the Queen, and in his confusion he bit a large piece out of his teacup instead of the bread-and-butter.

Just at this moment Alice felt a very curious sensation, which puzzled her a good deal until she made out what it was: she was beginning to grow larger again, and she thought at first she would get up and leave the court; but on second thoughts she decided to remain where she was as long as there was room for her.

"I wish you wouldn't squeeze so," said the Dormouse, who was sitting next to her. "I can hardly breathe."

"I can't help it," said Alice very meekly: "I'm growing."

"You've no right to grow *here,*" said the Dormouse.

"Don't talk nonsense," said Alice more boldly: "you know you're growing too."

"Yes, but *I* grow at a reasonable pace," said the Dormouse: "not in that ridiculous fashion." And he got up very sulkily and crossed over to the other side of the court.

All this time the Queen had never left off staring at the Hatter, and, just as the Dormouse crossed the court, she said, to one of the officers of the court, "Bring me the list of the singers in the last concert!" on which the wretched Hatter trembled so that he shook off both his shoes.

"Give your evidence," the King repeated angrily, "or I'll have you executed, whether you're nervous or not."

"I'm a poor man, your Majesty," the Hatter began, in a trembling voice, "and I hadn't begun my tea—not above a week or so—and what with the bread-and-butter getting so thin—and the twinkling of the tea—"

"The twinkling of *what?*" said the King.

"It *began* with the tea," the Hatter replied.

"Of course twinkling *begins* with a T!" said the King sharply. "Do you take me for a dunce? Go on!"

"I'm a poor man," the Hatter went on, "and most things twinkled after that—only the March Hare said—"

"I didn't!" the March Hare interrupted in a great hurry.

"You did!" said the Hatter.

"I deny it!" said the March Hare.

"He denies it," said the King: "leave out that part."

"Well, at any rate, the Dormouse said—" the Hatter went on, looking anxiously round to see if he would deny it too; but the Dormouse denied nothing, being fast asleep.

"After that," continued the Hatter, "I cut some more bread and butter—"

"But what did the Dormouse say?" one of the jury asked.

"That I can't remember," said the Hatter.

"You *must* remember," remarked the King, "or I'll have you executed."

The miserable Hatter dropped his teacup and

bread-and-butter, and went down on one knee.
"I'm a poor man, your Majesty," he began.

"You're a *very* poor *speaker,*" said the King.

Here one of the guinea-pigs cheered, and was
immediately suppressed by the officers of the court.
(As that is rather a hard word, I will just explain
to you how it was done. They had a large canvas
bag, which tied up at the mouth with strings; into
this they slipped the guinea-pig, head first, and
then sat upon it.)

"I'm glad I've seen that done," thought Alice.
"I've so often read in the newspapers, at the end
of trials, 'There was some attempt at applause,
which was immediately suppressed by the officers
of the court,' and I never understood what it meant
till now."

"If that's all you know about it, you may stand
down," continued the King.

"I can't go no lower," said the Hatter: "I'm on
the floor, as it is."

"Then you may *sit* down," the King replied.

Here the other guinea-pig cheered, and was suppressed.

"Come, that finishes the guinea-pigs!" thought
Alice. "Now we shall go on better."

"I'd rather finish my tea," said the Hatter, with
an anxious look at the Queen, who was reading the
list of singers.

"You may go," said the King, and the Hatter
hurriedly left the court, without even waiting to
put his shoes on.

"—and just take his head off outside," the Queen
added to one of the officers; but the Hatter was

out of sight before the officer could get to the door.

"Call the next witness!" said the King.

The next witness was the Duchess's cook. She carried the pepper-box in her hand, and Alice guessed who it was, even before she got into the court, by the way the people near the door began sneezing all at once.

"Give your evidence," said the King.

"Shan't," said the cook.

The King looked anxiously at the White Rabbit, who said, in a low voice, "Your Majesty must cross-examine *this* witness."

"Well, if I must, I must," the King said with a melancholy air, and, after folding his arms and frowning at the cook till his eyes were nearly out of sight, he said, in a deep voice, "What are tarts made of?"

"Pepper, mostly," said the cook.

"Treacle," said a sleepy voice behind her.

"Collar that Dormouse!" the Queen shrieked out. "Behead that Dormouse! Turn that Dormouse out of court! Suppress him! Pinch him! Off with his whiskers!"

For some minutes the whole court was in confusion, getting the Dormouse turned out, and, by the time they had settled down again, the cook had disappeared.

"Never mind!" said the King, with an air of great relief. "Call the next witness." And, he added, in an undertone to the Queen, "Really, my dear, *you* must cross-examine the next witness. It quite makes my forehead ache!"

ALICE'S EVIDENCE

Alice watched the White Rabbit as he fumbled over the list, feeling very curious to see what the next witness would be like, "—for they haven't got much evidence *yet*," she said to herself. Imagine her surprise, when the White Rabbit read out, at the top of his shrill little voice, the name "Alice!"

ALICE'S EVIDENCE

By Lewis Carroll

"**H**ERE!" cried Alice, quite forgetting in the flurry of the moment how large she had grown in the last few minutes, and she jumped up in such a hurry that she tipped over the jury-box with the edge of her skirt, upsetting all the jurymen on to the heads of the crowd below, and there they lay sprawling about, reminding her very much of a globe of gold-fish she had accidentally upset the week before.

"Oh, I *beg* your pardon!" she exclaimed in a tone of great dismay, and began picking them up again as quickly as she could, for the accident of the gold-fish kept running in her head, and she had a vague sort of idea that they must be collected at once and put back into the jury-box, or they would die.

"The trial cannot proceed," said the King, in a very grave voice, "until all the jurymen are back in their proper places—*all*," he repeated with great emphasis, looking hard at Alice as he said so.

Alice looked at the jury-box, and saw that, in her haste, she had put the Lizard in head downward, and the poor little thing was waving its tail about in a melancholy way, being quite unable to move.

She soon got it out again, and put it right; "not that it signifies much," she said to herself; "I should think it would be *quite* as much use in the trial one way up as the other."

As soon as the jury had a little recovered from the shock of being upset, and their slates and pencils had been found and handed back to them, they set to work very diligently to write out a history of the accident, all except the Lizard, who seemed too much overcome to do anything but sit with its mouth open, gazing up into the roof of the court.

"What do you know about this business?" the King said to Alice.

"Nothing," said Alice.

"Nothing *whatever?*" persisted the King.

"Nothing whatever," said Alice.

"That's very important," the King said, turning to the jury. They were just beginning to write this down on their slates, when the White Rabbit interrupted: "*Un*important, your Majesty means, of course," he said, in a very respectful tone, but frowning and making faces at him as he spoke.

"*Un*important, of course, I meant," the King hastily said, and went on to himself in an undertone, "important—unimportant — unimportant—important—" as if he were trying which word sounded best.

Some of the jury wrote it down "important," and some "unimportant."

Alice could see this, as she was near enough to look over their slates; "but it doesn't matter a bit," she thought to herself.

At this moment the King, who had been for some time busily writing in his note-book, called out, "Silence!" and read out from his book, "Rule Forty-two. *All persons more than a mile high to leave the court.*"

Everybody looked at Alice.

"*I'm* not a mile high," said Alice.

"You are," said the King.

"Nearly two miles high," added the Queen.

"Well, I shan't go, at any rate," said Alice: "besides, that's not a regular rule: you invented it just now."

"It's the oldest rule in the book," said the King.

"Then it ought to be Number One," said Alice.

The King turned pale, and shut his note-book hastily.

"Consider your verdict," he said to the jury, in a low trembling voice.

"There's more evidence to come yet, please your Majesty," said the White Rabbit, jumping up in a great hurry: "this paper has just been picked up."

"What's in it?" said the Queen.

"I haven't opened it yet," said the White Rabbit; "but it seems to be a letter, written by the prisoner to—to somebody."

"It must have been that," said the King, "unless

507

it was written to nobody, which isn't usual, you know."

"Who is it directed to?" said one of the jury-men.

"It isn't directed at all," said the White Rabbit: "in fact, there's nothing written on the *out-side.*" He unfolded the paper as he spoke, and added, "It isn't a letter, after all: it's a set of verses."

"Are they in the prisoner's handwriting?" asked another of the jurymen.

"No, they're not," said the White Rabbit, "and that's the queerest thing about it." (The jury all looked puzzled.)

"He must have imitated somebody else's hand," said the King. (The jury all brightened up again.)

"Please your Majesty," said the Knave, "I didn't write it, and they can't prove that I did: there's no name signed at the end."

"If you didn't sign it," said the King, "that only makes the matter worse. You *must* have meant some mischief, or else you'd have signed your name like an honest man."

There was a general clapping of hands at this: it was the first really clever thing the King had said that day.

"That *proves* his guilt, of course," said the Queen: "so, off with—"

"It doesn't prove anything of the sort!" said Alice. "Why, you don't even know what they're about!"

"Read them," said the King.

The White Rabbit put on his spectacles. "Where shall I begin, please your Majesty?" he asked.

"Begin at the beginning," the King said very gravely, "and go on till you come to the end: then stop."

There was dead silence in the court, while the White Rabbit read out these verses:

"They told me you had been to her,
And mentioned me to him:
She gave me a good character,
But said I could not swim.

He sent them word I had not gone
(We know it to be true):
If she should push the matter on,
What would become of you?

I gave her one, they gave him two,
You gave us three or more;
They all returned from him to you,
Though they were mine before.

If I or she should chance to be
Involved in this affair,
He trusts to you to set them free,
Exactly as we were.

My notion was that you had been
(Before she had this fit)
An obstacle that came between
Him, and ourselves, and it.

Don't let him know she liked them best,
For this must ever be
A secret, kept from all the rest,
Between yourself and me."

"That's the most important piece of evidence we've heard yet," said the King, rubbing his hands; "so now let the jury—"

"If any one of them can explain it," said Alice (she had grown so large in the last few minutes that she wasn't a bit afraid of interrupting him), "I'll give him sixpence. *I* don't believe there's an atom of meaning in it."

The jury all wrote down, on their slates, "*She doesn't believe there's an atom of meaning in it,*" but none of them attempted to explain the paper.

"If there's no meaning in it," said the King, "that saves a world of trouble, you know, as we needn't try to find any. And yet I don't know," he went on, spreading out the verses on his knee, and looking at them with one eye; "I seem to see some meaning in them, after all. '—*said I could not swim*—' you can't swim, can you?" he added, turning to the Knave.

The Knave shook his head sadly.

"Do I look like it?" he said. (Which he certainly did *not*, being made entirely of cardboard.)

"All right, so far," said the King; and he went on muttering over the verses to himself: "'*We know it to be true*'—that's the jury, of course—'*If she should push the matter on*'—that must be the Queen—'*What would become of you?*'—What indeed!—'*I gave her one, they gave him two*'—why, that must be what he did with the tarts, you know—"

"But it goes on '*they all returned from him to you,*'" said Alice.

"Why, there they are!" said the King triumphantly, pointing to the tarts on the table. "Nothing can be clearer than *that*. Then again—'before she had this fit'—you never had *fits,* my dear, I think?" he said to the Queen.

"Never!" said the Queen, furiously, throwing an inkstand at the Lizard as she spoke. (The unfortunate little Bill had left off writing on his slate with one finger, as he found it made no mark; but he now hastily began again, using the ink, that was trickling down his face, as long as it lasted.)

"Then the words don't *fit* you," said the King, looking round the court with a smile. There was a dead silence.

"It's a pun!" the King added in an angry tone, and everybody laughed. "Let the jury consider their verdict," the King said, for about the twentieth time that day.

"No, no!" said the Queen. "Sentence first—verdict afterward."

"Stuff and nonsense!" said Alice loudly. "The idea of having the sentence first!"

"Hold your tongue!" said the Queen, turning purple.

"I won't!" said Alice.

"Off with her head!" the Queen shouted at the top of her voice. Nobody moved.

"Who cares for *you?*" said Alice (she had grown to her full size by this time). "You're nothing but a pack of cards!"

At this the whole pack rose up into the air, and came flying down upon her; she gave a little

511

scream, half of fright and half of anger, and tried to beat them off, and found herself lying on the bank, with her head in the lap of her sister, who was gently brushing away some dead leaves that had fluttered down from the trees upon her face.

"Wake up, Alice dear!" said her sister. "Why, what a long sleep you've had!"

"Oh, I've had such a curious dream!" said Alice. And she told her sister, as well as she could remember them, all these strange adventures of hers that you have just been reading about; and, when she had finished, her sister kissed her, and said, "It *was* a curious dream, dear, certainly; but now run into your tea: it's getting late."

So Alice got up and ran off, thinking while she ran, as well she might, what a wonderful dream it had been.

*　　*　　*　　*　　*　　*　　*

But her sister sat still just as she left her, leaning her head on her hand, watching the setting sun, and thinking of little Alice and all her wonderful Adventures, till she too began dreaming after a fashion, and this was her dream:

First, she dreamed about little Alice herself: once again the tiny hands were clasped upon her knee, and the bright eager eyes were looking into hers—she could hear the very tones of her voice, and see that queer little toss of her head to keep back the wandering hair that *would* always get into her eyes—and still as she listened, or seemed to listen, the whole place around her became alive with the strange creatures of her little sister's dream.

The long grass rustled at her feet as the White Rabbit hurried by—the frightened Mouse splashed his way through the neighboring pool—she could hear the rattle of the teacups as the March Hare and his friends shared their never-ending meal, and the shrill voice of the Queen ordering off her unfortunate guests to execution—once more the pig-baby was sneezing on the Duchess' knee, while plates and dishes crashed around it—once more the shriek of the Gryphon, the squeaking of the Lizard's slate-pencil, and the choking of the suppressed guinea-pigs, filled the air, mixed up with the distant sob of the miserable Mock Turtle.

So she sat on, with closed eyes, and half believed herself in Wonderland, though she knew she had but to open them again, and all would change to dull reality—the grass would be only rustling in the wind, and the pool rippling to the waving of the reeds—the rattling teacups would change to tinkling sheep bells, and the Queen's shrill cries to the voice of the shepherd-boy—and the sneeze of the baby, the shriek of the Gryphon, and all the other queer noises, would change (she knew) to the confused clamor of the busy farm-yard—while the lowing of the cattle in the distance would take the place of the Mock Turtle's heavy sobs.

Lastly, she pictured to herself how this same little sister of hers would, in the after-time, be herself a grown woman; and how she would keep, through all her riper years, the simple and loving heart of her childhood; and how she would gather about her other little children, and make *their* eyes bright and eager with many a strange tale, perhaps even with the dream of Wonderland of long ago; and how she would feel with all their simple sorrows, and find a pleasure in all their simple joys, remembering her own child-life, and the happy summer days.